THE LUCIUS BEEBE READER

Also by Lucius Beebe

THE BIG SPENDERS

the Lucius Beebe reader

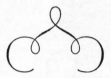

SELECTED AND EDITED BY

Charles Clegg

Duncan Emrich

HUTCHINSON OF LONDON

HUTCHINSON & CO (*Publishers*) LTD
178–202 Great Portland Street, London W1

London Melbourne Sydney
Auckland Bombay Toronto
Johannesburg New York

First published in Great Britain 1969

*This book has been set in Baskerville, printed Offset Litho in
Great Britain on Antique Wove paper by Anchor Press,
and bound by Wm. Brendon, both of Tiptree, Essex*

09 096050 5

ACKNOWLEDGEMENTS

Grateful acknowledgment is made to the following for selections reprinted in this book:

THE CURTIS PUBLISHING COMPANY

"The Fabulous Pump Room"; "Spendthrift Tour of London"; "Antoine's";
"Commander's Palace"; selections from "Good Eating in New Orleans";
"The Perfect Restaurateur"; "The Elegant Colony"; "I Saw the Elephant";
"The Savoy of London"; "Henry Poole: Gentleman's Tailor". All appeared
in *Holiday*, copyright © 1950, 1951, 1952, 1953, 1957, 1958, 1960, 1963
by The Curtis Publishing Company. Reprinted by permission.

DOUBLEDAY & COMPANY, INC.

Foreword from *When Beauty Rode the Rails*. Copyright © 1962 by Lucius
Beebe and Charles Clegg; excerpts from *Mr. Pullman's Elegant Palace Car*.
Copyright © 1961 by Lucius Beebe. Reprinted by permission.

E. P. DUTTON & CO., INC.

Excerpt from the book *Hear the Train Blow*, by Lucius Beebe and Charles
Clegg. Copyright 1952 by E. P. Dutton & Co., Inc. Reprinted by
permission.

ESTATE OF LUCIUS BEEBE

Article "On Packaged Breakfast Foods", reprinted from *The Territorial
Enterprise*. The following articles that appeared in *Town and Country*,
"Metropolis with Manners"; "Showcase Afloat (Cunard)"; "On the
Rocks"; "Brennan's"; "Commander's Palace" (selections from "Fare Thee
Well"); "Beef and Bourbon"; "San Francisco's Palace"; also "The Royal
Family". All reprinted by permission.

FORD MOTOR COMPANY

"Beverly Wagon Living." December 1958 issue of *Ford Times*; "Wakefield,
Massachusetts—The Town That Will Never Forget Me". August 1956
issue of *Lincoln-Mercury Times*. Reprinted by permission.

GOURMET MAGAZINE

Excerpts from *Gourmet* articles. Copyright © 1947, 1949, 1953, 1957, 1962,
1963, 1964, 1965, 1966 respectively by Gourmet, Inc. Reprinted by
permission.

To The Memory of
LUCIUS MORRIS BEEBE

Bostonian, New Yorker, Nevadan,
a thoroughly self-bespoke Londoner,
and not unknown to the Paris Ritz (Cambon side)

Gourmet, gastronome, transcendental oenophile
Member of the *Confrérie des Chevaliers du Tastevin*

Railroad Aficionado

Unique in having been expelled from both Yale and Harvard
at the signal insistence, respectively, of the dean and president of each

Columnist:
The *New York Herald Tribune* and the *San Francisco Chronicle*

Author

Publisher: *The Territorial Enterprise*

Bon Vivant, Viveur, Boulevardier

Collector of chefs, *sommeliers,* maîtres d'hôtel, and
the places of their works and devisings

Defender, against all comers, of the derby hat and the Cunard Line

Recoiler, as from a puff adder, at the sight or thought of milk, golf,
Democrats, the Wright Brothers' folly, Madison Avenue mendacity,
packaged breakfast foods, Bobby Kennedy, and le Grand Charlie

Co-owner, with his associate and partner, of two of the last
private railroad cars: the *Gold Coast* and *Virginia City*

Individualist and, by virtue of his own built-in time machine, Edwardian

Like many of the upper class
He loved the sound of smashing glass

HILAIRE BELLOC: *Cautionary Verses*

(reproduced by permission of A. D. Peters & Company)

FOREWORD

I feel an obligation to try to explain something of the nature of the man who wrote the pieces collected into this book. How did Lucius Beebe become "a legend in his own lifetime"? What was he like? We know that his extracurricular shenanigans on the Yale and Harvard campuses (he authored and circulated a petition demanding the exchange of two full professorships for a good running backfield) made him known in two hemispheres by the time he was nineteen. We know that at twenty-three he was the youngest lad in the country to be included in *Who's Who*. We know that during prohibition on the Harvard campus a great many undergraduates didn't believe there was actually such a person as Lucius Beebe. They thought the name was just a password to get into speakeasies.

The back matter of this book contains a good, bony, biographical sketch of Beebe so I will limit myself to a few vignettes in the hope of casting some flickers of light on a man who, in an age of conformity, was a bold individual.

He was a highly civilized nineteenth-century gentleman at odds with the mass uniformity and mediocrity he saw around him. He had been born to the twentieth century but he lived in the past, a chivalrous, gracious, and well-mannered age which he knew made him an anachronism, but vastly preferable to the present which he knew to be "a street accident," or to the future which does not exist. He never left the nineteenth century by the simple expedient of not acknowledging the twentieth, and when hard brought to task to confirm his present existence by amiable detractors he would smile gently and nod, but he never really believed his own reassurances.

People who read Beebe do so at their own risk. His writing is sometimes gentle, often hydrophobic, humorous when appropriate. He liked to think of himself as a Renaissance Man along with Harold Ross, Tallulah Bankhead, Henri Soule, Amy Lowell, Amon Carter, W. C. Fields, Belle Livingston, and Noel Coward, to mention a few—"and all these people were Renaissance Men and Women in that they did something well and never in their lives thought to consult anyone else as how to conduct their persons. They all possessed that one radiant qualification: the knowledge of excellence. They wrote, edited, acted, whored, drank, sang songs, served the nation, wrote history, and made enemies in their own pattern. If anything is worth doing it is worth doing in style, and on your own terms, and nobody's Goddamned elses!"

In New York in the early thirties Lucius literally invented something called Café Society in a syndicated column he had been conducting for a short time called "This New York" originating weekly in the *New York Herald Tribune*. There were, said Lucius, only five hundred people in the whole world qualified for membership or worthy of achieving these dizzy heights, and he laid down stern rules: "A general definition of Café Society might be an unorganized but generally recognized group of persons who participate in the social life of New York available to those possessed of a certain degree of affluence and manners."

Later, as unofficial leader of the Tong he wrote, in an effort to prod a few stragglers in the rear guard, "The Café Set of Manhattan firmly believes that if a given celebrity fails to show up at Morocco three or four times a week, he is dead, or even worse, he is out of town."

As a man well over six feet in height who bristled with the mien of an outraged archbishop slightly in wine, Lucius not only cowed his editors but also the poor people they sent him to interview. In restaurants his outrageous personal majesty was such that I have never heard a restaurateur dare ask him if he had made a reservation. It was apparent that he expected and intended to be seated at his whim at the best table and that instanter—and he always was. Michael Arlen used to watch and mutter, "That Beebe fellow has a restaurant face!" But Beebe would explain, under the cloak of a disarming smile, that it was all the result of being one of the few remaining true snobs in America. The waiters knew, he intimated.

Herb Caen says, "Lucius might be a square by today's viewpoint but he had great style because he had an unwavering awareness of what was right for him. He wasn't out to impress anybody. He was also unfailingly polite and class-conscious without being conscious of class. He even got drunk—'taken in wine' as he put it—with a terrible and laudable dignity."

Lucius was an almost unbelievably hard worker—he worked while others slept—and he took his newspaper jobs very seriously, although he always considered the American Newspaper Guild as a branch of the Mafia. He not only refused to join it but he attacked it in his own newspaper with such ferocity that the Guild considered suing for libel.

From the very beginning he refused to adopt the average newspaperman's tweed coat and slouch hat with press card stuck in the hatband.

What he did wear on duty popped his employer's eyes, and in self-defense he wrote, "I wear formal clothes, morning or evening whenever they are called for and regard them quite literally as the livery of my profession. I would no more think of appearing in a restaurant out of dinner dress than I would in swimming trunks." Then he thoughtfully added, "And anyway you get better tables and better service."

His syndicated weekly columns sent housewives in Des Moines, and Social Circle, Ohio, spinning on their ears. Never had such diamond-studded purple prose fascinated so many hungry folk—the Depression was barely over—and Lucius fed them on platinum-plated outrage both personally and through his column. For a whole starry-eyed decade Café Society was Utopia.

My first encounter with Beebe was at one of Evalyn Walsh (Hope Diamond) McLean's celebrated brunches at "Friendship" in Washington, D.C. The party was about over—most of the Supreme Court, Will Rogers, Jr., Leon Henderson, and other guests had already left—and Evie took Lucius and me by the arm, inviting us to join her in the bar "to dish the dirt" as she put it. I found Lucius to be an enormous, almost majestic man with a thunderous voice. Evie was, as usual, wearing an outsize Hedda Hopper hat "because she wasn't going anywhere" and was raising perfect hell with Lucius because (1) he had apparently, in wine, spent the night before on Evie's front lawn curled up with a cast-iron lioness and (2) he had only a few moments before been overheard by Evie from across the room bellowing, "And who the hell IS this Harry Drewmann?" At the moment Lucius was wearing the Hope Diamond as a gag and three Pinkerton men in badly fitting morning dress, their hands in their striped pants pockets, were slowly closing in. I was impressed. I also discovered that Lucius and I were both house guests and had to share a connecting bathroom in the west wing.

Very late that evening I returned to "Friendship" after a strenuous night on the town with old friends and headed for my bathroom. There, to my alarm, was Beebe fully clothed, sound asleep in some disarray in the bathtub, and covered with spots of blood and the remains of a gigantic china pig which had apparently caught his fancy as he passed unsteadily through the drawing room.

I roused him, undressed him, showered off the blood, swept up the pig, and put Beebe to bed with a stern lecture on how guests should behave in a nice private house. He had been a hotel child too long.

Then I went to my own bed smoking a cigarette, fell asleep, and set fire to myself and the house as well.

I think our mutual bad behavior enchanted each other and we began a friendship which lasted more than a quarter of a century. Mrs. McLean generously forgave us both (though she was mortally terrified of fire) and she invited us back many times—but NEVER again as house guests.

Beebe loathed and despised airplanes which he referred to as "thrice-damned flying machines" or simply "the Wright Brothers' folly," and he took fiendish delight in flailing the industry mercilessly in print at every opportunity. He advocated the establishment of a "Box Score" on the front page of his paper which would give the gruesome statistics of plane crashes, and deaths for the year to date on a daily-revised basis. But his ideals were overruled by "base ugly commercialism in the business office."

Once, however, I actually persuaded Lucius to accompany me on a short flight to Los Angeles, and when the boys in the airline's public-relations office heard of this they lost no time in escorting us along with a number of their vice presidents to the airport bar, where they plied us with charm, safety statistics (Beebe explained later that statistics are merely lies supported by affidavit) and strong waters in double measure. Jolly fellows all, they even kept the plane waiting five full minutes while we downed a last round on the house.

As Lucius and I entered the plane we looked down seemingly endless rows of curious and angry faces of people all strapped in and waiting to go. Lucius stopped short, looked again, swallowed hard, and turned about on his heels bellowing at the top of his lungs, "Let me out of his Hell-bound cartridge of death!" And he headed out the door and down the steps, followed by me and roughly one half of the paying passengers who had suddenly decided against flying that day. Needless to say, Mr. Beebe was never again solicited as a passenger by the airlines.

Lucius' deep hatred of the flying machine was probably augmented by his passionate devotion to railroads, and our St. Bernard dog, Mr. T-Bone, was staunchly promoted as the excuse for maintaining our own private railroad car. On most railroads, company officials are pleased to avert their eyes should a passenger sneak a dog into his stateroom without annoying other passengers. But a St. Bernard is unsneakable, so Mr. T-Bone acquired his own private car and maintained a growling acquaintance with yardmen and crews on a continental basis. Once when we arrived aboard the car in Seattle, where T-Bone had been born, he was pictured on the front page of the morning paper shaking hands with the Great Northern's President Budd. The caption: "Home Town Dog Makes Good, Returns on Own Private Car."

Lucius claimed the dog also served another humanitarian usefulness. "After a person has become accustomed to his violently bloodshot eyes they hardly ever notice ours."

A special delight to Lucius was the evening aboard our car bound for

Denver when the conductor came through to collect our fares and found his way blocked by Mr. T-Bone, curled up asleep in the middle of the aisle. The conductor tipped his hat and said, "Oh, please pardon me, sir," and stepped gingerly over the pup. Lucius was never sure whether the conductor knew it was a dog or if he was under the impression that anyone nutty enough to own their own railroad car would, of course, have guests in raccoon coats passed out all over the place.

After over fifteen years of reaping about every honor and fun-filled hour New York had to offer, his eyes began wandering toward the Western horizon. The war years had dimmed New York, and Café Society was evaporating back into the mist from which it had sprung. The Great Man's motto had always been to leave a party while it was still good; never to wait until melancholy drunks had begun singing off key. So he sat down and wrote a charming swan song to New York called "I Saw the Elephant," and we headed West for good, even though he considered California as an overcrowded nut hatch run by the inmates.

But just to the east of nutty California lies The One Sound State of Nevada. Here, high in the hills near Reno, rests the ghost town of Virginia City, replete with twenty gorgeous Victorian saloons. Lucius was smitten, and after checking out the population as a little over four hundred people he turned to me and said, "Keedo, do you realize that there is one saloon for every twenty men, women, and children in this town? Do you recognize the absolute ultimate in Progress when you encounter it? Well, I do. Why, the alcoholic proof here is so high, and the moral tone so low, that we can be absolutely inconspicuous. Let's see if there is a house for sale."

There was, and we adopted Virginia City permanently.

Lucius adored the West, its rugged vastness, and its outlandish history. And our books on the West did well. During his lifetime he wrote over forty books and I was proud to co-author seventeen of them. The diversification of subject matter is almost alarming: from *The Stork Club Bar Book* to a scholarly *Bibliography of the Works of Edwin Arlington Robinson*, from *Mixed Train Daily* to *The Big Spenders*, the latter on bestseller lists for nearly the past year. But his prime love was railroading; big, powerful, smoky locomotives; and his books on this subject were magnificent. Each one, as it was completed, was most definitely his last one, according to Beebe. But he was hard at work on another the day of his death.

Lucius' spelling was often downright hilarious and his passionate hate was Mr. Webster, whom he resolutely refused to consult. The result was, since he had been a brilliant student of Latin, a trail of quite likely-sound-ing but strangely unfamiliar words throughout his sentences which sent readers scurrying to their dictionaries—where the words were not. His dislike for Webster is directly responsible for many words which now appear there. Stanley Walker told me that "Lucius thinks in Latin and translates into English," and he added, "Once I sent two typed pages of Lucius' copy back to him with the suggestion that that much copy should have more than one period—the one at the end. He sent it back to me with a polite note suggesting that I as editor could put in as many periods as I wished. I tried but had to give up. The man had actually written one sentence, involved God knows, but one grammatically correct and complete sentence two pages long and that's the way it went to the composing room."

Not long after Lucius died I came across a recent memo to himself which he must have composed late at night, for its holograph was unsteady and smacked of the grape. But *in vino veritas*, it said:

"I have not cared greatly for nor been impressed too urgently by people or what they do or want or think. I haven't known many people, but those I have, have derived from, I think, the better vintages of professional competence. This is what has most impressed me and may well be a shallow thing, but I have admired most of all expertise, the quality of being strictly professional. This must be understood to extend to every aspect of living within the individual purview so that the business of having lived has been done, in all directions, with competence, its obligations discharged without blemish, its satisfactions achieved in the knowledge of their excellence."

These words were not penned by the Beebe the world knew: Beebe the millionaire boulevardier and dilettante, Beebe the wit and flamboyant gourmet. These lines were penned by Beebe the student and fantastic worker, Beebe the admirer of perfection seeking valid excellences in his own and other's works, or Beebe the poet, and there is poetry throughout his works, especially in his tender blank verse odes to the American epic of railroading, which was his true love. These odes may bring tears to the eyes but they will be tears of emotional wonder at the deep, pure beauty he could evoke from steel and steam with mere words.

This was the Lucius Beebe I knew and somewhat worshiped.

Charles Clegg

Virginia City, Nevada

CONTENTS

HIGH IRON

THE WEST: NEVADA AND CALIFORNIA

THE LUCIUS BEEBE READER

New England Youth

If vistas of enchantment beckoned in the form of swan boats, the Boston & Albany train yards, and Callahan conning the family cars through Back Bay traffic with endearments from the lexicon of horses, there were two splendors of supernal dimension that emerged to transcend even Mr. Medalina's ice-cream Thanksgiving turkeys. These were the fixed festival of Christmas as observed by Filene's store in downtown Boston, and the dateless but ever possible alarm of fire.

METROPOLIS WITH MANNERS

The distance that separates the present from the Boston of my boyhood cannot be measured with any assurance by the mere fifty years it represents. The distance of now from then can be measured only in a dimension of light-years, possibly in terms of galactic time. I do not say this in terms of dismay, for I no longer live there or, indeed, have ties of any degree of urgency with the Hub City of the Universe. My regret for yesterdays that I know were vastly better embraces Boston as well as other communities I knew in happier time. That goes in equal measure for London, Paris, and New York. Everything everywhere was better then, and the measure of all worldly wisdom attests it.

The Boston of my boyhood recollection was an only partly American city; it had overtones in manners, appearance, and social geography that made it half a suburb of London. It was a metropolis with manners; it had a character of breeding and poise that produced the politest taxi drivers this side of Trafalgar Square and signs that admonished one to "Please Refrain from Trampling the Grass." It was a city of only moderate haste and its defining characteristics, I think, were assurance and tranquility.

I am assured that things are different now in the city of Boston, but I do not know at first hand. I never go back.

Part, I am certain, of Boston's essentially English quality derived from its close identification with the Mother Country in colonial times; our institutions and habits did not change just because of Bunker Hill. Another aspect of Boston's essential Britishism derived fairly and squarely from the Boston Irish. In the years just after the turn of the century, they were still acting precisely as they had acted back in County Mayo or Sligo or Dublin or wherever. They were busily hating England in the State House and in the columns of the *Boston Post*. They were denouncing King George and, earlier, King Edward from the safety of Brimstone Corner, at Park Street, with a vehemence they might not have been permitted at home. They were active, tumultuous, vindictive, and noisy; and Eamon de Valera was the cause of civic disturbances that a predominantly Irish police force took no great hand in suppressing. The uproar of the Boston Irish made Massachusetts an outpost of the United Kingdom.

I hear it is different now, and the sons of the South Boston Irish who hurled chimney pots from the roof tops at Orangemen on St. Patrick's Day now sit on boards of directors of life-insurance companies and commute from Winchester or Concord every morning.

My first recollections of Boston's public aspect were of the city's happiest and most jocund moments—Commonwealth Avenue in spring with the crocuses showing through the lawn around the Sears mansion, in Arlington Street, and the Public Garden blazing with formal flower beds as a setting for the lagoons on which rode the swan boats. What joy to descend to the green-painted dock where the swan boats stopped and set sail on the tranquil waters, where all was serene until one's black varnished sailor hat blew off and had to be retrieved by the swan-boat man with a boat hook secreted on board, probably for that specific purpose! What fun to be allowed, with a dime supplied by one's governess in a long blue veil, to patronize the toy-balloon and pinwheel man, who tethered his wares to the ornamental fence around the Phineas Sprague house, in Commonwealth Avenue, and in button boots to run, screaming, up the Mall to activate the pinwheel until one fell on one's face, crushing the paper toy to pulp while the balloon soared off into the April sky, a symbol of ephemeral treasures yet to vanish in an unheeding world!

Just off Commonwealth Avenue, in that halcyon time, commerce held sway in small offices in the blocks toward Boylston Street. And one's first intimations of great affairs were lady stenographers, who were then gaining wide acceptance in business offices, with Gibson Girl hairdos and starched white shirtwaists performing on writing machines of amazing complexity. Three brands linger in the memory: an Oliver, whose keybars were ranked on terraces on each side of the frame and fell forward to smite the carriage like miniature guillotines; the L. C. Smith, whose primeval models had one bank of keys for caps and one for lower case; and a Blickensderfer, where the letters were embossed on a circular band of metal that rode a spindle and swooped down to make an impression on the unresisting paper with the impetus of the entire alphabet and many arbitrary type symbols behind it. My big brother Oliver, in a departure from strict truth, told me that he had invented the Oliver typewriter. I believed this piece of fiction and thenceforward regarded all attempts to tell me to the contrary as gross libels on the family.

My family home where I was born, and my father before me, was in Wakefield, then a remote and autonomous country hamlet fifteen miles north of Boston Stone and now a part of an unutterably dreary complex of suburbia. Communications being what they were at the turn of the century, we wintered inside the city confines of Boston for fully half the year, and my youthful allegiance was divided in equal measure among the horses, cows, and Irish farm hands of Beebe Farm, Lakeside, Wakefield, and the urban joys of the great city.

Bay State Road, at the turn of the century, was not a bastion of the old nobility as were, say, Louisburg Square or Commonwealth Avenue from Arlington Street to Massachusetts Avenue, but it sheltered substantial folk with a preference for comfort over ostentation. We lived in a corner apartment house with immense chambers and twelve-foot ceilings, a sort of Boston version of New York's legendary Dakota, with bay windows that afforded a matchless view of the comings and goings of Francis Clarke Welsh. Mr. Welsh, the ranking Nestor of all Boston estate lawyers, lived across the way in a true mansion flanked by the John Gastons and the Saltonstalls on the other corner and possessed a front lawn that might easily have accommodated a half-mile race track. He also owned a sailing pinnace, hung by davits over the Charles River from his back yard and manned by a Swedish sailor whose sole duty in the Welsh household was to take the old gentleman for a sail on Saturday afternoons.

Directly across the street from No. 96 Bay State Road and next door to the aristocratic Saltonstalls, who kept both a butler *and a footman*, was an enormous vacant lot that afforded an uninterrupted view, from our windows, of the Charles River from Harvard Bridge almost to Cottage Farm Crossing. In it, the small fry of the neighborhood who were my companions and I built shacks and snow forts according to season and waged unremitting warfare against a surly local policeman named Officer Bell, who despised us with reason and whose tall helmet—blue in winter, gray in summer—was a perpetual target for the guided missiles of the time and place. On this vacant lot eventually arose the first of all Sheraton Hotels, so that, in effect, much of my youth was spent in the primeval furnace room of a hotel whose series of structures I was later to inhabit in more elevated circumstances from Dallas to San Francisco.

The street lamps in our part of Boston, at the time, were lit every afternoon at dusk by a lamplighter whose wagon was equipped with a short stepladder, which he mounted when his intelligent horse paused at each post. In my mind's eye, backward over the decades, I can see Bay State Road stretching after a heavy snowfall at night from the Fenway to Cottage Farm, an unending vista of yellow gaslight on snow from curb to curb, unbroken by the passage of a single vehicle, the sidewalks barely scuffed by nocturnal pedestrians. On such nights, the sounds of the streetcar extra gangs and electric snowplows clearing the tracks a block away, in Kenmore Square, were the only sounds.

The three *eminenti* of Bay State Road at the time of which I write were William, Cardinal O'Connell, ranking Catholic prelate of Massachusetts, whose comings and goings were accomplished in a vast Pierce Arrow limousine presented him by grateful parishioners and suitably upholstered in bright papal crimson; Judge Robert Grant; and Dean Thayer of the Harvard Law School, whose home, at No. 77, was a modified version of Mrs. Jack Gardner's Italian *palazzo* in the Fenway, built around a central stairwell with a fountain and rockery where rare shrubs grew amid pools and waterfalls, in tropic temperature that must have entailed astronomical fuel bills during New England winters.

Dean Thayer, in a hard hat and white neckcloth, used to ride over on horseback from the Park Riding Academy on the far side of the Boston & Albany tracks and salute members of his family, gathered in admiration at the windows, with a ceremonious riding crop. When his body was found, presumably a suicide in the Charles River, Bay State Road felt it had lost a conspicuous ornament.

Judge Grant, a banty little man who was also a recognized novelist on the basis of *The Chippendales* and other works of decorous fiction, wore Boston's second most rakish silk hat—the first being that of Hooper Hooper, wine merchant—which he carried at such an angle of swagger as to be a caricature of dandyism. My father recalled having encountered Judge Grant, then a very young man, on the night of the great Boston Fire of November 1872, when our family leather business in High Street, like almost everything else in commercial Boston, was destroyed. Grant, in evening dress from a Saturday-night concert, had lost a prized dress walking stick with a silver handle down a drain in Washington Street. My father had small time for an acquaintance's lost property, since the roof was about to fall in both factually and metaphorically on the family fortunes, but he recalled that Grant had remarked he would come by in the morning and have the grate taken up. By next morning, that part of Boston had disappeared from the map.

Mayor of Boston at about this time was, of course, John Fitzgerald, known as "Honey Fitz," whose name and memory are perpetuated in John Fitzgerald Kennedy. The mayor had a fine tenor voice and was given to singing "Sweet Adeline" on the least provocation, until it became a political asset associated with his notably out-giving personality. Only once did I myself hear this oratorio—at the East Boston Cunard pier from which my mother was sailing for England, in 1911, on the old *Franconia*. Mayor Fitzgerald was also sailing—for Queenstown, of course—and sang "Sweet Adeline" as the steamer backed into the harbor. The strains of the mayor's music, combined with the deep maritime sound of the ship's whistle, reduced me to a passionate flood of tears.

In taking passage on the *Franconia*, my mother was departing from conservative Boston custom, which decreed that the only acceptable way of going abroad was with Captain Trant in the venerable *Devonian*.

The most desirable sailing on this ancient caravel was the first one after Harvard Commencement in June, and it was on one of these annual occasions that ships'-news reporters and others were amazed to see the ample form of Miss Amy Lowell, who had just gone aboard with her trunks and tiring maids, descending the gangway with the obvious intention of not sailing after all.

An explanation of this seemingly irrational conduct was demanded, and Miss Lowell had no hesitation in stating that she thought this sailing of the *Devonian* was a bad risk and that all on board might well be doomed. Miss Lowell despised the members of the Cabot family with a loathing that was legendary, and when she had scanned the sailing list outside the purser's office she had discovered no fewer than eleven Cabots among those taking passage.

"God isn't going to let slip any such opportunity as this!" she said firmly and marched down the plank.

Sundays in Bay State Road held opportunities for heavenly orgies amid the Sunday newspapers, especially on such occasions as I was not required to attend Sunday School at Emmanuel Church. These more or less coincided with my family's attendance at eleven o'clock services where my father, in morning coat and gates-ajar collar, occasionally passed the plate. In later years—together with the Baylies twins, Walter and Edmund, and Arthur Sharp—I was sometimes, at holidays, when the regular deacons needed succor, impressed into a similar function with an inevitable renaissance of my personal finances. Emmanuel could have showed a deficit if we had been asked to pass the plate often.

Sunday afternoon was devoted in its lovely entirety to the funnies. Because of the presence in its over-all economy of *The American Magazine,* which contained matters not suited to perusal by a presumably Christian youth, the *Boston Sunday American* was not supposed to enter the house. But my father shared my devotion to "Der Captain and Der Kids," "Abie the Agent," "Mutt and Jeff" and a feminine counterpart called "Viola and Vivian," "Hairbreadth Harry," and a strip that memory conjures up in its wonderment as though from yesterday called "Silk Hat Harry's Divorce Suit" in which all the characters were dogs in human attire and activities. It represented to me the sum of all human contentment. There was also a continued strip whose title escapes me over the years, in which a single precocious youth, retained by a railroad company, performed a variety of duties requiring him to appear in costume changes with a cap that read "News Agent," "Ticket Agent," "Porter," and "Western Union." I rather fancied railroading myself as a calling at the time and, after the Sunday funnies, debated offering my services to the Boston & Albany or the Boston & Maine as vagrant fancy dictated. I had given up attempting to induce my family to leave Bay State Road and move into the Lenox Hotel, in Exeter Street, whose rear suites directly overlooked the switching operations and coach yards of the Boston & Albany. I had a school friend named Arthur Sawyer who lived there, however, and we spent long afternoons in all seasons and weather leaning perilously over grimy window sills and becoming sootier by the moment watching the Boston sections of the *Lake Shore Limited* and *Wolverine* being made up for their long runs into the westering sunset to all the Newtons and, perhaps, Ultima Thule.

Sometimes Sunday afternoons were dedicated to calling on the various Beebes who flowered in suburban profusion along the North Shore of Boston and inland throughout Middlesex County. With my father in a sealskin-lined greatcoat and a sort of tufted bonnet of the same fur, we would set out in an open Pierce Arrow touring car, even in dead of winter, and make the rounds of his brothers, with whom my father came into continual business association six other days of the week. The Beebes of Boston were warm men in the Forsytian sense, with few or no interests outside their businesses and families. They belonged to the appropriate clubs—Union, Algonquin, the Brookline Country Club—but seldom used them. Home was their after-hours preoccupation. The Beebe circuit included Uncle Marcus in Malden, Uncle Decius in Melrose, Uncle Fred at Beverly Cove, Aunts Alice and Sylinda in separate establishments at Wakefield, where we ourselves lived in summer, and my father's cousin John Beebe at Wakefield, a racy individual with long yellow mustaches who drove the 1910 equivalents of today's sports cars and put up prizes for the town Fourth of July athletic events that could be staged on Wakefield Common and so viewed in comfort from his own front porch.

Uncle Cyrus lived in Framingham, a positively transalpine *faubourg* out toward Worcester that wasn't on the regular Beebe circuit of suburban Boston. My father took great pleasure in the company of his sisters-in-law, but, by the time we had made the rounds of Melrose, Malden, Beverly Cove, and Wakefield, my feet were cold and I was in favor of home where I knew tea was being served with cinnamon toast. I think my father regarded the open touring cars in which we rode winter and summer for years as an only partial departure from horse and carriage transport and, somehow, as falling short of complete capitulation to the effete decadence of the enclosed automobile.

Reversing the ceremonial tour of the North-of-Boston Beebes were the equally ceremonial visits, at unstated intervals, of my Aunt Hattie, my mother's sister who hailed from Walpole to the south of Boston. Just as Melrose, Malden, and Wakefield were peopled with Beebes, Walpole, Braintree, and Quincy were peopled with Merricks. Aunt Hattie could have stepped out of a radio soap opera, I am told, although I have never heard one. She was a roly-poly country-type aunt with silver-rimmed glasses—spectacles, she called them—and a bonnet that tied under her chin with ribbons, full of good will and obsessed with the notion that city folk did poorly at table. She would arrive, usually unannounced, in a horse cab from the New Haven Railroad that would begin to unload an almost unmanageable multiplicity of parcels, all of which turned out to contain pies, cakes, pastries, and other kitchen devisings from Hattie's neat hand and which, even in an age innocent of calories or Gayelord Hauser, suggested murderous overweight.

"June," she would address my father, "I know perfectly well that Eleanor never did set a proper sort of table. You look as though you hadn't had a square meal in a long spell. I've brought you some mince and pumpkin, and there's quince jam, too. Now you sit right down and eat hearty."

Father, who daily sat on a stool at the counter of Thompson's Spa in Washington Street to lunch on crackers and milk to avoid the rich fare at the Algonquin Club or Locke-Ober's Winter Place Wine Rooms, would visibly pale.

Transportation in and around Boston in the golden age of which I write was no problem. There were, of course, legitimate agencies of personal transport, family carriages and primeval automobiles and city-wide transportation systems of trolley cars, elevated trains, and subways on which, for five cents, it was possible to journey all the way across the metropolitan area from Everett Square or Malden to farthest Roxbury. For a slightly higher fee, there were ornate and wonderfully fast trolley cars that sped out Commonwealth Avenue—red for Auburndale, blue for Norumbega Park and the zoo. There were (and doubtless still are) elevated trains, from Park Street lower level to Harvard Square via the East Boston Bridge, on which you stood a fair chance of seeing President Abbott Lawrence Lowell of Harvard (this in slightly later times) wearing tan shoes with his morning dress and carrying a green cloth Boston bag to directors' meetings in State Street. In my extreme and most remote memory there was a surface trolley line from Harvard Square to town across Cottage Farm Bridge, then a spidery structure on wooden piles, which must have been the original Toonerville Trolley, a hilarious arrangement with only four wheels and lengthwise seats on which passengers faced each other as the conveyance rocked its way with a sort of sailing motion through the gaslit streets at night. Youths of my set considered riding this archaism an adventure into the primordial past, which indeed it was compared to the all-steel high-speed trolleys that went sixty miles an hour out Commonwealth Avenue in the direction of the many Newtons.

These, as I say, were legitimate agencies of locomotion. We much preferred those that involved the payment of no fare and embraced (a) avoiding the conductor or gateman, as the case might be, on the public utilities and (b) a clandestine ride on the trunk rack of the brougham-type closed cabs that were the universal hackney accommodation of the age. These were so constructed that the driver couldn't see behind him, and an agile youth might get a lift of several miles' duration before some fellow hackman or curmudgeon on the sidewalk spied him and shouted "Whip behind" to the driver, who then lashed out blindly over his shoulder with his horsewhip. In winter, when the same hacks were mounted on runners and known as "boobies," it was even simpler to loop the rope of a Flexible Flyer through the luggage rack and ride grandly as a sort of second section and, when discovered, simply loose the cord and fall out of reach of whip and blasphemy.

Riding the cars without paying the fare had its drawbacks. It required some native expertise and necessitated traveling at crowded times of day, and it eliminated the possibility of profitable commerce with a friendly conductor in the matter of old and presumably valuable coins. We all carried various handbooks of coin buyers, notably that of a William Hesslein, who operated at the corner of Tremont and Bromfield Street and assayed uncounted mountains of currency in search of silver pennies, three-cent pieces, ancient dimes, and twenty-cent pieces or double dimes, all of which were in some degree of circulation; and occasionally turned up a rarity that brought a dollar premium for its New Orleans, San Francisco, or Carson City minting. Our Holy Grail was a 1799 silver dollar, reputed to bring $1000 cash in hand, which nobody of my acquaintance ever turned up.

My authority on ancient coinage was a venerable watchmaker named Mr. Denton, who occupied space in front of a Bromfield Street pet shop hard by Johonot's Time Store. Together we schemed to write a definitive monograph on large U.S. copper one-cent pieces, then still fairly common even though many had been melted down during the Civil War. Somehow the book never materialized, but we experienced all the thrill of Sir Joseph Duveen unearthing a new Romney when we discovered a variation of the "1793 so-called fillet-head Liberty, crack in die by third star."

The first family chauffeur was, like many of his generation elsewhere, the family coachman promoted from pitchforks and saddle soap to a world of machinery but dimly understood. Of immense strength, Edward Callahan could lift the end of a 6000-pound limousine while a new tire was put on; but he continued to think in terms of horses and carriages and talked to the family Pierce Arrow, a great brute of a touring car, in the tones he had formerly addressed Blacky, Whiteface, and Brown Ned. When he gave vent to a shout of "Whoa up!" in Tremont Street traffic, we braced ourselves for an application of the brakes, and if the motor started missing he gentled it with soothing words like "There now! There!"

Callahan's ignorance of the economy of internal combustion was little greater than that of his employers. Once, on a long-ago Sunday, my father was minded to call on Henry C. Frick, who then summered in a magnificent North Shore mansion at Pride's Crossing or Beverly. The driveway was guarded by vast wrought-iron gates hung from medieval stone gateposts and, as we turned into the estate, the car somehow escaped from Callahan's control and rammed into the masonry with arresting vehemence. We were all precipitated out of our seats into the roadway whence we arose scatheless, but dusty and shaken.

Father addressed himself to Callahan: "What in tarnation did you do that for?"

Callahan's reply in later years became a family classic. "Something must have gone wrong with the carburetor, sir!"

The excuse was satisfactory to everyone. Nobody knew what a carburetor was or did, but it was widely understood to be unreliable.

If vistas of enchantment beckoned in the form of swan boats, the Boston & Albany train yards, and Callahan conning the family cars through Back Bay traffic with endearments from the lexicon of horses, there were two splendors of supernal dimension that emerged to transcend even Mr. Medalina's ice-cream Thanksgiving turkeys. These were the fixed festival of Christmas as observed by Filene's store in downtown Boston, and the dateless but ever possible alarm of fire.

Filene's was one of the first to promote the Yule season with magnificent electric effects five or six stories high and encircling their commercial premises with Santa Claus, the Magi, and other animated symbols of retail trade moving in simulated animation through waves of brightening and dimming bulbs. Any regional Macy's would today consider them unsophisticated. But, in 1905, animated spectaculars were far from commonplace and I was taken downtown one night a year, after dinner, to marvel at the benevolence of Filene's, which was at once the source of such aesthetic interludes *and* electric trains, Flexible Flyer sleds, and Boy Scout knives—all in a single bountiful season.

Fires were viewed with less approval by my elders, but, in an age of horse-drawn apparatus and red-helmeted pipemen clinging to the running boards of ponderous hook-and-ladder equipment, possessed an undeniable charm for young and old alike. Fires were frequent—indeed, almost daily—and in varying degrees of magnitude and, hence, charm.

Truly imposing holocausts, such as the one that destroyed the premises of the Massachusetts Automobile Club and, with it, a hundred or two vintage Loziers, Hupmobiles, and Kissel Cars that would gladden the heart of today's classic collector, usually took place at some remove from Bay State Road and at night, and hence were inaccessible to the Boy Beebe, an incurable fire buff although he had never heard the term. I was on terms of semiprofessional intimacy with the station firemen in the great stone firehouse in Boylston Street overlooking my favorite vista of Boston & Albany yards, a juxtaposition of delight which I ascribed to Divine Providence. Between blazes, I was allowed the freedom of the immaculate station house with its gleaming steam pumper, chemical wagons, hose carts, hook and ladders, and monstrous tower guns, all ranked behind a spidery chief's cart, which got on the road first with a single fast steed between its shafts when the alarm tolled. The beautifully groomed and petted firehorses, who were automatically released from their stalls and stepped under harnesses that hung from the ceiling, were known to me by name. And when the tocsin sounded I watched, with professionally appraising eye, the engineer of the big steam pumper sever the permanent steam connection by which its boiler was heated from the firehouse basement, toss an incendiary rocket through the furnace door to the firebox, and roll away with smoke trailing from the chimney before it had cleared the station doors.

In those times, a fire company called out at night was indescribably thrilling—something to make the hair stand on end with the sounds and sight of its going, as with the steam whistles of the pumpers, the bells of lesser equipment clanging, and fiery clinkers scattering from under the Amoskeag boiler in the darkness, its progress gave a reasonable preview of hell.

A first-class fire, then, was worth attending. By the time the ordinary spectator got there, an entire apartment dwelling or commercial premises could be enveloped in flames, burning with a rumbling roar of combustion, mingled with the shouts of firemen and the throbbing of the steam pumpers rocking and trembling on their carriages that, after half a century, raises the hackles and flutters the pulse. You knew you were getting close to a real three-alarm holocaust not only from the waves of apparatus rolling up from covering stations, but because you met the firehorses, blanketed and disengaged from their teams, being led back to places of safety in some side street. On the outer perimeter of disaster, the fat black hoses coiled and writhed through gutters flowing with hot water to distant drains. Chiefs in white coats, and engineers, pipemen, and laddermen in black, cascaded water down the long beaks of their leather helmets that slanted to the rear and, through the shattering uproar of smashing glass and disintegrating woodwork, you heard the shrill beeping whistle of the steamers signaling, in the midst of chaos, their whereabouts to their coal tenders. A steam pumper carried but little fuel on the footplate behind its boiler and, when settling in for a long siege, the engineer whistled for more coal, tolling the auxiliary apparatus in as ferries were tolled to their slip in a heavy fog. When you heard the engineer whistling for coal, you knew it was a fire of gratifying dimension.

I suppose that in everybody's retrospection there are events, in themselves not specially pertinent, that serve to demark the periods of life. Such a punctuation mark for me was, I think, the Great Fire of Salem, which occurred in June of 1914 and was, in the long light of hindsight, a preview of an even greater conflagration even then being kindled in Europe and which was, inevitably, to change everybody's life thereafter.

The Beebe family was in summer residence at our ancestral home in Wakefield when the news was circulated that Salem, only ten or twelve miles to the east, was the scene of an even then growing disaster. Indeed, from the elevated lawn behind the carriage house, we were able to see an enormous and ominous cloud of dirty smoke rising on the horizon, and an appropriate signal on our own town fire whistle signified that apparatus had been dispatched to an out-of-town fire.

I was mad with excitement in the realization that none of the fires of my previous experience could compare with this, but my father, home from Boston on the 4:30 Boston & Maine, refused to budge and remained placidly on the front porch where—in a seersucker suit and drinking cold lemonade, for it was a hot June day—he read the closing stock reports in the *Boston News Bureau*. He had seen fires before and of epic dimensions.

Suddenly, however, intelligence came that galvanized the entire family and sent a hurry call for Callahan to warm up the Pierce Arrow. My brother Oliver had heard on the Bell telephone, where our number was 16, the sixteenth telephone to have been installed north of Boston, that the State Militia had been instructed to dynamite the Salem railroad station and that the dissolution of this structure was expected within the hour.

The Salem railroad station occupied a special position in New England legend and folklore. Built in the 1840s when Gothic influence was everywhere, it comprised a vast shed flanked by tall, crenelated granite towers of menacing aspect and dimension through which trains disappeared in the direction of Portland. Opinion was divided on its aesthetic merit. One school of thought considered it easily the greatest architectural triumph since the Taj Mahal; another, to which my father subscribed, that it was a monstrosity of the first chop.

If the Salem station was to be dynamited, Father was going to be there to see, and off we went through the late-afternoon countryside past groups of farmers and their families assembled in the fields and all gazing to the east.

It so happened that the structure wasn't razed, after all. A change of wind gave it a reprieve, even after the charges had been laid whose detonation would have gratified an even half of New England sentiment. But the fire itself was a monstrous success, at least with the Boy Beebe.

The burning of Rome with Nero fiddling couldn't have been more satisfactory.

A month or so later the European flames, of which Salem had been the merest harbinger, erupted, and nothing was ever afterward exactly as it had been. Not even for a twelve-year-old Boston boy.

DIME NOVEL DESTINY

It is often difficult, and sometimes downright impossible, to trace a personal impulse, taste, or prejudice to its original source, its fountainhead. Freudians and headshrinkers go to arcane lengths to explore the subconscious. They make a production number of discovering why a man is addicted to collecting postage stamps, or why he prefers dogs to people. (The latter has always seemed to me so simple a matter of ordinary taste and intelligence as not to require discussion.)

But it took no complicated analysis for me to discovery why I love dining on trains—why, if there is a choice of taking a meal at a stationary point or en route, I will go to some lengths to arrange for eating in motion. I can trace the preference back with the flawless sense of direction of a salmon heading for its natal river and spawning ground.

It all dates back to my impressionable youth in Wakefield, Massachusetts, uncounted eons ago, when, like any other country boy of the time, I was an avid purchaser of that despised form of literature known as the dime novel. Unlike many of my contemporaries, I wasn't forbidden them by parental decree (although the Boston *Record American* and the old *Police Gazette* were frowned upon). My parents saw nothing more subversive in paperbacks than could be found in the novels of Mr. Henty and the recollections of Mrs. George Armstrong Custer, which often dealt with death and violence on an epic scale but were incontestably respectable on all social levels.

My bookseller was proprietor of the news and stationery stand across the tracks from the Boston & Maine Railroad's Upper Station in Wakefield, a hamlet which then seemed to me a metropolis because it boasted three railroad depots.

My custom was accorded the Upper Station shopkeeper because, as a bonus for my patronage, I was sometimes permitted to handle (but not to discharge) a Luger automatic pistol which he kept hung in a holster behind the counter as a warning to potential bandits. I doubt that his till ever held more than five dollars, as his business was almost entirely in Hershey bars, periodicals, tobacco, snuff, and paperbacks.

The theme and content of most of my dime novels (which seem in recollection to have cost not a dime, but a nickel) never remained long in my memory. But one of them is so indelibly recorded in my mind that now, forty-odd years later, I can still see it as clearly as I did the day I unhooked it from the wire rack and took it to my bosom as the late Joseph Duveen might have treasured a newly discovered Gainsborough. It was called *Love's Retribution,* but its cover illustration was one that, could it be reproduced, would deserve a place in the National Gallery in Washington. The cover showed, in glorious colors, the passage of the dining car of a splendid express train. Through a picture window, with its leaded Gothic transom, could be seen a beautiful young man dining with a radiant damsel. The table was laden with lobster Newburg, or, for all I knew then, terrapin Maryland, and the young man was holding out to the damsel a crystal chalice filled to the brim with what was undoubtedly Romanée-Conti '99 (although to my untutored eye it looked fetchingly like the raspberry syrup at the soda fountain in Bonney & Dutton's drugstore on the town square). And, as this scene of sybaritic splendor flashed across the lithographic page, representing to the Boy Beebe the fullest possible sum of human felicity, there knelt in the snowdrift that banked the railroad right-of-way a pitiful female figure, her garments sparse, her head protected against the elements by a seedy shawl. She held one arm supplicatingly toward the unheeding young man in the car window; the other arm cradled an infant, unquestionably the get and issue of the scoundrel in the Pullman.

Here was a complete story of romance, villainy, and tragedy, in a single four-color representation: woman wronged, innocent babe doomed to a name of shame, and perhaps to starvation, and the author of this misery awash with the good things of life, lavishing his wealth and seductive charms upon another.

In that instant, I was resolved to be the young man in the dining-car window, attired in a gates-ajar collar and a Prince Albert coat, pressing the best that money could buy on a beautiful damsel whom I would presently renounce for another even more seductive light-o'-love. I would find out what was the stuff that looked like Doc Dutton's raspberry syrup. Heaven willing, I would drink it all my life long, while reclining in the dining cars of the best extra-fare railroad trains *The Official Guide* could afford. In the twinkling of an eye, I was conditioned to railroad travel, and I have never had occasion to change my mind from that day to this.

UNCLE JOHN

Half a century ago, when I was a boy in Wakefield, Massachusetts, it was essential that every well-conducted American family claim at least one Uncle John. Some families had more than one Uncle John—in 1910, this was regarded in conservative circles as somewhat ostentatious—but one was necessary to any self-respecting New England household. Also necessary was an Aunt Hattie. The Beebes of Wakefield had, as a matter of course, both an Aunt Hattie and an Uncle John, and I doubt if we acknowledged the legitimacy of any family that didn't. Our Aunt Hattie lived in Walpole and was a notable old lady of good works and splendid apple pies. I believe her to have been the prototypical Aunt Hattie on whom all subsequent characters of that name in fiction and, I hear tell, on radio and television, have been based.

But my concern here is with Uncle John, because I never see fresh green corn in the markets without remembering him as a figure of sheer delight, the greatest consumer of fresh Golden Bantam corn on the cob the world has ever known. Chronicles of the era's high life were filled with the gastronomic achievements of Diamond Jim Brady, a notable consumer of high-pressure victuals in Rector's, Reisenweber's, Sherry's, and other lobster palaces of a gaslit and horse-drawn New York. Later, as a member of the *New York Herald Tribune*'s staff, I was to make the acquaintance of Henry George, head carpenter of the Metropolitan Opera Company across the street and celebrated as the big eater of Jack Bleeck's Artists & Writers Club, whose achievements among the entrees made occasional Monday morning feature stories for us. After Mr. George had eaten a dozen double Southdown mutton chops, an entire rib roast of beef, and two roast capons topping five pounds each, Bleeck would cut him off with stern orders to Fritz, the back-room waiter. "If Mr. George wants to top off his lunch with a Kentucky ham and six mince pies," Bleeck would say, "let him do it at the Greek's down the street. I don't want him dead on the premises."

Mr. George easily weighed three hundred pounds, and when he was occupied backstage at the Met with professional matters, two waiters would stagger across from Bleeck's with a laundry hamper filled with sandwiches and a fire pail of beer, to sustain him through the noon hour. When a dance floor was laid across the orchestra portion of the Met for a ball, the New York building inspectors considered it safe for public assembly if Mr. George had walked across it.

My Uncle John Beebe never achieved the formidable physical proportions of either Mr. George or Mr. Brady. In his mid-seventies he was a dashing fellow with as slim a waistline as you could ask, but his daily consumption of corn on the cob, in season, was enough, as Tilly, his Irish housekeeper, used to maintain, "to fill two silos."

Whatever he chose for breakfast and lunch (the latter was usually something frugal at the counter of the Thompson Spa in Boston, so as to leave plenty of room for dinner), John's evening meal, as long as the season lasted, was boiled corn on the cob and nothing else, if you except the accompanying fresh creamery butter, salt, and coarse black pepper, gunpowder grind. The butter came in round, one-pound pats with the image of a Holstein cow impressed on top; wooden boxes as big as kitchen-match boxes held the salt and pepper, one on either side of the plate, and there was a silver spoon for each. An Irish linen napkin, approximately as large as an unfolded copy of *The Wakefield Daily Item*, was tucked in over the wings of John's stylish gates-ajar collar. With it, he occasionally dabbed at rivulets of melted butter that coursed down his long yellow mustaches.

Tilly brought the corn from the kitchen, a dozen ears at a time, carrying them, swathed in the counterpart of John's dinner napkin, on a heavy ironware platter. "She cooks them in small lots," John would explain. "They taste better that way, and are fresher too."

Candor compels me to admit that I don't know how many dozen ears of corn John was good for at a sitting, but I'd say six or seven would be no exaggeration. I base my estimate on the fact that, at my father's order, Dennis Daly, our head farmer, brought two big square boxes of carefully packed ears down to John's house in a buggy every afternoon during the season at five o'clock. If the day was uncommonly hot, the ears were sprinkled lightly with a fine-spray garden hose before delivery.

As Tilly came and went with the steaming dozens through the pantry door, with its beautifully polished brass scuff board, there was convenient to John's hand a black, square-faced bottle of Lawrence's Grade B. B. Medford rum. This beverage was the true elixir of life to generations of New Englanders until an Episcopalian head of the family was elected a bishop, and promptly suspended manufacture of the family's most celebrated product. This was a moment of almost unparalleled calamity; a near panic ensued in Boston. Fanciers bought up all available stock at S. S. Pierce's and Cobb, Bates & Yerxa's groceries. John procured a supply that lasted the rest of his life, almost exactly, counting consumption at about a bottle a night, more during the corn season. People who drank Medford rum weathered the long New England winters into their eighties and nineties. It was the stuff Ponce de Leon had looked for.

John was one of the partners in my father's business, Lucius Beebe & Sons, Leather, located at 129 South Street, Boston. In later years he lamented the good times after the Civil War, when the West was opening up and a shrewd purchaser of hides could turn an honest dollar in the frontier cow towns of Kansas and Wyoming. He loved the howling wilderness of the railroad towns, the drummers' hotels, and the girls and the gold that had all been part of the leather trade in those halcyon days. When he was in his late seventies, he went to my father and asked for one last buying fling in the West he remembered. He wanted to take a pocketful of drafts on Boston banks and once more, perhaps for the last time, play poker and bargain for carloads of steer hides with derby-hatted drummers in diamond rings, in the dusty Western towns of his glory days. Father knew that disappointment awaited the old man, that the merchants and dealers he remembered had long since joined the majority, and that the railroad hotels and false-front saloons were only a memory. Times were not good, but he ponied up some fifty thousand dollars and told John to have his last fling. He knew John would come home empty-handed, for business wasn't done that way any more.

Uncle John didn't come home empty-handed. He arrived back in Boston with two freight carloads of buffalo hides. The year was 1930; the last buffalo lap robe had been sold in 1912.

John, of course, was radiant. "Real bargains, and prime merchandise," he announced jauntily. Nobody ever found out where he was able to acquire buffalo hides in the fourth decade of the twentieth century. They represented a last triumph for Uncle John's sagacity and acumen, a final radiant achievement for the biggest corn-on-the-cob eater of them all.

WAKEFIELD, MASSACHUSETTS:
The Town That Will Never Forget Me

The undisputed hero of my early youth in Wakefield, Massachusetts, was neither my uncle, John Beebe, who could and did, every day during the fresh corn season, eat thirty-six ears of Golden Bantam for a single course, clearing his long yellow mustaches of melted butter with an Irish linen napkin as big as a double spread of the *Boston Evening Transcript*, nor was it Buffalo Bill Cody whose Wild West show I had seen—chaperoned by the family coachman—in a vast tent pitched in Huntington Avenue, Boston. Both of them loom now, transcendentally wonderful, over the years, but at the age of twelve my heart belonged to Dennis Daly.

Dennis was the overseer or head man at my father's farm on the shores of Lake Quannapowitt in Wakefield. He was a graying native of County Mayo of slightly under middle height who had been a drummer boy under Burnside in Mr. Lincoln's War, and had served my father and grandfather before him faithfully among the haycocks and stables and strawberry patches and meadows of a New England almost insufferably tranquil and beautiful in memory. God light a good man in the dark.

Dennis was my man and I was, quite obviously, his. After my father had taken the 8:15 on the Boston & Maine to Boston for the day, Dennis was lord of everything in sight, viceroy of the cow barn, satrap of the stables, feudal proconsul of everything from the driveway in from Main Street to the farthest pasture which, truth to tell, was almost in Lynnfield a full two miles away.

Captain of an army with eight hirelings with pitchforks and overalls—more during the haying season—he had a tongue which combined a native Irish imagination that was highly anatomical with things he had learned in the Union Army, and the effect would light a coal-oil lamp at twenty feet. My father never heard Dennis at concert pitch or I would never have been entrusted to him.

Dennis, it was, who let me ride Patsy when his second in command, John Callahan, was doing the spring plowing. Dennis who, as soon as I was worth it on a hay tedder, paid me ten cents an hour cash on the barrel head every afternoon and, of course, charged me on the books at a full hired man's princely salary of $2.50 a day. Help was dear in 1914. And it was Dennis who taught me all I know about dynamite, which might surprise you.

The age of twelve found me a confirmed dynamiter who might have graduated to the estate of an anarchist if fate hadn't intervened. One of the established chores around any New England farm of the period was the blasting of tree stumps and the boulders which worked up with the frost into the vegetable gardens and hayfields every winter.

Blasting was primitive in those times. Although an electric blasting machine existed, a cap and fuse were cheaper. The charge of anywhere from a quarter stick of .75 gelatin up was tamped into position and a fuse good for, say, sixty seconds, left hanging out. Six or eight such charges were fired at a time through the agency of a red-hot poker carried swiftly by Dennis, and later me, from stump to stump with just time to get away before the first one went off. At the age of twelve any summer morning would have found me with an armload of the best product of Hercules Powder Company trudging a country lane toward a scene of destruction with a green tin box of fulminate-of-mercury caps in my Eton jacket pocket. A fall or brisk shock to the tin box would have put a noisy and perhaps providential end to me before ever experiencing the more mature satisfactions of adult life.

Dennis not only allowed me to assist at his blasting, an honor comparable, say, to Escoffier's permitting a kitchen piccolo to assist him in the preparation of a *sauce poulette;* he kept me in firearms and ammunition. I was the proud possessor of a remarkable arsenal of Civil War pistols and revolvers, most of them serviceable or nearly so; all of them, of course, of archaic and wonderfully muzzleloading construction. Any American country house in the years following the 1861 war was likely to be a repository of such material, discarded after Appomattox by countless Uncle Johns and Cousin Harolds in favor of more convenient weapons of precision for hunting or home defense. I had Starr's Navy revolvers, .50 caliber, mark you, that discharged a slug fairly comparable to a Krupp howitzer; Colt's dragoon pistols, fully as fearsome; pepper boxes for ladies' reticules; and little monsters of nickel steel which sold by mail in all the esteemed periodicals—say *The National Police Gazette*—for four or five dollars and would as lief blow up in your face as in the direction of the burglars they were always depicted as subduing.

The last of these fired ball ammunition, but most required fine-grained black powder and percussion caps for their multiple nipples, and these necessities of life George Taylor, the town hardware merchant, resolutely refused to sell me. "Your father owns this building I do business in. Do

you want to see me thrown, a beggar, into the street?" he used to say.
That was where Dennis entered, in the role of arms runner.

Our little understanding in the matter involved a game of diplomacy
which would have interested Sir Basil Zaharoff.

Wakefield was quite unaccountably dry, a desert of local option in the
rest of hilariously wet Massachusetts. Going outside Wakefield to neighboring Reading, Greenwood, or Stoneham, where limitless refreshment
might be obtained legally, wasn't considered sporting. The game was to
get a drink in downtown Wakefield, a mile from home, preferably at Doc
Dutton's drugstore which also retailed the largest banana split—it was
locally termed, for elegance, a banana royal for miles around.

The trick was to tease Dennis into an imagined errand for the barn, a
visit to the blacksmith in Mechanic's Street, or Beasley's Variety Store
for a horseshoe or saddle fitting. As we passed Doc Dutton's ice-cream
palace, Dennis would assume a dreamy look and I would suggest that
he be allowed to buy me a banana royal. As I was working my way
happily through the melted fudge, marshmallow whip, maraschino cherries, and strawberry ice at the middle, Dennis would disappear into the
back room where prescriptions were made up and emerge invariably in
mellow mood. Once I ate three banana royals and Dennis fell out the other
side of the buggy as we were getting in, just as the Reverend Dr. Rice,
minister at the First Congregational Church, was passing. No matter.

Secure in the knowledge that by this time Dennis was reeking of Old
Crow or whatever, it was no trick at all to blackmail him into getting me
a pound of shooting powder and small tin of percussion caps across the
street at George Taylor's. The game enchanted us both.

"Now you're all right for fair," Dennis would bellow for all the kitchen
help to hear as he deposited me at the back door after such excursions.
"Don't let your mother catch you pouring bullets or my name is Dennis."
Everyone screamed with laughter at this witticism.

Life was an uninterrupted lyric, molding bullets in the steel hand
molds in the attic, discharging doubly charged revolvers out back of the
pig barn, and every so often a saturnalia of dynamite—what boy would
not be in heaven?

But fate was preparing a mighty pitfall. Late in the month of June 1914,
while the world was preparing for a somewhat greater conflagration, Salem, Massachusetts, ten miles from Wakefield, was burned flat as a col-
lapsed opera hat.

My big brother Oliver took me to this Neronic occasion in his red
Peerless two-seater, and I never got over it. A joyous interlude of complete
madness during the height of the conflagration saw a squad of Army
demolition experts undertaking to destroy the Salem depot of the Boston
& Maine Railroad, a project which met with universal approval among

the spectators. The depot was a Gothic pile of dressed granite with four vast crenelated towers at the corners, and the trains ran right through it and out the other side on the way to Newburyport and farthest Portland. Ralph Adams Cram, the architect, used to say he could become actively ill by just thinking about it, and Salem had waited for years to see this primeval relic go. Even if the rest of the city had to go with it, it was worth it.

But it wasn't on the books. At the last minute, just as the militia was ready to touch off the charge, the wind changed and the Gothic pile was spared.

But the holocaust had given the Boy Beebe Judgment Day ideas. Smoke and flame and noise and destruction past the imagining. Flaming walls erupting under demolition charges. Powder smoke, bells, sirens, hoarse commands. The end of Rome under the invasion of the Visigoths. The Fire of London foretold by Solomon Eagle. Black Tom and Halifax were yet in the future or he would have included them in his blueprint of patriotism.

Next week Fourth of July came round, and I unfolded my plan to Timothy Ryan, a companion of youth and hellion of notable proportions from the adjacent North Ward.

Outdoor privies were still reasonably commonplace in the New England countryside in 1914 and their overturning standard practice on Halloween or other occasions of community malice. Farmer Cox, halfway to Lynnfield Four Corners, had just erected a notable specimen of utilitarian architecture, a three-holer whose convenience and pleasing design had aroused general admiration. A patriotic gesture of the first magnitude suggested itself to us.

The night before the Fourth saw Timmy and myself in a two-seater buggy powered by Whiteface, a presumably domesticated carriage horse from my father's stable, with enough dynamite in the back to have breached the Maginot Line, moving without running lights down country byways. Guy Fawkes on the way to abolish Parliament couldn't have been more conspiratorial.

According to previous plan, when we arrived at the scene of impending atrocity Timmy stayed with the horse and buggy a hundred yards or so down the country highway, its dust white in the moonlight, while I, with a full dozen sticks of Hercules best, capped and fused in a neat bundle, kept in the shadow of Farmer Cox's well-trimmed barberry hedge. It was the work of a moment to ignite the three-minute-length of fuse with a kitchen lucifer, drop it into the center aperture of the nonesuch, and streak it down the road to the waiting getaway car.

It had been our plan to be a safe spell down the road before the welcoming salute to Independence Day exploded, but somewhere I had miscalculated. Together with my co-conspirator I had no sooner gained the buggy seat and taken the reins from around the whipstock than Judgment Day with overtones of Vesuvius and Krakatau arrived. The midnight heavens sundered in a thunderclap clearly audible, as I later heard, in Reading Square eight miles away. A geyser of splinters, yellow smoke, and assorted other matters rose majestically to dwarf the hourglass elms of Farmer Cox's front lawn and descend in a rain of debris over a wide area of cow sheds and rhubarb patches.

And Whiteface bolted.

Since Gilpin's ride there had probably never been a double scurry comparable to our progress down the midnight highway. Sawing at the reins was a mere hilarious futility. The horse wanted out of there, and nothing was going to stop him. Where my companion left the careening rig I have no knowledge. I contrived to stay with Juggernaut as far as the grist-mill bridge across Saugus River, where the fore right wheel struck the guardrail, became engaged in some bolt or crossbeam, and was shorn from the axle. My father's best two-seater, lovingly built to order by a celebrated Newburyport carriage maker, disintegrated in hideous ruin with the wretch Beebe amidst the debris as the traces parted, and Whiteface spanned the bridge and was off into the night with a diminishing thunder of terrified hoofs.

No concealment of such a debacle seemed practicable. The arrival of the horse alone with trailing harnesses, to awaken the stableman, was sufficient to tell all, even were there not the wreckage of the vehicle and my own highly contused and abraded person.

Two days later I was shipped off to a boys' summer camp famous for its Dannemora discipline in deepest Maine. The train that carried me northward passed through the smoldering ruins of Salem and paused briefly in the detested but still intact depot. There was an ironical justice that, en route to exile, I should be confronted with the inspiration of my downfall.

I gave up dynamite and became an ardent builder of model sailboats. Middlesex County breathed easier when it heard about it.

UNCLE NED

This department is never able to read in other people's reminiscences or family memoirs of the heroic achievements of their relatives—usually uncles or grandfathers—in the fields of love, gastronomy, beautiful letters, or other noble sciences, but that it has a personal application for us. That, of course, is one of the technical devices of the writing trade known as "reader association," and we are available to it most persuasively in the category of wicked, worldly, and wonderful uncles.

We can never read about other folks' Uncle Jeff, who was a fast old party around Saratoga in the seventies when Mr. Vanderbilt was racing his *Maude H,* or Uncle Fred, who could command a dinner at Delmonico's just in pantomime so that the waiter-captain understood his order perfectly (although we always wonder about the motions to indicate *grenadins de boeuf béarnaise,* very rare), but we think of our own Uncle Ned.

Ned was a legend in the family long before we ever encountered him. "Never did a stroke of work in his worthless life," Father used to snort. "Lives off your Aunt Jessie's money and spends all his time staggering around with a lot of dukes and such in Europe." So of course Uncle Ned came with the highest practical recommendations in advance.

Ned and Jessie lived in a château that had belonged to one of Napoleon's less successful admirals in a little township called Celettes, near Blois in the Loir-et-Cher district of France. Jessie hailed from Framingham, Massachusetts, and so, of course, couldn't have been more Continental about everything, but Ned had been a New Yorker of some note at the turn of the century. His cousin, Center Hitchcock, had been first president of the Brook Club, and Ned had been a merry dog around the old Waldorf and Woodmanston Inn, and had written a popular music-hall song about Oscar-of-the-Waldorf Tschirky. He had also been a boxer of amateur note and a celebrated Fifth Avenue dandy in an age when competition was provided principally by the stock collars and morning coats of Evander Berry Wall. Aging salesmen from Wetzel and Bernard Wetherell still recall the wonderments of Ned's ratcatcher suits, high white linen spatterdashes, and crimson-lined Invernesses.

The 1920s found Ned and Jessie securely established among the county families of the French countryside. Jessie's proud old Framingham blood had been brought to a boil by the crude manners of people she chose to regard as *arrivistes* in American society whom she encountered in the society sections of the Sunday papers. Mamie Fish and Harry Lehr, if memory serves, particularly outraged her, and she never relinquished her allegiance to Mrs. Astor as the true queen. Ned's blood, conversely, had been perceptibly cooling, and he was willing to settle for a serene old age among his rosebushes, not too far from Paris and conveniently adjacent to the Vouvray vineyards of the Touraine.

In the bad old days in New York, Ned had been forever tooling coaches to Tuxedo Park with assorted Vanderbilts and riding in steeplechases in the right places, and now he discovered a new and somewhat more sedentary way of demolishing the human framework. The King of Spain introduced him to cross-country automobile racing, then enjoying a vast vogue in Europe, and Ned and Alphonse and a number of other highly placed personages terrified France, Italy, Spain, and parts of Austria for a full generation with their roaring Daimlers, Isottas, and De Dion Boutons.

A world war came and went, mostly unacknowledged by Ned and Jessie, and in the early twenties we went to France to see for ourself the central figures in a legend which, at home back in Boston, had assumed Dionysiac proportions. Ned's income checks kept coming back to the Old Colony Trust Company endorsed by various royalties; and military characters, returning from the wars around the Place Vendôme, told tall tales of having encountered Uncle Ned, surrounded by kings and generals in a blizzard of currency, at the Travelers' Club in Paris.

We could hardly wait.

A rimless single eyeglass and an amazement of plaids cut in the Edwardian pattern of what used to be known as an "English walking suit," a sort of bobtailed cutaway with golfing trousers, met the train at the depot at Blois. A few miles away at Celettes, the Château de Monrepos was a thing of real repose and loveliness. Its servants, of whom there were never fewer than fifteen, not including the shoals of garden boys, were of a liveried perfection never again to be encountered in this world. Life at Monrepos was an ordered and immaculately manicured progress from day to day.

But where were the disorderly grand dukes? Where the King of Spain? Where the auto racing, and when did we set out for Paris and *la vie sporting*? There was too much repose at Monrepos for a Yale undergraduate.

Alas, we had arrived too late. The years of the ortolans were over.

Ned and Jessie had seen the elephant, and all they wanted now was to hear the news of their grandchildren from the States. What we wanted from Ned were the details of the time the Grand Duke Cyril had made a champagne swimming pool out of the dance floor at Cannes. We were, in a word, a division chief who had arrived at the big fire just after the roof had fallen in.

But one great event, I found, remained. Its anticipation occupied the 364 days which intervened between its one celebration and the next. The time devoted to its planning was that time dedicated by the late Mrs. S. Stanwood Menken to her next year's costume for the Beaux Arts Ball of fragrant memory. It dominated conversation, demanded correspondence, and evolved stratagems in its pursuit which Metternich might have dedicated to the conquest of an empire.

All else might be dross in a world well lost, but the annual luncheon of Ned and Jessie at the Hôtel Univers in Tours! There you had something.

This epic convulsion of gastronomy assumed most of the overtones of the Field of the Cloth of Gold combined with the best features of the Grand Tour of Europe as practiced by rich provincials in the seventies. Tours was a scant one hundred kilometers from Celettes, a comfortable drive between late breakfast and luncheon. Tours might even have been available to the whimsical French telephone, whose switchboard was attended four full hours daily in the Touraine at that time and often made communication possible with Paris itself, if the call were placed two days ahead.

But such an approach to the big day would have been too frivolous. Luncheon at the Hôtel Univers was ceremonial, and only correspondence would do. Long, holographic correspondence conducted over a period of weeks and even months between Uncle Ned, as one of the high contracting parties, and the hotel management, in conference with the *chef de cuisine*, the *maître d'hôtel*, the head *saucier*, and the *sommelier*, as the other.

One could wish for a complete file of the Edward Center—Hôtel Univers of Tours letters concerning the service of a single year's luncheon. They would be printed in hand-set Caslon by the Merrymount Press and bound by Riviere in full crushed levant.

Although there were never more than two other guests at this function besides Ned and Jessie—usually a neighboring duke of fantastic age, who wore six-button jackets and a deerstalker hat, and his duchess—you might have been excused for imagining that the entire membership of the National Geographic Society had been invited. The opening skirmishes were of a minor order and usually concerned with establishing a date to the mutual satisfaction of the contracting parties. One year's luncheon had to be postponed until well into August because the *saucier* at the

Univers was visiting his sister in Paris. Upon another occasion, Aunt Jessie had to change a date at the last moment in order to attend a flower show in England, and the management of the Univers threatened to wash its hands of the Centers forever. Legend holds that it required the good offices of Myron Herrick, then Ambassador to France, to fix that one up.

It was the matter of the menu, however, that occasioned the most spirited exchange of contradictions, affronts, disagreements, provocations, and thinly disguised insults. If it was proposed by Ned that plain Russian vodka would be served ice-cold with the fresh Beluga, the maître d'hôtel at the Univers wrote his resignation, to take effect instanter, and deposed at a staff meeting that he would be party to no such barbarism, and that only Latvian vodka, lightly chilled, was thinkable in this circumstance. If the management submitted the suggestion that a mousse of *foie gras* might go well with the salad, Ned would point out with infinite hauteur that there would already have been *foie gras* on the toast under the *tournedos périgourdine*, and did they want him, Center who spoke, to turn into a diseased goose liver entirely?

When at last all had been adjusted after an exchange of missives which taxed the resources of the postal system at Celettes, Ned and Jessie settled down to matters of personal protocol. What attire was suitable to the season? Which car to take? What uniform for the chauffeur? The year your correspondent was present and witnessed these excursions, Ned finally settled for a dove-gray Prince Albert with black satin facings and a gray top hat. Jessie, who never wore anything else on any occasion, wore a white sola topee draped with an infinity of white motoring veils, a blouse with full-length white sleeves terminating in white glacé gardening gloves, a white skirt extending well below her ankles, and white suede shoes. The effect was of a monstrous, animated white toadstool. The car was, of course, the Renault touring, unearthed from the garages and given a full back-shop treatment. It was used only for this annual occasion and promised to last some centuries on this basis.

The day of departure from the Château de Monrepos was in the nature of a holiday. By the time Uncle Ned, with Jessie at his side, had ascended to the driver's seat, the household staff, together with the garden staff, tenants, and other adjacent and interested parties, had assembled in the driveway, and, as Uncle Ned raised his top hat in salute, there was a pretty fluttering of handkerchiefs and shouts of *"Bon voyage!"* The Renault, a splendid maroon monster, lurched fearfully, Uncle Ned screwed a glass into his face under the impression that it would really permit him to see anything beyond a radius of forty feet, and the cavalcade was off. It was a cavalcade because the chauffeur, at a discreet distance, followed the Renault in the family Ford just in case of engine trouble or other contretemps. Uncle Ned's logistics, in an age that hadn't yet heard the word, were impeccable.

What pen shall describe the progress of the Renault through the countryside of the Touraine, the peasants leaping for the hedgerows, the geese perishing miserably beneath the wheels in fountains of feathers, the householders clutching their young and retreating behind their doors in the small towns, the shouted maledictions of carters and teamsters as their horses took to flight at our passing? There was a general feeling that perhaps Von Hindenberg's uhlans would be preferable.

Or what lyric report shall chronicle the arrival at the porte-cochere of the Hôtel Univers in Tours, the management drawn up in an imposing array of frock coats (black), the solemnities of hat-raising and hand-shaking, the exchanged congratulations, respectively on owning and maintaining the Hôtel Univers and being privileged to patronize it?

Nor is it for this tyro of beautiful letters to depict the pageant of gastronomy that ensued, with Jessie at one end of a twenty-foot table and Ned at the other, with your correspondent in the capacity of a sort of telephone exchange halfway between. The courses succeeded each other as the seasons, presented, served, and their ruins removed by waiters in the dress livery reserved for royalty, the wines cherished and decanted drop by drop by the *sommelier* as though each were a sacrament, although but a few minutes previous they may have been tossed up from the cellarage like tennis balls.

Some three hours after having sat down, and amidst the stunned silence and satisfaction that are hallmarks of a superlative gastronomic adventure, Ned nursed a Jockey Club supercorona. Handy, too, were a fragile, solid-gold cup of *café des princes* and an inhaler which, paradoxically, exhaled the bouquet of an 1865 cognac from the bins of the Café de Paris at Monte Carlo.

"Next year," said Uncle Ned thoughtfully, "instead of the cold asparagus *vinaigrette,* I think we might have—"

A new cycle of time was inaugurated. The illimitable future beckoned. Ordinary people might have their January first or their Rosh Hashana, bankers their happy new fiscal year, but for Ned and Jessie, the time scheme started with the service of dessert at the Hôtel Univers in Tours. The glad new year of the calendar, according to Edward Center, came in with the cognac.

UNCLE NED'S WINE PREFERENCES

One has to go back several generations to find gentlemen who believed that the time for drinking claret was not during but after luncheon, and that the time for drinking Burgundy was not during dinner but after it. What, then, did these men drink with their meals? It is unlikely that they used hock and champagne as breakfast drinks, as was suggested by the early Palace Car menus of the Pacific Railroad. The chance of continuous and perhaps overwhelming alcoholism looms too large to be thinkable. Other solutions must have existed.

In the case of my uncle, Edward C. Center of the Château de Monrepos, Celettes, Loir-et-Cher, the solution was twofold: he drank a white Burgundy with his breakfast, and for luncheon Vouvray, a beverage that was regionally made and obtainable in the neighboring town of Blois. When I knew him in the early 1920s, Uncle Ned, so far as I could tell, regularly breakfasted on half a cold roast chicken and a full bottle of lightly chilled Chablis of established mark and approved vintage. After that, he was in prime condition to examine his rose gardens, which had been laid out by one of Napoleon's retired admirals (who, in *his* time, inspected them from a charette drawn by a trained goat), and to raise hell with the Scottish head gardener because some of the specialties of the Center gardens weren't going to be just so for the Paris flower show.

Although a man of strong opinions (one night at dinner, he set his trained police dog on my Aunt Jessie, and the ensuing interlude suggested one of the bloodier passages in *The Hound of the Baskervilles*), Uncle Ned forewent the whimsy of the goat-drawn charette. He descended directly upon the roses and the palsied under-gardeners. He wore for the occasion a bumfreezer-length tailcoat of articulate plaid (known to Edwardians as an English walking coat), plus-fours with high white linen spatterdashes, white wash gloves rolled back from the cuffs, and, in his left eye, a monocle of prismatic intensity. The corrective formula of this eyeglass seemed to attract all available luminosity and to project it in a concentration of objective disdainfulness that no other monocle could achieve.

A morning of incendiary language among the roses refreshed Ned, and he was then ready for lunch (served on the terrace in clement weather) and his Vouvray, after which he got down to the matter of clarets for the afternoon. At the conclusion of luncheon and dinner at Monrepos, the butler would pass a tall vase of scented water for washing the hands; he was assisted in the process by a footman with a broad basin. My sister from Boston, who had never seen such goings-on, at first encounter held her champagne glass out under the warm water. It was a moment that we never again mentioned in public.

One of the best established of the numerous fallacies associated with the drinking of wine is that its absorption, contemplation, and discussion exert a gentling influence upon the consumer. A thousand essayists have extolled wine as a tranquilizer of the emotions, and an agency for philosophic contemplation and the rationalization of differences between men. But the essayists did not know my Uncle Ned.

As the Cheval Blanc '04 went down, and the index of his system's blood sugar mounted, Ned became at first faintly luminous, and then positively incandescent. His rage at the less estimable aspects of humanity, at governments, and at income taxes assumed formidable proportions (for although he had become a French citizen, his sources of revenue were still in the vaults of the State Street Trust Company in Boston). Furniture and house footmen absorbed most of the damage. Aside from the night he set the dog on Aunt Jessie, there was the evening when he recalled a gratuitous insult that had been offered him a decade previous at the bar in the Brook Club in New York. Somebody either had blackballed a candidate for membership of whom Ned approved or had served him champagne in a chalice that held less than a full bottle, the minimum amount permissible in the Center code of courtesy.

Ned was moved to telephone the Paris manager of the French Line and to demand space on the next sailing. He was bound he would return to Manhattan and give his maligner a richly deserved thrashing. He would also justify this transatlantic mission by punching the nose of Reginald Rives, president of the Coaching Club, for some slight which dated back to the year Dewey took Manila. By morning, though, all had been forgotten.

Only once when he was in his cups did Ned put his terrible temper to practical application. It was in the autumn of 1914, and the Germans had pushed into France. A cargo vessel with several million dollars' worth of hides consigned for L. Beebe & Sons, Leather, South Street, Boston, had been embargoed in the Marseilles harbor. The French government had forbidden the ship to sail.

My father cabled Ned and instructed him to go posthaste to Marseilles and to drink up, and charge to Boston, as much Burgundy '86 as he could accommodate. He was then to call upon the Ministry of Marine in the interest of a clearance for the freighter.

For several days, silence reigned. Then the vessel was reported to have passed Land's End and disappeared over the western horizon under full draft, laying a wake of soot twenty miles long. Full details of its clearing never came to light, but it appeared afterward that Ned, armed with a shooting stick and two cases of Montrachet, had undertaken a one-man sit-down strike in the anteroom of the local Ministry of Marine office. There he had apparently made his opinion of French officialdom audible on a twenty-four-hour-a-day basis, in terms that evoked admiration even on the Marseilles waterfront.

When the ranking official opened the door of his inner office to see what was going on in the reception room, did a well-aimed bottle clip the plaster an inch or two from his head? Did the man then attempt to summon aid via the window, screaming in anguished accents for the police or the military? Was the street outside jammed with interested listeners who applauded at every chance, sharing my uncle's opinion of officials in general? Ned wasn't even into the second case of Montrachet when the ship's clearance, gingerly held in a pair of fire tongs, appeared from the inner sanctum. The French government had surrendered in the most abject defeat since Sedan.

THE *BOSTON TELEGRAM*

On being denied the Yale sacrament through the agency of Dean Jones's excommunication, delivered in as menacing an oration as ever the curse of Rome was pronounced by Sir Henry Irving as Cardinal Richelieu, I found myself not only cut off from communion with the humanities, but what was worse, locked out of my apartment in Vanderbilt Hall and thus deprived of a base of New Haven operations.

For a time I was able to maintain residence by the expedient of shacking up with undergraduate friends in the immemorial manner of Yale students seeking sanctuary when creditors were encamped upon their own doorstep and Kligerman & Mintz, the socialist furniture dealers, and other tradesmen were being unreasonable. Peter Arno had long since departed the campus, and I was able for a time to occupy a spare couch with his former roommate, Roswell Flower Taylor, of Watertown, New York, and one or two other charitable comrades. But word soon went out from the dean's office that giving shelter to Beebe was to incur the explicit enmity of the adamant Jones whose edict "Beebe must go" extended even to otherwise inviolable sanctuary and, at long last, credit and friends used up and every hand turned against me, I boarded the New Haven's *Merchant's Limited* for home.

To say that relations were strained at 96 Bay State Road would be the understatement of the century. My father communicated with me through the agency of written memoranda transmitted by the parlor maid or left on my bed. I was welcome to the shelter of the parental roof and might take my meals if I could stand the freezing temperature, but all financial assistance was at an end. Laundry and pressing were not included in my limited welcome.

Home seemed a good thing to be away from while the heat was on, and I set about looking for a job.

The first prospect that presented itself was in the field of communications which was destined to occupy the rest of my professional life. I called upon Robert Lincoln O'Brien, editor of the *Boston Herald*, hat in hand and on my company behavior, and asked if there was anything open like a nice reporter's job or anything else that would occupy my time, suggest penitential industry, and perhaps cultivate golden opinions, or at least gold-plated ones, at 96 Bay State Road.

Robert O'Brien was very much a Boston *eminento* of the time, a polished and urbane man of the world, in great demand as an after-dinner speaker and on first-name terms with everybody of consequence from Amy Lowell to Governor Channing Cox. To be sure, there were those who maintained that he was either errand boy or hatchet man for the First National Bank, the New Haven Railroad, United Shoe Machinery, and other predatory corporate interests of State Street, but he was in any event a somebody, and somebody was what I urgently needed at the desperate moment.

Mr. O'Brien, when I was announced, received me courteously and with apparent pleasure in his corner office in the *Herald* building in Avery Street. The office had two doors leading to different corridors and for some reason not apparent to me at the time, the editor of the *Herald* was wearing a hat and overcoat while doing his morning mail. I had just time, on entering, to see him close the top drawer of his desk in which there prominently reposed a large service revolver of what appeared to be Smith & Wesson design. I later heard that various errands Mr. O'Brien had run for the First National Bank, et al, had failed to endear him to everyone concerned and that sometimes he was subject to the hostile attentions of what were obviously fanatics and other misguided folk who arrived with the intention of violence to his person. Two doors seemed only a rudimentary precaution against such contingencies.

Mr. O'Brien made it plain to me from the outset that employment by the *Boston Herald* was not, perhaps, the equivalent to being a Morgan partner. Boston had the reputation at the time of being the poor farm of American journalism and the *Herald* the most parsimonious of its occupants. He took me down the corridor and pointed through a cracked office door into an untidy cubbyhole where a white-bearded ancient of seedy mien and beaten aspect was skirmishing with an Oliver typewriter of pre-Manila Bay vintage. The venerable Bede of the dust bins was, he confided to me, the *Herald's* chief editorial writer, Laurison Bullard, an *eminento* of the type cases who had twice won Pulitzer Prizes and was regarded as the very *beau ideal*, if also Nestor, of Boston journalistic letters. He received the *Herald's* top salary, Mr. O'Brien whispered, excepting only his own, and after half a century of faithful service received $5000 a year. It was intended to discourage me, but failed miserably.

Failing of discouragement, Mr. O'Brien took me to call on the *Herald's* then managing editor and later publisher, Robert Choate, who enjoyed a professional celebrity in newspaper circles approximating that of Simon Legree among the better plantation owners of the Old South.

Socially irreproachable as a relative of all the available Choate hierarchy that had produced Rufus and the Honorable Joseph Hodges Choate among others, Bobby Choate lacked the versatile wit of the first of these and the courtliness of the second and bluntly said no. He had no city-side openings and none were in prospect. He was about to discharge an entire coffle of serfs that very day and only my opportune arrival postponed the execution. He put on his hat. Mr. O'Brien had his. I retrieved mine and we all went across the street to Honest Parker Shannon's speakeasy, Boston's most celebrated resort of the muses and a sort of Mermaid Tavern under Borgia management.

I sensed at Honest Parker's that Choatie did not enjoy the esteem amongst members of his staff that some of even the most hard-boiled managing editors received in other newspaper shops I came to know. *Herald* staffers at the bar gave the three of us a wide reach of mahogany to ourselves and we enjoyed a splendid isolation like that of Catiline in the Roman Senate. A couple of the more subservient galley rowers knuckled a forelock but there was little of the pleasurable welcome that in years to come I saw manifested when Grafton Wilcox of the *Herald Tribune* or other members of the Ogden Reid hierarchy came into Jack Bleeck's. Choatie was a part owner of the *Herald-Traveler* and lacked the disposition to make himself attractive to his staff.

Under a couple of brisk jolts of Honest Parker's rifle whiskey, he thawed slightly, however.

"Tell you what," he said to me. "You go and see George Mandell at the *Transcript*. It's more your dish of tea, I'd say, than we are. You'd be happier there, but if he hasn't got anything come back in a week and I'll find something. It's like I say, you'd be better adjusted in the *Transcript*."

This was, of course, a compromise runaround and I knew it. I also knew Choatie wasn't in wine and was telling the truth. Liquor was not his vice, although I understood that he overate fantastically.

"Should I tell Mr. Mandell you suggested my seeing him?"

"I don't think it would do you any good."

I took my leave of the *Herald's* general staff not greatly discouraged and comforted for the road which led up Washington Street to the *Transcript* office by two jolts of Honest Parker Shannon's worst.

Boston in the early twenties, if the poor farm of journalism, was also fairly populous with newspapers. The *Herald, Post,* and *Globe* divided the morning field between them, the *Herald* appropriating the best people in the Back Bay and Brookline and the conservative suburbs, including Cambridge and Harvard University. The *Post* had a corner on the Catholic readers, while the *Globe*, a magnificent anachronism, derived its character from the ownership of one General Taylor, a Union valiant who in post-Civil War years had ruled its affairs with benevolent despotism. Its success was predicated solidly on the General's immutable rule that all advertising be paid for in gold currency previous to being composed and run, and the mention of every registered voter in New England at least once a year in its news columns.

In the afternoon there was the *Traveler*, companion and weak sister edition of the *Herald*, the *Evening Globe*, the *Record*, the Hearst *Advertiser*, and the *Sunday American*. There was also the *Boston Telegram*, of which more presently.

Somewhere, I figured, there would be a welcome mat, however threadbare, for the Boy Beebe.

The *Boston Evening Transcript*, although its affairs were sadly in decline and its circulation something less than forty thousand, was still the sturdy citadel of good writing and pretensions to journalistic integrity of Boston's Newspaper Row. It had been in the hands of the Mandell family for so long that it and the family bloodlines were alike running progressively thinner and their pulse declining until finally its heart ceased to beat entirely. It was still a bedsheet-size paper devoid of such concessions to modernity as banner headlines and, like all Boston papers, accepted a certain amount of front-page advertising. Its eight columns of front-page news each carried its own headlines in banks—that is, lines of heading in diminishing size summarizing in detail the contents of the story they concerned. The banks, beautifully literate and each of them a triumph of typographical ingenuity, were written, not by the copy desk, but by the reporter who wrote the story. They often reached to the fold halfway down the page.

The *Transcript*, whose golden age had been during the Civil War and which had been celebrated for its scrupulous coverage of the opening of the Old West and building of the Pacific Railroad, was a Boston legend and subject to innumerable witticisms with a body of folklore all its own. Hoariest of *Transcript* jokes was that concerning the Commonwealth Avenue butler who announced the arrival of the press: "Two reporters from the newspapers, madame, and a gentleman from the *Transcript*." A forgotten wag, in deference to the paper's widely famed habit of appropriating to its own columns news stories originating in other papers, spoke of it as "that fine old Boston kleptomaniac in a black bombazine dress." There was a limerick about a young maid of Back Bay with the culminating line, "And she once threw a *Transcript* away," an unthinkable action among its admiring subscribers.

The *Transcript* specialized in articulate and very literate essays on Chinese ceramics, colonial furniture, and shipwrecks in Boston Harbor. There was a full column daily on "Why the Weather," a ships' news department that was the peer of anything in the New York dailies, a genealogical feature that was treasured by every maiden aunt in New England who made a religion of ancestry, and there were the fiercely scholarly theater and music reports of the celebrated H. T. Parker, better or more bitterly, as the case might be, known by his initials, H. T. P.

The literary editor, Edwin Francis Edgett, was just that. Not a books editor as was the case elsewhere, but literary editor, a gentle and graying ancient with a William Butler Yeats cowlick of silver hair, Buster Brown tie, and Prince Albert frock coat of outmoded vintage and austere dignity. Book review space in the *Transcript* was fully as prestigious as its equivalent in *The New York Times* or any other periodical you could name.

If there was any single arbiter of Boston society it was Charles Alexander, the *Transcript's* own Ward McAllister without whose official approval it was believed no marriage alliance could be contracted in the rarified circles of Back Bay or Pride's Crossing. And if anything were required to complete the Alice-in-Wonderland pattern of the *Transcript's* editorial personality, there was the peculiar circumstance that its sports reporting was the best in town. The sports editor, George Carens, was dean of the confraternity, and Stanley Woodward, then on the *Herald* sports staff and later sports editor of the *New York Herald Tribune,* is authority for the sentiment that the *Transcript's* football extras were outstanding and authoritative achievements.

Only the business office, alas, failed to live up to the assorted wonderments of the paper's editorial side. The *Transcript's* readers were not the sort to patronize department stores and the big annual appropriations of Jordan Marsh, Raymond's ("Where you bot the hat"), Filene's, and the like went elsewhere. Such loyal partisans in finance as Lee Higginson, Stone & Webster, and Kidder Peabody were insufficient to keep the paper above water, and the authority of the all-powerful First National Bank, of course, was on the side of the *Herald.*

The *Transcript* in 1923 occupied the same editorial rooms upstairs from Dunn the men's tailor at the corner of Milk and Washington that it had occupied at the time of the Boston Fire when the melting lead from its composing room cascading down Milk Street had hindered efforts to control the flames. There was no elevator, and worn signs on the steep stair risers leading up from Washington Street read "Editors Two Flights," "Reporters Three Flights."

George B. Mandell, owner and publisher of the *Boston Evening Transcript* and last of the Mandell line, occupied a roll-top desk in what may have been an office but seemed more a part of the open corridor at the top of "Editors Two Flights." He closely resembled the late George Arliss made up for a performance of *Disraeli.* Ancient male functionaries and equally venerable females in black alpaca skirts and white shirtwaists with chatelaine watches hovered dustily in corners pushing cardboard letter files to the top of high ladders. Much of the newspaper's copy was still set from holograph by typographers dating from the American Revolution and skilled at deciphering the calligraphy of various members of the staff. The only typewriters in view were an L. C. Smith model that had separate keyboards for upper and lower case. The *Transcript* was a museum piece.

George Mandell, also dusty and brittle with age, was courteous but vague. He didn't think there were any openings at the moment. Did I know his son Ducky? I did; he'd been at St. Mark's and was shortly to kill himself and his entire family in an airplane accident of grotesque dimensions. Would somebody please ask the city editor if he could spare Mr. Mandell a moment? Was my family in health? He rejoiced to hear it. Had I graduated yet from Harvard? A Yale man? Sad, sad. There had never been any Yale men on the *Transcript*. Not that he could remember anyway.

The city editor, also a member of the GAR, with crumbs on his waistcoat from lunching at Thompson's Spa but still a far piece from senility, put in a deferential appearance. He confirmed his principal's gloomiest apprehensions. There was no opening at the moment on the city staff. There was a waiting list, one gathered, culled from the older members of the Union Club, of anxious aspirants to work on the paper. Perhaps in a year or so, but he couldn't be certain. A glimpse of the city room where graybeards were pushing pencils painfully across vast expanses of dark brown copy paper suggested there might be a vacancy earlier than he anticipated, but I prudently refrained from remarking as much. The average age of the *Transcript*'s copy boys would have entitled them to pensions in any other organization. Ranking executives and senior editors had obviously been contemporaries of the first President Harrison.

Still undismayed but with Honest Parker Shannon's inspiration dying on me, I went across the street to Thompson's Spa for lunch, presumably on the stool recently occupied by the city editor. Thompson's was famous for its fish cakes, baked beans, and apple pies, all served from behind small counters or bays by sensible and agreeable young women who were the local counterparts of the Harvey House girls in Kansas and New Mexico. Many of them married well. Most of the stools at lunch were occupied by State Street bankers and brokers and the highly substantial businessmen of downtown Boston. My father often walked up from his office at 129 South Street, a distance of well over a mile through city traffic. Happily he was not at Thompson's that day.

My third call was at the offices of the *Boston Telegram*, where, by late that afternoon, I was on the payroll. Three is a charm.

The *Boston Telegram* may well awaken memories only in antiquarians today, but it was once, and briefly, very much of a going concern with a circulation of well over 200,000 and a loyal following among readers who would have had to spell out stories from the *Transcript* while moving their lips.

The *Telegram* was the raffish whim of Fred Enright, publisher of the successful and solvent *Lynn* (Mass.) *Telegram* and probably an aspirant for political office in the state, although his career ended before he got a chance at the ballot box.

Staffed with a hastily assembled gaggle of journalistic oddments from the saloons of Newspaper Row ranged around a core of half a dozen more or less responsible practitioners from his Lynn establishment, the *Telegram* was published from a loft building at 99 Portland Street, near the North Station, with the reluctant participation of some of the most venerable printing machinery outside the Smithsonian Institution. If chemical analysis had been invoked to disclose that its editions were printed in a fifty-fifty solution of ink and whiskey, it would have surprised nobody familiar with its spectacularly irresponsible economy, least of all members of the editorial staff.

I waited upon Mr. Enright in his third-floor office and was hired as a city-side reporter with such celerity that anyone less naïve than Beebe in the year 1923 would have looked for hidden motives in Mr. Enright's instant availability. They lay, of course, in the circumstance that the Beebe family were involved in half a dozen of the more influential banks in town and that Mr. Enright felt that having a Beebe scion on his staff, no matter in how bad odor at home, couldn't be too much of a liability. As it happened, he never undertook to take advantage of my family connections and would have gotten short shrift had he done so. The *Boston Telegram* was not acknowledged in the circles in which Beebes moved.

My cheerful acceptance by Mr. Enright at a salary of twenty dollars a week on a basis of fair regularity of payment saw me on duty promptly at six-thirty next morning, an hour which until then I had associated with coming home rather than beginning the day. It meant leaving Bay State Road at five and taking the subway to Haymarket Square and having a preliminary breakfast en route. It was the custom of the editorial side to have a more substantial breakfast at ten in the morning after the first edition was on the street.

My duties, at the outset anyway, consisted of unlocking the front door at the aforementioned six-thirty as there was no night watchman and the janitor was a character so far submerged in a labyrinth of subterranean grottoes and furnace rooms that, to the best of my knowledge, I never set eyes on him in the year I worked there.

Climbing the cast-iron flights of stairs to the fifth floor where the editorial rooms were located, I turned up the lights, turned on the steam, which had been prudently abated at the close of business the day before, switched on the bank of teletypes in the telegraph room, being careful to see that each was properly fitted with a large roll of yellow copy paper that ground through its innards and coiled into a tall waiting basket, saw to it that mounds of copy paper were located at strategic points as indicated by the management, and spread out the morning papers of the competition and from New York on the city editor's desk where they would be handy when, if, and as that august functionary was able to make it up the stairs at seven o'clock.

There was nothing sybaritic about the plant of the *Telegram*. The editorial rooms had been used as some sort of storehouse before becoming a bower of the muses and the furniture was of a state of decrepitude that suggested it might have been acquired at fire-sale rates immediately after the Boston Fire. The reporters sat at museum-piece typewriters, not at separate desks as was the practice elsewhere, but at an immensely long deal table divided by foot-high partitions into individual compartments just wide enough to accommodate the typewriter carriage at its fullest travel. Over each of these cubicles hung a green-tin-shaded electric light bulb on a long cord.

The horseshoe-shaped copy desk, which as the day wore on would be occupied by half a dozen practitioners in green eyeshades whose general aspect suggested they were deserters from the Union Army after the debacle at Bull Run, communicated by a gravity slot with the composing room immediately beneath. So did an electric buzzer cunningly concealed just under the edge of the city editor's desk which sounded a tocsin audible to the compositors in case of riot or invasion. It was in frequent use. An outraged citizen who had made his way to the fifth floor with the announced intention of taking apart the executive branch of the shop, on turning around would find himself encircled by a menacing demi-lune of pressmen and compositors in square paper hats each with a heavy spanner in his hand and the hope in his eye that the stranger might start something. He seldom did.

As an afternoon paper the *Telegram*, the auspices being favorable, expected to print five daily editions, the first coming off press at approximately nine-thirty to meet the competition of the *Traveler* and *Evening Globe* which hit the street with a bulldog at approximately the same time. To fill eighty columns of typeset for the first paper there was usually an assist from overset remaining from the day before which could be brought up-to-date by rewriting the lead sentence and changing the dateline. The rest of the paper—the editorial staff, including the Boy Beebe— was expected to get over the copy slot by eight-thirty.

This was not as arduous a task as might at first suggest itself since the duty of the first editor to arrive was to attack the early editions of *The New York Times*, the *Herald Tribune*, the *World*, and the *Sun* with a pair of two-foot-long scissors, clipping out at random attractive-looking features and news stories and distributing them to the staff with instruction to "put a local lead" on them. This technique comprised taking, say, a story from Pittsburgh concerning the gross output of cold rolled steel for the week or a report from Omaha of a derailment on the North Western Railway and pasting it up in its entirety under a first sentence which read: "It will interest Boston readers to know that——."

To supplement this editorial brigandage which was by no means unique in the production of the *Telegram* but existed in most afternoon newspapers of the time, there was always an enormous square footage of boiler plate, comics, women's fashions, household hints, and even prefabricated editorials, which arrived in mats from N.E.A. (Newspaper Enterprise Association) ready to be cast and shoved into the paper in terms of acreage rather than lineage. As the day wore on and actual news of the moment came to hand, much of the purloined and filler material was displaced, edition by edition, with more legitimate copy, if the phrase could ever with propriety be used in connection with the *Boston Telegram*.

The arrival of the members of the staff who followed me on duty, so long as I was junior member of the city side and charged with opening up the shop, suggested nothing so much as the retreat of the Grand Army from Moscow. Hollow moans and sounds of deep breathing announced the advent up the stairwell of Norton Pratt, the city editor and a battered veteran of a thousand journalistic Trafalgars, who groped his way from one piece of furniture to the next in the direction of his appointed place and sat for some moments saying, "Oh, my God!" before bothering to remove his hat and coat.

Sometimes Norton discarded his outer garments before reaching into the bottom drawer of his desk for a bottle in the files marked "City Hall, Confidential." If strength was needed for hanging them up on the adjacent rack, he had his first drink of the morning while still attired for the street.

The transformation was as wonderful as it was almost instantaneous. In the space of two or three minutes during which I entertained the fear morning after morning that my boss was going to die with only myself to take down his final message, there emerged from the quivering human wreckage a well coordinated, cheerful, and entirely competent professional who shot his cuffs, composed his formerly anguished features, and picked up the day's work with easy expertise. The whole transformation was that of John Barrymore passing from Mr. Hyde to Dr. Jekyll and represented to me a greater recurrent miracle than the Resurrection.

Norton Pratt's advent was usually a sort of sneak preview for that of the other members of the executive and editorial staff who arrived in stages of disrepair running from what ship's underwriters would appraise as "total loss" to "perhaps salvageable."

Neal Moynahan, the managing editor, occupied a private office near the head of the stairs and we seldom saw him although we knew him to have arrived and be in residence by the slamming of his door and a series of shattering moans that came over the transom. A hugely fat man and an acknowledged if not practicing anarchist, he never appeared to the view of the staff until he, too, had taken restorative steps and was under more or less bodily control. I think he cherished the delusion that we imagined he arrived in perfect running order.

The social status of the individual members of the *Telegram* staff was not what I was later to come to associate with *The New York Times* or the *Herald Tribune* where Harvard and Yale graduates were the rule rather than the exception, Rhodes scholars fairly commonplace, and members of the titled nobility from foreign lands by no means unknown. Mr. Enright had ransacked the bargain basement of journalism to recruit the hearties who got out his paper for him, but if their appearance and conduct suggested at times a quorum in a Bowery mission, there was a remarkable professional competence about these seedy derelicts which suggested better days in more exalted professional circles. The chief of the copy desk, a courteous and knowledgeable old gentleman whose fine shock of coal-black hair suggested liberal applications of Three-in-One shoe polish, had about him a courtesy that implied he might have served under Colonel Marse Henry Watterson. I know that he had a speaking acquaintance, although whence it derived I never ascertained, with the great E. P. Mitchell of the *New York Sun*, and he initiated me into the technique of writing news copy as patiently as a court chamberlain might instruct a country boy in the duties of a page to royalty.

A less gentlemanly copy reader might well have accorded a feckless neophyte public reprimands for all to hear and appreciate, but this Chesterfield of the subheads would inconspicuously present himself at my elbow to point out some infringement of style or explicit libel in my story. I'm sure his reward is eternity on a celestial copy rim where no green reporters are ever broken in and where hangovers are unknown and even unremembered.

I remember his sad appraisal of the *Telegram's* style as somewhat wanting in what he must have considered perfection of syntax. "The word really is 'diplomatist' Mr. Beebe," he would say wistfully, "but in this shop I believe 'diplomat' is permissible."

Titles on the *Telegram* had little meaning amidst the rich disorders that accompanied its daily production and in the light of the razor-edge margin which separated getting out a paper from total alcoholic, professional, and mechanical dissolution. Leo Taffe, the head rewrite man and recently a tough top sergeant in the wars, was frequently called on to reach for his hat and sheaf of copy paper and hasten to the scene of a fire or other untoward occurrence in the role of ordinary leg man.

One news editor and makeup man often abandoned these exacting posts to participate in some uncommonly spectacular editorial fracas, especially if it involved love-life, alcohol, and low conduct generally. Witness the time when, through his underworld connections, he was able to set up light housekeeping with a female known to *Telegram* readers as "The Bandit Queen of Roxbury," living with her in profitable sin directly across from the Joy Street police station when she was in request not only by the local police but the more weighty Federal inspectors for Post Office robbery. At the end of an industrious week devoted, we gathered, on a fifty-fifty basis to amorous and editorial pursuits, he, without batting an eye, handed her over to the cops and the paper ran her autobiography as ghosted by this editor in a notable exclusive that had every other shop in town save possibly the *Transcript* and *The Christian Science Monitor*, consumed with envy. It wasn't exactly the *Monitor*'s dish of tea.

The *Telegram* profited on a not inconsiderable scale from tips on municipal and criminal matters brought into the office by shady characters and paid for in cash by Norton Pratt from a modest amount of petty cash kept handy for the purpose. I think five dollars was the going rate for oblique sidelights on misconduct in municipal judicial chambers and influential inmates of Charles Street jail who were, in fact, spending the weekends in the bosom of what may or may not have been their families.

Although all newspapers have of necessity their contacts and undercover sources of informed treachery, especially in the ranks of bail bondsmen, underpaid municipal servants, and undertakers, the *Telegram* was the only paper in my knowledge or experience where this traffic was so regular a commerce and the going rate for informers fixed by what amounted to union scale. Colonel William D'Alton Mann, the redoubtable publisher of *Town Topics* had established a sliding scale of fees to domestics turned informer on their socially exalted employers, a dollar for footmen, two dollars for personal maids, and five dollars for butlers and social secretaries.

To my observation the *Telegram* never went above five dollars or under two dollars. If there were bigger deals and more expensive treachery, they were consummated by Neal Moynahan in the privacy of the managing editor's office.

Purely and simply, the *Telegram* was a scandal sheet which made William Randolph Hearst's *Boston American* seem a tall tower of reticence and respectability in comparison. Common usage, if not an absolute editorial must, was the use of the word "orgy" in something bigger than 72-point Cheltenham on the front page of every paper that came from the delivery room. Lacking the two-collar presswork then in vogue to print alternate red and black banner heads among the better-heeled competition, we relied on bigger, bolder, and brassier headlines for shock impact on readers and for the promotion of street sales which is all the *Telegram* had. I don't believe we had a mailing list of any sort other than the tearsheets sent to advertisers.

Along the middle of the morning Frank Shannon, the police-headquarters man, a small, tough, shaggy Irishman who talked in headlines, would call in with his roundup from the station house blotters of the night before, and the inside staff at 99 Portland Street would go into action for the day, making subsequent editions bloom with orgies, stabbings, and marital contretemps of alarming dimensions. "House of Mirth Raided!" Shannon would shout into the telephone in 86-point Bodoni Bold tones. "Back Bay Debutantes Apprehended in Sensational Orgy," this in about 36 point. He would then launch into the story's lead, ready-written and only requiring that the rewrite man on the line take it down verbatim:

"Acting on tips of outraged neighbors, police from Station 16 under the leadership of Captain Pearly Neiland and Sergeant Harvey French raided a boudoir apartment where they arrested six men and six women described as society debutantes with Back Bay addresses and prominent club men. . . ."

The address, to be sure, would be in a neighborhood south of Huntington Avenue and the names of the society debutantes would turn out to be Suzie Slotnick and Rachel Dunkelfarb, but it made no difference in the *Telegram.* All our bagnios were perfumed boudoirs and their inmates social registerites from the Back Bay. The masculine accomplices to these skirmishes with Captain Pearly Neiland were usually in proper fact bootleggers off duty, ex-convicts, and shoe salesmen on the town but *Telegram* readers got the impression that, immaculately attired in full evening dress, they had gone directly from the police station, after posting bail, to the Harvard Club or the Tennis & Racquet, which was even handier, being next door to Station 16 in Boylston Street.

The patent circumstance that no copy of the *Boston Telegram* was ever allowed past the doors of any polite residence in Beacon Street or Commonwealth Avenue, although it may well have circulated below stairs, only suggested that we keep a stiff upper lip in the columns of the paper itself and see to it that it was peopled with folk of irreproachable social *ton.* Any subway stabbing that couldn't be elevated to the estate of a hereditary feud between Sicilian noblemen had no place in the paper. Our courtroom reporting seethed with duchesses and dowagers, playboy sons of industrial titans, and debutante daughters of members of the Chilton Club who had unaccountably taken up smoking opium in the main restaurant of the Copley Plaza Hotel. The conduct of

Boston society in the *Telegram's* brief interregnum assumed aspects of carnival it has never known before or since.

It was this editorial penchant for the better things of life and unabashed admiration of class on the part of the circulation department at 99 Portland Street that, ironically enough, finally obtained for me a Harvard degree.

My first few weeks on Norton Pratt's city staff were largely devoted to routine calls at the residences of proper Bostonians who somehow, and almost always embarrassingly, figured in the news. Uncle Henry had stolen a Paris taxi and driven it through the Arc de Triomphe, flattening a gendarme in the process; the daughter of the family at Vassar had been apprehended mounting the gangplank of the *Berengaria* with a bogus Rumanian duke; or a well-placed and eccentric relative, on whose gilt-edge holdings the entire family had counted eventually to bail them out of bankruptcy, had left all to a home for indigent Skye terriers. My appearance and manners, for I still had an ample wardrobe of New Haven fine raiment, largely itself unpaid for, could be counted on to get me past the butler or parlor maid until he could get an emphatic command from his employer to throw me into the street, during which brief interlude, I was expected to steal as many family portraits from the drawing room as could conveniently be secreted under my overcoat. "Take all you can get," Norton used to tell me with a seignorial flourish of his editorial scissors. "We may not use them all, but don't leave any for those bastards from the *Traveler*."

It is perhaps worth citing as a commentary on the reluctance the better people felt to tangle with the *Telegram* that once when I purloined from a lordly Commonwealth Avenue town house a charcoal drawing of a maiden that turned out to have been executed by John Singer Sargent and had intrinsic as well as sentimental value, no steps were taken to apprehend the offending party. The portrait, after appearing in a five-column front-page reproduction under the heading "Marries Her Father's Chauffeur," hung for as long as I can remember in the art editor's cubicle in Portland Street. The solid-gold frame which came with it was put to better use.

It soon appeared, however, that despite a modest talent for larceny in the best circles and a facility for rewriting other people's stories which permitted me to cover the Loeb-Leopold trial for the murder of Bobbie Franks without leaving Portland Street, my most radiant achievements might be accomplished elsewhere. The *Telegram*, which begrudged reporters a dime's carfare to Newton Lower Falls and would have gone a week without an orgy before sending a correspondent to Chicago, received widespread commendation for its Loeb-Leopold coverage, especially my moving first-hand account of Clarence Darrow's historic summary for the defense.

Harvard University, conveniently located within five-cent carfare of downtown Boston and therefore well within the *Telegram*'s possessive purview, was regarded by the management as an inexhaustible source of gratifyingly upper-class tumults. It was, it will be remembered, the darkest period of prohibition, and alcoholism in the groves of Academe was as requisite as English I or Music A (The History of Roman Band Instruments) at Harvard. Students were forever inciting to riot against the peace of Cambridge, inaugurating mass demonstrations at football rallies, or incinerating themselves on the College Highway in Stutz Bearcat roadsters.

That there might be an element of dedicated youths within the bounds of Harvard Yard whose interests and preoccupations were predominantly academic and who only got sailor-drunk on Saturday nights was beyond the comprehension of the *Telegram*. In Portland Street all students were playboys, cutups, stage-door johnnies, and elegantly upholstered tosspots who slept in their opera hats and brushed their teeth with a light Moselle in the morning.

There was, of course, just enough substance to this cheerful myth to facilitate its establishment on a universal scale and I was the obvious and perhaps divinely appointed agent for its perpetuation in the columns of the *Boston Telegram*. I became the paper's Harvard correspondent.

As a Yale ex., I had numerous friends and contacts among the undergraduates on the far side of Charles River. Many of my companions and contemporaries from the Connecticut prep-school circuit were now sophomores and juniors on the rolls at University Hall. As a practicing poet with a published volume of verses to my credit, I had access to other members of the poets' union such as Robert Hillyer, Foster Damon, and Dudley Fitts, the last of whom scorned English and wrote, as his best, verses in classic Latin. Fitts roomed upstairs in the back of *The Harvard Crimson* with an emaciated youth with soulful eyes lately of Kent School named James Gould Cozzens, who was destined for fame in the almost immediate future.

When Jim Cozzens' first novel *Confusion*, was published while he was still a sophomore and during my tenure at the *Telegram*, it was no trick at all to accord him full-page feature notice at regular intervals as the boy genius of American letters which he was, more or less. His and Fitts's chambers in Plympton Street became an outpost of the *Telegram* and we spent cheery evenings there plotting outrage and infamy which, when implemented into tangible action, would become front-page news and exclusives which even the *Transcript*, which had a college editor and regarded Harvard as privately posted territory, was unable to get.

Truth to tell, many of my beats were not the sort of thing the *Transcript* would have cared for at the end of the proverbial ten-foot pole. Did clandestine sex rear its head within the confines of Harvard Yard so that the dean's office was forced to take punitive action while shrouding the events in impenetrable secrecy? The *Telegram* had a play-by-play account within the laws of libel. Did revolt flare amongst the professoriate so that a dissident instructor in comparative literature appeared at faculty meeting wrapped in a Nazi flag and giving the Nazi salute until he was forcibly dissuaded? The *Telegram* told all.

Although university authorities would willingly have directed public attention elsewhere, a favorite with the working press of the time was a youthful Frenchman and undergraduate with the fetching name of Henri de Castellane. He was in proper fact a nephew of the celebrated or infamous Count Boni de Castellane, the international playboy and adventurer who had married Anna Gould and been divorced only after spending seven of the Gould millions in riot and extravagance in Europe. Count Boni himself was still alive and a favorite of Sunday feature writers and the society columnists, and Nephew Henri was entirely agreeable to basking in this reflected glory.

Young de Castellane was given to champagne breakfasts on Sunday in his college digs, to hiring horse cab processions to take himself and friends to *fêtes champêtres* in the Cambridge countryside, and to waltzing through French windows, glass and all, at balls at the Somerset Hotel in Boston, setting for the stateliest of Boston's social sarabands. He lived up to the fondest American notions of a dissolute member of European nobility by wearing a single eyeglass and sometimes attending class in a silk hat, thus setting a precedent for the later appearances of Prince Michael Romanoff at Cambridge.

The radiant press accorded these opulent disorders was understandably viewed with scant approval by President Abbott Lawrence Lowell of Harvard, especially in view of the circumstance that a segment of the readers of the *Telegram* began regarding Henri de Castellane as titular head of the university and Dr. Lowell as a sort of imposter. The misapprehension was not diminished when young de Castellane took to arriving at evening parties in Boston in an open barouche with footmen on the box and mounted outriders in military uniform with lances, recruited, of course, from the best undergraduate clubs of Cambridge, but open to misinterpretation among the peasantry.

It may be said in all modesty that an appreciable portion of the princely Monsieur de Castellane was the creation of the Harvard correspondent of the *Boston Telegram*. We regularly printed his opinions of Boston society, not all of them flattering, in leaded type and boxed on the front page and his pictured likeness, monocle, dicer, and all were as familiar to the *Telegram*'s readers as the porcine features of Mayor James Aloysius Curley.

When at length some particularly atrocious assault on the established proprieties enabled Harvard to be shut of de Castellane, his expulsion took on overtones of an international incident. The *Telegram* was able to report that the French Embassy in Washington was in receipt of a telegram signed by the French milord demanding diplomatic intercession on his behalf. It never was quite clear who sent the telegram.

To take his congé of Harvard, de Castellane rented every horse cab still available in Greater Boston for an entourage which accompanied him down U.S. 1 the entire distance to Providence, where French steamships still docked for the Atlantic run. The cavalcade took three days to make it, and forethoughtful bootleggers had established oases at strategic points along the way.

Need it be said that photographers for the *Boston Telegram* gave the pilgrimage adequate coverage while Dr. Lowell pondered fretfully on the meaning of life in his offices at University Hall.

My friendship with Jim Cozzens, Dudley Fitts, Bob Hillyer, Foster Damon, and the somewhat erratic Jack Wheelright was a source of satisfaction and entertainment quite aside from the advantage of their acquaintance as professional contacts. None of them were then as well known as they were to be in the near future, and met to recite their verses to each other under the auspices of a group called the Harvard Poetry Society. The influence of George Santayana, although he had himself long since departed Harvard for his native Spain, was a powerful one in the Harvard poetry of the early twenties, and Hillyer's early sonnets, if unidentified with their proper author, might easily be confused with the stately melancholy of the great Spanish philosopher. That Santayana's presence in Cambridge had not been without a taint of scandal did nothing to make him unfashionable in the rarefied literary atmosphere of Plympton Street.

Alcohol was, of course, the universal solvent of *belles lettres*. Hillyer and Damon shared rooms in a boarding house in Mount Auburn Street whose landlady had strict notions of propriety and locked the front door precisely at ten o'clock at night. Inmates locked out slept elsewhere until they discovered the availability of a fire escape whose bottom iron rungs terminated about nine feet from the ground, not so far as to be dangerous, but just out of reach for even a tall man unaided. Hillyer and Damon discovered that by one boosting the other and then reaching down a helping hand, the ladder could be used in emergency as a means of access to their apartment. If too much in wine they were unable to accomplish the necessary gymnastics and, as the gin circulated during poetry evenings, one would admonish the other: "Remember the goddamned fire escape."

On one historic occasion Hillyer had already gained the first landing outside the second-floor fire exit on this precarious arrangement when Damon contrived to get his legs through the rungs of the lower ladder where he hung upside down and crying piteously for assistance while a torrent of watches, keys, wallets, and small change cascaded from his pockets. A passing group of Cambridge port toughs took full advantage of the situation and their hideous laughter was swallowed in the night as they made off with all Damon's valuables with neither risk nor effort.

I had, at intervals, when the smoke of battle cleared sufficiently at 99 Portland Street, been endeavoring for some time to gain admission to Harvard College as a transfer student from New Haven, using my already-established academic credits to enroll me as a sophomore and pleading that the occasion for my dismissal from Yale, while perhaps provocative, had not represented any special moral turpitude and might well be overlooked by a broader-minded institution.

I had friends and partisans at University Hall. My brother Oliver's roommate as an undergraduate nearly a decade earlier, Ed Seymour, was one of the deans of the College. There were members of the English department who felt that the presence of an established professional in the calling of letters could do no harm to the literary tone of their classes. Others, like Robert Hillyer and Bernard De Voto, were just plain friends and well disposed on no other grounds. To all such intercession, however, Henry Pennypacker, dean of admissions, turned a notably cold shoulder. He took a dim view of refugees from other institutions where they had established a certain degree of notoriety for nonacademic behavior. My reputation stemming from New Haven was not of an altogether scholarly nature.

As time passed, however, it became apparent that the *Boston Telegram*, a paper which did the public image of Harvard as a grove of Academe no special good, had a built-in correspondent who had access to all and any skeletons that rattled around Harvard Yard. The *Telegram* was read with relish by undergraduates whose parents would only have handled it with fire tongs, as I had once actually seen done with a copy I inadvertently left on the reading-room table at the Algonquin Club in Commonwealth Avenue.

Somebody must have advanced the thesis to Dean Pennypacker that, enrolled as a Harvard student and subject to the discipline of the University, the Boy Beebe might be available to some sort of control and could probably be induced to give up his unfortunate professional connections altogether.

How much weight my family contributed in the matter I have no way of knowing. My father, although a profoundly respected and influential banker, was far from being a college man himself and, to the best of my knowledge, had no friends among the Harvard Board of Overseers. My brother, although a member of the class of '16 with a distinguished service record in the 1914 war, was in no sense a professional Harvard graduate and took no more interest in its affairs than using his privileged status to obtain football tickets.

I incline to believe that my eventual admission to Harvard in the class of '27 was a triumph of my own inadvertent diplomacy or, if you will, blackmail. It was made abundantly clear to me in an interview with Dean Pennypacker that severance of my obligations to Fred Enright was one of the conditions of his reluctant approval. A by-no-means-humorless gentleman, he remarked that if the *Telegram* could be removed from what amounted to required reading in Harvard Yard, almost no risk incurred in the transaction could be too great.

I had been on the staff of the *Boston Telegram* less than a year when I reverted to the status of undergraduate, but it had been an instructive experience in worldliness and I knew where I wanted to go and what I wanted to do when the time came. I knew a lot of things most college boys didn't and I was already a pro. I fear I didn't let anyone forget it.

BEVERLY WAGON LIVING

The exact role played by the Fords of Model T vintage in the lives of the Beebes of Beebe Cove, Wakefield, Massachusetts, I do not remember with total recall. This is partly due to the fact that they came and went in a continuous procession and to the fact that there were other cars (let's face it), some of which had a romantic hold on my imagination.

There was a magnificent Pierce Arrow, finished in solid-brass trim, which mounted like the boxes in a theater from the driver's level occupied by Callahan, our coachman promoted to chauffeur, through various levels to a peanut-gallery rear seat. There was my big brother Oliver's Peerless roadster, painted a fire-wagon red, in which we attended the Great Fire of Salem in June 1914. There was a car which must now be a collector's item, called a Bay State, which scores of Beebes drove when my father received the manufacturing company as security for a bad bank loan.

In such gorgeous and eccentric company, the Fords did not stand out as blossoms in my garden of memory until the advent of the first primeval Model T Beverly Wagon. The Beverly Wagon motorcar body, like the whip socket and cockaded chauffeur's top hat, was a vestigial but still direct link with horse and carriage transport. It was the direct descendent of the horse-drawn Beverly Wagon, named for the Massachusetts community of its origin. Behind the driver's seat there were two or three lateral bench seats like those in an open trolley car, entered from the side and open to the elements, seating three occupants each. It had been designed to take families of New England Yankees to Sunday meeting, county fair, or other communal *fête champêtre*. By the time of the motorcar, it was used by the well-to-do to send the servants to church.

Despite this function, the Beverly Wagon was possessed of no small chic and distinction. It was not a stock-model car in the early days, and had to be manufactured to order by the same firm of carriage builders on the North Shore that had evolved its horse-drawn predecessor. Only families or individuals possessed of an ample stable of other motorcars would dream of having a Beverly Wagon, and it was a sort of luxury item in the garages of the rural or suburban aristocracy. It was built of spruce or maple, of simple carriage-work construction, with a leather-surfaced top. No fringe.

The first car given me by my father for my very own at the age of eighteen or nineteen was a hand-me-down Beverly Wagon. In a conservative sort of way, excepting only for some months following my collision in the town square of Wakefield with a horse-drawn delivery wagon of the Crystal Lake Ice Company, I had had access to the other family cars, but the Model T Beverly Wagon was mine to have and to hold, to drive to the morgue or to jail as fancy might dictate.

At Harvard, where I was at the time serving a four-year stretch—with time off for bad behavior, as it turned out—the Beverly Wagon was viewed by my contemporaries with mixed emotions. The louts or peasants regarded it as a form of truck and were correspondingly contemptuous. My social peers recognized it for what it was, a conveyance of distinction but tainted with a suggestion of the servants' hall. They took to saluting me as "Hoskins" or "Jeeves."

I took counsel with a classmate named Bradley Fisk, a fellow of multiple clubs and great distinction of worldliness who had his clothes made by Dunn, the most expensive Boston tailor, and went to England every summer. Together we remodeled the Beverly Wagon into a carriage that won acclaim and envy on every hand.

Stripping it of its lateral seats, we added a striped awning to the edge of the roof engrossed with the words "Café de la Paix." Within its ample economy was space for three characteristic French sidewalk-café tables each with two chairs. A foot locker held cracked ice, bottled beer, and, on occasions of great gala, champagne. This was during prohibition when we thought that the flouting of the Nineteenth Amendment was a supreme act of devoted patriotism and carried with it a cachet of social distinction.

We arrived at lectures around Harvard Yard, the tables filled to capacity with bottle-waving classmates attired in raccoon overcoats and hard bowler hats, as thousands cheered. In the evening, for balls at the Somerset Club, debutante parties, and dinners in Boston, we rode grandly across the River Charles in opera hats and Inverness cloaks, saluting the passing traffic with lifted glasses and a courtly bow.

For the spring races at the Country Club in Brookline, the insigne on the awning was changed to "Royal Enclosure," and pearl-gray top hats and binoculars were required of our guests. Race week at New London, where the Yales strove mightily with the Harvards on the Thames, saw us in yachting flannels and caps with a décor of Japanese lanterns around the perimeter of our rolling clubhouse. The cocktail burgee trailed aloft, and the legend on the awning read "Corsair," a reminder to J. P. Morgan that he might have the largest steam yacht in the world, but that there was social competition.

The car notably elevated my invitational status, and I was asked to parties I would never otherwise have achieved. Owners of Stutz Bearcats and other equipages of splendor were eclipsed by our Beverly Wagon with its flowering slip covers in the summer and its occupants in hunting pinks with a groom blowing a long horn on the box for hunt meets at Essex Country Club. At Commencement it was filled with seniors singing "*Gaudeamus Igitur*" in caps and gowns, and I am sure, filled President Abbott Lawrence Lowell, who had only a guard of cavalry outriders, with envy.

It was this rancor in the breast of the president of Harvard University, I am to this day certain, which led to my undoing. Accused of a minor infringement of the University's rules—I had merely smashed a section of bookcase over a classmate's head in a moment of boyish spirits—my resignation was urgently in requisition at the dean's office. Friends in State Street, where Harvard was financed, carried it as high as the matter could go, to President Lowell in University Hall.

Dr. Lowell had heard that I was critical of his habit of wearing tan boots with a morning coat and he had, on occasion, seen the Model T conversion in full career. The verdict was an unqualified thumbs down, but I had a fine farewell to Harvard. With the assistance of the management of Jake Wirth's Germanic tavern in Boston, we decorated the Beverly Wagon as a beer hall with the advertising legend "Wirth's" on the awning, and ultimately were thrown into jail at Joy Street Station. To the very end the Beverly Wagon had what the French call *ton*.

AUNT ALICE AT THE OPERA

Although all Bostonians of her generation were familiar with Mrs. Jack Gardner by sight as, indeed, they were with another lady magnifico who was her contemporary, Miss Amy Lowell, my contact with the city's great patroness of the arts was accomplished on a single unique occasion, but one so blindingly splendid as perhaps to merit a place in the record.

At the time of which I write, the effulgent Boston opera company annually performed for a season in the farthest reaches of Huntington Avenue where the Boston Opera House lurched against the municipal skyline. My elderly and much-loved Aunt Alice Carpenter, a grande dame of formidable mien and overwhelming presence, and by every standard Isabella Gardner's peer save in the realms of fine arts, had asked me to squire her to an evening performance of *Aïda*, or perhaps it was *Carmen*. The billed performance was so inferior to my Aunt Alice's that it is lost to memory.

My aunt, in the prophetic mood of elderly ladies who had long outlived their husbands, felt that this might well be her last appearance in the Boston society of which she was so handsome an ornament, and, to lend style to the occasion, instead of soliciting one of my father's cars and a chauffeur, I arranged for what was certainly the last public horse cab in Boston to attend our going.

We dined grandly at the Touraine Hotel and there was a great deal of wine. Alice was arrayed in a pearl choker dog collar a good six inches deep which elevated her chin to a haughty degree, but in no way prevented her absorption of a large quantity of Mumm's '14.

It was a good dinner and we rolled grandly through the socially dubious purlieus of Huntington Avenue to the brilliantly lit porte-cochere. I had apprised Mr. Mudget, the courtly and equally elderly manager of the Opera House, of Alice's impending arrival and, full fit and glossy-hatted, a white satin-lined cloak over one shoulder, he was on the sidewalk to receive us.

It was a good entry, but nothing to what was to follow.

Alice's box was in the second tier. The maid on duty relieved her of her wrap and, on my arm, Alice stepped down from the dressing-room level to that of the box itself, which, in turn, was divided by still another step. Her progress was not unnoticed, and opera glasses were turned our way from all over the house.

That progress, however, was inhibited by the dog collar and the haughty angle of the Carpenter profile, so that, to my horror and that of half a thousand spectators, Alice kept right on going, firmly lifting a leg over the enclosing red plush rail and stepping grandly out into space.

I was able to apprehend her in mid-air just before gravity began to assert itself, and retrieved her to a well-bred patter of applause from the adjacent boxes and here and there a subdued "Well played, sir." From the box immediately below, however, into which she would inevitably have plunged, came the patrician and carrying voice of Mrs. Jack Gardner:

"Not tonight, Alice Carpenter," it said. "You know very well that this is your box only on Tuesdays and Thursdays. Stay in your own box on Mondays and Wednesdays."

BOSTON REVISITED: 1963

My affairs seldom take me to Boston nowadays, although for the first three decades of the century that metropolis was either my home or the center of my suburban activities at Cambridge and Wakefield. Family matters, however, did recently require of me a Boston trip, and it is pleasant to be able to record that, amidst the general decline of the city's façade, certain bright spots evidenced themselves. One was experienced—of all places—aboard *The New England States*, the only first-class train still maintained by the New York Central between Boston and Chicago. Although it is fast and convenient, *The New England States* has never been celebrated for any transcendental gastronomy. The Boston section of *The Twentieth Century Limited*, which anticipated it and which was discontinued in the thirties, was indeed famed for certain elegances of its dining cars—fresh Maine lobster, Cotuit oysters, and, inevitably, Boston scrod—but *The New England States* has enjoyed no such celebrity.

Nevertheless, when I recently used this train eastbound, then westbound two days later, the chef was serving a chicken pie so admirable that, having encountered it upon arriving, I ordered it again upon departing. It was a beautifully confected individual serving, with every justification of the menu's advertisement of its "rich, flaky crust." It contained half a good-sized bird, plenty of white meat, and the lovely "goozly" Southern type of gravy appropriate to the dish. And no green peas. Green peas have no more place in a chicken pie than does a silk hat on an Ojibwa. Whether or not this enviable entree is a regular feature on the Central's Boston run I do not know, but it was top-notch on the two occasions when I had it.

It is also pleasant to be able to report that the Boston Ritz-Carlton still maintains the almost unparalleled excellence of everything for which it was celebrated in the twenties and thirties. No signs of deterioration are visible to even the most critical eye. Its servants are still the match in Chesterfieldian manners of those in the best London hotels, or, for that matter, the Boston cab drivers, who, alone of their tribe in the United States, get out and open the door for patrons.

Twenty-four-hour-a-day floor waiters, serving from individual kitchens (which are in turn supplied from the main kitchen below), are still the invariable Ritz-Carlton rule. The valet presses jackets with the sleeves round and no crease, and the *Boston Herald*, with George Frazier as its principal editorial ornament, presents itself on every breakfast tray.

Throughout its life span, the Boston Ritz has been celebrated for its broiled scrod, and the legend has in no way diminished. A liberal cut of this most delectable of fish, beautifully "brown and bright to the heart's delight" and white-hot from the service kitchen, consumed for breakfast in a suite overlooking the Public Garden on a spring morning, is enough to make the visitor disregard the structural catastrophe of the city's skyline, and the emetic manifestations of what pass for "progress" in the Hub of the Universe.

Equally restorative, although not available to any but members and their invited guests, is luncheon at the Union Club, hard by Brimstone Corner on Park Street, a veritable cathedral of the proprieties and a citadel of the conservative conventions. Its only peer may well be the Boston Athenaeum just around the corner, which hasn't even dusted its stacks since the days of Ralph Waldo Emerson and Oliver Wendell Holmes. The Union Club's martinis, reportedly the best in Boston (although I had no opportunity for comparisons), are magnificent. A deaconess of a headwaitress in the main restaurant assured me they are compounded, when so requested, precisely according to the immutable formula laid down by the late Bernard De Voto.

After a nutritious collation of Cape Cod oysters (alas, they were not from Cotuit, for the beds there were destroyed in one of the recent Atlantic hurricanes and the reseeded oysters have not yet grown to maturity), larded tenderloin of beef, and a sultana roll (a dessert beloved of Bostonians, which I had forgotten over the years), I ordered a cognac in the bar. It was, for the record, Hine Triomphe, and it proved an excellent, tranquilizing digestive.

Equally restful is the view available to postprandial tarriers at the Union Club. It is The Granary Burial Ground, where sleep the not-so-rude forefathers of the hamlet. All of them are Carvers, Saltonstalls, Cabots, and Lowells, and they rest amid the downtown tumults, beneath decorous shafts of granite or Spartan slabs of memorial slate. Should disputation arise among the Union Club membership as to whose grave is which, a footman advances on catlike tread, and rolls down a vast and carefully wrought chart that identifies in jolly cartography each sepulcher of note in The Granary. The largest of all is the name, not of an ancestral patriot or a merchant in the China trade, but of Mary Goose. In the event that you are an ignorant outlander and don't know, she was the original Mother Goose.

New York

Father took the *Owl* home on the New Haven and was never the same afterward.

THE DEPRESSION YEARS

Every now and then in the public prints or in what pass for politics and government, and other circles where the horror story is considered the best for circulation and anything like pleasant reading is looked at askance, I encounter references to the great Depression that smote the nation late in 1929 and lingered on through much of the thirties. These allusions, invariably of a marrow-congealing nature, are used in numerous contexts, as grim warning against too much optimism in the realm of Syntex and Ford Motor Company, as a horrid example of the defects of risk capitalism, or as a reproach to the Republican Party, which happened to be in power when the great bust was inaugurated. Most people remember the Depression as a particularly blood-chilling sort of national street accident, more upsetting to read about at bedtime than Dracula.

I can only say that, while I may be one of a microscopic band of survivors, I lived higher on the hog through the disaster years of 1929 to 1934 than I ever have before or since. Stockbrokers might be tossing themselves from upper floors in numbers making it advisable to walk in the middle of Wall Street or William Street. The men might be coming for the pianos at the stately homes of Syosset and East Hampton, and the soup kitchens might be going at full blast from the Battery to the Bronx, but I, for one, rode it out tearing at pheasant *en plumage* like Henry VIII lunching with Cardinal Wolsey, and cuffing magnums of Bollinger '26, a particularly delectable vintage, from the Plaza in Fifty-ninth Street to the Bermudiana Hotel in Hamilton. I was repeatedly nominated for lists of the best-dressed and most versatile men about New York. My photo in glad evening attire glared at less fortunate passersby in Radio City, and Carino, the maître d'hôtel at El Morocco and the snootiest waiter captain in town, received me with princely honors.

None of these boons and usufructs cost anything, or if token payment was exacted, it was at the approximate rate of ten cents on the dollar. My weekly salary from the *New York Herald Tribune,* of thirty-five dollars, judiciously portioned out, enabled me to enjoy a way of life associated in more normal times only with Henry C. Frick and Diamond Jim Brady.

The secret of this five-year skirmish among the fleshpots usually reserved for our betters was that young and reasonably attractive people of both sexes were in greater demand as shills in the luxury spots of town than may be even faintly imaginable to the current generation. For peanuts I occupied a five-hundred-dollar-a-month suite at the Madison, the only condition being that half a dozen times a day I walk through the lobby looking prosperous, and dine, on the cuff, in the Madison Restaurant, then under the management of the now legendary Theodore Titze of the Ritz. I was supposed to look carefree and bountifully stoked with *foie gras* and forty-year-old Hennessy, which, in fact, I was.

Along with a lot of names that might surprise you, I partook of an arrangement with Gene Cavallero at the Colony Restaurant whereby I ate the best in the land at a discount of approximately sixty per cent, and a private-car rental agency pressed Rolls-Royces and Packard town cars on me if I would consent to be chauffeured to the best places, attired in a gibus opera hat with some reigning but hungry beauty on my arm.

It was a time when a casting agency was retained to send forty well-dressed couples nightly to the Starlight Roof of the Waldorf with instructions to order nothing but flaming desserts and wine in double bottles. Lone wolves like myself, with loftier aspirations than were represented by the Waldorf, could live in the rarefied atmosphere of the Ritz-Carlton as long as credit with their tailors held out. This was no hardship, since at least some of us were dressed gratis by three or four of the most expensive custom tailors so that we might be photographed at the opening of the opera for *Town & Country*.

Looking back on those straitened times, I wonder how many of the handsome folk who sailed weekly for sun and sand aboard the *Monarch of Bermuda* were the nonpaying guests of Furness Withy. It was an era when a young man who wanted to go places could do so in the presidential suite, if he had enough folding money for tips and could redeem his evening linen from the laundry. About the only places that demanded full payment at the scheduled rate were Jack & Charlie's "21" and Brooks Brothers. Rich friends took us to the former, and we went without Brooks until things were better.

Of the years of the great shirt cuff, about the only survivor still in circulation today is the durable Henry Sell, editor of *Town & Country* and, at that time, head of the agency that supplied the dinner-dressed shills to the Waldorf. "The place doesn't look half as wonderful now," he says, "as it did when it was losing seven thousand dollars a day." Henry and I, and a few others I might name, sat out the Depression in Peacock Alley. Neither of us at this stage of the game wants it back, but, while it lasted and we were younger, it was the Depression deluxe of all time.

THE GRAND CLOSING
AT 42 WEST FORTY-NINTH STREET

Few *beaux gestes* in the record of expensive real estate can top that of
Thomas Fortune Ryan's rose arbor, but its peer surely was the later departure from their original stand-in business as a speakeasy of the partners
of Jack & Charlie's "21" Club, easily the most austerely maintained and
most sumptuously upholstered of the many plush refuges from prohibition. The partners, Jack Kriendler and Charlie Berns, had prospered
greatly at the premises they liked to call the Puncheon Grotto at 42 West
Forty-ninth Street. The brownstone seat of their operations, like many
of its competitors in the West Forties had, in former times, been a home
of consequential people, in the case of the Puncheon of the family of
Benedict Quinn, Yale '26, whose patronage of the premises on a sort of
inherited basis was one of the assets of the management, since he brought
along well-heeled and influential classmates such as John Whitney, Peter
Arno (then known as Curtis Arnoux Peters), Rudy Vallee, Avery Rockefeller, Nicholas Saltus Ludington, and Henry C. Potter, a descendant of
the Episcopal bishop of New York who brought with him few overtones
of religion.

So greatly did the partners Kriendler and Berns prosper at the former
Quinn residence that late in the 1920s they sought more commodious
quarters at 21 West Fifty-second Street, an address slated for immortality
in convivial annals. The removal called for a grand opening at the new
address, a conventional gesture of good will to old patrons and freeload-
ers, but why, in the present special circumstance, shouldn't there be a
grand closing as well? The suggestion was made by Robert Benchley and
found instant favor with the management. Many of the fixtures of the
original premises it had been found expedient to duplicate rather than
remove, including mirrors, chandeliers, and fittings that were incorporated
into the architecture and didn't lend themselves to relocation.

On a given evening, therefore, a select group of invited regulars assembled at the original Puncheon Grotto. On their arrival they were
handed, with the compliments of the management, an assortment of fire

axes, crowbars, and other approved wrecking implements, and told to do as they would, the joint was theirs, and for the smashing of glass and destruction of furniture for this one evening there would be no charge.

The list of celebrants reads, even at this remove, like a synthesis of Dun & Bradstreet and the Social Register. It included as its bright and particular star John Hay Whitney, head of the august house of Whitney and future Ambassador to the Court of St. James's; Edward Reeves, heir to a fortune of grocery-store millions; Tommy and Bill Laughlin of Jones & Laughlin Steel; men of letters Benchley, Ernest Boyd, and Donald Ogden Stewart; art patrons Bill and Nick Ludington; Gilbert Kahn, Otto Kahn, Jr., William H. Vanderbilt, Frank Hunter, Elliot Sperber; George P. Marshall, the Washington socialite laundryman who took in the White House washing; Valentine Macy; and a member of the house of Harriman who is unavailable to posterity because, in his haste to have at the supply of fire axes, he omitted to sign his first name to the guest register. It merely and regally reads "Harriman," much as Mrs. William Backhouse Astor was accustomed to sign herself "Mrs. Astor."

It is improbable that so much destruction was ever accomplished by so blue-blooded a wrecking crew as that which closed one era of Jack & Charlie's and inaugurated another.

By virtue both of social and financial primacy, Whitney was accorded the honor of smiting the first blow and chose as his objective a twelve-foot expanse of plate-glass mirror behind the back bar. The satisfying carnage which followed inspired Joe Sheffield, heir to a name large in the annals of Newport, to take an overhead swipe at a massive crystal chandelier in the center of the main restaurant, after which Nick Ludington commenced an embattled assault on the door to the men's room which had once worsted him in a late-evening encounter when propelled from within by Ernest Hemingway. After that the destruction became so general that the noise attracted the mounted officer on the beat. He was bidden to enter and join the party by Jack Kriendler on condition that he bring his horse, an elevation which gave him an advantage in having at the light fixtures in the foyer with a bung starter provided by the management.

When at last the main stairway was sawed through, leaving Benchley and Roger Wolf Kahn stranded on the second floor and cut off from the basis of supply, it was agreed no greater disaster could be contrived, and everybody went up the street to the new address. Gilbert Kahn to this day cherishes a toilet seat that was ravished from the men's room and a bar flap of solid mahogany, probably the sole surviving tangibles from one of the most celebrated speakeasies of New York's drinking years.

The damage, Charlie Berns later was wont to assay at between $25,-

ooo and $40,000. "It was worth every penny of it," he says. "I wish we could do it all over again."

It seems worth noting as a footnote to this most resounding of all grand closings that the engraved announcements of Jack & Charlie's at their new address where they became the town's most spectacular speakeasy read: "Luncheon at Twelve, Tea at Four and Until Closing."

CAFÉ SOCIETY

The phenomenon of American society, it is almost a cliché to remark, has always provided for the impious-minded observer the best features of Halloween at the madhouse and Ringling Brothers' Barnum & Bailey Circus at its most gaudy pitch of hurrah in the days of the consulship over its destinies of John and Buddy North. Since the first pair of substantial pewter nose stilts were purchased by an early Dutch madam in Maiden Lane the day after she emerged from a lower Manhattan house of mirth to marry a wealthy sea captain with genuine silver buckles on his shoes, the nose-stilt industry, along with the interlocking directorates of the tiara bazaars, lorgnette foundries, and coat-armor forgers, has paid enormous dividends and is allowed as gilt edge investment, even for trust funds, in most states.

The manifestations of patrician circumstance have varied naturally enough with the seasons and the place. In the earlier colonies there was an association with landed property and feudal obligations. After the Civil War and to this day it is possible to identify a true Southern aristocrat by his professional poverty and dexterity in bad manners and the Northern nabob by a faint aroma of William James and the Grand Tour. The real boom, of course, which brought on the finest excitements and biggest bathtubs in society derived from the bonanzas and Golcondas of the wonderful West.

During the thirties of the twentieth century, as a consequence of a number of causes and occasions touched upon later, New York society, which has always set the national *ton* of deluxe living, despite agitated head tossings and anguished cries of "Me, I'm the prettiest" from Boston, Philadelphia, Washington, Charleston, and other suburban points, found itself living frankly, unabashedly, and almost entirely in saloons.

It wasn't any very startling revolution, but the exploitation to which the night-club era was exposed, more than anything else through the agency of intimate photography of celebrities in the tonier taprooms, soon caused it to become known as café society, and the rise and flowering of this particular generation of a café society that had always been in existence was the occasion of a vast deal of publicity, pother, and, of course, profit to all concerned.

The balance of this chapter depicts the closing years of the thirties, while the lights of the world were still dazzlingly ablaze, and is recalled from the oblivion of the files as a nosegay, a period picture, as dated and archaic as Grandfather with his hand thrust into the folds of his Prince Albert. The period in Manhattan's tinsel progress through the years is as clearly defined and as easily distinguishable for its own characteristics as the Florida Water age of Ward McAllister or the years of the great tea dance of Scott Fitzgerald, and it is left in the spirit in which it was written to emphasize its part in a period pattern. Almost every one of the physical premises in which its characters have their setting are today flourishing as the haunts of another generation of café society, but the spirit of the age that produced it is something for the attention of the historians and the champions of lost causes.

The swarthy carriage starter in the blue uniform of the Foreign Legion, complete with kepi and pugree, saluted you with a *"Bon soir, m'sieu, madame,"* as the line of limousines' shiny bonnets edged up to the marquee on the south side of East Fifty-fourth Street. He was Senegalese and spoke no English, but there were two other liveried doormen and as many uniformed police officers on duty who were adequate in both speech and action, should either be required. There was never any trouble at El Morocco, perhaps New York's costliest and most representative night club, and in the thirties, it was generally acknowledged, the world's most opulent parade ground for the celebrities of fashionable "café society."

Inside the door there were several hard-faced gentlemen in dinner clothes and two or three coat-check girls of positively iridescent beauty. And beyond them was Carino, most urbane of waiter captains and a diplomat on whose favors and discretion hung feuds and romances, careers, aspirations, and the very foundations of the most bitterly jealous and competitive social hierarchy of our generation. Fortunes and professional careers were made by sitting at the right table at Morocco, believe it or not, and people were known to leave town because Carino had said he was sorry, but all the tables were reserved that evening.

The tangible décor of El Morocco might not have impressed you. Neither would the floor show, for the reason that there wasn't any. It was a long, low room—once a store—decorated in deep blue and white, with palm trees of gold leaf along the walls and tiny stars winking on and off in the azure ceiling. There was a modest-sized dance floor and at one end a stand-up bar presided over by half a dozen expert youths in spotless white. There were many more spectacular night clubs in New York, but El Morocco seemed at the time *the* night club—that is why it is being described here at length—and when you looked at the people who were patronizing it, you at once knew why.

Naturally, El Morocco was not the one and only night club in Manhattan to which the elite of the social and professional front repaired for midnight-to-breakfast merriment and parade. It was unique in that it offered no show or entertainment, but there were half a dozen other night clubs and hotel restaurants where the carriage trade flashed their lorgnons over the bird and cold bottle of tradition after the theater: the infinitely smart Persian Room at the conservative Plaza Hotel; Sherman Billingsley's Stork Club; the Iridium Room at the St. Regis, or the Rainbow Room on the tip-top floor of the RCA Building at Radio City. Then, too, there had been a revival of the after-theater supper as a serious meal without music or entertainment of any sort, and at the Colony Restaurant, at Theodore's, and at Jack & Charlie's, folk who had dined hastily off a highball before the show might be seen setting to work on Scotch grouse, pheasant *en casserole*, firkins of Strasbourg *foie gras*, quail in aspic, vanilla soufflé, and gilt-foiled bottles of heroic proportions.

But somehow, perhaps by some process of sheer emergent evolution, John Perona attracted to his El Morocco the patronage of the most spectacular celebrities of America's café society, and café society was the only society of that day that amounted to a hill of *haricots verts*.

It was a gala night at Morocco, although the difference between a *fête de grand luxe* and an evening of regular business was discernible only to the trained eye of an expert reporter of the urban scene, like Maury Paul or Nancy Randolph. Surging in a flood tide of imperial sables and diamond-and-ruby necklaces, caressed by squalls and cat's paws of costly perfumes, was the most glittering parade of names that made news, of chichi and chinchilla, since the days of Peacock Alley, when the Waldorf was at Thirty-fourth Street and Fifth Avenue.

Morocco was maintained on the basis that the most exciting floor show in the world was provided by the patrons themselves. Two crack orchestras provided continuous music from dinner till dawn. As the evening progressed and the press of patrons became greater, tables were set up on the border of the postage-stamp dance space, farther and farther infringing upon the parquet until, on a really full night, the entire floor was covered and there was no dancing at all. Folk went there to see and to be seen, to be photographed by the first of the "candid cameramen" to invade the privacy of society and to make notes on who was keeping company with whom.

The most opulent furs, wraps insured for fifty and sixty thousand dollars, a wide predominance of white ties over the informal dinner jacket, emeralds and sapphires so costly that insurance companies kept the premises patrolled at all times by guards in evening dress, the single eyeglasses of titled foreigners, and the appraising glances of a stag line of beautifully manicured youths at the bar were the commonplaces of the house. The café set of Manhattan firmly believed that if a given celebrity failed to show up at Morocco three or four times a week he was dead, or, worse still, out of town.

On the dance floor at one time might be seen such a social mixed grill as Hope Williams, of stage fame, in a short ermine coat and blazing necklace of emeralds, dancing with Whitney Bolton, debonair and dapper managing editor of the *Morning Telegraph* and one of the two New York reporters to sport an imported motor car; George Djamgaroff, mystery man of the White Russian colony, with the boyishly monocled Edla Frankau, a leading fashion expert; Moss Hart, most successful of musical playwrights, his arm around the shoulder of Tallulah Bankhead; Paul Draper, youthful tap dancer, with Mrs. Harrison Williams; the adolescent Jimmy Donahue, brother of the better-known Woolworth Donahue, with Babe Palmer of the famous Chicago tribe of Potter Palmers; and Peggy Fears, wife of A. C. Blumenthal.

Archetypal, perhaps, of the ultra-fashionables who had, in a manner, abdicated from "Cave Dweller" society—or the "Four Hundred"—in favor of the gayer activities and more elastic contacts of café society, was Mrs. Williams, often tagged by news writers "New York's smartest woman." Reported to spend $150,000 a year on her wardrobe alone, Mrs. Williams was far from being a mere mannequin gracefully revolving in a chromium mist of cocktail party sophistication and the florid gestures of publicized mediocrities.

So sound was her taste in matters of art that she was once taken by a London shopkeeper for a fellow professional as a result of her knowledge of Chinese ceramics. Having parted on the best of terms from two previous husbands, she was the wife of a public utilities magnate and was as much of an arbiter in social vogues as he was in the world of light and water power.

The famous "white" drawing room of her magnificent mansion on Fifth Avenue, set a style in white furniture and décor which swayed the taste of every interior decorator in the land, and her four hundred-foot German-built yacht *Warrior* were the scene of the smartest entertaining of the seasons, as the tide of finance and fashion ebbed and flowed from Long Island to Palm Beach and to Newport.

"Birth," Mrs. Williams once said, "no longer is the prime requisite of society. If there is a society, it has leveled to personalities of intelligence or cleverness or interest, or to those who are just well liked and have enough money to maintain themselves with reasonable conventional comforts. And that is as it should be."

At a table facing the door, which was reserved for the proprietor and his guests, were a group of the ranking society reporters of the town, as beautifully dressed as the paying guests, earning their daily plover's eggs. Without their presence, and that of the dinner-jacketed photographers, no evening at Morocco would have been complete.

An aspect of the social comedy as it was played in the thirties which would have grieved the members of "Cave Dweller" society of the Murray Hill and gaslamp era was the attitude of café society toward the reports of its activities in the metropolitan press. Social prestige in 1937 was rated by lineage in the papers, and such society reporters as Maury Paul, Mme. Flutterbye and Reggie (Baron George Wrangel) of the *Journal,* or Nancy Randolph of the *Daily News* fulfilled much the same function at a party as do reviewers at a new play.

No hostess considered her party a success, no matter how much pleasure she might have afforded her guests, unless it received favorable notices in next day's newspapers. Just as there was a Critics' Circle of drama reviewers which included such luminaries as John Mason Brown, Gilbert Gabriel, Richard Watts, Jr., and Brooks Atkinson, there might very well have been a Society Reporters' League of Helen Worden, Barclay Beekman, and George Lowther III, the last of whom sometimes doubled for George Wrangel. Their functions, in their special fields, were very similar.

In many cases society reporters were themselves accredited members of the circles in which they moved, while others were *ex officio* participants in the smarter routs and revels of the *faubourgs.* The late Maury Paul, stoutish, jolly, and an amazingly informed chronicler of metropolitan doings, was recognized as the leader of all social scribes. He was a member of a Philadelphia family whose legend and coat armor went back beyond the Revolution. Molly Cogswell Thayer (Mme. Flutterbye) was married to a son of the Reverend William Greenough Thayer, long the venerated head of St. Mark's School at Southborough, Massachusetts, one of the two most churchly and aristocratic boys' preparatory schools in the country. Baron Wrangel was a member of the Continental family of that name.

But to return to Morocco—where the stags *pro tem* lined the bar downing highballs or champagne cocktails. Among them on a given evening might be seen Morton Downey, the Irish thrush; Jack Velie of Kansas City, a nephew of Dwight Deere Wiman and one of the proprietors of the Deere plow works; Emlen Etting, the Philadelphia modernist painter; Bill Hearst and his young brother, Randy; Delos Chappell, producer who revived the Central City Opera House in Colorado for a week's run of *Camille,* which set him back $250,000; Winsor French, columnist of the Cleveland *Press,* on a Manhattan jaunt; Bill Okie, display designer for a Fifth Avenue jeweler; "Junior" Wotkyns, a dazzling youth from Hollywood and the heart throb at that moment of Libby Holman Reynolds; Quentin Reynolds, the fictioneer; Jack Kriendler of "Jack & Charlie" fame, and Nat Saltonstall, most eligible bachelor of Boston, over for the weekend.

Later, the stags would be augmented by Dwight Fiske, who had just finished singing his wickedly satirical ballads over at the Savoy-Plaza; Arthur Cooley, the champagne salesman, with the Marquis de Polignac, his boss; Joe O'Donahue IV, and Shipwreck Kelly; Howard Hughes, the film producer, and Stanley Sackett, the hotel man, said to be the original of Peter Arno's surprised-looking gent with the bald head and waxed mustaches who is always finding himself in such peculiar jams.

The bar was well thronged by two o'clock, but nobody needed to stand there longer than he wished, because every one in the room knew almost every one else, and any personable somebody was asked to sit at some friend's table every other minute.

Let us for a moment, however, desert the mink and monocles of Morocco and glance deeper into the past to see if there is visible there the origin of what the thirties called café society.

It is impossible to date arbitrarily the beginning of an important social trend, but to say that the arrival of Addison and Wilson Mizner on the Manhattan scene marked the start of the evolution of café society is close to being the truth. These rowdy, tumultuous, and gusty brothers from California descended on formal society—what was known as the "Four Hundred." Their fabulous adventures and spacious gestures became a national saga.

Before they got through, Wilson had married Mrs. Charles T. Yerkes, who had inherited $50,000,000 the month before from her traction-magnate husband, and Addison turned out to be the architect who laid out Palm Beach as it is today. And the two of them had laughed so hard at formal society that society started laughing at itself.

That was the beginning of the end. Society as it was then constituted laughed itself out of existence, and after the smashed opera hats and ruined conventions had been cleared away, it was found that something new had come into being. It was becoming known as café society.

Like any other social manifestation, café society was evolved over a considerable period of time and as the result of a number of otherwise unrelated forces, motives, and circumstances. It existed in its purest form in New York and New York's closest suburb, Hollywood.

It had its counterpart in what were known as the "bright young people" of London. Its first authentic flowering was in the speakeasy age of the twenties, but its full-blown maturity came with Repeal and mass entertainment in public resorts.

There had been signs and portents as far back as the nineties that the impeccable respectability, or at least the superficial conventionality, of the Edith Wharton era was in a decline. The most historic of these was an

event ever since known as the "Awful Seeley Dinner," a masculine fore-
gathering which today would scarcely cause comment among the
participants, but which in the brownstone Gotham of 1896 assumed the
proportions and awful glory of a Babylonish revel.

It was discovered that at the ushers' dinner of Clinton Seeley, grandson of P. T. Barnum, served in a suite of private rooms at Sherry's, a
dancer named "Little Egypt" had appeared before the guests in what,
for those times, passed as the nude.

The dinner was raided by the celebrated Captain "Whiskers" Chapman
of the Tenderloin Squad, an officer whose bear and umbrella—the latter
carried in lieu of a nightstick—won him a kind of local immortality, and
the resulting scandal surpassed all bounds of probability. The public
prints, hitherto unaccustomed to indulging in details of this sort, were
given full license by the court proceedings which followed, and the town
was fascinated with the first complete coverage of a notorious interlude
in the life of the *foie-gras faubourgs.* Forward-looking city editors and
society reporters, up to that time restricted to anonymous paragraphs
where names were suggested by initials and asterisks, or to conventional flattering chronicles of balls and private routs, began to see a great
light.

Coincidental with the rise of journalism based on gossip and scandal,
almost universal later, there awakened among the more responsible members of society some appreciation of the uses of publicity. Newspaper
reporters were even admitted to drawing rooms, although at such times
a close watch was kept on the overcoat rack in the hall, and notables
who had hitherto scorned the public prints began actually to smile at the
camera from the boxes of coaches-and-four or behind the wheels of Pope
Hartfords set for hair-raising dashes to roadhouses in the wilds of Pelham.
Old standards and reticences were crumbling, and the stage was being
set for the dominance of the professional celebrity.

Membership in café society as a rule presupposed sufficient personal
means to support a presentable metropolitan scheme of living, although
many familiar figures in its midst might come by their keep in oblique
ways. The limousined mistress, the handsome gigolo, and the pensioner-
friend had recently returned to the scene in increasing numbers. But the
dominant requisite for membership in the loosely coordinated circle of
café society was a name that was news, a warrant for existence.

Everyone had to be able to point to some occupation, achievement,
distinction, or even notorious frailty that made identification possible. The
person might be a painter, a press agent, a lover of uncommon appeal, a
film actress, the president of an aviation company, the principal patron
of a particular restaurant, a society photographer, a professional hostess,
or a night-club promoter. The old generalities of "clubman," "millionaire,"

"society woman," and "internationally known figure in the world of art and politics" were no longer meaningful, valid, or acceptable.

The recruits of café society stemmed from a number of sources, but its principal luminaries were of the generation that achieved maturity in the era following World War I. Whether or not its members fitted into so nice a chronological category, a general definition of café society might have been: an unorganized but generally recognized group of persons whose names made news and who participated in the professional and social life of New York available to those possessed of a certain degree of affluence and manners.

The contrast in the attitude toward publicity of horse-cab and side-whiskers society and café society was not the least outstanding difference between the two orders. Personal gossip was by no means the invention of Walter Winchell, but he lent the retailing of spicy news a bright new technique when he first started his column in the *Evening Graphic* in the early twenties, and he was the first practitioner of a style later widely and sometimes successfully imitated. Other New York columns specializing in Broadway and café paragraphs concerning the private lives of the famous included those of Leonard Lyons in the New York *Post,* Ed Sullivan and John Chapman in the *Daily News,* Louis Sobol in the *Journal,* Whitney Bolton and Dorothy Dey in the *Morning Telegraph,* and George Ross in the *World-Telegram.*

Louis Sobol, recognized as the dean of afternoon paper paragraphers, was the despair of rivals and the wonder and admiration of his colleagues, if only for the incredible territory he contrived to cover. A mousy little man with horn-rimmed glasses, a big nose, and a nice taste in Shetland and cheviot suits, he managed to fill five columns a week of two thousand words each with names, news, anecdotes, color, and comment that was invariably fresh and, in its field, important. Half a dozen cocktail parties, dinner at "21" or Jack Dempsey's or La Hiff's Tavern, a first night fairly awash with celebrities, glamor, and good copy, a visit to two different Forty-fifth Street bars at the intermissions, and finally a tour of the night clubs which would include Leon & Eddie's, El Morocco, the Stork, the Kit Kat, the Cotton Club, and the Onyx were his standardized nightly routine before he sought out his Greenwich Village apartment and sat down to his typewriter. Nobody knew how he did it.

Too, Sobol enjoyed a considerable popularity with his professional associates, as he consistently refused to run items of news, witticism, or correction at the expense of other newspapermen.

In the case of fashionable entertainment and the social activities of the café set, it might safely be asserted that the type of reporting of these aspects of the Manhattan scene which prevailed then was an obvious result, rather than a motivating cause. When entertaining was a private-affair privately conducted for the pleasure of people one knew, it was possible for a hostess such as Mrs. Fish, Mrs. Astor, Mrs. Alexandre, or Mrs. Gould to give out only what details she considered suitable for publication. But in a generation whose dinner parties, after-theater suppers, and dances were conducted in public restaurants, in night clubs, or in the ballroom suites of luxury hotels, the antics, manners, and departures from decorum of the guests were easily chronicled.

The focal point of New York's entertaining was no longer the noble Vanderbilt mansion on Fifth Avenue, nor was it the drawing rooms of Mrs. Hamilton McK. Twonbly and Mrs. Orme Wilson or the opera box of Miss Annie Burr Jennings. It was probably the front second-floor restaurant of Jack & Charlie's in Fifty-second Street, or the intimate gold-and-blue bar of the Colony Restaurant, or the postage-stamp floor at El Morocco, that glittering synthesis of a Cecil B. De Mille opium dream and a paragrapher's heaven. Nor were the headlined performers any longer Mrs. William Watts Sherman, Mrs. Robert Goelet, and Miss Louise Iselin, even though these amiable and distinguished ladies were still featured as opera-box holders and in the reports of the Society for Improving the Conditions of the Poor.

The names were more apt to be those of Woolworth Donahue, John O'Hara, Mrs. Brock Pemberton, Libby Holman Reynolds, Noel Coward, Tallulah Bankhead, or the Louis Bromfields, some of whom were associated with the theater and only a few of whom would have appeared on Ward McAllister's celebrated list for Mrs. Astor's ball.

The transition from private balls and dinner parties of three hours' duration, from the Metropolitan Opera, cotillions, supper parties in private homes, and the various levees like the Charity Ball, to public appearances of the socially prominent at restaurant and night-club parties, to the cocktail routes of such wits as Nicholas de Molas and Clifton Webb and their chronicling in the newspaper columns next day, really required only fifteen years. Dates became casual, dinner receded from a flood tide of Burgundy and innumerable game courses and entrees to a simple four courses and champagne in double magnums; formality became a thing of the past in almost every field save that of personal attire, where standards remained much the same as they had always been among people of breeding and circumstances.

It was this amiably demented whirl of scrammy entertainments, Fifty-second Street morris dancing, whoopsing, screaming, and clogging it to Eddie Duchin music at the Persian Room of the Plaza, making pretty faces for the cameramen at Gilbert Miller first nights, bicycling through Central Park to charity carnivals, keeping luncheon trysts at the Vendome in Hollywood and being at the old desk next morning, gossiping by the hour on the London phone, and living in a white tie till six of a morning before brushing the teeth in a light Moselle and retiring to bed, which constituted the life of Manhattan's café society.

It was a strenuous business, and right thinkers and forward-lookers said it would end in nothing good. Said New York: Live half as long; see twice as much!

CAFÉ NAMES MADE NEWS

The glamor which surrounded New York's café society derived, more than anything else, from the willingness of its celebrities to be constantly on parade. The names that made news were those of individuals whose lives visibly typified all the romance of urban civilization. They lived in luxury hotels, dined in restaurants and night clubs whose opulence had become a legend, and made no pretense of hiding their million-candle-power light under any bushes whatsoever.

Never before, probably, had New York been snowed under by such a blizzard of money as was then drifting through its streets, piling up at its night clubs and in the ateliers of its court jewelers, furriers, couturiers, and luxury tradesmen. There was a rare perfume on the market priced—and selling—at $500 for an ounce flask. There was a positive shortage of matched sables and chinchilla; diamond boutonnieres for men were being passed over the counter at $10,000 a copy; waiter captains were playing the market once more, and it was possible for two to dine at the Colony and have very little change out of a half-century bank note.

Let us select at random from the ranks of the town's café society a few individuals and institutions that were a part of the glittering scene.

Because he was so cosmopolitan as to be as much a New Yorker as a Londoner, we shall take Noel Coward, actor, playwright, musician, accomplished and versatile artist in half a score of mediums. Mr. Coward was the ranking professional celebrity of the English-speaking world. He spent about twelve weeks of every year in New York, and the term of his stay might well have been known as the Coward Season. The smart activities of the town revolved around his presence, his newest play, his latest witticism or cocktail party, almost to the exclusion of all other manifestations of daily life.

Mr. Coward had not always been the richest man of the Anglo-American theater. He once came very close to starvation in a midtown garret, and he might well never have been heard from except for the friendship of Alfred Lunt and Lynn Fontanne, who weren't so well off themselves at the time, but who still could have an unknown but ambitious English boy in for dinner two or three times a week and give him the key to their apartment when they were on the road.

The success of Mr. Coward's plays, his own stage appearances, his songs, like "Mad Dogs and Englishmen" and "Some Day I'll Find You," and his limitless personal charm and enthusiasm for going places, doing things, and being fascinating to everyone he met were the component parts in a rags-to-riches romance which had no counterpart in the contemporary theater.

While he was no night-club rounder, there was seldom a private party of account which Mr. Coward missed during his annual New York interlude, and if he could be induced by his hostess to sit down at the piano and play a few of his long-familiar but ever-popular songs, the evening became a part of history.

The hold that Mr. Coward exerted on the imaginations and loyalties of a vast and sophisticated following was chiefly attributable to that elusive quality "charm." To him the world was an immense gag, sometimes wistfully sentimental, sometimes pathetic, but never to be treated too seriously. Amazingly youthful of person (only in his middle thirties), he had been known to hold such a difficult audience as New York's Dutch Treat Club—a convocation of cynical, show-us advertising men and executives—spellbound by the adroitness of his patter. He made fun of everything, himself first of all, and was, at heart, the kindest person imaginable.

"Marie Grand Duchess, 30 Beekman Pl." was the way she was listed in the telephone directory, and if you had been of a mind to chat personally with the first cousin of the late Czar, daughter of the Grand Duke Paul, sister of the Grand Duke Dmitri, Marie Pavlovna, ranking Russian exile of the United States, there would have been nothing to prevent you from dialing her number. Or you might have visited her at her commercial photography studio, where she made camera studies of persons, flowers, jewels, perfume bottles, evening wraps, or fashionable hairdresses.

In the Grand Duchess Marie was most dramatically visible the synthesis of economic necessity, professional competence, and social assurance that made for recognition in café society.

"My brains are of more use to me than my title," the Grand Duchess was fond of saying, "and conditions have changed so much in recent years that society has grown to respect personal effort more than any other qualification in the individual." And this adequately summed up the requirements of professional society.

In appearance, Marie lived up to the most exacting expectations of what a Grand Duchess should be. Tall, brown-haired, and with a gait and carriage slightly on the imperial side, she was no razzle-dazzle figure in the night clubs, no overexploited ringside spectator at the town's gilded and less inhibited carnivals. She was chary of her person, preferring to lunch at the Colony with intimates—Prince Serge Obolensky, perhaps, or Princess Ketto Mikeladze—and to dine at home in her Beekman Place apartment with its walls covered with autographed photographs of royal and otherwise notable or noble celebrities.

She was at her best on such evenings as the Russian Naval Ball, the celebration of the Russian New Year the second week in January, and the ball of the Corps des Pages, when, under the influence of gleaming candlelight, old Slavic tunes, and the flow of vodka and champagne, something of the atmosphere of other times was re-created in the ballroom of the Plaza, and the one-time officers of the Czar in their skirted coats, high Cossack boots, daggers, and ribboned orders performed the Sword Dance.

For nearly a decade Marie had been the town's ranking member of Continental nobility and a personage without whose name no list of charity patrons, art sponsors, or ball guests was complete. By refraining from facile commercial exploitation of her title and person, she maintained a degree of dignity in keeping with her charm, integrity, and horse sense.

For the better part of a decade the brownstone mansion with the floriated iron grille and gateway, sunken entrance, and seasonal window boxes, known as Jack & Charlie's, had been one of the four or five most distinguished restaurants in town. Its address was 21 West Fifty-second Street.

It was as a restaurant and bar that "21" had its primary reason for existence, but its fame derived from the fact that its modest façade concealed a celebrity hideaway which had only three rivals in the United States: the Colony Restaurant, El Morocco, and the Vendome Restaurant on Sunset Boulevard, Hollywood.

There was nothing about the exterior of Jack & Charlie's to distinguish it from the other resorts which made West Fifty-second the Rue de la Fontaine of America. Nor was the interior particularly palatial. There was a lounge tastefully furnished in green and white, with an open fire, a divan or two, and a rack of English sporting periodicals and daily papers. Beyond that was an oak-timbered taproom with a semicircular bar, and above this were two restaurants, at the front and back of the house. A white wooden-railed stairway lined with green carpet led upstairs, and there were a barbershop, a gymnasium, and the usual retiring and powdering rooms. Nothing else. Nothing, that is, but the clientele.

If you were a recognized and approved patron of the house, as soon as you stepped in the door, Jimmy, the concierge, said, "Good morning, sir" or "Good evening" as the case might be, and half a dozen sleek youths bustled forward to take your hat and coat. If Jimmy didn't look up from his desk nobody made any move in your direction, and if you persisted further in trying to be recognized and attended, Jimmy remarked with an infinity of sorrow in his voice that the house was filled to capacity and that there were no reservations to be made.

Now and then, of course, folk did get into "21" who weren't particularly wanted. For them there was a back room known as the "doghouse" and a special menu on which all the items were just double the prices on the regular card. The management comprised Jack and Mac Kriendler and Charlie Berns. Of this triumvirate, more later.

If you stepped into the bar to see who was on the premises one noon in the thirties, one or, rather, two of the first things you would see would be the twin beards, red and gray respectively, of Ernest Boyd, litterateur and boulevardier extraordinary, and Edgar Montillion Woolley, director of the production of *Fifty Million Frenchmen* and theater celebrity of the first order. If he was in town, Cole Porter, composer of innumerable hit songs, would be with Mr. Woolley. Ranged farther along the bar were Alfred G. Vanderbilt, invariably talking horse; Jefferson Machamer, the illustrator; Hal Phyfe, foremost of the town's professional photographers; Prince George Shebatoff; Steve Hannagan, ace press agent; Gene Tunney, the Connecticut squire, Ernest Hemingway, John McClain, top-notch ship news reporter for the New York *American* and friend of more international celebrities than you could shake a gold-headed stick at; Dudley Field Malone, noted divorce lawyer and one-time Collector of the Port of New York; Keats Speed, managing editor of the *Sun;* Damon Runyon, Eddy Duchin, George and Valentina Schlee, the distinguished couturier; Freddy Beckman, married to Jules Bache's daughter; and Clifton Webb with Marion Tiffany Saportas, flaming-haired beauty and a celebrated hostess in her own right.

Nowhere was there any suggestion of ostentatious luxury, but there was that intangible thing called "atmosphere" about the front restaurant upstairs. It was visible in the dexterity of the waiters; in the silver mesh of wine baskets and the sheen of champagne coolers at every table; in the masterful eye of Philip, the maître d'hôtel, and in the accomplished gestures of his captains, whether they were spreading Parmesan on your *marmite* Henri IV or achieving a pain's fireworks effect with oranges and cognac over a flaming platter of *crêpes Suzettes.* Wine corks were never permitted to pop too loudly; dessert appeared at just the proper interval after the salad and mousse of *foie gras;* the Armagnac was served in sniffing glasses big enough for the unwary to fall into.

This was luncheon hour of a no-matinee day, and there was a good representation of theater folk visible. At the center table just inside the door were Noel Coward and Gertrude Lawrence, sharing pompano and fresh asparagus with Jack Wilson, Mr. Coward's producer and business manager, and the amazing Princess Paley, to whom Mr. Wilson had been paying chivalrous attentions for several seasons. At the next table were

Mrs. Brock Pemberton, wife of the producer and hostess at the town's most representative cocktail levees, with Dick Aldrich, lanky Harvard graduate and producer in his own right, and round-faced Donald Oenslager, whose stage sets were visible in no fewer than six Broadway hits during one season.

Elsewhere, busy with alligator pears, crabmeat *au gratin*, and slim bottles of Steinberger-Auslese '21, were Lois Long, former wife of Peter Arno and "Lipstick" on the staff of the *New Yorker;* Johnny Weissmuller and Lupe Velez; Ted Husing, ace radio announcer; James Montgomery Flagg, the illustrator; Donald Ogden Stewart, the humorist, with Joseph John O'Donohue IV, gilded Park Avenue youth, and Frank Sullivan and Corey Ford, humorists, magazine writers, and the closest of professional associates.

To trace the emergence of a group of tavern proprietors who became such important factors in the café-society scene that their influence could not be ignored by any amateur of social evolution, it is necessary to go back to the dark days of the early twenties, the Ordovician Age of speakeasy geology.

Café society came into being in the form in which it was finally recognized, through the agency of the speakeasies, and a small handful of their more farsighted, ambitious, and urbane proprietors were, in a way, the arbiters of its earlier destinies.

The first of the speakeasies to command a national reputation and a clientele of reputable patrons was Dan Moriarty's famous men's bar at 216 East Fifty-eighth Street. Dan and his two brothers, Mort and Jim, were the salt of the earth. They were influential citizens on the upper East Side, where they owned large real-estate holdings.

Their unostentatious bar, located in the basement of a brownstone house, became known as a safe and respectable resort of masculine fashion. The liquor was the best obtainable in a dangerous time; the premises were free from police molestation and all but the most infrequent Federal raids; and no shady characters, toughs, or ugly drunks were allowed inside the door. Dan was banker, confidant, bail bondsman, and friend to half the distinguished blades of the town.

Of an evening youths were accustomed to run over to Dan's from the balls and debutante parties at the luxury resorts along Park Avenue. The bar was populated with snowy shirt fronts and gleaming top hats set at the rakish angle. The place became a sort of outpost of the Racquet and Tennis Club, the Union League, the Yale Club, and Harvard's aristocratic Porcellian all rolled into one.

Everyone who was anyone was there of an evening: it was the regular resort of Paul Palmer, then editor of the *American Mercury;* of Sherman Hoyt, most famous of all American yachtsmen, who was accustomed to

wear oil skins and sou'wester over his tails on stormy nights; of Peter
Arno, then a Yale undergraduate, and of his classmates, John Hay Whitney, Avery Rockefeller, Count Henri de Sibour, and Rudy Vallee. To be
a member of the regulars at Dan's was the equivalent of being a recognized fixture at White's or one of the dandy coffeehouses of eighteenth-
century London.

The last three or four years of the thirties saw a great revival of the
luxury hotel and restaurant trade in premises once permeated by legality
and gloom, and a number of smaller but infinitely smart restaurants such
as the Colony, Jean's French delicatessen in Sixtieth Street, the Aperitif,
run by Leon and Gregory, and Theodore Titze's Theodore's came into a
renewed prosperity.

The real-estate trend which transformed all but the very richest Man-
hattanites into apartment- or hotel-dwellers ended the long tradition of
home entertainments on a magnificent scale. Cocktail parties and small
dinners were the only generally observed types of private parties to survive.

New York, of course, had always lunched in public, and great debutante
parties had for years been held by tradition at the Ritz, Sherry's, Pierre's,
or the Colony Club. Now New York society was getting accustomed to
doing everything of an entertaining nature in public.

Publicity, too, was becoming a valuable commodity, and editors preferred pictures and names of actresses, screen stars, and radio celebrities,
who knew from their professional experience how to make news and how
to pose, to the blank expressions and maladroit utterances of the average
debutante. Dwight Fiske, Eve Symington, Cobina Wright, and other professional entertainers and entrepreneurs with plush overtones suddenly
discovered that the social activities of New York were revolving about
them and their friends and acquaintances, and that the actual individuals
of the *Social Register,* unless they were amusing, successful in their own
right, and amenable to changing times and institutions, were headed for
oblivion.

Close upon the heels of society's emergence from the mists of privacy
and exclusiveness came the reporters, paragraphers, and columnists, and
behind them came the photographers. No longer was it even plausible
for folk of fashion to shield themselves from the flashlights as they
scurried across the sidewalk. A few old-fashioned irreconcilables still affected the gesture, and often as not actually didn't get snapped for their
pains, a contingency which never failed to make them furious.

The first "candid cameraman" to get exclusive shots of notables in
Manhattan's café society was retained by Editor Harry Bull of *Town &
Country* to procure photographs of celebrities in moments of unconven-
tional intimacy. So great was his success that within two years half a score

of imitators had sprung up. The only one to parallel his success was Marty Black of the New York *American,* but close behind them were Tony Sarno of *International News,* Gloria Braggiotti, fashion expert of the New York *Post* and photographic free lance, and a youth named Dan McNutt. In Hollywood, Hyman Fink was an established social fixture among the stars.

The lensman became a not inconsiderable figure in the social midst. Tail-coated and top-hatted of an evening, his presence was solicited at the best tables at any party, and the cocktail shebang or dinner dance at which no press photographer was present was considered an unequivocal failure by host and guests alike.

The ultimate hallmark of social success in the Manhattan of 1937 was a four-column cut of one's self in the *American,* posed against the distinguishing zebra stripes of the Morocco décor, with a cooler of wine on one's table and an eligible companion. The credit line would read, "Photo by Black," and the implications of achievement in the New York parade were precisely those which, a generation before, reposed in the chaste script lettering of a card reading, "Mrs. Vanderbilt requests . . ."

Take a gander at one of the more sensational barn raisings of the era.

Unlimited quantities of champagne were poured freely at the bar. Ray Bolger, star revue dancer, whisked around the ballroom floor with Edith Gray, sister of the Dowager Duchess of Marlborough, who was dressed in a milkmaid's costume and wearing more than $100,000 worth of diamond and emerald bracelets.

Mrs. "Mudge" Howard, who was in trade and knew everybody in Manhattan by his or her first name, was in a vague parody of rustic clothes and wearing the Howard pearls, which were by way of being something. There was a papier-mâché cow bedded down on real straw in a stall in the corner opposite the most expensive orchestra available.

"What," you gasped, seizing the arm of a passing wine steward, "what in the name of holy hoopskirts is it all about?"

It was Elsa Maxwell's "Barnyard Frolic" on the Starlight Roof of the Waldorf-Astoria, Park Avenue, New York—that's what it was. And it was attended by every café-society celebrity who could possibly beg, wrangle, or borrow an invitation to the season's most dazzling costume ball.

Lady Iya Abdy, spectacular Russo-British beauty, had on red tights and a headdress made of a very dead stuffed crow. Prince Serge Obolensky, in peasant garb, led a fat, squealing pig on an expensive dog leash. Mrs. James A. Corrigan, who had outgrown Cleveland society and who had preferred that of King Edward VIII until he became overnight the Duke of Windsor, was dressed as a Russian moujik, but with an enormous emerald set in twenty-carat diamonds on one arm and three ropes of Oriental pearls around her neck. Mrs. Ogden L. Mills wore a blinding diamond tiara above blue denim overalls.

Leonard Hanna, Cleveland multimillionaire, had imported a genuine Ohio hog caller, who was making his strange native cries heard above Fairchild's new swing band, and Mr. and Mrs. Douglas Fairbanks, Constance Bennett, and Gilbert Roland were in identical farmer suits, looking for all the world like a group of synthetic rustic quadruplets.

It would take two full columns of news space to list all the people who attended one of Miss Maxwell's more pretentious parties, but a few more of those participating in this parody barn dance were the Fredric Marches of Hollywood; Lauritz Melchoir of the Metropolitan Opera; Princess Natalie Paley; Charles Hanson Towne; Mario Braggiotti, the band leader; Harry Payne Bingham; George Jean Nathan, the drama critic; Mrs. Vincent Astor; Charlie MacArthur, of the famed Hollywood team of Hecht and MacArthur; Beatrice Lillie, fresh from her performance in *The Show Is On;* Winthrop Aldrich; Averell Harriman of the Union Pacific, and Cornelius Vanderbilt Whitney, cousin of the famous Jock Whitney.

For Elsa Maxwell, short, snub-nosed, and almost as frumpy in her attire as the late Hetty Green, was the ranking hostess of two continents and sponsored the New York parties which were the 1937 equivalents of the balls and cotillions of Mrs. Astor in the mustache-cup era.

Her parties were vast and inclusive and were tremendously publicized. About the only similarity between Miss Maxwell's routs and the stately parties of a generation before was their hold on the public imagination, but there is no denying that they were the parties of that moment, and very magnificent parties they were, too.

Every season the photographers' flashes revealed the emergence of numbers of youths whose primary warrant for attention was good looks, a reasonable range of topical conversation, and a sufficiency of clean linen to don a white tie and waistcoat every evening. Their sole objective was entertainment, dinner at the Colony, and a bowing acquaintance with Tallulah Bankhead, and most of them achieved this reasonable end.

This much at least is apparent: the café society of New York was infinitely more democratic, more open to achievement, than the older social order. The requirements for membership in it were primarily those of professional success, personal distinction, and willingness to subscribe to the vaguest of formal codes. Almost anybody with something to offer stood an excellent chance of becoming somebody in café society.

New York in 1937 was a city of luxurious resources never before so attainable by ambitious youth with something to give. Its motto might very well have been: "Here it is; come and get it."

BLEECK'S "FORMERLY CLUB"

Tarriers at the bar at Bleeck's Artists and Writers Restaurant in Fortieth Street have been forever turning to one another and remarking that somebody really ought to write a book about the place! It really was worth a book!

Although nobody has ever written the book, Bleeck's is not unknown to beautiful letters and is a standard of currency with newspaper columnists and paragraphers. For Bleeck's, like all unique things, defies classification and maintains a raffish individualism which baffles all attempts at formalized portaiture. It is a club, a tavern, a public deadfall, an address, an arena fragrant with the souvenirs of mighty contests with bottles, wits, and fists, a repository of immemorial legend, and a monument to the supremacy of the vital life of the town of the whiskey bottle and the rotary press.

As solid and respectable in its every visual aspect as any gentleman's club on Murray Hill, Bleeck's is still possessed of a sly and latent atmosphere of hooray. Located on the littoral of Manhattan's Ghetto, the garment district, it has nourished and comforted with its resources the lofty intellects of chief editorial writers and managing editors. Its regulars have ranged from the best minds and most corrupt kidneys of the staff of the immediately adjacent *Herald Tribune* to Crazy Bob Clifford, the Merry Mortician, and on one occasion, Mrs. S. Stanwood Menken, a fashion queen and great lady of dowager proportions. It was before its slightly soiled mahogany that Stanley Walker muttered his immortal aphorism: "Cirrhosis of the liver, the occupational disease of the reporter!" It was in its rear room that Henry George, the big eater, consumed, one Christmas Day, six entire roast capons, twelve Southdown mutton chops, a four-pound chateaubriand, and then, when Bleeck flatly refused to serve him further, shook an angry fist at the management and stamped across the street to the Greek's "where they wouldn't turn a man away hungry on Christmas!"

It was at Bleeck's that Harry McCormack, the demented barkeep, imagined he maintained a complete poultry farm and apiary behind the bar. The premises, in his fancy, were filled with white leghorns and bees in clover, and he was forever scattering imaginary cracked corn to his flock among the duck boards back of the ice bins. He was an excellent barkeep.

It hasn't been hard to build Bleeck's into a legend.

From the point of view of an internal decorator, the Artists and Writers Restaurant (formerly Club) isn't such a much. Its heavy mission furniture and fixtures were designed with an eye to the occasional tantrums of bemused copy readers and the legerdemain whims of the late Edward Dean Sullivan, the Lionel Strongfort of New York reporters of his era. Affixed to the mirrors are the accustomed array of memorabilia-wireless messages from Byrd at the South Pole, photographs of celebrities, and all the usual museum pieces which arouse wonder, conversation, and thirst in bars the world over, plus (1) the only oil painting by the late Clare Briggs believed to be extant; (2) a reconditioned sailfish of uncertain history; (3) the cement-filled suit of armor which has broken many a playfully swung fist.

Originally the Artists and Writers (Club) was a speakeasy of notable proportions run by a strangely excitable Hollander named Jack Bleeck. It was almost entirely dominated by the staff of the *Herald Tribune,* although a few stylish outlanders like Skipper Williams and the august Charlie Lincoln of the *Times* were always made handsomely welcome. The city editor on duty in an age when Stanley Walker used to head the assignment sheet with the daily entry "Calvin Coolidge: Cover Northampton Situation" (Cal was a contributing columnist at the time) was certain to be able to assemble a fabulous staff of reporters in an emergency simply by calling the bar downstairs. At one time he had his pick of Alva Johnston, Dennis Tylden Lynch, Beverly Smith, Henry Cabot Lodge, Jr., Edward Dean Sullivan, William O. McGeehan, Don Skene, Percy Hammond, Ned McIntosh, John O'Reilly, Ben Robertson, and Herbert Asbury. Some of these luminaries were members of other departments and highly specialized feature writers but all and any were glad to pitch in on city assignments if the occasion demanded.

The front footage of Bleeck's in those days was camouflaged by a fruit stand under Levantine management, and the bar was in the back room along with the restaurant proper, the men's can, and Harry McCormack's ghostly Plymouth Rocks.

The change from a speakeasy run exclusively for men to a legitimate restaurant open to the wholesale public grieved Bleeck and gave the regular customers a bad turn. It also confused Miss Dorothy Thompson, at the time a starred contributor to the *Tribune's* feature columns, who, one night after her initiation to the wonders of the former poultry rookery, now open to bugeyed *gobe-mouches,* told friends that she had been taken to a fabulous place called Jack Bleeck's Formerly Club! Hadn't it said so on the sign outside the door?

The regulars at Bleeck's have ranged from Ogden Reid, editor and publisher of the *Herald Tribune,* and his editorial janizaries, to waifs and strays from *The New Yorker* and stage notables such as Noel Coward and Tallulah Bankhead, Jimmy Walker, Jimmy Cagney, Frank Sullivan, John Garland, Owen Davis, Jr., and an assortment of Hollywood celebrities have made it a stamping ground. Katherine Vincent, the *Tribune's* resident Lady Diana Duff Gordon Cooper, was for years the undisputed empress of its mahogany. When Judge Crater disappeared, headquarters detectives regularly combed the premises for the absentee jurist on the theory that sooner or later, as at the Café de la Paix in Paris, all the world passed through the Artists and Writers.

At the time of repeal, one of the qualifications for licensing establishments like Jack's was the production of evidence to show that the institution had actually existed before that time as a *bona fide* club, so the inmates of the Artists and Writers went to work to fabricate a book of spurious minutes to testify to the essentially private character of the spa. Langdon McCormick, the stage designer and author of more than a hundred blood-and-thunder melodramas, was elected president, Stanley Walker was elected librarian (the only periodical ever subscribed to was the *India State Railways Magazine*), and Roy Chapman Andrews and Heywood Broun constituted a billiard committee. There was, of course, no billiard table, but its exact physical disposition in the middle room occupied endless debate, all of it fully recorded in the *ex post facto* minutes. Voting of funds for various humane, patriotic, and scientific enterprises was a constant testimony to the public spirit of the members. Did old Joe Doax, the printer, fall down a coalhole and break his neck payday night? "Defray all expenses of the funeral" was the immediate fiat of the committee. The sum of $1000 for the annual clambake and chowder party of the club appeared regularly in the minutes.

Ordinarily a midst of almost pastoral tranquility, Bleeck's has occasionally been the scene of stirring encounters and hairbreadth 'scapes. The reverse of Sherman Billingsley's famed Stork Club—where fisticuffs are so frequent that a standard Broadway gag entails saluting its proprietor with the line, "Hey, Sherman, who's fighting at your place tonight?"—the peace is kept with a loaded nightstick behind the bar and is seldom violated.

It was about this time that Dick Watts, an inveterate amateur of Irish whiskey and practically nothing else, went on the wagon for some obscure reason. After the passage of a few unhappy days, the hanker, characteristic of all tosspots of any standing, for sweets began to agitate his person and he sneaked, with coat collar up and hat turned down, into a neighboring Schrafft's and boldly commanded a chocolate ice cream soda. To his surprise and no small dismay, he liked the arrangement and found himself ordering another. When this was consumed he smacked the glass resoundingly down on the soda counter, looked the young man who had served him squarely in the eye, and demanded: "Well, what about one on the house?"

Another favorite is Bob Clifford, the Newport undertaker, known to the clientele at the Artists and Writers as Crazy Cliff, the Merry Mortician. Cliff, who has buried the Newport ornaments of the worlds of aristocracy, fashion, and wealth, and is entirely aware of the abysmal gulfs that separate these categories of society, possesses the added enchantment of looking like an undertaker out of Cruikshank and has most of the ghoulish attributes of his calling. He carries a pocket rule and is forever sneaking up behind drinkers at the bar, who are for the moment happily unaware of mortality and the worm; applying a folding ruler to their persons, he announces: "Ha! A good six-foot-six job. I'd suggest bronze handles! Something costly but in perfect taste!"

"Death, it's hilarious!" he is accustomed to shout with graveyard overtones, weaving among the palsied drinkers at the bar.

A frontier legend practically intact from the era of Pawnee Bill and Buffalo Bill Cody occasionally descended on the terrified palefaces among the cuspidors in the form of Ned Alvord, the old-time carnival press agent, a celebrity in every saloon in North America from the Hurry Back in Salt Lake and the Crystal Bar in Nevada City to the Switch Key in Fort Worth and the Palace in San Francisco. Alvord's claims to immortality are many and varied, but his outstanding achievements are in the spheres of attire and profanity. His accustomed costume when he appears at Bleeck's, usually on the arm of Dick Maney, is a seersucker cutaway with trousers to match, a pearl-gray top hat of Mississippi River gambler proportions, Texas boots and spurs, and an assortment of diamonds profusely and tastefully scattered about his person.

It is reliably reported that printers dived through the composing-room windows on the occasion that he attempted to secure proof of a four-column ad in a Tokyo paper when on tour with a nonesuch called *A Night In Paris*. This was the confection, a dreary routine of Bronx grandmothers in flyblown spangles, which Alvord shoved down the reluctant gullets of three continents, billing it as "a stupendous carnival of sex and abandon, imported at vast expense directly from the Folies Bergère of Paris. Not since the dawn of time has there been convoked such a congress of beauty." To illustrate and guarantee these promises Alvord plastered Shanghai, Sydney, Madrid, Mexico City, Cape Town, and Antofagasta with three sheets depicting the charms of a quite undraped nymph—from the rear. The caption under it read: "At eight o'clock tonight she will turn around!"

Never tethered by facts, Alvord and Maney, abetted by Amon Carter, plastered the entire state of Texas with propaganda advertising the fascinations of Billy Rose's first *Aquacade* on the occasion of the Texas Centennial celebration at Fort Worth. They evoked a Babylonish vocabulary, hitherto unencountered by the guileless cowhands and oil drillers, wherein every B-girl, late of the Wabash gin parlors in Chicago, became "the favorite of the late Emir of Afghanistan, an houri of legendary voluptuousness snared from the seraglio of the Sultan to ravish your senses with her exotic fascinations." When Dallas, the traditional rival of Fort Worth in all things civic, put on a somewhat more abated exposition of its own, with less accent on gunfire, whiskey slings, and the fatal charms of harem voluptuaries, Maney and Alvord dreamed up a slogan which illustrated every billboard from Aransas Pass to Nogales and from El Paso to Brownsville: "First go to Dallas for culture, then come to Fort Worth for fun!"

On another occasion Alvord tried to induce Anderson to help him with the projected tour of a girl show in Japan.

"Whatever do you want to go back to Japan for?" asked Anderson. "You know the time you were there you didn't even see Fuji!"

"I know," quivered Alvord, "but I want to be the only person alive who has never seen Fuji twice!"

But of all the occasional inmates of the Fortieth Street zoo during the entire decade of the thirties, the most glittering, zany, and legend-shrouded was Charles Stanley Sackett, a fabled raconteur, and a leering exquisite whose entry into almost any bar in Manhattan was greeted with happy howls of "Here comes Uncle Stanley!" and a great and universal setting up of drinks. Stanley was only infrequently in funds, save, of course, for the time he inherited $10,000 from somewhere or other and spent it in a week, but so gaudy was his personality and so ingratiating his stories that he was welcome in circles that embraced grand duchesses and truck drivers.

He was the super-front man of such posh hostelries as the Lombardy, Elysee, Vanderbilt, and Madison, and later, for a brief but undeniably gala interlude, managing director of the Palace in San Francisco. His tail coats, of which he possessed literally scores, his hand-kissing, and his lordly commanding of supposedly gratis magnums of Perrier-Jouet which might later be found unobtrusively but profitably lurking in a guest's bill—a technique perfected by Rosa Lewis in her Cavendish Hotel in London—endeared him to patrons and managements alike, and under the flowering Ascot tie and urbanity of approach, he knew at a glance most of the skippers, bad-check artists, swindlers, and other public enemies of the hotel business in two continents.

"Why shouldn't I know them?" he used to say. "They're all of them my best friends out of working hours!"

Uncle Stanley's undeniable weakness was going on toots. Not just one or two-day binges which ended with remorse, Bromo Seltzer, and a chastened return to duty, but big, vital three and four-week screamers conceived on an epic scale and accomplished with éclat.

Upon one occasion, when he was at the Madison, Uncle Stan had a great falling-out with the proprietors, resigned with a suitable flourish, and arrived at Bleeck's with a mound of Vuiton luggage, suitcases, hat-boxes, and valises, and announced grandly that he was through with the hotel business forever and was sailing for England at midnight.

In point of fact, he had his passage in his pocket, and it was apparent that some of his more valuable household possessions had gone to the flea market. In effect, he was flush, merry, and in a mood to command wine. By the middle evening word of this expansive farewell-forever party had circulated, and thirsty friends and even mere acquaintances had come to bid Stan a fond *bon voyage*. The queue reached through the doors and out into the street, and, as midnight approached, Stan was hoisted into a taxi, his baggage tossed in after him, and directions were given to convey him to his pier in the North River.

"Don't any one come with me, please, boys," he pleaded. "I can't stand good-bys!"

The next morning the international traveler awoke, still in his dinner clothes and on a berth in what was undoubtedly the stateroom of a steam-ship. He rang weakly for assistance and restoratives and was only mildly surprised when a large and amiable Negro in a white jacket answered his summons.

"Cunard changed to colored stewards, eh!" remarked Uncle Stanley. "Well, that's nice, although I must say I hadn't heard of it!"

"This ain't no Cunarder, sir," beamed the darky. "This am the Norfolk boat and we're there now. You better get up and dressed, sir."

There were times in Stan's life when the Norfolk boat was only very vaguely distinguishable from the *Berengarial*

The foregoing are, of course, only a few highlights and low woodwind noises from a Manhattan saga which, while not, perhaps, possessed of his-toric greatness, is still representative of the spirit of an era and a locale. Many verses and chapters must survive, like the Homerica material, only by word of mouth, such as the occasion when a prominent Boston indus-trialist, on the town for the marriage of his son, was inadvertently locked in the men's washroom at closing hour and, having lost his spectacles down the drain and not being entirely sure of where he was, was unable to find his way to the front door to summon help: he remained closeted with himself until next morning at eleven, when John Gallagher, the day barman, opened up and released him.

Helen Hayes has always maintained that Bleeck's doesn't exist at all; that it is simply an Indian rope trick and the figment of somebody's disordered imagination. Escorted there one evening by her husband, Charlie MacArthur, of *Front Page* fame, she discovered that life in Fortieth Street was every bit as demented as had been represented to her, worse perhaps. At one table Nunnally Johnson, Darryl Zanuck's most expensive vicar, was beating his third wife, whom he had married that afternoon, over the head with a silver-handled umbrella, a wedding present from Fred Wildman, screaming the while: "You'll never have my autograph, woman!" Dick Maney with his hair in his eyes like an English sheep dog, was matching passages from *Troilus and Cressida* with Dr. Henry Rowell of Johns Hopkins, also a notable recitationist. Crazy Cliff, the Merry Mortician, was measuring folk for imaginary coffins with his undertaker's measuring tape, and Bleeck himself was shaking an admonitory finger at two terrified and entirely blameless sailors who had wandered in under the impression they could enjoy a quiet glass of beer, and telling them that no overly intoxicated people were allowed on the premises. Bleeck always takes it for granted that all members of the armed forces are stewed on general principle. Miss Hayes was, understandably, persuaded that the worst she had heard wasn't a patch on the real thing and that Halloween in the madhouse would be a rest cure by comparison.

But much of doing and undoing has passed before its mirrors. It was at its back table that most of Stanley Walker's *Mrs. Astor's Horse* was conceived and written; it was from Bleeck's that Gene Fowler set out, loaded with canned goods and copy paper, for a winter of solitary labors on *The Great Mouthpiece* on Fire Island, a winter frighteningly destructive to the morale of his only neighbors, the members of the Coast Guard. Dexter Fellowes, with his plaid overcoat and silver-headed stick, first stopped in there to announce the annual descent on the town of the Circus and there Tallulah Bankhead was known to stand on her hands while singing "God Bless America." George Buchanan Fife, the dandy reporter of the *World*, used to sport his square bowler and come-to-Jesus collar for the admiration of younger reporters.

There was, too, Minnie, the house cat, who was beloved of stars from the Opera across the street when Bleeck's was originally situated at Fortieth and Seventh Avenue. She knew Scotti, Caruso, Lawrence Tibbett, and Mario Chamlee intimately and liked to lap up a refreshing martini herself if it were placed for her in a saucer on the bar. She knew William J. Fallon when he was a rising young lawyer. She even made friends with

Albert Payson Terhune, a professional lover of dogs, and she was on the best of terms with Joe Cook, the comedian, Winsor McCay, the cartoonist, Clare Briggs, and W. O. McGeehan.

Now Minnie is with the ages, along with many of her friends, a player in an allegory of lost causes, but still participant in a sort of bright and raffish immortality, along with all the boys before the bar and singing "Clementine" in the back room.

FATHER VISITS BLEECK'S

Once, and only once, I took my father, a Boston banker of formidable dimensions, to Bleeck's. Father had been down to do some business with the firm of Morgan & Company, a bank he always distrusted since he had had an eight-dollar Collins & Fairbanks hat blown off his head when emerging from its portals during the Wall Street bombing of 1917. He viewed the ribald company at the bar with cold distaste.

At one point he asked me if I could identify the two burlesque figures crouching at the corner of the bar in parodies of evening attire and obviously about to be thrown out by the management.

"The tall one, sir," I told him, "is my employer, Mr. Ogden Reid, publisher of the *New York Herald Tribune,* son of Whitelaw Reid, former Ambassador to the Court of St. James's. The other is Mr. Reid's cousin, Ogden Mills, Secretary of the Treasury of the United States. I think in a little while they'll leave and go to the Brook Club."

Father took the *Owl* home on the New Haven and was never the same afterward.

DOROTHY KILGALLEN'S VICTORIAN DRAWING ROOM

Trends in the direction of things Victorian have been not infrequently noted in this space in the past, both because they engage the fancy of the writer and because they represent such a gratifying rebellion against "modern" décors, "functional" designs of all sorts, and all the depressing reminders of a utilitarian and industrial age. The Victorian age, especially as it grew increasingly mellow and opulent, evolved a character of leisured charm and elaborate manners and attire so foreign to an age of geopolitics and television that any vestigial trace of Victorian tranquility is a welcome manifestation.

A few issues ago in this department, we noted that among the ranking amateurs of things Victorian in Manhattan was Miss Dorothy Kilgallen, lady columnist, wife of Richard Kollmar, the highly successful producer, and very much a woman about town. Miss Kilgallen, immediately upon the appearance of this sentiment, endorsed and substantiated it in an almost unbelievably sumptuous manner by showing off to her friends what is probably the most beautifully conceived (and also probably the most costly) Victorian drawing room in the grand manner anywhere in the land. This department knows of some very lovely apartments in the later Victorian spirit, especially in such communities of Victorian origins and flowering as Central City in Colorado, Virginia and Carson Cities in Nevada, and in San Francisco. But for palatial overtones of crystal and watered silk, tufted damask and cloth of gold, Miss Kilgallen's new Park Avenue drawing room tops anything outside the fakements available to the studios of Hollywood.

The occasion for the room's unveiling was a party of such splendors for fifty or sixty stunningly fashionable guests, including the King and Queen of Yugoslavia and a number of top-ranking theater folk, as hasn't been since the wonderful days of the Hutton-Manville-Stotesbury flag raisings in the Palm Beach of the twenties.

Some notion of its devisings may be had when it is reported, quite literally, that up to the time your reporter tottered into the dawn at five o'clock, music had been available from no fewer than eleven name bands;

dinner and supper had been served in elaborate profusion of champagne
and Prague ham, highballs, vodka, and pheasant à la king, and breakfast
in a similar vein was promised; there had been a floor show, lasting a full
hour, in whose economy Bert Lahr and Ethel Merman had been casual
performers; and the jewelry on tap had required the presence of a posse
of armed Pinkertons quite in addition to the escort of Federal detectives
accorded the King and his entourage. Just potluck with the Kollmars and
some old kings and queens.

It is probably possible, with the aid of guides, St. Bernard dogs, and
fresh changes of horses at post stations, to make a complete tour of the
Kollmar-Kilgallen premises in less than a ·day, but most of their guests,
titled and untitled, but all of them pretty regal for the occasion, were
content to promenade in and admire the two most classically Victorian
apartments of all, which, in themselves, take up a mere half block of Park
Avenue front footage. By the time this appears, there will probably be
full-color reproductions of the Kilgallen palace in *Life* Magazine, but it
will do to note here that its entire length and breadth of mahogany, satin,
ormolu, marquetry, and cloisonné are lit from crystal wall brackets to
which no electric current has access; that every print, sampler, and ob-
ject of virtu from Dresden shepherdesses to china collie dogs, life-sized, is
a museum piece; and that it took New York's most expensive collector of
Americana five years to assemble its silver fire trumpets, Civil War pano-
ramas, and other fascinating items of nineteenth-century ornament.

The only remaining touch of Victorianism that Miss Kilgallen and Mr.
Kollmar have left to achieve is to arrive at Broadway first nights in a
landau with cockaded footment, frilly black parasols, and a swirl of Inverness capes. That will raise no eyebrows among folk who know them
and expect almost anything.

THE PLAZA: 1947

On the first day of October—the year was 1907—Secretary of State Elihu Root arrived in Mexico City on a good-will tour according to the *New York Daily Tribune*. On the front page of the same paper was an alarming dispatch from Newport to the effect that Mrs. Alfred G. Vanderbilt's automobile had been in a low scuffle with a butcher's wagon and its "front end somewhat damaged." At Princess Anne, Maryland, an Army balloon had remained in the air for an endurance record of four hours and traveled eighty-seven miles, while from Friedrichshaven came the intelligence that an aircraft piloted by the Count von Zeppelin had remained in the air for seven hours. In Washington an earlier Mrs. Roosevelt, the wife of the President, sat in a box at the Belasco Theater for a performance of *The Lancers* with Lawrence D'Orsay and Cecilia Loftus in the leading roles, while at Baltimore Mr. Otis Skinner was trying out a new play called *The Honor of the Family*. Sir Thomas Lipton had refused to race for the America cup, declaring that "cup races were a thing of the past." The bears in the market were uneasy over heavy supporting orders for Great Northern, Northern Pacific, and United States Steel. The North German Lloyd Line was advertising the fall sailings of the *Kaiser Wilhelm der Grosse* and the *Kronprinzessin Cecilie*. McCutcheons was having an autumn linen sale, and Mrs. William Goadby Loew had arrived at Tuxedo Park for the season.

Thus, in a serene and mannered world, marred only by the presence of misplaced butcher's wagons and bears in the market, the nations went about their lawful occasions, and the massive bronze and crystal portals of the new Plaza Hotel swung open upon an era of magnificence and splendor of life whose end, even in a mannerless world of mounting taxes, is not yet.

No hotel in the world ever opened its doors to such a gratifying thunder of publicity as accompanied the debut of New York's $12,000,000 Plaza, set up kitty-corner from the splendid Vanderbilt château in Fifty-eighth Street at Fifth Avenue. The sum of $12,000,000 was the figure officially re-

leased by Fred Sterry, the first manager, but this improved with distance
so that in the *Boston Evening Transcript* it was elevated to $13,000,000,
and in Omaha, a not very conservative town sprawled along the North
Platte, it was reported at a flattering $15,000,000. The Plaza replaced a
hotel similarly named and erected on the same spot in the early nineties
which had cost a mere $3,000,000 and had caused some dismay by in turn
dispossessing an ice skating rink where the beaux of Mrs. Astor's fashionable world had foregathered in wintertime for genteel figure eights while
skating waiters distributed noggins of Tom and Jerry and hot buttered
Medford rum, much as they still do at the winter resorts of Switzerland.

No hotel comparable to the Plaza's magnificence and resources of luxury
had ever been seen in New York before, although Senator Sharon's fabulous Palace, destroyed the year previous in the San Francisco fire, had
been its peer at least in Western prestige. But it was not its nineteen floors
rising above three subcellars in a glorification of French Renaissance style
nor its multiplicity of ballrooms, marble staircases, hydraulic lifts, restaurants, wine cellars, wireless rooms, mirrors, mosaics, and potted shrubs
that bugged the public eyes to their widest and played havoc with the
general imagination: it was the names of the people who were to occupy
and populate these Babylonish wonderments.

Until the era of the Plaza, hotel life on a permanent basis was almost
unknown among persons of means and refinement. Until then fashionable
folk had, to be sure, frequented resort hotels such as the United States at
Saratoga Springs and the Royal Poinciana at Palm Beach, and occasionally
they had patronized the restaurants and ballrooms of New York's more
conservative hostelries, but up till now persons of circumstance had
homes, and a home definitely was not an apartment in a hotel, however
distinguished might be its patronage.

When, however, it became known that permanent residents in the
town's newest hotel would include George Gould and his family, the Alfred G. Vanderbilts, Colonel and Mrs. William Jay, Mrs. Albert Tilt, "Bet-
a-Million" Gates, C. K. G. Billings, Julius Fleischmann, Mrs. Oliver
Harriman, and Mrs. Wallace Shillito, a palace revolution, quite literally,
was accomplished overnight. Permanent residents of distinguished position in the world began flocking to the old Waldorf, the St. Regis, the
Gotham, the Belmont, the Knickerbocker, the Imperial, and the New
Netherland, and the belief went into the discard that hotels were for
people with no homes of their own.

The Plaza came into official and expensive being on the last day of September 1907, with a dinner of expansive proportions for the press who
were first gentled with magnums of Bollinger and Perrier-Jouet and
soothed with sixteen courses including terrapin Maryland, grilled plover,

lobster aspic, and a staggering assortment of *pièces montées,* and then inflamed with oratory in splendid periods with ornate flourishes and superlatives in unexampled profusion.

The resulting press notices on the morning of October the first were gratifying and tumultuous. Spreads of epic dimensions appeared in the *World* and *Tribune. The Times* listed the first apartment lessors, not alphabetically or in the chronological order of their arrival but in order of their estimated personal incomes. The *Journal* showed an elevation of the hotel's façade cut away to indicate the locations of the suites of John W. Gates, the Alfred Gwynne Vanderbilts, and the Young-Heyworths and Master Otto Young-Heyworth, and the *Telegraph* referred to the Plaza chummily as a "snug tavern adjacent to Central Park."

The public was reminded all over again that the Plaza was a $12,000,-000 enterprise, a tidy sum in valid and 1907 dollars, and was informed that the first names on the register were those of Mr. and Mrs. Vanderbilt "and servant," who had been assigned to rooms 521 through 529, while the closely following William S. Roelkers "and maid" were ushered into 1141 and 1145. The Young-Heyworths got in on the show money and went haughtily upstairs to 237 through 245.

As a matter of fact, the Plaza and its important guests had been the recipients of a deluge of publicity for months before the date of the hotel's actual debut. Reports of the rentals received for residential suites, eye-popping in 1947, were of positively light-year proportions forty years ago, and the public, already inflamed and alarmed by the reported rental of "Bet-a-Million" Gates, at first quoted at $42,000 a year and later placed at the more conservative figure of $35,000, was deliciously outraged at transient rates running from $100 to $500 a day for the state apartments.

The doings of the Plaza's guests have been for forty years the stuff of which news and romance are made, and its chronicle as recorded in the public prints alone outglitters a thousand and one nights of Baghdad. And, of course, there are those chapters, some of them transcending fiction and making mock of melodrama, which will never be printed.

The Plaza's first large public function was the dinner given by the Pilgrims of America to the Right Reverend Arthur Foley Winnington Ingram, D.D., Lord Bishop of London, who had recently beaten President Roosevelt at tennis, and bragged about it, no end. Four hundred persons, on October 15, sat to table in the Grand Ballroom of the Plaza, and despite the Lord Bishop's disapproval of alcohol, drank his health in champagne when President Nicholas Murray Butler of Columbia University proposed the toast. Senator Chauncey M. Depew added his bright whiskers and sparkling wit to the occasion. That epicurean repast included:

Huîtres

Tortue verte olorose Crème Argenteuil

Amandes salées   Feuilles farcies Céleri

Olives

Diablotin à la Duchesse

Flétan farci de homard Newburg

Pommes de terre persillade

Filet de boeuf à l'arlequin

Haricots verts sautés au beurre

Medaillon suédois

Perdreaux rôtis sur canapé

Salade panaches

Glacé Napolitaine

Petits fours

Gaufrettes aux amandes

Sweets   Fruits   *Pièce montée*

Café

And these vintages: Braudeberger, Vino di Pasto, Pontet Canet, Champagne, and Beaune.

All this and hand-painted souvenirs at fifteen dollars a plate.

When Mrs. Patrick Campbell arrived from England, November 8, for a theatrical engagement, she went to the Plaza; with her went her monkey-spitz poodle, seventeen years old and blind but essential to the peace of mind of the actress. She was so ungracious to the press that Frank O'Malley of the *Sun* told her he regretted he was an opera critic and would therefore have to cover her *Hedda Gabler*, "which is a comic opera."

To the Plaza went Enrico Caruso, and, exasperated by the sound of the electric clock, tore out its innards and so put the 225 clocks in the Plaza out of business, for in those days when one clock went out, all did.

Caruso was something of a trial to hotel managements which were sometimes hard put to live up to his ideas of florid magnificence, and when in San Francisco in 1906 the first Palace had burned and Caruso had made an exit from the Montgomery Street entrance attired in a top hat with a Turkish towel around his middle and carrying a signed portrait of Theodore Roosevelt under his arm, there were wags, even on that day of doom, who remarked that it had been easier to burn the house down than adapt it to the tenor's demands.

Mrs. Julia Watts Curtis took a suite at the Plaza and soon was explaining to bug-eyed reporters that she was not extravagant, but duty made her spend $200 a day, because "an income is like a reputation—one must live up to it."

In the basement of the Plaza, George A. Fuller, Jr., the ten-year-old son of the Fuller Construction Company, had a speedway, one seventh of a mile long, on which he drove a boy-size electric automobile at a speed of twelve miles an hour.

A New York tradition at the turn of the century held that all coaching meets and other horsy events should have their inception at the old Fifth Avenue Waldorf-Astoria, and it was here that celebrated whips like Reginald Rives and William Vanderbilt posed in white top hats and paddock coats for the news photographers of the time to immortalize them in silver salts through the agency of the Graflex focal-plane shutter camera. In 1909, however, modernity caught up with New York, and nine automobiles, driven by women, set out from the Plaza on the perilous four-day trip to Philadelphia and back, a distance of 220 miles, and *The New York Journal* was able to remark smugly that "the trip proved that women in the aggregate are as careful and sportsmanlike as men."

The war, not that between men and women later immortalized in *The New Yorker* by James Thurber, but between the hay-burning horse and the internal-combustion engine automobile, had, as a matter of fact, been fought with unremitting fury beneath the Plaza's porte-cochere ever since the night of its grand opening in 1907. At that time a delegation of New York hackmen had protested to Fred Sterry the placing in service on the Fifth Avenue cab rank of "a fleet of twenty-five taximeters painted bright red with green panels and the charges for riding in which are recorded on an odometer." Auto-taxis had, however, already appeared outside Rector's and the Imperial Hotel, and the jehus were not to have their innings again until the Second World War when gasoline suddenly was discovered to be at a premium and the ancient hansoms and victorias beside the Pulitzer Memorial were once more in great and general requisition.

There were times when the Plaza's progress, as chronicled in the public prints, resembled nothing so much as a Court Circular, and New Yorkers came to associate the hotel with almost every available degree of transient nobility from the Old World. In 1911 the *World* was able to amaze and delight its readers with an account of dinner as served in her private apartment on the Fifty-ninth Street side of the house by the Princess Vilma Lwoff-Parlaghy of Berlin and Vienna. The Princess brought with her her own complete service of crested gold dinner plates and accessories and her own table linen of Irish lace, and her guests were served by her personal staff which included five butlers, two footmen, and a bodyguard, who, while on duty, were attired in crimson satin liveries with black satin breeches, silk hose, and silver-buckled pumps.

More decorous and, therefore, less fascinating to the press were the Count Aponyi of Hungary, who was honored by Mayor Gaynor and Mrs. Andrew Carnegie at a state dinner at the Plaza; Earl Gray, the Governor General of Canada, who was entertained by the Theodore Roosevelts; Lord Clifford of Chudleigh, who was of the opinion, for the reporters, that American civilization as represented by New York's skyscrapers "was getting completely out of hand"; and the British King's messenger, the Honorable Frederick Grahame Curzon-Howe, who excited dramatic attention by arriving in New York with a state message for President Taft which was carried in a dispatch case chained to his wrist and which he never discarded "even during the intimacies of bathing and shaving."

Glittering, magnificent, trivial, dramatic, and sentimental by turns, life at the Plaza has never been dull, and the reports of it have proved fascinating alike to readers of the papers and to city editors at their wits end over the wherewith, the fill-in, the space remaining in their Monday mornings' columns between the transcript of Chauncey Depew's address to the members of the Lotus Club and the inevitable report on the state of the Central Park Zoo.

In the early years a close runner-up for the reporters' attentions with Mr. Gates and the Lord Bishop of London was Consuelo, Dowager Duchess of Manchester, who was variously reported as being in residence, in transit to Newport and Tuxedo, and the dinner guest of Mrs. John Jacob Astor and Moncure D. Robinson. As a pretty gesture characteristic of a gaslit time, A. E. Merrall of Acker, Merrall & Condit Company presented a loving cup to Miss Elsie Janis in the course of a champagne supper. In the men's bar, a cocktail was specially named for Sheriff Bob Chanler of "Who's loony now?" fame, and the coming and goings of Mrs. O. H. P. Belmont, James R. Keene, and Berry Wall, "King of the Dudes," made pleasant breakfast-table reading. Once, to the provocation of a universal gasp, a rival appeared for Wall's sartorial honors in the person of Louis Newman, a broker, who made an entry in a purple evening tailcoat and white-topped patent-leather shoes. He was not taken seriously by Mr. Wall. A Mrs. J. B. McDonald lost her "priceless" pearls in the dining room, and they turned up in the Plaza's vacuum cleaner. Mrs. George Gould returned to the stage for a single performance in the interest of charity and did it in the Plaza's private theater to the accompaniment of whoops and hurrahs in the papers that would interest a Hollywood film star today.

Gradually, there came into being among the Plaza regulars and with the enthusiastic endorsement of the town's society editors—Howard

White, Maury Paul, and F. L. Baker—a group of women who came, over the years, to exercise almost complete dominance over New York society: Mrs. Whitelaw Reid, Mrs. William D. Sloane, Mrs. Ogden Mills, Mrs. Elbridge T. Gerry, Mrs. John Jacob Astor, and Mrs. Cornelius Vanderbilt. Where, but a few years before, Mrs. Stuyvesant Fish and Mrs. William Astor had reigned supreme, these insurgents assumed authority, and the name of the Plaza became synonymous with a stronghold of fashionable conservatism, a significance that it has never altogether lost.

Indeed, the Plaza came into effulgent being in an era when the grand manner was in vogue and has never, to this day, lacked a continuity of *bon ton*, a tangible link with the heroic past when the unforgettable champagnes of 1899 were still on the best wine cards and terrapin was as essential to a well-selected menu as caviar is today.

The Plaza became a regular port of call for district reporters and society paragraphers and it was possible to read in the columns of the *New York Commercial* that "James R. Keene was drinking Great Elephant Water last evening at the Plaza with a group of capitalists," or that the Count Szechenyi, an aspirant for the hand of Gladys Vanderbilt and, therefore, *per se,* a name that made news, had been "trailed by reporters in meter taxis" from the Plaza to Grand Central Depot where he embarked for Newport aboard the private car of Mrs. H. McK. Twombley.

In 1928 the late Evander Berry Wall, "the kindest gentleman in France and the best-dressed gentleman in the world," returned to revisit the New York of his salad days when, as he himself described it, "terrapin were not used for racing and nobody confused sherry with Madeira." He put up at the Plaza, naturally, and the writer of this account called on him, having often been his guest in Paris in other years. Berry was depressed by the New York he rediscovered. It was in the declining years of prohibition, and manners were not what they had been. He remembered when there had been only four hotels in Manhattan which had any claims on the patronage of people of refinement and taste, long before the day of the Plaza, St. Regis, and the other then current hotels of social acceptance. His top hat with a wide weed and stock collar attracted amused smiles on Fifth Avenue when he wore them on days other than Sunday, and he was outraged by the vogue, then universal in a country-club generation, of wearing soft shirts with dinner clothes. Berry never drank water at any time, preferring a brut champagne with breakfast and vintages of increasing dryness and consequent acidity as the day wore on. The Wall system never revolted, and by bedtime, which, in his eighties was about four in the morning, he had usually consumed half a case of Bollinger or Perrier-Jouet and his stay in the Plaza never necessitated any abatement of this habit. But he was profoundly depressed by New York and the necessity for drinking behind closed doors, and after a few weeks he returned to Paris, never again to set his well shod foot on his native land.

During the forty opulent years of its existence, the Plaza has kept on an average of five restaurants in more or less constant operation, the service at a given era being conditioned by the general times and public taste. The least mutable of these have been the Terrace Restaurant, the great formal dining apartment of the establishment, and the Plaza Restaurant as the café at the Fifty-ninth Street corner is known. At the moment, too, there is the Persian Room, which is one of the most modern of the Plaza's public apartments in décor and its showcase for Manhattan society in its lighter moods. Under the waiter captaincy of the Plaza's famed M. Paul, the Persian Room flowered into opulent being as the scene of repeated triumphs by Eddie Duchin, the de Marcos, Emil Coleman, Paul Draper, and the incomparable Hildegarde. Today the room is in charge of Fred, and there dancing in the evening is institutional and in summer time the most magnificent cold buffet on the Avenue is furnished forth at lunch.

The Oak Room, in the rear of the house, is on weekdays a preserve of masculinity until the market closes in the afternoon, and luncheon is also served in the richly decorated men's bar which formerly was the premises of E. F. Hutton & Co., the stockbrokers. It is now on the cards that in the early fall of the current year, the Plaza Grill will be reopened in the basement on the Fifth Avenue side under the special guidance and supervision of Col. Serge Obolensky and the Count Cassilli Adlerberg, a team of expert practitioners charged with revitalizing the current estate of the Plaza through the agency of reviving its glories of other years.

To New Yorkers who recall the early years of prohibition, defined by the late Scott Fitzgerald as "the Years of the Great Tea Dance," the Plaza Grill is pregnant with memories and fragrant with a lingering odor of romance and juniper. Here, when the toddle was in vogue and the academic existence of a generation known as "collegiate" was orchestrated to the tune of "Valencia" and "Kalua Bay," the fashionable youths of Harvard, Yale, and Princeton were accustomed to foregather, especially on Friday and Saturday afternoons, fortified with Matt Winkle's or Dan Moriarity's gin and heartened by the presence of Miss Constance Bennett and other notable prom-trotters of the Stutz Bearcat age.

Miss Bennett was a symbol of a world that has vanished as completely as the fauna of Miocene times, an oriflamme of youth in a time of Brooks Brothers four-button suits, of monster pilgrimages to New Haven for football games, of epic routs and valiant skirmishes with the police at Cynthia White's routs at Webster Hall, of breakfasts in a Reubens that was in Columbus Circle, and of Beaux Arts Balls that made the name of Gretchen Menken a hallmark of extravagance and fantasy of costumes. Ah, dead and gone, never to be relived, the green days and fair of youth when gin was seven dollars a bottle and Helen Smith was mistress of ceremonies at the Pre Catalan!

It was the Plaza's Palm Court that witnessed the opening engagement of what was to become one of the most sensational controversies of its time when Mrs. Pat Campbell lit the cigarette which caused almost as much excitement as an earlier Mrs. O'Leary's cow had in Chicago. In compliance with an established house rule, a desolated manager persuaded her to extinguish the offending gasper, but the torch was lighted for a crusade which was to rock society, in the broader sense of the word, on its heels and furnish more newspaper copy and topics for more embattled sermons than any New York scandal since the Awful Seeley Dinner at Sherry's in the almost-forgotten nineties.

The Palm Court, too, was destined to be the occasion of an only slightly less publicized tumult when the new management of the Hilton Hotels, who had recently come into possession of the property, undertook its decorative modernization. The older element of Plaza residents such as Mrs. Clara Bell Walsh, who had moved in the day the house was opened, looked upon the efforts of L. Alavoine & Company in this direction, for all that they had been the original decorators of the hotel, as akin to the sack of the temple. The cries of outrage and sacrilege achieved space in the papers, and Gotham conservatives, who had been convinced that revolutionaries were loose in the palace every time a carpet had been replaced during the past four decades, metaphorically averted their gaze when passing the scene of outrage and denounced the Count Vassilli Adlerberg, in charge of the renovations, as a tool of the Kremlin.

In the end, however, when the Palm Court emerged renewed in splendor but intact in spirit and feeling of the past, even the old guard of the palace were reconciled and, before his death, Jules Bache, to whom change of any sort was synonymous with infamy, was seen to adjust his monocle and give the gold and silver screens and monster crystal *torchères* his complete approval.

Uncrowned, perhaps, but nevertheless universally recognized queen of the Plaza is Mrs. Clara Bell Walsh, who is herself all but institutional both in the Kentucky of her birth and in Fifth Avenue. Mrs. Walsh, widow of Julius Walsh of Royal typewriter fame and fortune, moved into the Plaza the day it opened, and, despite impassioned threats to leave the premises every time there is a new potted shrub in the Palm Court or the economy of the breakfast menu is revised, has remained in majestic and diamond encrusted residence from that day to this. Her demesne is a seventh-floor apartment alarmingly populated with several live dogs and scores of china fidos, and the great and near great of the theater and allied worlds of professional society overflow her brocaded chairs and sofas and empty decanters of her overproof bourbon while consuming fantastic quantities of her home-grown Kentucky hams which are sent on from Bell House, Lexington, with chronometric regularity.

The same day that Clara Bell moved in, Romeo Giannini, the hotel's chief bellman, took charge of his desk in the lobby and has never left it. Nellie Golden, hat-check girl at the Plaza Café, refuses to divulge the length of her service among the top hats and homburgs, but veteran patrons can recall her at the same post thirty years ago. William Hartery, chief house officer, has been guarding the guests for so long that were he to write his reminiscences there would be a deal of heart searching among the town's carriage trade. Jack Koch, headwaiter in the Plaza Restaurant, has been there since the first dinner cover was laid in 1907, and, indeed, it may be said that probably the youngest important member of the hotel's staff is Frank G. Wangeman, the general manager, who came to the Plaza with an enviable hotel-management career both here and abroad.

Within the past few years something new, however, has been added to the Plaza in the form of what are probably the most lavishly upholstered editorial offices in the world when the twenty-two-room penthouse was leased as its headquarters by Earle MacAusland, editor of *Gourmet, The Magazine of Good Living*. Originally the New York residence of Harry S. Black of the construction firm which built the hotel, *Gourmet's* impressive offices boast an oval, marble-floored foyer, a sixty-foot drawing room, bathrooms with solid-gold plumbing fixtures, a terrace giving on the most expensive skyline in the land, and a dining room and kitchen capable of seating and serving forty guests and completely staffed with the magazine's own chefs and housemen. This side of a Cecil B. De Mille production-number editorial rooms, there is nothing like the home office of *Gourmet* anywhere.

Sunday is a big day at the Plaza and especially a snowy Sunday in midwinter, for, be its corridors never so populous on long, cool evenings in spring or its window boxes never so inviting in the July noontide, there is an affinity in the New York consciousness between snow and Central Park and the Plaza. It is debatable whether parents taking their well-furred moppets for a ride in Pat Rafferty's sleigh or hansom, as the case may be, from the Fifty-ninth Street cab rank are doing so for the instruction of youth or for the indulgence of a pleasant sentimentality on their own part. But there is no doubt at all that to command hot rum and tea in the Oak Room or the Palm Court afterward, with wonderful cakes for the moppets, is to establish a link, at once tangible and gratifying, with the storied past when carriage call on Broadway had a literal meaning and the "taximeters with odometers" were merely a novelty and certainly not here to stay.

Sunday at any season is the day that Jules Villani, the Oak Room headwaiter, has more morning-coated personages to accommodate than on any other day of the week, and Sunday evening is when James McKiernan, the wine steward, deep in the third subcellar of the house, insinuates more foil-topped bottles of Mumm's and Bollinger into silver wine buckets than at any other time. And, of course, Sunday is the day when François Gouron, the executive chef, knows that there will be an almost insatiable demand for the Plaza's cream of chicken soup, a restorative and comfort to mankind, acknowledged by the most celebrated authorities on Saturday night among the pots to be without peer or equal.

A knowledgeable fellow, this Gouron, a student of Brillat-Savarin, a pious follower in the footsteps of Escoffier, and heir to a regal tradition of forty years of terrapin and pheasant, canvasback and chateaubriand richly devised and lovingly cherished deep in the culinary heart of the Plaza. No single person in all the complex economy of the hotel's management is so influential in its prestige and bears such a burden of responsibility for its fair name, and no one is so intimately acquainted with the tastes and preferences, whims, and gustatory mannerisms of the notables who populate its restaurants.

This then is the Plaza, a repository and trustee of many things to many people, a microcosm of immutability in a changing world, a bond between the storied past and opulent present. There are presences in its galleries and ballrooms which may be apprehended by the truly perceptive: Goulds and Vanderbilts, "Bet-a-Million" Gates and Berry Wall, General Pershing and Marshal Joffre, Mrs. Patrick Campbell, Scott Fitzgerald, and Consuelo, Dowager Duchess of Manchester. Here the past is as valid, almost as tangible as the present.

As has been suggested before, it is this continuity with the past, more than anything else, which lays hold upon the imagination at mention of the Plaza, this quality of intactness from a time that is even now, to a whole generation of Americans, only a wistful souvenir of an age of graciousness and glamor. Seven years before Sarajevo was, in reality and measured in terms other than those of years, a very distant period indeed. The world has grown gray in that time, and its brighter lights have been dimmed by the mediocrity and the fussy devisings of little men.

But the lights of the Plaza, somehow and miraculously, have been undimmed. Even tonight they gleam in welcome across the asphaltine stretches of the wealthiest avenue in the world, and in many and many a heart is the hope that they will so continue to gleam, tranquil, warm and unabated, for many and many a year.

Printed as a souvenir brochure by the management of the Plaza on the occasion of the hotel's fortieth anniversary celebration, October 1, 1947. The wish contained in Beebe's last sentence has continued true for at least the last two added decades, and the hotel celebrated its sixtieth anniversary on October 1, 1967. For an up-to-date story of the Plaza see *The Plaza 1907–1967: Its Life and Times,* by Eve Brown (Meredith, 1967).

LE PAVILLON: 1953
5 East Fifty-fifth

To remark in so many words that Le Pavillon is New York's superlative French restaurant is at best the expression of an opinion. The sentiment is, however, entertained by the author of this article and enjoys the support of an impressive number of perceptive diners-around and amateurs of gastronomy in its more exalted aspects. *Revue du Vin de France,* official organ of the vintners of the Republic, for example, with no qualification at all, hails Le Pavillon as "the finest restaurant in America," and such various personages and personalities as Walter Bedell Smith, Myrna Loy, the Duchess of Marlborough, J. Edgar Hoover, and Sir Alexander Korda subscribe, by implication, to the superlative.

An even wider clientele is agreed, also, that of all Manhattan's restaurateurs none—and this without dissent or exception—is more notably a perfectionist than Le Pavillon's rotund, smiling, and infinitely diligent Henri Soulé. They concur that the transcendental gastronomy of which Brillat-Savarin wrote is Henri Soulé's objective, and there is a hard and not too small core of gourmets who are of a mind that he achieves it.

There are, of course, drawbacks attached even to perfection in the restaurant business. One is that it is breath-takingly expensive and that, as a result, its enjoyment is limited to a small clientele. Also, preparation and service can be conducted only on a scale far below demand. Both these circumstances give rise to implications of snob appeal. As a matter of fact, Le Pavillon can and does serve 150 persons at lunch and half as many at dinner, and this, Mr. Soulé states for the record, he would cut by, say, two thirds if it were economically possible.

"I want my customers to have only the best of everything the world affords," he says.

Soulé's Pavillon has been a New York institution ranking roughly with Van Cleef & Arpels and the House of Morgan since the New York World's Fair. As the bright jewel of its exhibit, the French government designed a restaurant to embody the best of everything French which, as all the world knows, is in the field of food and drink. The staff of this advertisement for the deluxe way of life was the veritable flower of French kitchen chivalry—a *saucier* here, a *garde-manger* there, a wine steward from the old Lafayette, a chef from the Café de Paris in Paris—men of vast culinary excellence.

Manager of this embassy of edibles was Henri Soulé. *Chef saucier* was Jean Louis Christophe, for twenty-one years with the now-immortal staff of the Hôtel de Paris at Monte Carlo. Both of them are today associated, Mr. Soulé as proprietor, Mr. Christophe as executive chef, of Le Pavillon in Fifty-fifth Street, across the street from Vincent Astor's St. Regis Hotel. Without disloyalty to the merits of the St. Regis, some of its regulars are also admirers of the cuisine at Le Pavillon; in fact, the hotel's managing director, Pierre Boltink, himself sometimes lunches there.

Like its clientele, conduct, and cuisine, the Pavillon's address is in the more exalted brackets: 5 East Fifty-fifth.

The décor of New York's most impenetrable cathedral of caviar is severe with the opulent severity of the very rich. Its chairs are upholstered in cherry damask. Its carpet is deep enough to be negotiated best with snowshoes. Huge masses of long-stemmed, crimson American Beauties reek pleasantly of well-being. A florist spends six hours a day arranging them, and the annual bill for roses alone is more than $15,000.

The walls are trimmed with dull gold and silver, and the largest wall space in the room is filled with a map of France in gold leaf on glass, showing the regions notable for viniculture and gastronomy. Perigord, where the truffles originate, and the Champagne region are specially decorative. Knowing patrons sometimes look at the map and order on a regional basis instead of consulting the menu.

Directly at the left of the street entrance is a small restaurant in which the bar is located and which is often reserved for private parties by such notables as Sol Hurok, the impresario, and the Duchess of Windsor.

Of approximately fifty tables at Le Pavillon, half or more are regularly reserved for constant customers: the Duke and Duchess of Windsor, Mrs. Fleur Cowles, Mrs. Millicent Hearst, Colonel Sosthènes Behn, Mrs. John Barry Ryan, Harvey Firestone, Jr., Mainbocher, Cole and Linda Porter, Henry Ford II, Mrs. Winston Guest, Count Vasilli Adlerberg, and George Mabardi, Soulé's old friend the wine dealer from the St. Regis. These tables are held until an arbitrary hour, approximately one-thirty at lunch, and, if not by then claimed, are released.

The Duke of Windsor, as one of the oldest and most distinguished friends of the management, enjoys what amounts to top priority. Even though he is known to be in Paris or on the Riviera at the moment, his table is always held until the established hour for its release, much as in the London mansion of the elder J. Pierpont Morgan, the bed was turned down, a bed lamp lit, and an assortment of literature arranged at hand every night of the year, even when the master was assuredly dining in his Murray Hill establishment in Manhattan.

A complete stranger to the premises—at least during conventional hours of lunch and dinner—has only a microscopic chance of securing a table, no matter how opulent the mink. A representative survey on a January afternoon would disclose such headliners as Bernard Baruch; the Duchess of Marlborough; Prince Serge Obolensky; Jean Dalrymple with Edmund Goulding; Mrs. Frederick Blake Payne, the explosively beautiful blonde; the walrus mustaches and old-style, four-button suits of Ben Sonnenberg, the super-publicist; Elsa Maxwell; Mme. Alma Clayburgh, the retired diva; Clara Bell Walsh, of Bell House, Lexington, Kentucky; Hedy Lamarr; the Marquis of Milford Haven; Cornelius Vanderbilt, Jr.; Robert Sherwood; and Louis B. Mayer.

Admittedly this is a fairly concentrated essence of high life, but it is also a representative cross-section of Mr. Soulé's clientele, and the concentration remains constant from day to day.

"I am reluctant to have acquired a reputation as a snobbish restaurant," says Mr. Soulé, "but I have to protect my valued patrons against four-flushers who would like occasionally to make a big flash or consummate a business deal, but who have no proper knowledge of how to eat and drink. To them the answer is reluctantly but unequivocally: 'No!'"

Aside from the necessity for running an establishment on a selective basis, the culinary doings at Le Pavillon can be described by only one word: superb.

The menu lists all the recognized items of *haute cuisine* in the classic manner of Vatel and Escoffier: fresh Malossol caviar, truffled *foie gras*, English Channel sole flown in that day; melon, asparagus, strawberries at their out-of-season best; grouse, partridge, duck, and pheasant in season; soufflés, ices, and desserts beyond number; and, at all seasons, a cold buffet as photogenic as a Powers model. This, however, is only an introduction to the resources of the house: for Mr. Soulé and Mr. Christophe can produce anything within the bounds of culinary reason, which, at Le Pavillon, are uncommonly spacious.

Largely, the daily selection of dishes is based on the preference of established regulars. Sir James Dunn, the Canadian tycoon, is devoted to soft-shell crabs, while Lady Dunn, *à l'anglaise,* is an eater of notable proportions of beef. Cole Porter demands grilled quail or *poulet Beau-sejour;* Leland Hayward wants mousse of ham, *pot-au-feu,* and the white meat of chicken sautéed in heavy cream sauce. Margaret Truman can't get through either lunch or dinner without chocolate soufflé; Jock Whitney has no inhibitions about caviar and steak *au poivre;* Mrs. Carmel Snow wants *oeufs brouillés estragon,* and Marlene Dietrich will go for *pojarsky.* Most of these items appear regularly on the menu. More exotic tastes, such as that of Henry Sell for entire roast suckling pig, and Sosthènes Behn for whole baby lamb, are not so easy to accommodate as that of Fleur Cowles, who demands hamburgers (and gets them, too, by golly) flat and completely cooked, with carrots. Mr. Soulé pales slightly at mention of this sort of thing. Most Pavillon customers want their beef rare.

In the matter of drinks, the Pavillon has an enviably high average of consumption. Almost all customers, both at lunch and dinner, consume at least one cocktail, and nine out of ten order wine at dinner. The Pavillon wine cellars were built to Mr. Soulé's specifications and maintain an inventory of more than $85,000's worth of the best vintages and spirits, which is augmented every two years when Mr. Soulé goes abroad for the purpose.

In the classic tradition of restaurant keeping, Mr. Soulé does almost all daily purchasing of provender, making the rounds of his favored tradesmen six days a week with a metaphorical basket over his arm.

Until Arsène Tingaud died a few months ago, an almost daily scene each morning in his Sixth Avenue establishment was the arrival, often simultaneously, of his two most aristocratic customers, Mr. Soulé and Joseph Donon, *chef de cuisine* to the late Mrs. Hamilton McK. Twombly. Mr. Tingaud was, and his firm still is, the Cartier's of baby lamb, mallard duck, and fillets of beef so costly they should be guarded by time locks, and *poussin*, or baby chicken, of such delectable texture as to defy description in prose.

Mr. Donon, whom Mrs. Twombly retained at a reported salary of $25,000 a year, and who was a Newport cottager and yachtsman in his own right, almost invariably came in search of *poussin* by the dozen, or by the hundred, as might be required by the day's schedule of his employer. (Mrs. Twombly's purchases of lobster, made elsewhere, sometimes ran to forty dozen for luncheon alone.)

When Mr. Tingaud died ("with a quarter of beef on his shoulder," according to Mme. Jeanne Owen of the Wine & Food Society), his passing was mourned by the Messrs. Soulé and Donon as would be that of a patron saint.

Another respected wholesaler who values Mr. Soulé's patronage is Lucien Prince, of 204 Front Street, himself a *viveur* in the town's better restaurants where his lobster, shad, and oysters are fixtures on the menu.

"Of all the buyers I have ever known," deposes Papa Prince, as he is known in salmon and sea-bass circles, "Soulé is at once the most meticulous and the most liberal. Smoked fish, such as salmon and finnan haddie, are cured according to his specifications. If they aren't just right, they never get past the service door at Le Pavillon. On the other hand, Soulé never asks the price of anything. When the merchandise is what he wants—I swear he can tell if a terrapin has led a happy childhood—its cost is no consideration.

"Salmon for Soulé must be smoked slowly a whole week. His smoked sturgeon is taken only from the center cut, the most expensive part of our most expensive fish. His smoked eel is done for us by an old Dutchman who has been smoking eel since before Dewey took Manila. Crab meat for Le Pavillon must be in large lumps, so fresh that it's practically alive. Frogs' legs are flown up daily from the Everglades. Brook trout he selects for their eye appeal as well as flavor: they must be speckled just so.

"He buys sea urchins—our only customer for them. He must have a special patron who likes them. [Inquiry disclosed that Le Pavillon has not one sea-urchin fancier, but two: Bernard Lamotte and Jean Gabin.] Soulé is both a pain in the neck to satisfy and our most wonderful customer. All he wants is the best of everything."

Papa Prince regularly supplies three varieties of seafood for the Duke of Windsor: striped bass to be prepared *Dugléré*, frogs' legs which will appear *poulette*, and the Scottish finnan haddie which is the Duke's special weakness. Finnan haddie is basically codfish caught in the cold waters of the North Atlantic and derives its name from the town of Findon, near Aberdeen, where generations of Scotsmen have passed from father to son the secret of properly smoking fillets. Scottish finnan haddie costs Mr. Soulé approximately three times the price of the domestic product, which he claims is more pickled than smoked.

The Duke is also partial to fillets of beef, broiled woodcock, and Scottish grouse, some of the latter coming to Le Pavillon from the preserves of the Queen of England, a relative.

A dinner for thirty guests of the Duke and Duchess a short time ago began with caviar (almost invariably the first movement in all Pavillon symphonies), smoked salmon, smoked sturgeon, and cherrystone clams on the side; followed by striped sea bass with mousseline sauce; and swept into its third movement with roast fillet of Colorado beef, puréed potatoes, green beans, and green salad. For dessert, a *bombe* Pavillon. This simple but nourishing bill of fare was accompanied by Puligny-Montrachet '47, Château Lafite-Rothschild '34, and that rarest and most delicate of all champagnes, Moët & Chandon's Dom Pérignon Cuvée '34.

Lauder Greenway, a knowing social notable, improved somewhat on the Duchess when he invited dinner guests to sit down to the inevitable caviar followed by clear turtle soup, striped sea bass broiled *en bordure* with parsley potatoes, roast pheasant with *coeur de céleri demi-glacé*, green salad, a soufflé *au parmesan*, and assorted cakes, sluiced with (again) Puligny-Montrachet '47, Château Lafite-Rothschild '34 (this in magnums, however), and the Dom Pérignon '34.

Each summer when Le Pavillon reopens after vacation, Mr. Soulé gives an invitation dinner for regular patrons.

Last summer's menu offers a study in classic simplicity tempered by luxurious sufficiency: Beluga caviar, consommé Henri VI, *homard* Pavillon, *carré d'agneau,* potatoes *fondantes,* green beans *au gratin,* lettuce salad, and fruits *au kirsch.* The wines weren't listed, but Mr. Soulé recalls that they included Dom Pérignon Cuvée toward the end, a commodity with which, at seventeen dollars the quart, Le Pavillon is as plentifully supplied as with sparkling water.

Obviously, Le Pavillon serves enormous quantities of caviar, and its procurement is often a matter of some concern to the management. Mr. Soulé has for years maintained contact with a specialist in the fish-eggs field, a Syrian gentleman who understands doing business with the Russians.

Two or three times a week the caviar man appears with ten or a dozen tins (caviar comes in round, 4¼-pound tins worth approximately $106 each, at the present market). Mr. Soulé samples each tin and purchases one—at the most, two. "Only one container in ten is worth my having," he says. Le Pavillon's caviar Malossol, which has no price after its listing on the menu, but which comes at better than five dollars a spoonful, is composed entirely of the large, pale gray, perfectly globular eggs, almost the size of buckshot, and each egg separately defined from its neighbors.

The person and personality of New York's ranking perfectionist are both complicated and at times contradictory. Mr. Soulé is short and very round, as becomes his occupation. His benevolent moon face surmounts an *embonpoint* testifying to a thousand losing skirmishes with *homard Pavillon, faisans sur plat,* and *soufflés glacés* in borders of wood strawberries, as well as untold temptations in bottles marked Ausone '37 and Dom Pérignon Cuvée '21, all of them unsuccessfully resisted. Mr. Soulé has a suspicion of difficulty in folding his neat small hands across his beautifully tailored double-breasted suits, and his neat, astonishingly small feet fairly twinkle in a minuet dedicated, conceivably, to *filets de boeuf périgourdine* flanked by *haricots verts au gratin.*

Mr. Soulé has a trick of appearing never to delegate the affairs of his restaurant to his staff which, for the record, would be entirely capable of handling such duties. He takes all wine orders himself. He believes the presence of a *sommelier* is an imposition. When he isn't busy with wine or receiving customers or advising them in matters of menu, Mr. Soulé is industriously carving the *carré d'agneau* which is the *plat du jour,* or rearranging the already well-ordered roses on the table of Sir Alexander Korda.

The operation of Le Pavillon, as should be true of an honest house, has been without change discernible to the patrons from year to year.

Many members of the staff came from the original corps of the French Pavillon at the conclusion of the New York World's Fair and are still on duty amidst the roses and wine coolers.

Next under Mr. Soulé comes Martin Decre, a veteran with the title of manager, who is almost as familiar with the feeding of patrons as is Mr. Soulé himself. There are six captains: Pierre Parini, Henri Rouget, Fred Decre, Gabriel Joffre, Pierre Géraud, and Robert Meyzen. The bartender, André Gros-Daillon, an authoritarian who shakes his martinis vigorously against all established precedent, is a dreamy Gallic fellow. He mutters into his glassware about Adirondack lakes and the simple life, but admits to being desperately lonely out from behind his bar. Jacqueline Casanova, the cashier mounted at the end of the bar, carries on a multilingual conversation with most of the regulars, and is institutional at Le Pavillon.

Although probably a closer approximation to perfection than anything available this side of Judgment Day would seem to have been achieved at Le Pavillon, Mr. Soulé is not content.

"Perfection is an illusion," he says. "Here I have what I know very well is the finest restaurant in the best-fed city in the world, where everyone of consequence turns up sooner or later, and the wealth of the gardens, vineyards, and game forests is available.

"Do you know what I would like? I'd like this restaurant with just twelve tables—with forty-eight covers—and orders for every meal two full days ahead! But America is not geared to this, so we do the best we can."

Mr. Soulé looked wistfully into space, ignoring the simultaneous arrival of Millicent Hearst, Joseph Kennedy, and Ed Sullivan, and there was a dreamy quality in his gaze, as if it lit on visions of *homard Pavillon* and Dom Pérignon—served for no more than four, and ordered forty-eight hours in advance.

THE ELEGANT COLONY: 1958

There are a good many distinguishing aspects of the Colony Restaurant which set it aside from even such exalted establishments as Henri Soulé's Pavillon, Jack & Charlie's "21," and the Plaza Hotel, although it shares variously in the attributes of all these luxury restaurants.

For one thing, the Colony is the only resort of fashion in the record that, a good many years ago, found a Madison Avenue address too ostentatious for its requirements and modestly assumed one around the corner in Sixty-first Street. The Colony, too, is practically unique in that while other fashionable restaurants gain prestige from their customers, several Colony regulars without a shred of claim to celebrity have achieved fame solely by occupying the same table at the Colony year after year.

Another trait which has won the Colony the loyalty of a good many influential customers is the unvarying accuracy with which the management recalls their preferences in food, drink, and cigars. It has been able to duplicate for an old friend a luncheon that was held ten years before, right down to the brand of sherry in the green turtle and the selection of flowers in the centerpiece.

Other restaurateurs—and the legend of good living is full of them, from Olivier of the Paris Ritz to Theodore Szarvars of the New York Ritz-Carlton—have flattered prime ministers and tycoons by remembering details of their preferences. Indeed, Marco Hattem, the Colony's legendary barkeep, prides himself on being able to reconstruct the special dimensions of a patron's fizz or swizzle a decade later.

The Colony management, however, does not trust memory. Long ago it established a record of the tastes and favorite menus of its regulars. It is a card-index system, and it is consulted the instant a distinguished patron checks his hat. It isn't as theatrical or as flattering to the customer as having a waiter captain recall that three years ago there had been too little curry powder in his *crème Waterbury*. But it is more reliable and, over the years, it has paid handsome dividends. The Colony, its regulars believe, is here to stay.

The fact that the Colony in its earliest days took on an aura of social exclusiveness has not hurt the reputations of its proprietors, Gene Cavallero and Ernest Cerutti, as purveyors of fine food. Its name has always carried with it a cachet of upper-case grandeur and carriage-trade *éclat*. But this would not have been possible if the management had not been dedicated to the food and wine that are the basic reason for the Colony's existence. Gene Cavallero has a winning way with celebrities and aristocrats, but it is his fanatic standards of quality when shopping for Nova Scotia salmon or white muscat grapes that have placed the restaurant in the firmament of the world's fine eating places.

This blue-blooded aspect has, indeed, sometimes been a headache of major proportions to Cavallero. The architecture, acoustics, kitchen availability, and even the décor of its main red-and-pink saloon were designed so that no one table was more advantageous than any other. Service at the end of the room farthest from the Sixty-first Street foyer is identical with that at tables No. 1 and No. 2 just inside the door. The flowers are as fresh, the captains as attentive. But the word got around over Park Avenue's back fences that a position well forward in the restaurant was infinitely to be preferred over those in the rear, and sometimes, on spring days, it has been necessary to set up tables in the front lobby.

To point up his snob approach, a New York society reporter spoke of the rear portion of the Colony as "the doghouse," implying that its occupants were less aristocratic than those in the front of the house. It probably caused the management more trouble than anything since prohibition, and the doghouse indictment spread to other restaurants, notably "21," where for two full decades the management had to contend with the superstition that the rear restaurant on the second floor was a social pesthouse.

The story of a restaurant's success is usually more fascinating than that of a rolling mill or a shoe factory because it is based on small, touching acts of faith on the part of its sponsors—the little heartbreaks when a splendid *homard à la cardinal* is neglected by a petulant patron, or a cross word is spoken by an influential customer on whose good will so much depends. The façade of maître d'hôtel must be impervious to anguish.

The years during which the Colony emerged from the jungle night life of New York in the age of prohibition were eloquent with heartbreak, disappointment, and sacrifices on the part of the three founding partners. They were also characterized by interludes of hilarious incongruity. Before it was discovered by the William K. Vanderbilts and Jules Bache, the Colony's most munificent patron was Arnold Rothstein. It first shared the premises it occupies today at the corner of Sixty-first and Madison with a small but discreet gambling establishment (upstairs) and a man who specialized in various tranquilizers of a pre-Miltown age.

The restaurant was opened by Joe Pani, sometime proprietor of Wood-manston Inn, and almost overnight became popular with professional gamblers and gentlemen who wished to entertain ladies not their wives. The twenties were the golden age of kept women in Manhattan, and an account at the Colony soon became a badge of successful availability along with Paquin gowns and Minerva motorcars.

Ernest Cerutti, Pani's maître d'hôtel, and his captain, Gene Cavallero, were on bowing terms with most of the town's *poules de luxe*, while the chef, a dedicated Alsatian named Alfred Hartmann, ran up superb *poularde à l'estragon* for the *poules de luxe*. The Colony was nothing you'd recognize today.

But Cerutti and Cavallero had other ideas. Both had long backgrounds of more elevated surroundings which included the Savoy in London and the aloof Astor-owned Knickerbocker Hotel in New York. Pani was a man of moods, morbid discouragement alternating with wildest optimism, and Cerutti, Cavallero, and Hartmann, who by now had pooled their resources, waited for the proper moment in the boss's fortune. There came a day when, for a variety of now-forgotten provocations, Pani was ready to cut his own throat. Through an intermediary—for they feared Pani would never sell out to his own staff—the partners asked his going price. It was $25,000—$7000 more than their combined resources. The balance was providentially provided by Sylvester Haberman, the landlord, who liked Ernest and Gene, and secretly longed for Vanderbilts and Otto Kahns where there were now Rothsteins and Larry Fays.

It would be pleasant to record that overnight the Colony won social recognition and prosperity, but such was not the case. The ladies of the evening and the well-manicured card experts were soon discouraged by the aloof moral tone of the new regime and took their business elsewhere, but, alas, few new customers arrived to fill their places. The slender resources of the partners were reduced to nothing, and their credit became strained among the Danish pastry barons and shad-roe earls of Fulton Fish Market. Hartmann, in his kitchen, resorted to various measures of economy known only to hard-pressed restaurateurs, but never compromised with the quality of his food. In later years the partners were glad to recall that even when things looked darkest they still paid sixty dollars a crate for their asparagus, an astronomical sum in the early twenties, and that the waiters wore evening shirts with sleeves and cuffs, instead of the dickies suggested as a measure of economy by a restaurant-linen-rental firm.

And then the wheel turned full cycle, and the ivory ball paused at the right number for Cerutti-Hartmann-Cavallero & Co.

Mrs. William K. Vanderbilt came for dinner. It was as simple as that.

Today, when New York upper-case society names mean less than they did thirty-odd years ago, it is hard to appreciate the triumph implicit in this haughty visitation. The presence of this formidable lady, in a single evening, erased the tarnish of the Rothstein years. The William K. Vanderbilts were not only blue bloods beyond the wildest dreams of the Colony's proprietors, they were also gourmets of the first chop. Their patronage was at once a social triumph and a gustatory victory of impressive proportions.

Gene and Ernest made no bones about pointing out Mrs. V. to the other patrons on that auspicious evening. They wanted witnesses lest unscrupulous rivals should say it was all a promotional canard. Before she gathered up her wraps to leave, Mrs. Vanderbilt's presence was well attested by other reputable diners, and the next day the New York restaurant world buzzed.

The management's efforts today are dedicated strictly to the perfection of its chicken Marengo, but it has never failed to be gratified by the arrival of Doris Duke or Mrs. Merriweather Post; and Gene has come to regard the food and the customers in a manner complementary to each other, as if Col. Serge Obolensky were somehow an ingredient of the chocolate soufflé and vice versa.

Once approved by the impeccable William K. Vanderbilts—who maintained their status as first family of the Colony for many years and, until Mr. Vanderbilt's death in the thirties, were a fixture to the right of the entrance—names arrived to rejoice the heart alike of Cavallero and New York's society paragraphers: Reginald Vanderbilt, Tommy Hitchcock, Lord Northcliff, Jules Bache, Mrs. Edward Hutton, the Angier Biddle Dukes, Alfred Hitchcock, the Duke of Marlborough, the Winston Guests, Alfred P. Sloan, Clara Bell Walsh, and the Grover Loenings. With the passing years, these primal grandees were to give place to a generation of perhaps less formidable Newport and Southampton names, but the turnover has always been of well-upholstered background and good breeding.

Inevitably time left its traces on the economy of the Colony. In 1927 the great Alfred Hartmann sold his share in the partnership to Ernest and Gene, and returned to his native Alsace, a tolerably wealthy man. He was the only chef in the long history of the restaurant to be personally exploited, and thereafter Gene insisted that the chef de cuisine remain comparatively anonymous. For many years the headwaiter had been a tall, sad, gentle-mannered Italian named George Fiorentino, with something of the air of an extremely well-bred undertaker, and when death struck the original partnership, Gene was ready to admit him to the firm.

Ernest Cerutti died, en route to Italy for his annual vacation, aboard the Rex in 1937, and the New York newspapers recorded the event in terms of national importance. By then the Colony was, with the possible exception of Jack & Charlie's "21," the city's most celebrated restaurant, and its affairs were news of the first order. Cerutti left an estate of approximately half a million dollars, which may be taken as an index of the financial status of the partnership. Two years later, George Fiorentino became Gene's partner and he has remained part of the firm, to everyone's satisfaction, to this day.

George has at his command a sort of grand bedside manner. His presence is both soothing and reassuring, and customers with the shakes credit at least fifty per cent of their recovery from the night before to a few minutes spent in conversation with him. The other fifty per cent, of course, goes to the medicinal arrangements of Marco Hattem at the bar.

The Colony early became a favorite with O. O. McIntyre, a wide-eyed country boy from Gallipolis, Ohio, the author of the most widely syndicated New York column ever to be written. McIntyre—who drank nothing, but ate well—indulged an insatiable craving for Sulka cravats and bathrobes, and arrived in a sky-blue Rolls-Royce town car that, second only to the basketwork Rolls of Mayor James J. Walker, was the best-known motor in the streets of New York. His column brought the Colony and its patrons home to people who would never go there, and ultimately dog wagons and obscure saloons called "the Colony" began appearing all over rural America.

The love affair between Mayor Walker and the Colony became national news when the mayor changed the direction of traffic from east-west to west-east in the Sixty-first Street block between Madison and Park. In theory, this reversal of the city's established traffic pattern made the Colony more accessible to the mayor's block-long Rolls-Royce, and the whim tickled a town which admired Walker more than it did those who eventually accomplished his ruin. After Jimmy Walker's departure from office, Sixty-first Street reverted to east-west traffic, as the police department originally intended.

Due to the ingenuity of the Colony management and the ambassadorial assurance of Cavallero in moments of crisis, contretemps were infrequent during prohibition at the corner at Sixty-first and Park. For one thing, Marco Hattem, even in those primeval times the Colony bartender, kept the larger part of his stock in the freight elevator which served other parts of the building, and at the slightest alarm the Louis Roederer '16 and Gordon's gin soared majestically into upper regions where they might be overlooked by revenuers. The Colony was seldom molested and never seriously discommoded.

Marco Hattem, one of the few staff members who remember the days of the old Madison Avenue address and the gamblers, is celebrated for at least one departure from the conventional mixing ritual of bartenders: he shakes a martini. "This talk about how a martini should be stirred for fear of bruising the vermouth is for the birds," says the genial Marco, who is

Turkish and a man of greater cultural background than you might suspect. "What the martini needs, vermouth and all, is a good beating up, like this." Whereupon he gives his shaker a tremendous workout, and the drink comes out into the glass as clear as one of the Van Cleef & Arpels diamonds in the Colony's lobby display.

Two of the Colony's most enthusiastic and recurrent patrons for whom Gene has a warm place in his heart—no matter how their social status may have skidded elsewhere—are the Duke and Duchess of Windsor.

Like the society columnist's troublesome reference to the Colony's "doghouse," the Duke was to have a marked effect upon the conduct of the restaurant. Once when he was having a luncheon cocktail with Robert Young in the front bar, the captain announced that the Duchess was served in the formal restaurant. The Duke asked Gene if, as a special favor, his guests couldn't lunch where they were. "It's so cheerful out here, and we don't get stared at so much as in your grand salon," he told Cavallero. The innovation created an immense vogue for ordering lunch at the tiny cocktail tables in the bar, which was an inconvenience to everyone until the next season when Gene had the cocktail lounge redecorated, with larger tables. After that, the service of meals there, luncheon especially, became part of the Colony routine.

Between them, Gene and the kitchen card-index can throw a good deal of light on the character of a number of notables if you subscribe to the hypothesis that the food on a man's plate is as reliable a key to his personality as the books on his shelves.

Bernard Gimbel, for example, has the taste of a merchant prince for roast Scotch grouse, rare, white hot, and well hung, though possibly not to the point decreed by Professor Mahaffey of Dublin that game is ready to serve only when it falls away from its own legs when hung in the woodshed. Mrs. James P. Donahue, reportedly the richest woman in the world, often orders selected baby pheasant roasted and served *grandmère*. Lobster-claw salad with an intricate special dressing of her own devising which she mixes at table is the whim of Mrs. George U. Harris, while Aristotle Onassis prefers spaghetti and his favorite Greek bread to all the *foie gras* ever shipped from Strasbourg. The Duchess of Windsor runs true to racing form with a nice preference for caviar, partridge, and terrapin, and Joan Crawford insists on a "Crawford Special" salad of spinach leaves with chopped-bacon dressing. Elsa Maxwell—and the staff will make book on her ordering it—is passionately addicted to well-browned lamb hash.

A Colony regular, a generous part of whose fame derives from having held down Table No. 21 so long that the memory of living man runneth not to the contrary, is Miss Beth Leary, a close friend of the late Mrs. James Farley's. Miss Leary lives at the St. Regis, seven blocks removed from the Colony, and is a passionate bridge player. Often, when games in her St. Regis apartment become of stirring proportions, she telephones Gene and has dinner sent down with a couple of waiters in a taxi, a practice which it may reliably be reported meets with no great favor from Pierre Bultinck, the St. Regis' managing director, who maintains a superb kitchen of his own.

Through wars, depressions, and the inevitable tides of change that are the patterns of New York's existence, the staff of the Colony has remained remarkably cohesive. Of the original staff which came together in the twenties, Felix the maître d'hôtel, Bianchi the senior captain, Marco the bartender, and seventeen waiters are still on duty. The entire staff today comprises eighteen chefs and sous-chefs, ninety-five other kitchen employees, ten captains, thirty-two waiters, seven bus boys, and the conventional complement of doorman, washroom attendants, and pages. *Chef de cuisine* is Jean Vergnes, a native of Grenoble, who came to the Colony nine years ago from the Waldorf as *saucier* and has been *chef de cuisine* for the past six.

The Colony maintains an inventory of $175,000's worth of wine and spirits in its cellar, guarded and cherished by a professional cellarman and dispensed by William Mascarotti, the *sommelier*, who is no mere waiters' waiter invested with a chain of office, but a scholar and amateur viniculturist and oenophilist.

Menus are handwritten by Bianchi and reproduced daily by an old-fashioned gelatin process so archaic that Gene believes he can detect signs of Indian warfare about it.

One of the secrets of the Colony's stature in the realm of fine food is the purchasing, which has always been supervised by Gene himself and often actually accomplished by him. He buys caviar from Romanoff, or from the subsidiary of his rival down the street—Jack & Charlie's "21"—the Iron Gate Importing Company. Fish largely comes from the dean of New York fishmongers, Papa Lucien Prince of Fulton Fish Market and an old customer of the Colony, where he admires to order his own shad, pompano, scrod, and Cape oysters, according to the season. Beef and baby lamb, among the most costly items, mostly come from Knickerbocker Foods in downtown Manhattan, and for years came from Shaffer's Market, then located right across the street.

Shaffer's has now moved farther uptown and Gene is upset about it. Not only was Shaffer's a sort of emergency supply in case the Colony found itself short of terrapin or ring-necked pheasant, but the Colony had its own key to the premises and access to the refrigerators after business hours; the steward just left a chit on the cashier's desk to show what he had taken. Gene recalls that once he hurriedly sent across late one evening for a hundred partridges which the late Clarence Mackay, Irving

Berlin's father-in-law and heir to the fabled wealth of Nevada's Comstock Lode, demanded for a dinner party on the spur of the moment. Without Shaffer's, Gene could never have made do in this crisis, and he doesn't like to contemplate the possibility of one like it.

Most recent addition to the partnership of the senior Cavallero and George Fiorentino is Gene Cavallero, Jr., a personable young man of abundant charm and manners whom his father was determined not to bring into the restaurant business through the front door with the customers. As soon as his formal education was completed, Junior, as he is known to almost everyone, was packed off to learn the business of food and wine the hard way, and spent two years following the established *cursus honorum* in some of the best kitchens, wine cellars, and steward's offices in the world.

He polished pots in the George V in Paris, and did duty on the telephone switchboard at the Paris Ritz to perfect his French. He learned the secret of noble sauces from the venerable *saucier* at the Suvretta House in St. Moritz, boned up on the service of game at the Buffet de la Gare in Zurich, and practiced handling the world's finest wines at the Ambasciatori in Rome.

Today Junior is one of the three partners of the Colony and enjoys the professional confidence of his father, no mean achievement as anyone in the New York restaurant business will tell you.

There are those to whom the Colony seems of fairest aspect and most beguiling mien on nights during the season when opera or the horse show calls for tailcoats and tiaras, and the reassuring plop of gibus hats in the foyer is background music for the service of pheasant Souvaroff in a setting where the emeralds of the patrons shame the Van Cleef & Arpels showcase by the door. Solvency, propriety, and good breeding, all being served up along with the *hachis de volaille glacé argenteuil.* What more can you ask?

CAFÉ SOCIETY REVISITED

It may well be possible for the informed sociologist or political scientist, if indeed the latter term is not self-contradictory, or other ex-post-facto entrail watchers and after-the-event soothsayers to leaf through the pages of *El Morocco Family Album* and find in the inmates of its sumptuously upholstered banquettes and ringside tables the outriders of a doomed society poised on the brink of the abyss or, at the very least, participants in a long Gibbonesque decline and terminal fall.

That the then-impending events and portents of world catastrophe (*Family Album* was published in 1937) may have cast shadows visible to melancholy necromancers is credible, but I must confess that, on reviewing its pages after the passage of more than a quarter of a century, I find in them no auspices of doom, but only visible evidences of good times and often attractive people in a world innocent of guile. John Perona's elegant nocturnal trap has nothing obviously in common with the Duchess of Richmond's ball on the eve of Waterloo.

El Morocco's significance in the golden midnight of its fame and fashion is that it was the cathedral where there foregathered nightly the higher echelons of what at the time was known as café society, which has since disappeared from human experience as completely as the Sixth Avenue El or the horse-drawn patrol wagon. *Family Album*'s significance is that it is the tangible iconography of a small, self-limiting group of attractive people who got a great deal of attention simply because they wore beautiful clothes beautifully, drank a great deal of vintage champagne, and took a good picture.

Café society itself was the emergent product of a number of interlocking factors which comprised, among others, the disappearance in the market debacle of 1929 of much of the basic wealth of an older and more formally organized society, the repeal of prohibition, and the perfection of a technique of personalized photography known as "candid camera."

The new photography, which made interior lighting for the first time possible without either ponderous batteries or the Burning-of-Rome effects of the earlier magnesium flares, portrayed personable people demonstrably having a good time in luxurious and pictorially exclamatory surroundings. To secure publication in the Sunday supplements and periodical coated-paper press, the participants in these largely innocent alcoholic and gastronomic scuffles had to be reasonably easy to look at, and cheery of mien. Mrs. Stuyvesant Fish would never have qualified. Neither would Mrs. William Backhouse Astor.

Willing stand-ins for the by-now-obsolete seagoing social battle wagons were available from the ranks of stage and screen, the fringe professions of letters, journalism and advertising, decorating, women's fashions, and the vending of old masters, antiques, *objets d'art*, and champagne. There were princely parvenus from foreign places and parvenu princes from even more distant and unidentifiable climes, Swedish tycoons, hallroom boys from advertising agencies, acceptable stockbrokers, Yale men, and debutantes who would later be nominated for Miss Rheingold. And there were enough old-line names deriving from families of empire builders, merchant princes, and financial buccaneers to pass across the copy desk under the ambiguous heading of "society."

To corral, ride herd on, and vaguely to domesticate and tranquilize these elements, Perona invoked three associated agencies which made El Morocco overnight a concentration camp of competitive celebrities. One was the genius of a decorator who evolved an identifying backdrop of cobalt blue and silver palm fronds which screamed the premises' name without its mention in the letterpress. A second was the house photographer who was possessed of a gall of rhinoceros-hide dimensions and a personality that was intrusive without offense; and could usually be relied upon to suppress the photo that caught you with your eyes closed, mouth open, and the flies going in and out. And the third was Carino, a maître d'hôtel who was beyond peradventure the most adroit practitioner of the diplomat's calling since Metternich.

Carino was probably the largest single factor in the resounding success that El Morocco turned out to be. Essentially a genius of the first order, Carino was the presiding master of revels, arbiter of elegances, cotillion leader, and tailcoated Petronius. El Morocco without Carino would have been just another trap, though of course it was Perona himself, of all the night-club proprietors in the world, who discovered that the fanciest floor show imaginable to a chic and witty audience of New Yorkers is themselves. Not only, he discovered, were they fascinated with looking at each other, libeling each other conversationally, and bowing to themselves in the mirrors—they would pay fabulous sums to do it. And the fame of their personal appearances, the feuds, occasional loyalties, witticisms, and general after-dark conduct of the celebrities who flocked to El Morocco became symbols of urban magnificence wherever Sobol and McIntyre were lovingly spelt out one word at a time.

There were, to be sure, contretemps and occasional physical disagreements among the inmates, ending with the thud of falling bodies being tossed into East Fifty-fourth Street; but the bodies were invariably attired in dinner clothes, and the hats that were tossed after them into the night were opera hats, which made it possible, in reporting the engagement next morning, for the press somehow to invest it with the old-time heartiness of Jack Dunstan's with overtones of the Patriarch's Ball.

Perona enjoyed a glittering press, which may have been attributable to the circumstance that every New York newspaper publisher and magazine executive of any stature at all was at least an occasional patron, while the more personable members of their editorial staffs found the bar at El Morocco fully as productive of entertaining and sometimes gee-whiz copy as an earlier generation of reporters had found the men's bar at the Waldorf and the Windsor.

The generation of dedicated playboys and play-actors, theatrical producers and *foie gras* consumers that made El Morocco the inheritor of the lobster-palace tradition of an earlier Broadway is no longer commanding magnums of Bollinger and crossing Carino's palm with shares in Minnesota M & M. It has evaporated from the public gaze even as the formal society of Frank Crowninshield, the last great gentleman, disappeared to make room for the saloon set.

But it has left such a pictorial record of its going as was never the lot of the dynastic hoedowns of Vanderbilts, Gerrys, and Millses that antedated it. Archeologists a thousand years hence may be excused if they confuse café society with the real thing.

I SAW THE ELEPHANT

In San Francisco, where they do everything in the grand manner, they have a happy phrase that is the equivalent of the French *faire la bombe*. When one goes out to do the town and experience its wonderments, he is said to be "seeing the elephant." In closing the books on the twenty years of my own private Manhattan Project, I feel that the phrase is completely appropriate. I have seen the elephant!

I came to the *New York Herald Tribune* from Harvard in the fall of 1929, and last spring [1950] I resigned to go to Nevada to live and fill a number of book assignments. In that period of time I was, variously, a city staff reporter, ships'-news reporter, editor of and contributor to the now-vanished "Op Ed" page of Sunday essays, contributor to the editorial page, assistant in drama, and conductor of a syndicated column called "This New York." With few and infrequent exceptions I had nothing to do with politics, crime, or foreign news. My concerns were all with the ornamental and amusing aspects of life, and my copy was principally concerned with glamor, good living, and the more prosperous aspects of what passes for civilization. I was referred to, by other newspapermen, as the *Tribune's* saloon editor, and I considered my function that of a connoisseur of the preposterous.

In the terms of the newspaper cliché, I *did* meet a lot of interesting people. I did have a fabulous time. I did drink more champagne and get to more dinner parties and general jollification than I would have in almost any other profession. On the strength of my *Tribune* by-line, I wrote or photographed ten books on improbable subjects, four of which turned up with gratifying frequency in the best-seller lists. I became a Chevalier of one of the oldest orders of knighthood in Christendom, the *Confrérie des Chevaliers du Tastevin*. I found myself, somewhat puzzlingly, listed for several years among the ten best-dressed men. I endorsed whiskeys, shaving soaps, and other merchandise to my great profit, and I got to be on speaking terms with the maître d'hôtel of every restaurant of consequence in the United States. I met some truly great and distinguished men and a large number of comedians and otherwise relaxing persons.

I have seen a round cycle of events in a round period of two decades, and now I am breaking up this continuity as a professional New Yorker. The green valleys and chocolate-ice-cream hills of Nevada are calling, and I have sent my boiled shirts and Inverness to storage.

On Monday, the twelfth of August, 1929, when I reported for work to Stanley Walker on the city desk of the *New York Herald Tribune,* it was abundantly apparent that God was in His Heaven and all was right with the world. The week previous had seen 20,000,000 shares change hands on the New York Stock Exchange, with Atchison selling at 272 and Auburn Motors at 425. During the day, United States Steel gained eleven points to reach an all-time high of 220½. Lady Lowther was the guest of the Drexel Biddles at Newport, and Mrs. Julia Berwind had entertained stylishly for the Franklyn Huttons. The Sandy Hook steamers were advertising a round-trip twilight sail, the full length of New York's incomparable harbor, for $2.50, with a six-course dinner thrown in. Theatergoers could have their choice of the Ziegfeld Follies, Eddie Cantor in *Whoopee* at the New Amsterdam, or a show called *Bird in Hand.* Payne Whitney had just ordered a new private Pullman car at a reported price of $175,000.

I was further convinced that I had landed in clover when the reporter whose desk adjoined mine, Beverly Smith, now head of *The Saturday Evening Post*'s Washington Bureau, introduced himself and asked if he might have the honor of buying me a drink at Bleeck's, a handy saloon where I was introduced to the owner and publisher of the *Tribune,* the late great Ogden Reid. Most reporters, I reflected, didn't have drinks with the publisher the first day on duty. Things were certainly looking up.

Other newspapers with which I was familiar had been written, edited, and published from conventional editorial and publication offices, but I soon found this was not the case with the *New York Herald Tribune.* With the exception of such minor details as its composition and printing, the paper was conducted from the adjacent premises of Jack Bleeck's Artists and Writers' Restaurant, which was then, of course, a speakeasy.

Bleeck's is a superior newspaper saloon with some of the best food and most generous drinks in New York, and it has long since become a legend. The very best reporters of the generation made Bleeck's their home. Such characters as Alva Johnston; Joel Sayre; the *World*'s stylish George Buchanan Fife, who always wore a square derby and wing collar; Skipper Williams, the great *Times* ships'-news reporter; Harold Ross and Wolcott Gibbs of *The New Yorker;* Red Dolan of the *Daily News;* and, of course, the *Tribune*'s own Bill McGeehan, Percy Hammond, John Lardner, Howard Barnes, and Joe Alsop were in practically constant attendance. So were the *Tribune*'s executives: Geoffrey Parsons, chief editorial writer; William Morris Houghton, his assistant; Walter Millis; Harry Staton, of the syndicate; Howard Davis, the business manager; and Mr. Reid himself. At one time Stanley Walker had an extension of the city-desk telephone at one end of the bar.

Now and then, the news of the day was not only edited in Bleeck's but had its factual origins there. One Saturday afternoon in midwinter, the gleaming silk hat of Hugh Brown, house manager of the Metropolitan Opera down the street, put in an agitated appearance. The matinee performance had been an opera whose last scene was a Spanish street fair in which a number of gaily colored, gas-filled balloons had been released by the merrymakers, and a freak draft had carried them out over the footlights and up into the farthermost reaches of the Met's rococo ceiling. There was no harm in this, but the evening performance was to be *Faust* or some similarly massive affair with no time out for levity, and the management foresaw that, as the gas leaked out of the balloons, they would descend into the orchestra stalls and boxes and, if the management knew anything about Saturday-night audiences, it wouldn't be long before tail-coated old sirs would be bouncing the things back and forth.

It was no time for vacillation. Harry McCormack, the chief barkeep, pulled a double-barreled shotgun from under the bar and shoveled two boxes of dustshot loads into my hand, and everyone raced back to the Met. There I took a stand in the Ogden Mills Estate Box and opened fire. The balloons came down all right, sometimes two or three at a time. So did small plaster cherubs and other bits of ornamentation. There was more dust and noise and smoke for half an hour than ever accompanied a performance of *The Roundup*. The day was saved, but members of the evening audience commented wonderingly on the smell of nitro loads which perfumed the premises.

The city staff of the *Tribune,* in the early thirties, had only a vestigial trace of the urgency associated with newsrooms in the minds of filmgoers. In that distant day, the walking stick and the green covers of *The American Mercury* protruding from the overcoat pocket were the hallmark of the New York reporter, and Stanley Walker's personal philosophy was embraced by two remarks, the latter quoted from Chauncey Depew: "When I feel like exercising, I lie down until the feeling goes away," and "Walking downstairs for breakfast is enough exercise for any gentleman."

I was given occasional assignments covering the activities of Mayor James J. Walker, whose charm, courtesy, and loyalty to his friends have become one of the legends of American politics. On one occasion I was with the mayor on a junket to Long Island, and it was his whim to play a fast game of roulette at an interdicted but, to this day, flourishing parlor. I knew the proprietor of the game, who maintained an even more elaborate and extensive layout at Miami Beach, and the management was enchanted to see the mayor clattering happily around in colors, columns, quarters, and *en plein*. Word of the mayor's presence, however, was carried by some political enemy to the state police, and a sneak raid was organized. When the smashing of glass and shouts of "Everyone stand where you are!" apprised us of the arrival of cossacks, the mayor, a couple of other reporters, and myself hastily draped napkins over our dinner-jacket sleeves, seized piles of handy dishes, and walked out into the night in the guise of waiters. The cops never did recognize the mayor of the world's largest city with his hair slapped down in a cowlick over his forehead. A few minutes later, our entourage encountered the police muttering darkly in the lobby of a nearby hotel. "Gambling around here?" said the mayor. "That's terrible. It should be suppressed at once."

It was at about this time that Peter Arno indulged in his only skirmish with the dramatic muse. He wrote something called *There Goes the Bride*, and it was staged with a great deal of social fanfare at the Majestic. There were more opera-length gloves on hand that evening than the Metropolitan's Horseshoe usually rates, and the thunder of opera hats must have been audible at the Battery. After the show, Jock Whitney, a classmate of Arno and myself at Yale (I had matriculated at Yale but graduated from Harvard to everyone's confusion), was giving a little supper for the cast and four hundred other guests for which he had taken over the Starlight Roof of the Waldorf. It was to be the party of the year.

In its way, it was, too. The play turned out to be such a stinker that the more mannerly of the guests were far too embarrassed to show up at the party. Not so the reporters and Broadway paragraphers. Twenty or thirty of these harpies showed up and brazenly told their hosts the play was a sure-fire smash and where, please, was the champagne? I was among them. So was Howard Barnes and so, to my best recollection, were Percy Hammond and Dick Watts. The *Tribune* was adequately represented. Between midnight and five in the morning, and to the music of a Meyer Davis society orchestra, we devoured all the caviar and quail, and drank all the champagne that had been planned for nearly five hundred guests. Everyone took home a hundred Corona Corona cigars, and the play closed that night.

My first association with the really great of the age was with Noel Coward, then the king of the English-speaking world. I was doing ships' news, a dreary assignment calling for chilly pilgrimages down the harbor on the 6:30 cutter on winter mornings to get fussy interviews with celebrities like Otto Kahn and William H. Woodin, when Coward arrived aboard *The Empress of Britain* to commence rehearsals with the Lunts for *Private Lives*. I had breakfast with Coward in his suite and wrote a chatty two thousand words in which he told about his early poverty and struggles in Greenwich Village, and how he and the Lunts had agreed someday to do a world-beater, and *Private Lives* was going to be it. The Associated Press picked up the story and next morning it was all over the country.

That evening I attended the opening of some now-forgotten play. Coward was seated at the other side of the orchestra and, at the intermission, stood up to survey the house in the Continental manner. Every eye was on him in envy and admiration when he spotted me. He made handshaking motions of appreciation and then, excusing himself from his party, came all the way across the house to tell me what a beautiful story I had written. A less generous or imaginative actor might have written a polite note of thanks for the interview, but Coward, knowing that at that moment his friendship was prized in New York and London above rubies, chose a public and spectacular way of flattering an unknown reporter. I have always thought of him as the most gracious celebrity of my time.

My literary agent for several years before he left New York for Hollywood and a torrid marriage with Ida Lupino was Collier Young of the firm of Brandt & Brandt. A child of whimsy, he liked to do things in costume, so I was not surprised one day when the phone on my desk rang and he said: "I'm getting married in an hour. Hurry over to Sniffen Court, and please wear a Confederate uniform." This was his marriage to his first wife, Valerie Edmonds.

I paused at Bleeck's to get my courage up and then went to Brooks, the costumer, from where I emerged in a General Lee suit and slouch hat and headed for Murray Hill, followed by the hoots of urchins. Sure enough, Collier was also in a general's suit but could find no proper cavalry boots and so was barefooted. Charles Hanson Towne was in Rebel attire and so, if memory serves, was John Marquand, author of *The Late George Apley*, whose agent Collier was. Mayor James J. Walker was in a conventional morning coat, Valerie was in a hoop skirt, and nobody was in very great pain. Sometime later in the day, as the reception was becoming fevered, Valerie backed up to an open fire in the studio. Unaccustomed to the extent and inflammability of hoop skirts, she at once caught fire and had to be put out by the guests who used seltzer, champagne, or any handy extinguisher. Just the wire frame for the hoop skirt remained. It was a wonderful wedding.

Along in the middle thirties, when my syndicated column was having considerable success in such suburban communities as Cleveland, Fort Worth, Kansas City, and Washington, I found myself on terms of most agreeable friendship with Mrs. Evalyn Walsh McLean, owner of the Hope Diamond, a sparkling character in her own right and the nation's most deluxe hostess. From then until her death I never missed one of her Washington parties.

There was never a dull moment at Evalyn's parties, particularly those at "Friendship" on Wisconsin Avenue far out in Washington's suburbs. An enormous and aristocratic farmhouse that had been the property of Ned McLean when Evalyn had married him, it stretched in illimitable vistas of drawing rooms and dining salons, and could accommodate house guests literally by the hundred. There was a solid-gold table service for sixty, and silver service plates, wine buckets, and epergnes for three times as many. There were the private golf course, the Berberini tapestries, and the great oil portrait of President Harding. There were invariably the British Ambassador; Cissy Patterson in a floppy hat that none of her scrubwomen at the Washington *Times-Herald* would have had as a gift; Senator J. Ham Lewis in his bright pink whiskers; Sir Willmott Lewis, correspondent of *The London Times;* John L. Lewis; Thurman Arnold; Henry Cabot Lodge; and Joseph Hergesheimer. There were also, because of the presence of the Hope Diamond and approximately a million dollars' worth of other free-floating baubles, a dozen or so Pinkerton men.

The first evening I was a house guest at "Friendship," the hour bell sounded at seven, and everyone went upstairs to dress for dinner. There was a burglar alarm in the form of an elaborate mother-of-pearl push button on the bed table in each guest suite. Around it were other buttons for footmen, valets, and ladies' maids, and in Joe Hergesheimer's room a special one marked "Hennessy and Soda."

I was in my shorts and dancing pumps, shaving, my face a mass of suds, when a thunderous disturbance broke out. Gongs exploded; there was a muffled sound of doors being slammed and a leitmotif of smaller bells tinkling hysterically. Armed with a straight razor and a determination to strike stoutly for my hostess should the occasion offer, I opened the door and stepped into the corridor. There was no sign of excitement, only a continued tumult backstairs. A footman in snuff-colored livery, marching serenely past with a highball on a tray, set my mind at rest. "It is nothing, sir. You need not be disturbed," he said tranquilly. "Mr. Hergesheimer invariably sets off the alarm while ringing for a drink. He does it every evening, sir. The butler will soon disconnect the gong."

Evalyn McLean was afraid of nothing, and took an almost sensual pleasure in the perpetration of minor social outrages. In 1938 the second Joe Louis-Max Schmeling fight was scheduled to take place in Harlem, and rumors were freely circulated that anything in the nature of a victory for Schmeling could lead to race riots. Evalyn was enchanted and at once commanded a block of ten of the best seats.

We had dinner in Harry Dougherty's apartment in the Waldorf, and a police escort waited for us in Park Avenue. There were five in the party and five bodyguards supplied by a detective agency, and, dressed to kill, we went in a pair of the most ostentatious Rolls-Royces I ever hope to see. After a while we got to the fight. It lasted less than one round, and Louis knocked the German cold after an elapsed time that had to be measured in seconds. In the tumult and confusion that ensued, Evalyn and I were separated from our posse of detectives and roamed around the streets of Harlem for an hour and a half before finding a taxi. Since Evalyn was wearing the Hope as well as the Star of the East and several hundred thousand dollars' worth of other trinkets, I was understandably perturbed. But not Evalyn.

Not all Evalyn's best parties were at "Friendship." In 1937 she visited her native state of Colorado to attend the opening of the drama season at Central City, Colorado's celebrated and lively ghost town. She hadn't been in Colorado in many years, and old-timers who had known her and the Walshes and McLeans in Ouray, Leadville, and Creede turned up in shoals, many of them miners from Colorado's spacious days who had also struck it rich. On the spur of the moment one Sunday morning, Evalyn decided to have a hundred old friends in for dinner that night. How the management of the Brown Palace Hotel, in Denver, accomplished it, I will never know, but at eight o'clock that evening—in the middle of July, mind you—her guests sat down to dinner served by knee-breeched footmen with champagne in double magnums; ice elephants, requiring two servants to carry them, full of fresh caviar; solid-gold plate and service, and two name bands. Everyone was in full evening dress, and the display of diamonds would have shamed the Metropolitan on opening night. All the guests except Polly Grimes and me were elderly, rich, and reminiscent. I knew that Evalyn saw in them a parade of the long-dead years and Colorado's pioneer times, before ever her father was a partner in the Camp Bird mine with King Leopold of Belgium, and she herself was absolute monarch of Washington society.

It was inevitable, writing a column about the good life in which wine and food often figured, that I should do a great deal of dining out, and after a while a dinner jacket became as much a uniform for me as it is for a waiter. One of the pleasantest dinner groups I belonged to was composed of half a dozen friends of Albert Keller, the late managing director of New York's Ritz-Carlton Hotel, and a wit, oenophile, and gourmet of great distinction. An elegant and portly fellow, Keller was shaved in bed every morning by his personal barber, brushed his teeth in a light Moselle, and once every two or three months would pick up an extraordinarily fine basket of woodcock or Scotch grouse, or a couple of dozen bottles of really wonderful claret. When he did, he asked O. O. McIntyre, Karl K. Kitchen, Bob Davis, myself, and another tosspot or two in for the evening. Never more than six: that was as many as he would carve for. Kitchen and Davis were spectacular raconteurs, had seen all the world that was worth seeing, and known everyone worth knowing, and we were often still at table at six in the morning. The consumption was fantastic, and I once asked the waiter captain in charge of Keller's dining room what it had amounted to the night before: six of us had accounted for twenty-six bottles of claret, Burgundy, and champagne, and seven bottles of cognac, Armagnac, and other *eaux de vie*.

McIntyre's vice wasn't so much at table as it was in the field of haberdashery. He practically put the firm of A. Sulka, of Fifth Avenue, on the map, and I have seen him command ten dressing robes at a time, each costing more than $200. Odd and Maybelle McIntyre were fond of Italian food, and another establishment they made into an institution was Monetta's restaurant in Mulberry Street. The sight of Odd's blue Rolls-Royce parked in that shabby district would bring out crowds who knew the car by sight and loved Odd for his friendly column and friendship for the neighborhood. There would be cheers when he and Maybelle emerged from Monetta's after dinner, the only newspaperman I ever knew to be so loved and respected.

Selmer Fougner, of the *Sun*, was another of the town's leading gourmets, and organized for his own amusement a group of table *aficionados* known as *Les Amis d'Escoffier*. They met, usually, at the old Lafayette, in University Place, now but a fragrant New York memory, and the only rules of the club were that you had to tuck your napkin in your collar, and there must be no speeches. Selmer's speeches at these dinners were some of the longest in my recollection.

Throughout the years when I was writing a New York column, one place supplied me with more color and copy than any other, despite the fact that, to *Tribune* men, Bleeck's was home, club, and professional resort. Jack & Charlie's "21" Club has always been a stamping ground for names that make news. Back in my New Haven days, along with Peter Arno, Jock Whitney, Steve Etnier, and Benedict Quinn, I had been among the first regulars at its bar, when it was located at 42 West Forty-ninth Street. By the time I came to New York to work, it was the town's leading celebrity trap, and remains so to this day. It was here that Valentina, the *couturière*, made her famous remark which appeared next day in my column, deprecating the cheapness and universality of mink: "Meenk, meenk?" said Russian Valentina. "Meenk, it is for footballs games!" It was at "21" that I dined with Libby Holman the night she took off her stockings at the table and we went to a Metropolitan Opera opening, she to be photographed extensively as the first woman ever to appear there with bare legs and painted toenails. It was at the bar that John Krimsky and I planned and pooled our resources to open the American Music Hall, a saloon of our own in Fifty-fifth Street, where we presented such gag shows upstairs as *Naughty-Naught*, *The Drunkard*, and *The Fireman's Flame*. And it was at "21" that Bob Benchley introduced me to a stranger with a fierce beard whom he presented as *"le barbe qui parle,"* and who turned out to be Ernest Hemingway.

It was in the front upstairs room one night, as I was dining with Madeleine Carroll, that a clumsy bus boy dropped an enormous wine bucket full of ice and brine right over the tiaraed head of Mrs. Mae Manwaring Plant Heyward, mother of playboy Phil Plant and wife of Colonel William Heyward of World War I fame. The catastrophe was so awful, so incredible, that for an entire minute nobody in the restaurant spoke, and forkfuls of *foie gras* were arrested in mid-air. When animation returned to the scene, the bus boy fled and never even returned for his street clothes. Colonel Heyward removed the bucket from the head of his wife, who had providentially fainted, and then, stuffing a napkin in his mouth to stifle his potential roars of mirth, left the room. Philip, the imperturbable maître d'hôtel, surveyed the wreckage, tucked a menu under his arm, and walked out into the night. There just wasn't anything anyone could say, and the rest of the meal was passed by those present in a sort of trance. Mrs. Heyward was all right by the next day, but the morale of the staff at "21" has never completely recovered.

Probably next to Jack & Charlie's, Bleeck's, and the Oak Room of the Plaza Hotel presided over by the incomparable Jules, I have spent more time, in the past twenty years, in the Turkish baths of the Biltmore Hotel. Besides possessing therapeutic qualifications for anyone leading the life of a *viveur*, there used to be a pleasant sort of informal Saturday afternoon club which foregathered in its steam room and tepidarium, and passed the time of day around the pool. Al Smith, Jim Farley, and Gene Tunney were regulars, and a sort of nonresident membership was enjoyed by Ben Sonnenberg, the publicist, Steve Hannagan, also a high-pressure agent, Nick Kenney, of the *Daily Mirror*, Edward Stettinius, and myself. With the death of some of its foremost members, the steam-room club has, in a measure, dissolved.

Over the years, there have been a good many people shaking the dust of New York from their boots, for a variety of reasons, most of them with declarations of distaste varying in intensity with the occasions for their going: my old friend Evander Berry Wall because New York's club life was deteriorating and people no longer played bridge-whist; James Hazen Hyde, in recent years repatriated, but who once departed because the stockholders of the Equitable Life Assurance Society didn't see eye to eye with his dinner parties; and Stanley Walker because the place was getting coarser, cruder, noisier, and dirtier every day.

There is some truth in almost all criticism of the Manhattan façade in the year 1950. The place is fantastically overpopulated; New York's state taxes add one more confiscatory item to the Federal total; its traffic is an abomination; and the city is slowly strangling in its own murderous and sooty breath. Old landmarks are disappearing, even such a completely modern structure as the Ritz-Carlton Hotel being doomed for another superfluous, monolithic office building which will add nothing but congestion to an already-established paralysis. Formal society doesn't exist at all, and New York manners are a street accident.

None of these considerations affects my choice in going elsewhere. I am, personally, impervious to soot, bad manners, and street accidents, and to me New York is, as it always has been, wonderful. A little tarnished and showing soup spots on its dress-shirt front, but strictly fabulous. In twenty years it has given me everything I wanted and had the minimum determination required to reach for, and I wanted a great deal. It is the greatest free market for talent and ambition in the world today. It will give anyone anything and everything he hankers for, almost for the asking. The defamer of New York is no more than a defamer of his own personal abilities and capacity for meeting competition.

I am taking it on the lam for the same reason the wise guest goes before the party is over. The last part of every party is *not* the best, and the discerning person leaves before the band gets tired and he himself starts walking with legs akimbo.

I've seen the elephant, and a fascinating elephant it was, too. It gave me a ride in a platinum howdah and accepted the peanuts of my gratitude politely.

England

I am stayed not with apples, but with Colchester oysters and Southdown mutton; I am ennobled by the mere triumphant achievement of crossing Piccadilly or the Strand in the face of a traffic scheme never sanctioned by heaven; and I am humbled by people who, in a degenerate time elsewhere, still have about them both style and substance.

". . . FOR ME ENGLAND MEANS LONDON."

. . . There is spiritual solace in Rome; Paris is a sacrament of the arts; one's own natal heath revisited establishes the sense of continuity so deeply craved as a paliative to mortality.

My own deep need for regional communion is for England, and for me England means London. Except through the agency of literature, I have never been exposed to English country life. I have spent no appreciable time in the shires or among the county families, but as the hart panteth for the water springs of legend, so, at stated intervals, do I pant for Alsopp's pale draft lager ingested amidst the sights, sounds, and smells of the metropolis that to me, more than any place else, represents continuity, order, manners, the secure and ordained inheritance that sometimes suggests that *homo sapiens* is not a misnomer.

I am stayed not with apples, but with Colchester oysters and Southdown mutton, I am ennobled by the mere triumphant achievement of crossing Piccadilly or the Strand in the face of a traffic scheme never sanctioned by heaven, and I am humbled by people who, in a degenerate time elsewhere, still have about them both style and substance.

THE WISDOM OF POLONIUS

In May 1922, I first took passage to cross the Atlantic in the Cunard steamship *Aquitania,* then at the apex of its celebrity as a luxury vessel of the type spoken of in the public prints as "an ocean greyhound." As a youth traveling alone, I was assigned, as was the custom of the time at capacity sailings, to share a stateroom with another gentleman whose identity was revealed as that of Claude Graham-White.

At this remove the name may mean little except to students of aviation, but Graham-White was a flying pioneer of impressive dimensions, so valued by the English government as an expert and consultant that he was paid an annual sum, reported to be $25,000, never to set foot in an airplane. He was a handsome, sophisticated, and urbane *viveur* in whose debt I shall always stand for many kindly offices of worldliness.

Learning, conversationally, that I was an undergraduate at New Haven and that this was my first trip abroad, my roommate was quietly amused and remarked: "I think you will learn more that will be useful to you in life in six days aboard a Cunard steamship than in a semester at any university in the world."

Claude Graham-White couldn't have been more right. Others may sit at the feet of Yale or Oxford or the Sorbonne as their alma mater, but although I am a graduate elsewhere and have Latinate documents to attest it, I own to being a graduate first and foremost of transatlantic travel and the University of Cunard.

A good deal of gin has flowed under the bridgework since Claude Graham-White instructed me in some of the basic facts of life: gentlemen wear shawl-collar dinner jackets, peaked lapels are for musicians (this was 1922); only show-offs drink more than one bottle of champagne at breakfast; the most costly cognac on the wine list isn't always the best; don't ask for Maine lobster on an east-west passage or English channel sole going from west to east; tip the carver at Simpson's no more than threepence.

Don't get in fist fights with Frenchmen, which is degrading: strike them with your walking stick; try not to use the words "bottom" or "bum" in polite English society: they mean something else. When the King of Spain asks you to have a drink in the Ritz Bar, which he will probably do if you are a regular, it's more polite not to order a King's Death, which is what he himself will be drinking, but to call it a Royal Highball.

Nearly forty years afterward these instructions may, to some, seem vaguely frivolous. In 1922 they were the wisdom of Polonius.

SHOWCASE AFLOAT: 1959

There was a time, not so long gone as human reckoning goes, when a good dinner approached being a unit of currency or standard of value. "To hear this debate [in the houses of Parliament] is worth three dinners," wrote the Earl of Clarendon to a friend in the reign of Charles II and, even today, to owe a man a good dinner is often a more acceptable form of indebtedness than one involving cash in hand.

The Earl of Clarendon was putting a value on English dinners a full two centuries before Samuel Cunard, a Nova Scotian by birth, first began to carry passengers on the Atlantic run and, in his own turn, to establish Cunard cuisine as a standard of excellence ranking with that of Savile Row, Rolls-Royce, Huntley & Palmers, Claridge's, and other hallmarks of the British superlative.

And today, a full century after Cunard chief stewards were first occupied with gentling travelers aboard such legendary paddle steamers as *Europa, Brittanic,* and *Persia,* and although the company advertises a variety of categories of travel, "going Cunard" implies going first class and nothing else.

Perhaps the basic reasons for this acknowledged pre-eminence as an agency of transport are Cunard's radiant traditions of seamanship and navigation, but the show window of Cunard operations has, for some decades now, been the Cunard cuisine. For magnitude and volume in strictly deluxe brackets, there is probably no operation in the world today comparable to the victualing of the Cunard fleet. Caviar is served by the hundreds of pounds every week in the year. And a ship's inventory, such as that of the *Queen Elizabeth,* includes forty-two kinds of cheese and enough wine and allied beverages to require the full-time services of twelve *sommeliers* in the first-class restaurant alone.

This is a mere random selection of tangibles. The Cunard *esprit* and philosophy toward the customers are expressed in the company's order to its service staffs: "The word 'no' is not to be in your vocabulary." It is implicitly observed.

Good food, fine wine, and irreproachable service have been a determining factor in the good way of life in any generation. But today, when institutionalized management, packaged foodstuffs, cost accounting, and union demands have laid clammy hands on so many aspects of civilized conduct, they are, for Americans especially, at a premium.

Aside from the cathedrals, historic shrines, and natural wonders—not to mention the alleged cultural and broadening usufructs of travel—there is the perfection of service and dining no longer available at home, which a ponderable number of Americans of means and perception head for Europe to find annually. Luncheon at Simpson's almost equates a painting at the Tate Gallery; the vineyards of Bordeaux are a must on a par with the châteaux of the Loire.

To all these pleasures of the senses, Cunard cuisine, eastbound, provides a gratifying overture; westbound, a coda in terms of Prague ham, Romanée-Conti, and soufflé *amandine*. Not for nothing is the Cunard advertising in the best coated-paper periodicals couched in terms of *aiguillettes* of Rouen duckling *aux cerises*.

"We try to be guided as much as we may in our purchasing by the seasons, despite the obvious possibilities of freezing," says J. R. Smith, Chief Steward of the *Queen Elizabeth*. "It's possible, I know, to serve Delaware River shad in October and Scotch grouse in May, and we keep a minimum supply of almost everything frozen, against the possible out-of-season demands of the passengers. But, in general terms, we regard the deep freeze as an expedient of necessity, not of everyday convenience. Nothing, but nothing at all in this world, comes out of a deep freeze so good as it goes in, not even beef."

Because food in the mass, through some special quirk of human psychology, is possessed of a fascination lacking in even the most perfect single culinary masterpiece, it should be of interest to know that, in a single round trip across the Atlantic, the *Queen Elizabeth* serves something over 200 pounds of the finest gray Malossol caviar, making Cunard the largest single purchaser of this exalted commodity in the world; an equal weight of the best Strasbourg truffled *foie gras;* 450 pounds of smoked Scotch, Irish, and Canadian salmon; 1200 pounds of fresh asparagus; 200 pounds of fresh strawberries; and 1200 pounds of Hamburg and Malaga grapes. Additional statistics reveal that the *Elizabeth*'s steward stocks twenty-one different bins of French champagne; fifty-two vintage still wines from Bordeaux, Burgundy, and the Rhine; forty varieties of cigars, and sixteen different ales, lager beers, and other brewed potables.

There is always a reserve of frozen game in the form of venison, woodcock, quail, wild duck, English hare, and South American ptarmigan and, if a Cunarder is sailing from Southampton on the evening of the Glorious Twelfth of August—when the shooting season opens in Scotland—there are Scotch grouse aboard, rushed by air from the moors in sufficient quantity to supply exacting diners from there to New York and back.

To American travelers, inhibited and vexed at home by closing hours, the annoyance of unions, and the superstitions of diet fanatics, the very volume, variety, and availability of Cunard provender are reassurance of abundance and stability.

Rising from a breakfast of minced spring lamb and pickled walnuts, Yarmouth bloaters, or deviled beef bones and cottage-fried potatoes, he discovers lounge and smoking-room stewards providing against malnutrition with large ham sandwiches, Carr's table biscuits, giant ripe olives, and six kinds of cheese under glass. No sooner does he push himself from a luncheon table—where he has consumed chicken Kiev, a few slices of Prague ham, fresh asparagus, and wood strawberries with clotted cream —than he finds the apartments of public assembly devoted to the service of the universal British sacrament of afternoon tea with watercress sandwiches, thin slices of buttered white bread, and approximately a million alluring calories in the form of iced cakes. After three hours at dinner— where he has overcome fresh Malossol caviar, clear turtle soup, poached Scotch salmon, Long Island duckling flamed in cognac, a terrine of *foie gras,* chocolate soufflé, and Stilton cheese, washed down with a Niagara of Bollinger and Hennessy 1865—he finds supper being spread in the smoking room to sustain him while bidding in the ship's auction pool.

To the "tycoon" who for months has gone through the transparently fraudulent ritual of lunching at his desk on orange juice and Melba toast and to the housewife who has long bored herself and conversational acquaintances with the abominations of her diets, this sort of thing is heartening indeed.

Outside Edwardian memoirs and period novels, Cunard ships are perhaps the last repository in actual practice of the legendary English breakfast in the grand manner. Where else, on either side of the Atlantic, will the refugee from matutinal infamies of orange juice and shredded butcher's paper that masquerades as breakfast food encounter such a bewildering plenitude of broiled Irish salmon, Scotch kippers, London finnan haddie, broiled butterfish, lemon sole, fresh brook trout, smoked chipped beef in cream, Irish bacon, Southdown lamb kidney, liver and Irish bacon, roast-beef hash, grilled Danish ham, deviled beef bones, Cumberland sausages, galantine of chicken, seven kinds of omelettes, twenty hot breads, and, for exotics, French onion soup *gratinée* and cold Oxford brawn?

"We like to think that, within reason, we can serve a passenger any dish he can name from the conventional categories of American, English, and Continental cuisine," says affable Patrick Mullins, manager of the first-class restaurant on the *Queen Elizabeth* and feudal overlord of 140 waiters, six headwaiters, twelve wine stewards, two carvers, and door-men, bus boys, pages, and apprentices almost past counting.

"We even have forty-five Kosher dishes and twenty-five Japanese specialties, including bamboo shoots, lotus seeds, and water chestnuts. Our *chef de cuisine*, Edward Wrenn, has an inventory of more than two thousand substantial articles of diet. And I don't mean herbs, spices, and small-time incidentals either. There are very few things on the menu that come aboard ship prefabricated. Our ice creams—forty-two varieties —are an exception; they come on ready frozen. But all our bread and pastry is made at sea—the bread by a night shift, sweets by the day side. Even our fresh fish at both ends of the run comes aboard whole and is cleaned, filleted, and otherwise readied on board."

Mr. Mullins, an ample man in the evening tailcoat of his office, looks as though he enjoyed his own food, and he points with pride to the beau-tiful cold buffet that is arranged daily by the *garde-manger*. "Take these Maine lobsters," he says lovingly. "You couldn't get better at a shore din-ner in Skowhegan! Or our Channel sole; Scott's in London doesn't have finer! Take that cold side of Black Angus beef, from Scotland! Cuts like butter, it does. The best beef, bar none, in the whole wide world. It has to be, if Cunard buys it!"

We tried the Black Angus that had moved Mr. Mullins to lyric flights, and he was right. The same was true of the special Stilton cheeses set aside for Cunard, of the chef's gingered gooseberry fool, the Wiltshire bacon, and the Rouen duckling *aux cerises*—supernal testimonials, all, to the genius of Chef Wrenn and the veracity of Pat Mullins.

In the long folklore of the Atlantic sea lanes, a brief but deathless para-graph is devoted to the memory of Monsieur Gatti, the maître d'hôtel aboard the *Titanic* on its primal, fatal voyage. Attired in the silk top hat and morning coat of his calling, Monsieur Gatti was last seen by mortal eyes on the boat deck of the sinking vessel, bowing his regular patrons into the lifeboats and meeting, with complete aplomb, a rendezvous with immortality as calmly as he would brush aside a fallen soufflé.

It is to be hoped that such a gesture of ultimate heroism will never be required of Mr. Mullins. But, if the occasion should arise, regulars aboard the *Queen Elizabeth* have a feeling that he would match the urbanity of Monsieur Gatti and, chancing to encounter a former first-class passen-ger on the other side of Jordan, remark: "I trust, sir, that the shoulder of Pauillac lamb, last evening, was up to Cunard standards."

SIR JAMES CHARLES

Going Cunard as a friend of the company or an important personage with letters from Sir Ashley Sparks, the line's American manager, in the early twenties entailed almost as much inconvenience as it did prestige. The institution of cocktails served every night while at sea by the captain as is the practice today did not exist, and the ultimate in social recognition was to be asked to sit at the captain's table, which had about it overtones of royalty. Captain's tables differed in their conduct at the whim of the master of the vessel. Cunard didn't select its captains on a basis of gregariousness or Chesterfieldian courtliness, although most senior sea dogs were fairly well indoctrinated, by the time they reached this exalted rank, in the social and financial status of the line's clientele.

It was possible to sail with a strict disciplinarian like Sir Arthur Rostron, who had been in command of the *Carpathia* at the time of the *Titanic* rescue, whose table was a tall tower of maritime proprieties but small geniality, or a voyager of importance could be invited to sit with Sir James Charles, commodore of the Cunard Line and a legend of seagoing joviality and bonhomie.

Sir James's pennant flew from the masthead of the *Aquitania* and represented the ultimate cachet of nautical rank and dignity combined with voluptuary table practices which were a preview of Maxim's and the Café de Paris in an age when Americans were refugees from prohibition with an illimitable thirst for champagne washed down with Niagaras of gin, vodka, arrack, tequila, cognac, slivovitz, and bourbon, whatever was handy in the most substantial quantities.

Guests at Sir James's table lived by protocol. It was an age when the dinner jacket was not in universal acceptance among Englishmen as evening attire, and one's steward, on instructions from the bridge, laid out smoking or tails as the commodore might have decreed and left a note naming the dinner hour. You didn't dine at your convenience but the commodore's, and on evenings of the Captain's Dinner full evening dress was required with decorations, which put Americans, unless they were of military background, at a disadvantage in the matter of crosses, ribbons, and miniatures.

Sir James's tastes at table were vaguely those of Charles Laughton playing Henry VIII. Stewards wheeled in carcasses of whole roasted oxen one night and the next evening small herds of grilled antelope surrounded a hilltop of Strasbourg *foie gras* surmounted with peacock fans. Electrically illuminated *pièces montées* representing the Battle of Waterloo and other patriotic moments made an appearance while the ship's orchestra played Elgar. Chefs in two-foot-high hats emerged to make thrusts in tierce at turrets of Black Angus beef that towered above the arched eyebrows of the diners, and soufflés, the size of the chefs' hats, blossomed toward the end, like the final set pieces of a Paine's fireworks display on the Fourth of July. Throughout these flanking movements and skirmishes, champagne circulated in jeroboams, Mumm's '16, Irroy, and Perrier-Jouet, ditto.

Sir James Charles, a grandee of the sea lanes so portly and full of honors that his mess jackets required structural bracing in their internal economy to support the weight of his decorations, died in line of duty, at sea, almost literally leading an assault on a citadel of pastry moated with diamondback turtle stew *au Madeira*. When they took him ashore at Southampton, it was necessary to open both wings of the *Aquitania's* half ports to accommodate his going. It was the exit of a nobleman and a warrior.

SHIP'S POOL

Auctioning the ship's pools in the great days of the Atlantic runs aboard such fast vessels as *Mauretania* and *Berengaria* and *Aquitania* were memorable events both for the amounts of money involved and for the excitement which accompanied the bidding for twelve potential winning numbers each evening after dinner in the gentlemen's smoking room. The possible mileage for the next day's run, established every noon from the bridge, could be foretold with reasonable accuracy, give or take a few miles, by the ship's company, and ten numbers were sold in its immediate range, the collective amount for which constituted the day's pool. If the estimated run was, say, 635 miles, the numbers sold were 630 through 639, which, when included with the high field and low field, covered all possible contingencies. If the engine room had trouble and the vessel stopped or slowed down, low field won. If, on orders from New York or Liverpool, it accelerated its speed, high field was the one to have.

The twelve possibilities were sold at open auction by some celebrity from the passenger list, usually a theatrical personality or someone well known in sporting circles who would lend the occasion an aura of distinction. Claude Graham-White, the pioneer aviator and a celebrated *viveur,* was a favorite in the role. So was Dudley Field Malone, the theatrical lawyer and barrister whose trade in Paris divorces for notables kept him constantly in transit. Perhaps the most celebrated of all pool auctioneers in the early 1920s was William A. Brady, the Broadway producer, father of Alice Brady and married to Grace George, a brilliant comedienne. An inflammable Celt with a bottomless capacity for liquor, Brady was also a student of parliamentary law and a witty orator, in short the ideal man to auction a ship's pool in those affluent and uninhibited days.

On occasion, when carried away by his own eloquence, not to mention ample potations as he labored, Brady would order wine for the entire smoke room out of his own pocket in order to beguile his audience into ever higher bidding. Daily pools well in excess of 1000 pounds ($5000 in those times) were not uncommon when Brady sold them, and on one memorable occasion when his wife bid in what turned out to be the winning number, it seemed wise for her to spend the entire sum next evening on drinks for everybody—to refute loudly voiced charges of collusion. A lot of drinks could be had for $5000 in those days.

Unabashed in their admiration for a spectacular pool auctioneer were the smoking-room stewards. Ten per cent was their conventional cut for holding the stakes.

"IT IS AN ARTICLE OF FAITH . . ."

It is an article of faith with this writer that, just as maritime excellence is generally the supreme expression of the English genius for perfection, so the very essence of this supremacy is the Cunard Steam-Ship Company.

My heart belongs to Cunard because it is one of the last links between the deplorable here and now and the time before August 1914 to which most of the civilized world wishes it might return. Cunard passage is still, in microcosm, an embodiment of the manners and amenities which were taken for granted when Edward VII was the last of the magnificent monarchs—when currency meant coined gold, and the bartender stood the bottle in front of the customer. I am assured on every hand that we will not look on such an age again. But I can always vicariously re-enter it by taking Cunard passage to a foreign port where I will have neither business nor the intention of tarrying for long. When I travel Cunard, I want the added luxury of knowing that I'm going for the ride only, as the younger Bennett did.

I am assured, too, that time is running out for the *Mary*—that twenty-six years, some of them through war, is a long time for complex machinery and structure to be exposed to the multiple strains of passage. When her time comes, she will probably be replaced with ships of mean apartments and ensmalled resources of service and dignity. There will be fewer braces of grouse on the autumn stores requisitions, and the number of dining-salon stewards will no longer be standard at four to a table for two. The metal plaque directing the *Queen Mary's* passengers to communications says: "To the Wireless Telegraph Transmission Room." On her successor, it can only say "Radio," and I shall not be there.

THE OLD CUNARD CLUB HATBAND

Nothing it would seem has ever even approached the measure of devotion accorded by partisans of the Cunard Line. Perhaps the P & O of the great days and the Kipling years may have approximated it, but a truly indoctrinated Cunard passenger is never really at home aboard anything else.

It is an affectionate contagion that neither ships' companies nor passengers are immune to. Old-time smoking-room stewards with battle ribbons obscuring half their mess jackets look wistful when they mention serving in "the old *Saxonia*" or "the old *Mauretania*," just as the memory of long-vanished but endearing wonderments are evoked in graying passengers by mention of the *Aquitania* or *Samaria*.

Perhaps the most dramatic demonstration of the regard in which Cunard has been held by Americans over the years was that evoked by the sinking of the *Lusitania* which aroused the American public to a pitch of incandescent fury and led ultimately to the end of the German Empire. A much-loved ship whose speed and beauty were household legends, it was the barbarous destruction of the vessel itself, as much as the loss of life entailed, that branded the Kaiser's military hierarchy as Huns and monsters. American public opinion was far more incensed by the *Lusitania* than by the invasion of Belgium.

If there were such a thing as old ships' ties or hatbands, the Cunard Club colors would be worn by men who would consider wearing a Harvard Club band or that of the Racquet Club on their boaters a naïve ostentation.

They are a little band of brothers who may very well, when the time comes for the final crossing, dig in their heels and refuse to go until Charon hoists the reassuring house flag with the golden orb and lion. Folk who wouldn't dream of an Atlantic crossing by any other agency than going Cunard are unlikely to settle for less when they come to embark for the Styx.

HENRY POOLE, GENTLEMAN'S TAILOR

The firm of Henry Poole & Company at No. 37 Savile Row is not only a cathedral of waistcoats and hunting pinks: it is a repository of Victorian grandeurs establishing continuity with the past and the great names of English legend.

Brooks Brothers in New York likes to remark that when Lincoln was inaugurated for his second term he was wearing a Brooks overcoat lined with fine twill silk and embossed with a figure of the American eagle carrying the legend "One Country, One Destiny." Poole's can, with equal veracity, point out that when Napoleon III ascended to the throne of France, he was wearing (on credit) a uniform from Poole's, and that Benjamin Disraeli, when he presented Queen Victoria with the gift of the Suez Canal, was in Court dress by Poole. According to legend, when Henry M. Stanley uttered his classic salutation to Dr. Livingstone in the African jungle, he was wearing a belted poncho wrapper, the forerunner of today's raincoats, by Poole.

Nearer home, the late Evander Berry Wall once emerged from his suite at the United States Hotel at Saratoga Springs and paraded in forty changes of attire in a single afternoon, thus achieving for all time the title "King of the Dudes." Every outfit bore the Poole label, and newspapers from Bangor to San Diego carried the tidings of the London firm the next day.

When you have a dinner jacket cut by Poole, you are thus skirmishing with history. You are also getting the finest workmanship and expertise of a firm whose experience dates back to Napoleonic days. This bright ascendancy in a highly competitive field in the nineteenth century was, like so many other aspects of history, the result of the right man being at the right place at the right time. The right man was Henry Poole, son of James Poole, a linen draper in Everett Street, Brunswick Square, who had stumbled into being a tailor in the panic that engulfed England after Napoleon's escape from Elba. The country was mobilizing to resist invasion, and patriotic James Poole hastened into the ranks of his militia regiment in a tunic cut by himself and sewn in equal haste by his wife.

Its neatness caught an officer's eye and, after Waterloo, James set himself up as a military tailor.

Henry, who was born in 1814, inherited his father's business in 1846. He had a great love of sporting properties, horses, hunts, pink coats, and the earls and dukes who wore them, and he had a great flair for getting on with the right people. Not only did he learn as an apprentice to flat-braid a coat and face a lapel, but to associate himself on terms of decorous sporting equality with the owners of great ancestral stables. Formal London drawing rooms and the Court were something else again, but they were in the offing, too.

Fashionable tailors were taking over Savile Row, until then sacred to the medical profession which was now moving to Harley Street. Poole's Italianate premises, which the firm occupies to this day, became a recognized gathering place for young bloods and swells who smoked Henry's irreproachable cigars and drank his impeccable port while being measured for hunting pinks or the new Court dress, introduced by the firm, of mulberry velvet. In nineteenth-century English sporting circles, an alliance with a good tailor was as important as a marriage approved by *The Morning Post,* and Henry Poole was soon driving his own splendid horses in Rotten Row and following races on the Thames in his own stylish steam pinnace.

Poole made himself agreeable to men of influence and promise everywhere, including the rising Jewish bankers, Rothschild, Levy, Behrens, and Montefiore, who weren't yet in Society but certainly were about to be. Among Henry's long shots was an improbable political opportunist, Prince Louis Napoleon, who claimed the throne of France. Henry and Baron Meyer de Rothschild between them ponied up $50,000 to further his cause and hit the jackpot when he suddenly emerged as Napoleon III.

Henry Poole & Company were now Court tailors to one of the most brilliant if insecure thrones in Europe, and the celebrated stag hunts of the Imperial Court at Compiègne became largely a dress parade of Poole's wares. From the rifle-green jacket with gold lace, gold-laced tricorn hat, doeskins, and jackboots of the Chief Ranger, the Baron de Wimpferen, to the uniforms of footmen and grooms and the riding habits of the Court ladies, everything bore the hand-sewn label of Poole & Company.

According to the firm's official biographer, it was at a performance of *Ruy Blas* at the Princess's Theater, where the Prince of Wales admired the dress coat of one of the players, that Henry fell in with the stout little autocrat who was one day to be King Edward VII of England. His Royal Highness in those days was perennially and embarrassingly hard up. Mamma, the Queen, didn't see eye to eye with his way of life, his tastes, some of his friends, and cash was in short requisition at Marlborough House, the Prince's residence. Neither was his credit good with conservative London wine merchants, purveyors of plovers' eggs, or race-track operators.

In this pass what was more natural than that the Rothschilds and Henry Poole, who had won with Louis Napoleon in precisely similar circumstances, should bail out the Prince of Wales? His overdrafts were honored by the banks, and uniforms by the vanloads (and on credit) were delivered to the various palaces and country homes of the Prince and his equally aristocratic but insolvent friends of the Marlborough House set. Do you imagine for a minute that the carriages of the Rothschilds and Henry Poole's phaeton with its chestnut horses and scarlet footmen were not far behind the vans?

By the mid-1870s Henry Poole was a London institution basking in wealth, adulation, and the friendship of the authentic great he had always sought: the Prince of Wales, the novelist Anthony Trollope, the artist Millais, the equivocal Lord Cardigan who had led the charge at Balaklava, and, of course, the ever-helpful Rothschilds, Napoleon III, and the Empress Eugénie. "Old Pooley" became a living legend. "The most beautiful horses I remember were Lord Calthorpe's and those of Mr. Poole, the Savile Row tailor," wrote the Duke of Portland in his memoirs. The Duchess of Bedford, arch-arbiter of London society, invited him to her Belgrave Square house. Gilded youth glowed in his sartorial approval. His greatest claim to literary immortality came when Disraeli included him in his novel *Endymion* as Mr. Vigo: "The most fashionable tailor in London . . . consummate in his art . . . neither pretentious nor servile, but simple, and with becoming respect for others and for himself."

Henry died as he had lived, a little theatrically, in 1876, when his carriage was caught in an unseasonal April snowstorm and pneumonia followed. His obituaries in the British press might have aroused the envy of an earl.

The line of continuity, however, was direct and strong. Old Henry had taken on his first cousin, Samuel Cundey, as general manager, later followed by Howard Cundey, who lived until 1927. The business today is dominated by three directors, Samuel Cundey II, Hugh Cundey, and Joseph Mead, who has been with Poole since 1912 and frequently travels in the United States. Still a fifth generation is represented by Angus Cundey, a son of Samuel II, who is completing his apprenticeship in the cutting room.

Over the years, the writer has had a number of suits tailored by the master builders at No. 37, to whose atelier he was long ago directed by the belief of Berry Wall and his own Uncle Ned Center that there was simply no other gentleman's tailor in practice and that suits by craftsmen other than Poole's were little better than the garb of Happy Hooligan in the funnies. Berry had long been an American expatriate in Paris, and lived in a vast apartment in the Hôtel Meurice, where his wing collars with stocks made for him by Charvet, his chow dogs, and his full-time career as an unreconstructed Edwardian dandy were known to newspaper and magazine readers all over the world.

My Uncle Ned was a parallel case, having been one of the original members of the Brook Club in New York, a celebrated amateur boxer and coaching whip, and an integral part of the Manhattan glamor scene in the Diamond Jim Brady era. He spent his declining years growing exhibition roses at his Château de Monrepos on the Loire. Ned, whose gaming at Saratoga had been part of the table talk of the smart sporting cosmos in the first decade of this century, had entree everywhere. He claimed to have been present on the dreadful occasion when Lily Langtry slipped a piece of ice down the collar of Edward VII, an association with history which gave him as much prestige in 1910 as though he had been present at the signing of Magna Carta. A cynical group of detractors-of-everything claimed the episode never happened, basing their dissent on the almost complete absence of ice in England at the time. But no matter.

Poole's representation in my own wardrobe is limited to two business suits, two sports jackets, a suit of morning tails with striped trousers for ceremonial occasions, and what the management prefers to list as a "dining suit." The jackets of the business suits are cut from doomsday fabrics with notched lapels and four buttons, precisely on the lines, only somewhat expanded in dimension, of the first suit cut to my order by Wetzel in New York, the American version of Poole, nearly forty years ago.

Poole receives my modest patronage graciously, and about once a year I turn up among the dusty glories of No. 37 Savile Row if only to communicate with the ghosts of Lord Cardigan and Napoleon III trying on long-vanished Inverness capes, raglan and chesterfield coats, taglionis (caped street cloaks), sacs, reefers, boat cloaks, Prince Alberts, and velvet Court dress complete with stars, orders, and jeweled swords.

Like many other patrician English commercial establishments, the façade of Poole's is extremely modest, a study in understatement that contrasts in dramatic fashion with the implications of the name it shelters. A single story finished in mustard-yellow plaster, some of it in a state of uneasy adhesion, it is without windows. In a recessed alcove in this unimposing façade, a red-and-gold plaster crown, also in some disrepair, might be taken to symbolize the estate of the royalty upon which Poole's once depended for a large measure of its business. A crepuscular entrance, lined with dark wood panels and creaky floor boards, suggests an almost primeval antiquity. The salesrooms, cutting rooms, and business office, with open fires in wintertime, are roofed but not lit by glass transoms in which generations of dust were not even disturbed by the wartime bombings. Without in the least suggested contrived archaism, Poole's is well aware of the uses of a venerable setting.

An assortment of Court swords still glitters dimly in an armory in the main salon at No. 37. So does a representative selection of the blue-and-plum-colored Court tailcoats, frogged in gold, faced with watered silk, buttoned in crested gold—mute reminders of departed levees in London and dinners at Windsor Castle. Hundreds of bolts of prudent fabrics are stacked on vast mahogany tables dating from the days of the founding Henry. In winter, a coal fire burns in the grate, its light reflected in the brass jockey scales on which the shrinkage and expansion of the peerage are recorded over the decades, and on a huge bronze eagle brought from Paris by Henry as a tribute to an exalted customer.

Half a dozen cutters in jackets and waistcoats stand at cutting tables, and the whole is presided over by Hugh Cundey, first gentleman of Savile Row and repository of a legacy of overpowering, if respectable, magnificence.

On the walls are about fifty framed warrants, testifying to the patronage of emperors, kings, sultans, emirs, czars, rajahs, archdukes, princes, lord lieutenants, and defenders of various faiths and keepers of privy seals past all tally or reckoning.

"If you were to go through the pages of *Burke's Peerage* and the *Almanach de Gotha*," says Mr. Cundey, "from 1850 to the end of civilization in 1914, I think we could match you page by page with our old ledgers."

Prices at Poole's have, generally speaking and in keeping with their times, been steep by English standards. J. S. Rarey wrote in 1858, in *The Art of Training Horses:* "Poole supplies more men and masters of hounds than any tailor in London, but his customers must be prepared to pay for perfection." When he was finally confronted with Poole's bill, the Prince of Wales approached the first Mr. Cundey with the suggestion that perhaps the firm might arrange to charge less exalted customers double, while royalty be allowed to pay in warrants and lordly patronage. Make the solvent pay for their insolvent betters, suggested the Prince in a curiously Marxian moment.

Current prices at No. 37 range from approximately $150 for a business suit to $180 for evening tails, with morning suits and dinner jackets ranged in between. The management prefers three or four fittings spaced over as many weeks, but will cheerfully arrange a briefer schedule for hurried patrons.

Entries in Poole's vast ledgers kept in meticulous Spencerian script reveal the prices of other times in a harder currency than we will ever know again. In 1875, William C. Whitney, whose grandson is our Ambassador to the Court of St. James's, gave his address as 20 Nassau Street, New York, presented a letter of introduction from H. A. Cooper, Esq., and commanded a dahlia-colored velvet beaver frock coat with velvet cuffs and lapels, and edges braided with the same material, for forty dollars gold. J. P. Morgan was more conservative: he ordered a black twilled Angola frock coat, superfine silk lined, for thirty-five dollars gold. Mr. Morgan, apparently, needed no letter of introduction.

The Prince of Wales's purchases for the same year cover pages of meticulous entries, including one for a brown vicuña stalking cape with hood and leather belt and buttons and velvet collar for fifty dollars, and one for a crepe mourning band for dress uniforms, priced at four shillings. The unsmiling record makes no indication of how or when the bill was settled.

Emerging from a fitting at No. 37 today is to step from a world of Levantine frock coats and checked Angola trousers into the pin stripe present. Gone from the shadow of the venerable red-and-gold crown that is the glory of Poole's yellow façade are the top hats and tailcoats of London's yesterday, now replaced by the bowlers and briefcases of bourgeois commerce. Gone the parade of footmen and grooms, in mulberry and whipcord, emerging from Poole's on their master's errands, now supplanted by the liveried chaffeurs of republican Rolls-Royces and Bentleys.

Savile Row itself is a blend of the old and the new, the former represented by the immutable façade of Poole's, modernity by the Ministry of Health and a new metropolitan police station. Perhaps the police station is a precaution, taken after suitable deliberation, against repetition of an unfortunate occurrence in 1816, when two villains made off with a number of bolts of cloth from the shop of James Poole and were hanged for their trouble.

"We asked for added police protection," says Mr. Cundey, "at the time and, as you see, we got it."

"THE END OF CIVILIZATION . . ."

It may be worth noting that the two most widely accepted dates for the total end of anything approaching civilization in the twentieth century both have overtones of men's dress. One period to the continuity of society as it once existed is unhesitatingly assigned by Hugh Cundey, head of Henry Poole & Company and first gentleman of Savile Row, to August 1914, when English gentlemen exchanged their civilian attire for uniforms. The other, pinpointed by Walter Lord in *A Night to Remember,* was the sinking of the *Titanic,* an event in itself characterized by imposing sartorial overtones.

The *Titanic* sank under the highest imaginable social auspices, its sailing list having included such veritable grandees as Colonel and Mrs. John Jacob Astor and their personal servants, Sir Cosmo and Lady Duff Gordon, the Countess of Rothes, Harry Widener, Major Archie Butt, the President's military aide, the Isidor Strauses, Benjamin Guggenheim, Charles Hayes, president of the Grand Truck Railroad, and other notables by the score. Because it was Sunday evening when not all passengers dressed for dinner, a number of fastidious persons, who would have had it otherwise, faced eternity in business dress. Unwilling to make an exit on this note of informality, the aged Benjamin Guggenheim summoned his valet and retired to his stateroom, presently to reappear in full evening dress with tails and his best pearl studs. "Now we are dressed like gentlemen," he said, "and ready to go."

No nobler last sentiments are on record anywhere.

SPENDTHRIFT TOUR OF LONDON: 1960

The purpose of a spendthrift tour is not the disbursement of money for the mere sake of extravagance. Its aim is to devote four days in a given locale to the whims and caprices of the reporter without reference to cost. Only his taste in food and drink, shelter and entertainment is consulted. We selected London as the objective of our next deluxe inquiry into the best of everything. Our hotel was Brown's in Dover Street, a premises of such excellences that to recount them would occupy the space allowed for this entire article. Suffice it to say that Brown's is unhurried, superbly comfortable, and, above all, resoundingly British, an establishment known as a private hotel because it can select its patrons with a fine glass. Nobody simply walks into Brown's and registers. Its fewer than two hundred rooms and apartments are bespoken in some cases years in advance, and always by persons acceptable to the management.

Brown's was started early in the nineteenth century by a former butler in the service of Lord Byron's family and soon established the impeccable respectability and unostentatious luxury that recommend it to the most discerning.

The restaurant at Brown's, like the rest of the house, has character and a style all its own. The St. George Bar, which in primeval times was a separate establishment that was eventually absorbed into the economy of the hotel, is presided over by London's handsomest bartender, Dennis Hawkes, a good man to consult in matters of food and drink.

To live at Brown's is to live by a window giving onto Edwardian London. It is located in London's West End where, nearby, lie aristocratic Mayfair and Berkeley Square and, beginning right outside its Albemarle Street entrance, are the fine shops, services, and institutions that have made London metropolitan since the time of the Second Charles.

Our sitting-room window on Albemarle Street commands a fine view of Gieves, the gentleman's furnishers on Old Bond Street, and, by leaning a little over the sill, of Quaritch's and Sawyer's, two celebrated bookshops at the Grafton Street end of the vista. Around the corner, in Dover Street, is a stone façade with a bronze plaque reminding passers that here lived

Henry Peter, Lord Brougham, originator of the stately carriage that bore his name. Around the corner, too, are Truefitt and Hill, the exclusive gentleman's hairdressers; the world-famous tailoring establishments of Kilgour, French & Stanbury, Pope & Bradley, and Henry Poole & Company. It is a *faubourg* that reeks of distinction.

Our sitting room, bedroom, dressing room, and bath on the Albemarle Street side of Brown's came to nine pounds, eight shillings a day, or approximately $26.50, plus $2.10 daily for the regular house breakfast for two. This brought our fixed daily charges at our hotel to $28.60, considerably less than the $150 a day rental for the presidential suite at the Sheraton-Palace in San Francisco.

Where to lunch the first of our four days in London? Where, indeed, but that house long reputed for its seafood—Scott's in Coventry Street just off Piccadilly, a ten-minute walk from Dover Street. Scott's has been going, in one form or another, since 1851, when John Scott became a shellfish monger, starting with a faithful clientele who knew him as a popular headwaiter in that part of town. In a few years Scott's Oyster and Supper Rooms were a London institution, and much of the Victorian solidity of the house is still in evidence. Massive beveled French mirrors and mahogany-paneled walls, polished brass on the doors, and snowy linen everywhere set a motif of subdued opulence. There is a buffet upstairs for quick snacks, but the main café beckons a following of businessmen who would consider less than two hours and two wines for lunch an impertinence.

"Real Turtle Soup 7/6," proclaimed the menu, making turtle the most expensive soup in the house and we ordered it, liberally laced with fine sherry, while our companion commanded a Dublin-prawns cocktail. Scott's lists fresh Channel sole in seventeen different ways, including *crevette*, Walewska, Mornay, plain grilled, and Goujonette. We agreed on two whole soles *meunière*, new potatoes, and Lauris asparagus, which, it being early spring, was a luxury of the first order.

Londoners sensibly eat their way around the calendar and take little stock of frozen food so that asparagus is in great request from the first of April, strawberries six weeks later, and Scotch grouse starting smack dab at dinnertime on the evening of "the Glorious Twelfth of August," the day the season opens.

With the sole we ordered a bottle of Bâtard Montrachet '52, an extravagance which set us back thirty-five shillings but secured the attentive regard of the management, and for dessert, fresh sliced pineapple and Stilton cheese. There was also Scott's special bottled cognac and coffee, and we rejected with gestures the captain's suggestion that such splendors deserved a coda in the form of a savory. The charms of the English savory —usually grilled sardines on toast, Welsh rarebit, or shad roe—at the end of the meal are, generally speaking, lost upon American taste and we contrived to pass our entire time in London without once having mushrooms on toast or angels on horseback after the ice cream.

The luncheon tab at Scott's came to just six pounds which, with something for the waiter, amounted to an even $20. Satisfactory without being sumptuous, and altogether good.

Dinner in London is late—eight o'clock at the earliest, if one is not going to the theater, ten-thirty if a play is contemplated. Our first evening we decided against theater and selected the Savoy Grill for a leisurely dinner in surroundings haunted by some of the most delightful ghosts of Edwardian times.

London's spacious days of discerning gastronomy had their actual inception with the opening of the Savoy Hotel, the dreamboat of the Irish entrepreneur D'Oyly Carte, where it stands today in the Strand and for which he imported the ranking culinary genius of modern times, Auguste Escoffier, and his equally radiant impresario, César Ritz.

In an age of limitless wealth and imperial dimensions of urbanity, the success story of the Savoy was written in such names as the Duke of Orléans, Pretender to the Throne of France, Lily Langtry, Lady de Gray, Adelina Patti, Sarah Bernhardt, Sir Henry Irving, Mrs. Keppel, and the rest of the Marlborough House set gathered under the three ostrich plumes of the Prince of Wales, later Edward VII. It was on the menus of the Savoy that there first appeared such now established classics as Peach Melba, Fillet of Sole Coquelin, *Cerises Jubilée, Cuisses de Nymphes à l'Aurore,* and *Filet de Boeuf Lucullus.*

Cocktails in the Savoy's American Bar (a cynic once remarked that it was so named because it was the only place in London that actually had ice) made a pleasant prelude to a table on the Savoy Court side of the grill next to the windows, and on being seated we ordered a bottle of Mumm's, *sans année,* and a bowl of plovers' eggs.

Plovers' eggs, which reach the British market seasonally in April, have about them a cachet of Edwardian elegance and are specially prized. Plovers' eggs have their origins in Scotland where they are laid by the birds (which can't be too bright) in the ruts and wagon tracks of country roads, whence they are retrieved by hunters who pay landlords for the concession of combing private lanes and byways.

Larger than a pheasant's egg and smaller than a pullet's, plovers' eggs are pointed at one end, speckled dark green, and handsome to behold. Hard-boiled, they are served intact in their shells, which are removed by the customer, and eaten with salt and pepper at a tariff of about four shillings an egg. They are indescribably delicate and, personally, I can think of nothing to drink with them but the driest and coldest champagne.

Following the overture of plovers' eggs, we went for a *petite marmite*, *contrefilet* of Black Angus beef, served from the wagon, with creamed mushrooms, cold asparagus, and a Biscuit Glacé Savoy with a splendid claret, a Domaine de Chevalier '26, reverently decanted after all these years of wars and bombings in the Savoy's own vast cellars. These, with a forty-year-old Hennessy and coffee and remembrance for the waiter and captain, came to $42.50.

The morning of our second day in London was unable to show any expenses against our spendthrift account. It was largely occupied with Mr. G. R. Polley, the urbane and knowledgeable manager of Fortnum & Mason's wine department in Piccadilly. At the time we were in London the firm was inviting old customers to taste a fantastic collection of Madeiras which had recently come to hand, and bottles ranging from an 1815 Bual to 1880 Sercials and Malmseys were put out in the spacious cellars. We sampled the 1815, the wine complete and intact when Napoleon was alive, and felt the river of history merging pleasantly with our blood stream while Mr. Polley conversed learnedly on vintage cognacs.

For luncheon that day we selected À l'Écu de France in Jermyn Street, a restaurant recommended both by popular regard and our own previous experience as a result of well-heeled accounts. A chef in the tall hat of his office circulated among the waiter captains and lesser flunkies at the entrance as though daring the customers not to order from the display of his offerings of the day handily on a buffet, including cold Bresse chicken, Scotch salmon, mushrooms the size of billiard balls, giant strawberries, and, of course, it being the season, asparagus. It was a dare we couldn't resist and we ordered *foie gras au Porto*, fresh poached Scotch salmon, new potatoes, fresh Lauris asparagus with drawn butter, the showpiece strawberries, and a Brie cheese. The strawberries were continentally served in orange juice and powdered with confectioner's sugar; the cheese came from a huge wheel with an almost ecstatic consistency. We drank a carafe of the house *vin rosé* and with coffee two glasses of a vintage port selected by the management, a Fonseca '27.

With an appropriate *pourboire* for the staff, the damage came to $25.50, which we felt was modest compared to the euphoria induced by so admirable a collation.

Because we were going to the theater that evening and London curtain is at a time which precludes any thought of dinner first, tea was a more critical matter. It was served in one of the numerous lounges of the Berkeley Hotel around the corner from Brown's, and provided, in addition to the conventional watercress and thin buttered white bread, sandwiches of Prague ham and slices of Wensleydale cheese.

Theatergoing in England is something to be reported with a good deal more pleasure than its equivalent excursions in New York, but space forbids its mature consideration here. Suffice it to say that two orchestra stalls at the Old Vic, where a roaring production of *Macbeth* was current, with Michael Hordern in the title role, together with cab fare to farthermost Waterloo Road and pink gins between the acts, not to mention programs at a shilling each, came to $11.50, and we were off to supper at Le Coq d'Or in Stratton Street, Piccadilly.

Immediately we got the news that Malossol caviar cost thirty-four shillings, with blinis, thirty-nine, and we ordered the pancake job. This is deluxe going in a big way in England and we continued in the gilded groove with a single order of Dover sole with white grapes, between the two of us, and followed with that standard of English luxury fare, Aylesbury duckling *à l'orange*, an endive salad, and pineapple in the manner of the house, which turned out to be a heavenly arrangement of liqueurs and sliced fresh figs.

Vodka with the blinis, Château Margaux '34 with the Aylesbury, and Mumm's '49 with the dessert. As a come-on for the American trade, apparently, the Coq d'Or makes a specialty of American coffee, and we ordered it with the last of the wine and forwent the brandy. The tab came to a tidy $49.50, with tips to $57.

No survey of good London restaurants could be compiled without Simpson's-in-the-Strand, a landmark ranked with Bow bells. For Simpson's is the archetype of chophouse, the abode of the roast beef of Olde England. Simpson's has been a going concern for so many decades that it is part of the folklore of the realm. It has figured in jokes in *Punch* and debates in Parliament, and a single venerable carver of its monumental joints and roasts, Charlie Brown, was a London landmark and personality for almost sixty years.

Because it is a favored lunching place of many London men of affairs as well as a must for visitors, noontime reservations are obligatory. Its menu is simple and changes little from season to season, but its steak, kidney, and oyster puddings, sirloin of beef with Yorkshire pudding, saddle of Southdown mutton, Dover sole, and Stilton cheese are a hereditary birthright of Englishmen, like the Magna Carta.

Our lunch at Simpson's was the simple three courses conventional with regulars: smoked Scotch salmon, boiled silversides of salt beef with dumplings, and mutton; we came together again over Stilton and port. Beer is the accustomed drink at Simpson's, served in pewter, although claret, *rosé*, hock, and Chablis are all available at carafe prices. We drank chilled lager and with cheese and coffee Sandeman's 1934 port, bottled in 1936. The check was less than $8.

To say that Simpson's is a good house is an inexcusable cliché and yet, more almost than any other place in London, it is one to which hungry and thirsty men return habitually, not only for incomparable beef, beer, mutton, and cheese but for the spiritual refreshment that comes with communion with the past and the long continuity of established things.

The afternoon of our third day was spent fitting suits at Poole's, an exhausting ritual albeit a satisfying one, and teatime found us in the stately purlieus of Claridge's in West Brook Street, perhaps the top-notch residential hotel of London and since time immemorial a rendezvous of royalty and visitors of state and circumstance.

The restaurant at Claridge's, alas, is not noted as a Mecca for epicures, but tea in its pilastered foyer, served by house footmen in knee breeches and frogged crimson tailcoats of a more stately age, is something not to be missed.

For dinner that evening we had invited guests to join us at the Connaught Hotel, a magnificent repository of Edwardian splendors just off Grosvenor Square, where the atmosphere suggests an earlier day of leisure and repose and the food is of better than good report. Having ordered in advance, we sat down with our company to chilled Mediterranean prawns and plovers' eggs as our hors d'oeuvres; clear consommé, poached turbot with *mousseline* sauce, chateaubriand *béarnaise*, artichoke hearts, soufflé potatoes, and a *bombe* soufflé which at home is known as a baked Alaska.

The wines, in their proper succession, were champagne cocktails with the hors d'oeuvres, a magnum of Musigny, shipped by the Comte Georges de Vogue, of the vintage of 1948, a magnum of Perrier-Jouet '49, and Hines's Triomphe with the coffee and cigars. Because the conditions of the spendthrift tour restrict expenses to two, and our company made four, we halved the addition which, with tips in all directions, came to a grand total of $59 for two.

The morning of our last day we hankered for fish. The three ranking seafood restaurants of metropolitan London are generally agreed to be Scott's, Bentley's, and Overton's. Having patronized Scott's already, we tossed a coin between the other two and drew Overton's in St. James's Place.

Our guide, Dennis the barman at Brown's, had warned us not to miss the bisque of lobster at Overton's, and we report with assurance that no one will contradict us when we declare that lobster bisque to be not alone the soup of the world—but the transcendental wonderment of galactic gastronomy—a sacrament of communion with the ocean deeps, laced with thick cream and butter, plentifully seasoned at table with coarse black pepper, a votive offering to confound the calorie counters and be marked with a star in anybody's diary of great sensations.

Almost anything would be anticlimax after the bisque, but somehow we managed a very palatable *scampi maison* with French peas and finished with pineapple fritters and coffee. A carafe of excellent Niersteiner provided against thirst. For these supernal culinary doings the tab was sixty shillings or $8.40, which, with $1.50 for the waiter, brought it just under $10. Incredibly, the bisque of lobster, a dish that could lend immortality to a Vatel, is just five shillings.

The delusion that business is more important than eating or drinking has never laid hold on English men of affairs. The hours from twelve-thirty until after three, in the day of any important London executive, are earmarked for fillet of Dover sole, lobster Thermidor, *tournedos périgourdine*, double mutton chops from Southdown sheep, Toulouse sausages with Lyonnaise potatoes, *crêpe à l'orange*, and Brie cheese, the whole pleasantly saturated in Pommard, Richebourg, Pontet-Canet, Mumm's Extra, and vintage port, followed by Londres cigars.

This will hold a man together for the ride back to the shop, where tea will be served at four with bread-and-butter sandwiches, Huntley & Palmer's sweet biscuit, strawberries and cream, and, perhaps, even tea. You can't expect a man to last until eight o'clock dinner on nothing more than supreme of chicken Kiev and *entrecôte minute au cresson*. Not in London anyway, and from the Tower to Temple Bar a hundred luxury restaurants, at which reservations are necessary every day, testify in the form of capacity business deriving from the bowler-hat-and-briefcase set that Englishmen have the good sense never to let business interfere with their digestion.

As in New York's "21" and St. Regis, the customers are all men, all on expense accounts, and all doing themselves handsomely from the hard-boiled pheasant eggs among the hors d'oeuvres to the *bombe praliné* at dessert, and it is your reporter's impression that more vintage Bordeaux and champagne is drunk by businessmen at lunch in London than in all New York in twenty-four hours.

Informed Londoners will tell you that all this display of prosperity, like the multitude of gorgeous Rolls-Royces and Bentleys manned by liveried chauffeurs and footmen in the West End, is paid for by vast industrial corporations whose executives avoid taxes and live well on their expense accounts. The private means of the average British business-man wouldn't foot the bill. Be that as it may, it makes the luncheon hour an impressive parade of uninhibited calories all over London these days.

Who's for Aylesbury duckling à l'orange, chateaubriand for two (thirty-five shillings), *soufflé au Grand Marnier,* and a couple of bottles of the bubbly? Your reporter is, for one.

We saved our last night on the spendthrift tour of London for the big blowoff, a skirmish with the fancy victuals and well-nigh-incredible wine card of Mirabelle in Curzon Street, a premises that combines in synthesis the celebrity of Maxim's, the *éclat* of Chasen's or "21," and the gustatory resources of Soulé's Pavillon, a veritable Taj Mahal of truffles and *caviar au blinis*.

To condition ourselves for a heroic assault on the barricades of Mirabelle we instituted a special training table at teatime—only tea with lemon and a single watercress sandwich. Thus unfortified, we walked through the pleasant English evening of Berkeley Square to a rendezvous with the best that London provides.

Like many great restaurants, Mirabelle is a few steps below street level, with a low ceiling and trellises of flowers separating its various passages and alcoves. After a single champagne cocktail each, we ordered from one of the most opulent menus in the world. Mirabelle offers a choice of twenty-five varieties of fish, served in any manner within the gift of human imagining, thirty-five nightly entrees and *grillades*, and eggs and roasts in proportion, while, over and above this array of wonderments, there is a closely set column devoted to *Les Plats des Gourmets* and another, only slightly less breath-taking, of *Les Specialités de la Maison*. On every hand happy customers were awash with *Le Homard Deauvillaise, Poularde Sautée au Champagne*, and *Les Aiguillettes de Caneton aux Truffes*. Every waiter who passed with a tray made decision more difficult.

Finally we settled for *Croustade de Langouste* for my companion, *Moules Marinière à la Poulette* for me, and for each of us *Filet de Boeuf Lucullus* with *Pommes Amandine*, both of which we knew were specialties and superb, as indeed they were.

The wine card at Mirabelle is of variorum dimensions and, if you want to know how grand, it devotes one entire page to magnums only of Bordeaux and a similar category to wines of the Domaine de la Romanée Conti. German wines being outside our sphere of information, we allowed the captain to suggest a Forster Langenacker Riesling Auslese, followed, at our own selection, by a 1952 Richebourg, and left dessert and its accompanying vintage open for later consideration.

There is no need to belabor the lexicon of superlatives to describe the food at Mirabelle. Everything was as it should be in a restaurant of *grande luxe* and it would be invidious to report that the *filet* surpassed the *croustade* simply because this would be impossible.

Surprisingly, the time appropriate to dessert found us still in the fullest vigor of appetite and we settled for a *Soufflé Grand Marnier* and a bottle of that incredible if recurrent champagne, Dom Pérignon '47, followed by coffee and Sandeman's '34 port.

The bill was worthy of the occasion: 265 shillings or $37.10 for wine; the food, ninety-five shillings or $13.30, with three pounds to appropriate recipients, a total of $58.80, or about half the tab for the same dinner in a comparable New York restaurant.

Thus came to a close our term of four spendthrift days in London's West End with a total expenditure on the books for hotel, transport, wine, food, and good cheer of $415. Add $25 for imponderables, such as unaccounted-for transport, cigars, and oddments, and you have a grand total of $440. It is not the function of this report to provide comparative analysis of this sum beside the amounts disbursed on similar expeditions in New York and San Francisco, except in the most general terms, which indicate that, through the agency of advantageous exchange and other favorable factors, luxury life in London is approximately half as dear as its parallel in the United States.

A salutatory here's how in soda bicarb!

THE SAVOY OF LONDON

The location of the United States Embassy in England is well established in the aristocratic precincts of Grosvenor Square, in London's residential West End. Equally well established, even if unsanctified by diplomatic usage as an outpost of the United States, is the Savoy Hotel, a hostelry of such prestige, dimensions, and august repute that it is generally regarded as a repository of continuity reaching back to an era peopled with names that have become legend. The Savoy, in fact, is ranked with the great hotels of all time—the old Waldorf-Astoria in New York, the Adlon in Berlin, the Hôtel de Paris in Monte Carlo, the Paris Ritz, and the old Palace in San Francisco.

The Savoy is perfumed with an aura lingering from the rich and regal England of Edward VII. It glitters in the approval of contemporary royalty and enjoys what is perhaps the most extensive bibliography of any hotel in history. Books devoted to it are a commonplace and, by reason of its association with the greatest chef of all, Auguste Escoffier, it occupies conspicuous space in every book on gastronomy written since the beginning of the twentieth century.

Archaeologists a thousand years hence may dispute the place occupied in a vanished civilization by the structure whose ruins ramble beside the serene Thames, but they will be right if they surmise it to have been a temple of sorts. For the Savoy was and is a place where perfection is worshiped. The philosophy of its management might be summed up by an aphorism of the late Michael Arlen, in his time a patron of the Savoy. "I want very little in this world," he said. "All I want is the best of everything, and there is so little of that."

If you consider that over the years the administrative management of the Savoy has been vested in César Ritz, its cuisine directed by Escoffier, its dance orchestra led by Johann Strauss, and that Anna Pavlova danced in its floor show, you may get some idea of the exalted plane on which the affairs of this hotel are conducted.

The Savoy Hotel was the creation of Richard D'Oyly Carte, the original producer of Gilbert and Sullivan operettas which were the mainstay

of his Savoy Theater to such an extent that they became known as the
Savoyard operas. An entrepreneur in the grand manner, D'Oyly Carte
not only discovered the immortal authors of *H. M. S. Pinafore* and *Patience*, he was the first property owner in the world to light a public
building with electricity. On the opening night of *Patience,* to reassure
the audience, he appeared on stage with a lighted electric bulb which
he smashed to show there was no danger of fire.

In 1884, D'Oyly Carte was seized with the idea of a hotel for London
that should outdo in convenience and elegance anything the world had
ever seen. He had recently been in New York and had noted the kind of
living encouraged by the luxury hotels and restaurants—a scale of upper-
class patronage quite unknown in England.

Entertainment for the rich and aristocratic in London was limited to
private homes and governed by conventions of the most inhibited Victorianism. Hotels were a matter of necessity for foreigners or county families without town houses, while visiting royalties were put up at the
several palaces available to the British crown. Public dining was largely
a masculine affair and a gloomy one at that, with strict closing hours
which sent men to their clubs or homes in search of food and drink at
midnight. Compton Mackenzie recalled that his grandfather died of a
heart attack brought on by sheer rage when the waiters, promptly at
twelve o'clock, started to close a restaurant over the heads of guests he
had invited to a supper in honor of Henry Irving.

D'Oyly Carte set about changing all this.

The Savoy Hotel, which arose at his command on the ground between
the Savoy Theater and Thames Embankment, in many ways paralleled
the innovations of the Palace Hotel which, only a few years earlier, had
risen in San Francisco at the behest of the magnificent William Ralston.
Both dominated the surrounding community by their physical stature.
Both were so far advanced that they had to effect a change in public
habits to justify their existence. Each excited the public imagination with
unprecedented conveniences, elevators, bathrooms, and spacious private apartments for permanent occupancy, and the life of both the Palace
and the Savoy centered about a great central courtyard where arriving
guests were set down in the very heart of the hotel.

The Savoy presented to London and the world an entirely new concept
of public entertainment and architecture. It was the first hotel to be
fireproofed, with all floors and partitions of "cement concrete." Continuous day and night service was available for the first time, as it is today.
A private powerhouse supplied electricity, and private wells the hotel
water. Speaking tubes connected all floors, and every suite of two or
more rooms had its own bathroom. While this sort of thing is taken

for granted today, it popped eyes at a time when a contemporary hotel, the Victoria, had four bathrooms for five hundred registered guests.

The joint general managers of the Savoy, Mr. Griffin and Mr. Contarini, maintain that the hotel is a national institution operating on the scale of the finest private residences. Today, as in the past, it is operated in a manner which they venture to say few private houses in the world can equal. Where nowadays would you find, for instance, a home with three staff members for every guest? The Savoy's operational ratio is fifteen hundred staff members to the booking capacity of five hundred clients.

The Main Restaurant of the early Savoy was reached by a double staircase, and guests were ushered in and turned over to the maître d'hôtel by a seneschal wearing a silver chain and carrying a white wand of office. Private dining rooms bore, as they still do, the names of Savoyard operas: *Iolanthe, Gondoliers, Pinafore* and *Mikado,* each with its characteristic décor. Waiters remained in the corridors outside, again as they do today, and were summoned by a bell, saving the diners from the uneasy feeling of having servants lounging behind them.

Bright jewel and showcase of the Savoy from the very beginning was its Main Restaurant. D'Oyly Carte intended that it should attract not only the limited patronage of hotel residents, but the potential of the fashionable world which now dined behind the stately portals of the great town houses of London. To this end the management stressed not only English cooking, which had until then been the established backbone of London dining, but the best table fare of Russia, India, Germany, France, and even the United States, so that canvasback duck, terrapin, sweet corn, and Little Neck clams amazingly appeared on the menu. Not only was dinner a function at which full dress was required of all patrons, but the institution of after-theater supper came into its fullest flower, served every weekday save Saturday (when closing hour prevented) from eleven to twelve-thirty. Supper at the Savoy became legendary. It remains to this day a formidable tradition of London night life.

To preside over the kitchens of what was fast becoming a celebrated Mecca of food, D'Oyly Carte summoned a perfectionist whose name was to be enshrined with the Savoy's own in the bright lexicon of gastronomy. D'Oyly Carte was taking the cure at Baden-Baden when he encountered César Ritz and convinced this ambitious Swiss that his star hovered over the Savoy Hotel. Ritz was installed as general manager four months after the Savoy opened its doors in 1889, and with him he brought another expert of transcendent magnitude: Auguste Escoffier.

In the early years of the twentieth century, the Savoy began taking on the character that has distinguished it ever since as a living repository of things Edwardian, a vital institution with its first flowering in the most spacious era England was ever to know. Primarily the hotel represented the imperial wealth which caused Queen Victoria near the end of her reign to remark to the Duchess of Sutherland: "I have come from my house to your palace."

It was an era that saw more than five hundred persons under the roof of "Chatsworth," residence of the Duke of Devonshire, for weekends. Lady Warwick's guests for a shooting party arrived by private trains. Alfred de Rothschild maintained a private symphony orchestra in his home.

The seasonal cycle of the King himself was represented in arrivals and departures from the Savoy. Spring, Edward spent at Biarritz, Paris, and a brief time in England; winter was occupied by a Mediterranean cruise and then home for the Derby at Epsom, the Ascot, and London's fashionable season; then to Cowes for the regatta, a cure at Marienbad, Balmoral for the fall shooting, and November and December at Windsor. Within the range of their means and inclinations, the Savoy became the mirror of these progressions of Edward's subjects.

It was to this willing audience of uninhibited admirers of worldly ways, of royalty, nobility, and of great Jewish bankers whose affairs were on the rise, of courtesans of fashion, diamond millionaires from Kimberley, champagne salesmen, turf notables, and Americans with limitless resources from mines, railroads, and cattle that Escoffier found himself billed as the star performer in the Savoy kitchens.

He was no man to shirk such a responsibility.

The two dishes inseparable from the name of Escoffier in his creative years at the Savoy were *Cuisses de Nymphes à l'Aurore* and *Pêche Melba*, dreamed up for the Prince of Wales and for Mme. Nellie Melba, respectively. The *Nymphes à l'Aurore* created something of a problem of presentation and identification since they were, of course, frogs' legs served cold in a jelly of cream and Moselle tinctured with paprika. The management was afraid, in view of the circumstances at the moment—the Prince was having a flaming affair with Lily Langtry—that gossips might read sardonic intent into the suggestive dish; but it passed off without challenge and everyone in both front office and below stairs breathed easier. If the Prince had detected a suggestion of impropriety in the creation, the Savoy might have been obliged to close its doors then and there.

The peaches for Melba entailed neither such a threat nor such invocation of Escoffier's genius, being nothing more complicated than fresh peaches poached in vanilla syrup served in a timbale on a layer of vanilla ice cream coated with raspberry purée. The initial presentation took place one evening after the diva had sung Elsa in *Lohengrin,* and it was Escoffier's happy conceit to bring the new creation to the table in a magnificent swan carved from a huge block of ice borne by four tottering footmen in knee breeches, to the applause of the entire restaurant.

Melba was in ecstasies but Escoffier merely smiled at her delight. To his thinking, mere peaches and ice cream were nothing to get excited about. Unhappily, peach Melba is perhaps the most widely imitated and dreadfully libeled of all Escoffier's creations.

Another special guest whom Escoffier treated with the deference due royalty was the Duke of Orleans, the ranking Bourbon exile dreaming of lost splendors and living on the best of everything, thanks to a substantial private fortune. César Ritz had manufactured for him a special service of deep-blue Vallauris china with the fleur-de-lys crest of France, and the ducal menu was personally engrossed every day by Escoffier on special paper watermarked with the appropriate crest.

Few students of gastronomy or mere amateurs who today order *les Suprêmes de Volailles Jeannette,* those delectable breasts of cold chicken in jelly, enfolded in *foie gras,* know the origin of the dish.

In 1881 the Arctic exploration vessel *Jeannette,* preparing for a voyage of discovery to the North Pole, became icebound and its entire crew, save only a handful of surviving sailors, perished off the Siberian coast. Fifteen years later Escoffier unveiled a monument to their memory when he first introduced *Suprêmes Jeannette* at a Sunday evening dinner for three hundred in the Main Restaurant of the Savoy, the individual portions being served amid barriers of crushed ice reminiscent of the floes which had spelled the doom of the ship's company. Nobody seemed to feel there was any incongruity in the celebration of a major maritime catastrophe with the creation of a new adventure in gastronomy.

Among the great names of the Edwardian *belle époque* who were attracted to the Savoy in its early years and who assured its success for many decades thereafter were the most brilliant reigning stars in the theatrical firmament: Bernhardt, Ellen Terry, Henry Irving, and Beerbohm Tree; singers such as the de Reszke brothers, Adelina Patti, Mme. Nellie Melba, Emma Eames, and others who couldn't wait to get off their makeup backstage at Covent Garden to hasten to supper parties at the Savoy where Scotch grouse and salmon, magnums of Moët & Chandon and applauding friends awaited them.

Henry Irving lived permanently at the Savoy. James McNeill Whistler, who carried on a feud with Sir Henry, lived down the corridor from him, and they studiously ignored each other in the lift. Whistler made an etching of the hotel in the process of construction, claiming it would never look more beautiful. Sarah Bernhardt nearly died in her suite from an overdose of sleeping medicine. Chaliapin took his supper every night after performances not in the sanctified precincts of the Grill but in the chef's office in the kitchen. Tschessinskaya, *prima ballerina assoluta*

of the Russian Imperial Ballet, practiced *entrechats* in her suite, and
Tetrazzini, Gigli, and Caruso bowed to admirers as they entered their
carriages for Covent Garden under the statue of Count Peter of Savoy,
which dominates the courtyard.

Charles Frohman once was stalled in a lift between floors for more
than an hour. By the time workmen released him, the management was
apprehensive of his temper. But he emerged grandly, swept the assembled members of the staff a bow with his top hat, and remarked that
it was the first time in months that he had been able to enjoy a vacation
uninterrupted by would-be soubrettes.

A legendary figure in the Savoy chronicle is the late Sir George Reeves-
Smith, managing director of the company from 1901 until 1938, when,
at the age of seventy-eight, he was knighted as the foremost English
hotelier. When D'Oyly Carte first encountered Reeves-Smith, he was
under contract to manage the Berkeley, so D'Oyly Carte grandly bought
the hotel and Reeves-Smith's services along with it. He already had added
Claridge's, and today all three hotels remain as the Savoy Company,
which also owns Simpson's chophouse in the Strand, for good measure.

The Savoy today, in a world of vast uncertainty, still bears a reassuring
similarity to what this great hotel was in the glory days of an empire the
world envied.

"We are the only hotel in London," explains G. B. Potts, assistant to the
managing director, "where every whim of the most exacting guest can be
gratified at four in the morning as satisfactorily as at four in the afternoon.
It isn't often, of course, that we do that sort of thing, but the late Dorothy
Paget regularly was served a full-course dinner at three o'clock every
morning in her apartment, and we stand ready to do it for any guest
with the same desire."

"We were a New York hotel in terms of shower baths, elevators, and
extension telephones before these things existed on any appreciable scale
in New York itself," says morning-coated Mr. Griffin, "so that when the
new Waldorf was building in Park Avenue, Lucius Boomer came to us
for tips and incorporated many of our conveniences in the present hotel
of that name. I can't say offhand what proportion of our guests are
Americans, but it is very large—probably over half—and we feel we are
definitely an outpost of the United States. Just for the record: the first
golden sovereign taken in by the hotel in 1889—there were no cash registers then—was paid by an American, Harry Rosenfeld. Symbolically, it was
for a bottle of champagne, and we still have the coin in the safe."

As in the very beginning, the Savoy's restaurants are the inner core
of its being. Two entirely separate kitchens serve, as they always have,
the Main Restaurant giving on the Thames Embankment, and the Grill,
whose service was first inaugurated for guests who didn't wish to dress.

Two autonomous *chefs de cuisine,* Mr. A. Laplanche and Mr. Silvino S. Trompetto, preside over the Main Restaurant and its contiguous private dining rooms and the Grill, respectively, and separate menus are available in each.

The Savoy is first and last a luxury establishment. It serves approximately half a ton of fresh Beluga caviar annually, for which it pays £10,000 at wholesale, and fourteen tons of smoked Scotch salmon worth £31,000 at the fishmongers. Unlike the practice in American hotels where competitive bids for all comestibles are submitted daily to the purchasing department, the Savoy awards its patronage on a basis of quality alone and has dealt in Dover sole and Southdown mutton with the same purveyors for decades.

The company imports thirty-nine tons of butter from Normandy every year because it considers French butter superior to any other. The Savoy serves fifteen dozen plovers' eggs a day, during the two weeks' season in April, when they are available. Two tons of Strasbourg *foie gras* pass over its tables every year, and thirty-five hundred dozen quarts of champagne, not to mention half a million Colchester and Whitstable oysters in the *r* months. The legendary high point of the English gastronomic year comes on August 12, "the Glorious Twelfth," when grouse shooting starts on the Scottish moors, and on that afternoon a few hampers of the birds are flown in for choice customers at an average cost to the management of thirty-six shillings a bird. After that, they come by train and are consumed at the rate of about two dozen a day.

"The standard-bearer of the British luxury world is, of course, Scotch salmon, both the fresh and the smoked," says Mr. Potts reverently. "The best of the catch is London smoked, emanating from Billingsgate fish market where the profanity of the fishmongers has been proverbial for four centuries, but the fish itself, like malt whiskey, is the product of waters that bubble from granite through peat. The superbest of the lot is salmon from Craigellachie on the Spey."

On the Savoy menu, smoked salmon as an hors d'oeuvre is priced at ten shillings sixpence, and broiled fresh, *au beurre Parisien,* at double this amount. That's not cheap.

"Our fastest moving champagne is Bollinger," says Mr. Potts, "with Moët & Chandon second. We would sell more of Krug's Private Cuvée if we had it, but distribution is limited. In the claret department, we keep one hundred thousand bottles of Bordeaux on hand in the hotel all the time, more in reserve at our warehouses."

Supper in the Savoy Grill, still ritual after nearly three quarters of a century of *Sole Grillée Sauce Béarnaise* and *Selle d'Agneau Rôtie aux Pommes de Terre Byron,* is late. The room doesn't fill until well after nine o'clock and is still doing business after midnight. A substantial portion of its custom derives from the town's theater on both sides of the footlights, and the gleaming Rolls-Royces and Bentleys of managers and producers are the accustomed traffic in its courtyard driveway, the only artery in London where drivers keep to the right-hand side of the road.

Institutional, too, is the Savoy American Bar, an oasis of many satisfactions, first of which is an array of highly personable barmen who are celebrities in their own right. Sir George Reeves-Smith after World War I made a big thing of the American Bar, and with the advent of prohibition in the United States hired Harry Craddock, already the highest-paid barman in the world. Today the customers, regular and transient, are served by Joe Gilmore, Vic Victors, and Dennis Kelly, and the combined names of their familiar customers is a roster of notables of the English-speaking world. Many American visitors to the English capital don't feel they are officially on record as being in London until they have checked in at the Savoy Bar.

Such spacious gestures as those of George Kessler, a champagne magnate, who flooded the courtyard so his guests could be served dinner aboard gondolas, have pretty much disappeared, although as late as 1959 the hotel arranged to have 150 pounds of a rare fish called tilapia flown in from Lake Victoria in Tanganyika for the annual Ismaelia Dinner given by the late Aga Khan.

But in the details of its guests' comfort and convenience, the Savoy has by no means declined from the standard it established in more magnificent times. It keeps an exhaustive card file of the preferences of every patron of importance and attempts to assign them to suites that have given pleasure on previous visits. A Spanish grandee once evidenced a superstition about yellow roses, so now all yellow roses are assiduously culled from the welcoming bouquets that adorn his drawing room on arrival. Another guest dislikes answering telephones, so every extension is carefully removed from her rooms whenever she is in residence. Even in the last war when London was in a state of siege, the Savoy sent Christmas cards to all its old patrons throughout the world, cheerfully anticipating their return to London at an early date.

The passing of the office of managing director from the hands of Sir George Reeves-Smith to those of Hugh Wontner represented a very considerable change in the attitude of the Savoy's management toward its own institutional status.

Sir George had steadfastly refused to admit the existence of the hotel's past or of its historic mission to establish continuity with the great days of Victoria and, later, Edward VII. To him the past was a closed book and the only matter for concern was the immediate here and now.

"I have brought a little different approach to the matter of the place the hotel occupies in history," says the urbane and polished Wontner, on whom the mantle of dean of British hoteliers rests as gracefully as his beautifully cut pin-striped business suits. "We feel we can afford to acknowledge the past and recognize the Savoy as an institution that is now a part of English history and the annals of civilization. I myself am extremely conscious of my responsibility, not only as the director of a considerable organization but as a custodian, as it were, of remembered glory. The Savoy really is history, and we have come to feel that this is an asset, not something to be discarded like a worn rug."

That the hotel's glorious past may indeed be a very concrete asset is suggested by the fact that the over-all operation of the Savoy and its associated hotels and restaurants under Wontner's management has regularly paid the shareholders at the rate of twenty per cent.

"We are even in a small way a repository of *belles-lettres*," says the managing director, whose handsome person, cultured accents, and assured presence suggest a university don rather than an efficient man of affairs. "You know we have in the safe the manuscript of Arnold Bennett's *Imperial Palace*. Makes us on bowing terms with the Bodleian Library. The book itself, incidentally, was responsible for shaping the career of one of your own most distinguished American hotel men, Dan London of the St. Francis in San Francisco. London read it when he had yet to select a career for himself and was so impressed with the enviable distinction of being a successful hotel man that he immediately undertook to become one himself."

So seriously does Wontner take the responsibility of the Savoy as a cultural agency in the field of gastronomy that he offers a few select wines almost at cost, to insure their reaching an appreciative public.

"We regard it as an obligation to promote the best vintages we can procure," he says. "And we often reduce their markup to a mere fraction in the interest of seeing them drunk."

Significant of the Savoy's awareness of the United States is the apartment designated as the Abraham Lincoln Room, a spacious chamber where a great deal of history has been made. Here is where Herbert Hoover, during World War I, organized the American Citizens' Committee which arranged for sending home some twenty thousand stranded American tourists; it was here that the American colony in London gathered to celebrate the entrance of the U.S. into the conflict. Here in 1917 Sir Winston Churchill, then Minister of Munitions, made his appeal to a significant Anglo-American gathering for "the supreme intensity of effort" to end the war. Eventually so many transatlantic associations gathered about the apartment that it was finally dedicated as the Abraham Lincoln Room with a bust of the Emancipator unveiled by the Marquis Curzon of Kedleston, Secretary of State for Foreign Affairs.

In today's Anglo-American affairs, the Abraham Lincoln Room is the scene of such events as the monthly luncheon of the American Chamber of Commerce, the luncheons of the American Correspondents' Association, the Pilgrims' Dinner, the annual banquet of the Royal Society of St. George, founded to keep alive English traditions in America, and the meetings of the Monday Luncheon Club, a group headed by the U. S. Ambassador to the Court of St. James's for the discussion of international business problems.

But of all the organizations that regularly meet at the Savoy, the one that is probably the most distinguished is also the least known. Founded in 1911 by Sir Winston Churchill and the late Lord Birkenhead, and reputedly more exclusive than any of the celebrated gentlemen's clubs of St. James, the Other Club reportedly has about fifty members and its rituals are more closely shrouded in secrecy than those of a Yale senior society. The club's only admitted purpose is to dine, which it does behind closed doors in the Pinafore Room. The names of its members are wrapped in impenetrable mystery, as are the conversations that take place there, but it has been noted that significant government policies have been announced from time to time shortly after meetings of the Other Club, and it is widely suspected that a pipeline exists from the Thames Embankment to No. 10 Downing Street.

This is as it should be and maintains a tradition dating back to the middle of the fourteenth century when the King of France was a guest of Savoy for several months on end. "The King of England visited him frequently," wrote the historian Froissart of this pleasant time. "There were several times great feastings between them and other entertainments at this Hotel of the Savoy."

Six centuries have seen a lot of "feastings" under the gilded statue of Peter of Savoy, and the end is not in sight.

SOUTHDOWN MUTTON

The holy sacrament of my London can be partaken at a wide variety of places of worship, but its devotional sharing seems most appropriate at Simpson's, the Mecca of the mutton world to which all true worshipers of Southdown turn their faces when the spirit moves them, murmuring the litany: "Rare, please, carver, with the fat left on."

The roast beef of Old England may be the advertised national culinary triumph; London smoked salmon from Craigellachie on the Spey and plovers' eggs at the Ritz the hallmark of worldly affluence; Lauris asparagus specially grown in France for the early English market the delight of epicures supping in the Savoy Grill after the theater; but it is for Simpson's Southdown mutton served from the trolley with boiled greens on the side that I will make a round trip of sixteen thousand miles and count it time and miles well spent.

Over the years and decades, I am spiritually one with William Dunbar of Scotland:

> Rich be thy merchauntis in substaunce that excellis,
> Fair be their wives, right lovesome, white and small;
> Clere by thy virgyns, lusty under kellis:
> London, thou art the flour of Cities alle.

It is, as it was in the time of Richard III, still to me "the flour of Cities alle," but I am at a loss to know why Dunbar failed to mention mutton. Of all things English, I count it the rightest lovesome.

PEAL & COMPANY, AND ALAN MC AFEE

Passed along to me from John O'Hara is the saddening intelligence that Peal & Company of London, bootmakers to the English aristocracy for the last 173 years and probably the most celebrated firm of shoe cobblers in the world, has gone out of business, at least as custom purveyors of the finest handcrafted footwear the world has ever seen.

"The Directors of Peal & Co. Ltd. announce with regret the closing of their bespoke workshops due to the ever-increasing difficulty experienced over the past few years in obtaining skilled labor to replace their long-serving staff who have left due to retirement and deaths. It is very distressing to have to close down this side of our business that has been in control of the Directors in direct lineal descent of its founders for so long a time."

The author of *Butterfield 8* and *Pal Joey* goes on to remark that for the past thirty years, ever since he could afford them, boots from Peal have been his sole extravagance. He should by now have a sufficiently ample supply to last him for even a Churchillian lifetime, for no pair of Peal boots has ever been known actually to wear out or come apart beyond being repaired for more years of service.

I have never fallen under the spell or mystique of Peal, although I have had numerous suits from Henry Poole, the tailor always linked with Peal for reasons of quality and alliteration. Addiction to custom-made boots, however, is a habit no easier to shake off than smoking opium and is almost equally as compulsive.

One of my old-time principals was the legendary Arthur Clark, venerable Sunday editor of the *New York Herald Tribune* in the thirties and a magnifico of journalism in its more spacious days. Clark used to tell about his father, an Englishman who, like O'Hara, was an admirer of Peal footwear. He had a standing order for two pairs of new Peal oxfords made to his last and delivered every year. They were delivered, too, notwithstanding the circumstance that for the last fifteen years of his life the old gentleman had been bedridden.

Second only to Peal and still very much in business is the London establishment of Alan McAfee. The rather dingy shop, in the best British tradition of diffident antiquity, is just across the street from the Dover Street entry of Brown's Hotel. McAfee has made my evening pumps for many years. Because I am their only regular customer with a Nevada address, my infrequent visits to their dusty premises give them, I think, a certain pleasure. Their preconceived notions of the American West have a cachet of the Wells Fargo years about them, and the fact that I do not wear fur trousers and a brace of shooting irons is a surprise and disappointment to the clerks in long yellow dustcoats and whiskers to match.

"But what *do* you do, sir, with evening slippers in your part of the world?"

One must mourn the disappearance of Peal's custom-made boots as one does the vanished art of the carriage builder, the saddlemaker, and the artisan who understood the art of luring a silk hat into high gloss with a hot iron and wax. They are a part of a vanished time of gentility and leisure. It is doubtful, however, even if Peal could have found the craftsmen to perpetuate its special expertise, that there would be sufficient custom to maintain it economically. There are all too few customers for handmade shoes, although millions in today's affluent society could afford them if they would.

TOURIST TRAVEL LITERATURE:
Scotland, 1965

Although it may strain gullibility in its gussets, I ask you to believe the following. Planning a brief trip to England with my partner Charles Clegg, I conceived the idea of chartering a yacht to cruise off some of the little-visited islands of northern Scotland—the Hebrides and the like. The Clegg butler is a high-proof Scot who misses no local celebration of Bobby Burns's birthday, and throws the caber and toots the pipes with the best of his clan. He volunteered to write to his sister in Edinburgh on the chance that she might turn up some travel literature not available to the several British travel agencies in this country.

In a week or so a reply came to the effect that, while the Scottish travel bureau had exhaustive material on the Riviera, the Costa Brava, Lake Louise, and Pagopago, they had very little on Scotland. Such as they had, she affirmed, would be shortly forthcoming, compliments of the government. Sure enough, in a week or two there arrived, under British frank, the most up-to-date travel literature available. It was a copy of the English edition of Volume No. 387 of Everyman's Library: *The Journal of a Tour to the Hebrides, with Samuel Johnson, L.L.D.*, by James Boswell.

Honor bright.

ROLLS-ROYCE

In the six decades that Rolls-Royce has been produced, first at Derby, later at Crewe, and briefly in Springfield, Massachusetts, a number of explanations have been advanced for the mystique which surrounds it as is associated with almost no other end product of human devising. One is its comparative scarcity. Figures are not available over its entire life span, but in the first fifty years of its existence only twenty-five thousand cars were outshopped altogether, a figure which assumes perspective when viewed in the light of the production of thirty thousand cars in Detroit in a single week of March 1965.

Another is Rolls-Royce's imperviousness to change and uncompromising refusal to downgrade its product from the plateau of absolute excellence it achieved in the lifetimes of the two men whose name it bears, the Honorable Charles Rolls and Sir Henry Royce. Its radiator shell, bonnet outline, and Spirit of Ecstasy mascot on the radiator cap are essentially what they were half a century ago.

Rolls-Royce, although the firm has made a determined effort since the mid-1950s to abate "chauffeurs and baronial halls" in the car's collective image, has remained over the years and the decades primarily a car for heads of state, towering social grandees, and the upper-bracket one-thousandth of one per cent of the very rich of the world. In 1958, the New York advertising firm of Ogilvy, Benson & Mather was commissioned to "show Rolls-Royce in the context of American life," presumably being driven to cookouts by housewives in curl papers, and while the concept did indeed dramatically increase the sale of Rolls-Royces and Bentleys in the United States, it did absolutely nothing to abate the almost unearthly splendor of their associations.

Long after other of the world's car manufacturers assumed that all but a microscopic fraction of their products would be owner-driven, Rolls-Royce, both factually and by implication, assumed that owners of its cars would have limitless resources of servants both to drive and maintain their automobiles. The management adopted a very high tone with its patrons, and a handbook of comparatively recent years directed the unfailing manual lubrication of thirty points in the mechanism to be greased every five hundred miles, eighty-four points at every thousand miles, and twenty-nine at every two thousand miles, not to mention routine over-hauling and adjustments, checking of filters, tappets, and spark plugs, and the periodic removal of wheels for greasing. This sort of thing presup-posed Rolls-Royce ownership by people for whom the servant problem simply didn't exist, and the assumption was flattering to those who not only drove their own cars but emptied the ashtrays as well.

Rolls-Royce found itself elevated far above the estate of a merely ele-gant and well-appointed agency of personal transport into an article of faith and a way of life itself.

The first Rolls-Royce, a ten-horsepower, two-door saloon of 1905, sold for $1080. Today it is possible to purchase them in a price range from $16,800 to $26,000 with conventional fittings and the standard ameni-ties of deluxe transport. As with private Pullmans, the sums that can be expended on special effects and interior décor are almost without limit. They run from jeweled traveling clocks on the dashboard to in-dividually controlled air-conditioning, sun roofs, built-in bars, and tele-phonic communication between passengers and driver. In the late twenties a dealer in rare period furnishings saw no reason his Rolls-Royce, a Phantom I brougham model with carriage work by Clark of Wolverhampton, shouldn't be as luxuriously furnished as his home, and upholstered the interior with Aubusson needlework tapestry, the cost of the fabric alone coming to $3000 in a time of gold currency. Mrs. Hamilton McK. Twombly's favorite limousine contained a gold and emerald built-in vanity by Cartier valued at $10,000. Solid-silver drink-ing tools, Abercrombie & Fitch picnic baskets, and Baccarat glasses in the bar are a commonplace. Gold-plated motors in the James Bond tradition were never a matter of record, but gold-washed radiator shells and mascots have been executed, one such job by Mappin & Webb, the London gold and silversmiths, coming to $4000 in weight of metal alone.

The most expensive car ever seen in California and one which, in world comparatives, ranked in costliness with both Andrew Mellon's $40,000 car built exclusively of products of the Mellon enterprises and Sir Bernard Docker's $35,000 gold-plated Daimler, was shown at the Pebble Beach *concours d'élégance* at Del Monte Lodge in 1961. It was a Phantom V model Rolls-Royce owned by Martin Martyn of Beverly Hills which had cost its owner $54,000. The body was designed by Os-mond Francis Rivers, a celebrated craftsman who had for many years been chief body designer for the house of Hooper and architect of many of the cars used by the British royal family. The two-tone black and beige body was fabricated by the Paris firm of Henri Chapron, one of the last great bespoke body builders still in business. It required more than a year to build, and to supervise the work three trips to the Continent were made by Rivers and four from the United States by Mrs. Martyn. A working bar was furnished with drinking tools from Van Cleef & Arpels and glasses and decanters by Baccarat. There was an air-conditioned humidor for cigars, three-length radio reception controllable from each seat, individual armrests, and a locked compartment for the owner's binoculars and parasol on race days. "It has an English soul and a French body," said Mrs. Martyn, dusting its already-immaculate bonnet surface with a small dustcloth sewn of matched mink skins. Unknown at the time to the owners was the fact that before they took delivery on the car in Paris, the workmen who had labored over it had had a private christening party of their own and sent the car into the world wreathed with roses and formally christened with champagne. Some of the workers had wept to see it leave the shop.

Perhaps the most radiant of all chapters in the saga of social Rolls-Royce in the upper-case sense concerns Mrs. Hamilton McKown Twombly, whose death in 1952 at the age of ninety-eight put a final period, according to Cleveland Amory, to Newport's era of elegance. Mrs. Twombly's memory is still green in the upper brackets of the New York Four Hundred for her determined effort in 1935 to attend the Hollywood wedding of her grandson to Florabelle Fairbanks, a niece of Douglas Fairbanks.

Already in her eighties, Mrs. Twombly was forbidden to fly. The family private Pullman car had long since been discarded and Mrs. Twombly wouldn't even toy with the idea of renting one from the New York Central, let alone ride in a public train. Driving the entire three thousand miles from Newport to the church was the only solution, but it, too, was fraught with grave perils and the ever-present dangers of the Great Plains and other accidents of violence in the howling wilderness west of St. Louis. The James boys, she understood, were no longer in operating condition but who knew about others—the Daltons, for instance? And there was always the chance of hostile Indians. If they recognized her she would be held for ransom, a most inconvenient possibility.

Finally a solution presented itself. For three thousand miles going west and an equal distance coming back, the last grandchild of Commodore Cornelius Vanderbilt, dressed as her maid, rode in the front seat next to the chauffeur in one of the Twombly Rolls-Royces, while for an equal time and distance, Mrs. Twombly's maid, dressed as Mrs. Twombly, rode in lonely state in the back seat.

It was a triumph of ingenuity and determination still mentioned with pride in Park Avenue as a gesture the Commodore himself would have applauded.

Like all Vanderbilts, Mrs. Twombly rode in sometimes seedy but inevitably grand Rolls-Royces which she kept *en suite* at "Florham," her incredible estate near Convent, New Jersey, to match her mood and attire of the moment. John Mason Brown recalls being present at one Sunday morning when, returning from church, Mrs. Twombly was holding court, receiving her guests in the foyer under the sculptured likenesses of twelve Roman Caesars. "She stepped out of her violet Rolls-Royce," recalls Brown, "and swept inside wearing a violet hat, violet gloves, and carrying a bunch of violets. It was unforgettable."

The climactic example of the owner-driven Rolls-Royce came seven years after the campaign was first launched to make "the Finest Car in the World" a property of the masses, and must have been viewed with mixed emotions of frustration and gratification by Rolls-Royce itself. Returning, soon after the new year of 1965, from the funeral of Sir Winston Churchill, in itself enough to give the event a cachet of resounding privilege, the sixty-four-year-old Duke of Gloucester, an uncle of Queen Elizabeth and eighth in line for the British throne, managed to drive his Rolls-Royce into a ditch in the township of Eaton Socon about fifty miles north of London.

It had long been the Duke's practice, said the head of his household, Major Simon Bland, to have his chauffeur drive him to state and official functions and for the elderly nobleman to take the wheel himself on the way home. As a result of failing to make a turn, the ducal car went into the ditch, hospitalizing the Duchess with a broken arm and concussion, breaking the arm of the Duke's valet, and severely shaking up the chauffeur. The Duke himself was discharged from the local emergency ward with a badly skinned nose but no more severe injuries.

The mishap landed on the front pages of the press of the world in a fine farrago of strawberry leaves and coronets, bandages and arnica, and may well prove to have been the most distinguished owner-driven event in the long history of Rolls-Royce. It flattered both aspects of the Rolls-Royce saga, involving as it did an owner-driven car in which the owner-driver was heir to a title that has thrown a long shadow in English annals since the times of the Plantagenets.

The press of the world was at pains to follow the Duchess of Gloucester's fortunes in the hospital at Bedford, and every day bulletins, none of them failing to mention the ducal Rolls-Royce, apprised the newspaper readers on two continents of the progress of her recovery. On February 8, 1965, a United Press dispatch recorded that she had been discharged from her suite at Bedford and gone home. In the family's spare Rolls-Royce. The accident Rolls-Royce was still undergoing repairs.

The high interior construction of Rolls-Royce by most bodymakers and especially for heads of state and magnificoes of finance was, of course, largely predicated on the wearing of high silk hats by their occupants and retained as a vestigial heritage from the past into an age when silk hats were less universal than they once had been. In *Portugal and Madeira,* Sacheverell Sitwell recalls an anecdote in point. "The writer remembers meeting a certain Indian potentate at a luncheon party. The host said to him: 'May I ask why you commanded your new fleet of Rolls-Royces built with such high roofs?' The maharajah replied, 'Oh! I don't know. I might want to wear an aigrette.'"

ROLLS-ROYCE:
Horsepower

Always a pushover for Rolls-Royce stories, I like to recall one about the American customer who, when contemplating the purchase of a Rolls Silver Cloud, had some difficulty in ascertaining the precise horsepower of the car from his local Rolls dealer, and got no more satisfaction when he applied to the firm's chief agency in the United States, Inskip of New York. Rolls is extremely reticent about horsepower for a variety of reasons: it doesn't aim to compete in massive motive power with American cars, and never has; in addition, cars in England are taxed on the basis of their horsepower, and manufacturers undertake to keep it as low as possible, for the record. Typical English understatement.

Anyway, our boy, finally vexed beyond endurance, sent a weekend cable, for economy, to Rolls-Royce in Conduit Street, London, to this effect: "I'm not asking for a preview of the Holy Grail or even an invitation to a Royal Garden Party at Buckingham Palace. All I want to know is the exact brake horsepower of your Silver Cloud motor."

Days passed with no reply. Another weekend came around, weekend cable rates were again available, and finally the reply came from Rolls-Royce. It read:

"Sufficient."

Just to show that Rolls-Royce has no monopoly on British aloofness: a San Francisco acquaintance of mine recently encountered seemingly insoluble trouble with his Aston Martin and wrote to the factory in England, voicing his bitter complaint that the gear shift was defective and the springing of the front axle out of balance.

"We will not dignify your unseemly language with a reply," was the answer *he* got.

France

"I will tell you, Mr. Beebe," he said, "with whom you used to drink in this very room in 1923 and 1924. You often drank with a young Yale man with the peculiar name of Tipton Blish. Sometimes you came in with your uncle, Monsieur Edouard Center, and on one occasion you were in the company of Berry Wall, King of the Dudes, and His Majesty King Alphonso of Spain. Correct?"

THE PARIS RITZ: MEN'S BAR:
Georges and Frank

The news that Georges of the Paris Ritz (Georges Schauer is his full name, though few know it) is retiring, after forty-three years' service in and around the men's bar on the Cambon side of one of the world's finest hotels and most enduring celebrity traps, marks an epoch in the history of social drinking and drinking society. It doesn't, as the headline writers are so fond of proclaiming when a venerable celebrity dies or retires, "mark the end of an era," a cliché that seldom has justification and possesses none in the present instance.

Georges himself survived several "ends of eras" in the history of the Paris Ritz and, merely by his presence, accomplished a continuity with the past that was remarkable for its comprehensiveness. During prohibition, Georges had been the boy in buttons on the men's-bar door under the regime of Frank, and his memory for names was phenomenal even then. He survived the great change in American travel and drinking habits that accompanied repeal. He lived through World War II, and, finally, as manager of the men's bar, he witnessed an entire new generation of Americans and manners, of which he must have disapproved heartily.

His memory was, indeed, a fantastic mechanism of total recall, as the following anecdote will reveal. During the period from about 1928 to 1954, I didn't go to Paris at all. I was employed in New York, and the Manhattan scene provided all the delights and excitements a newspaper reporter could desire. It was a full quarter of a century since I had last been through the Cambon doors when I stopped by for an eye opener in the mid-fifties. Georges had been a *commis* when I last saw him; he was manager now, urbane and ubiquitous in a flawless white linen jacket, and he addressed me by name and gave me a good day as though I had left only yesterday.

I, not unnaturally, suspected collusion or some sort of fakery. Spying Art Buchwald, then a member of the editorial staff of the Paris *Herald*

Tribune, at the bar, I remarked that he must have apprised Georges of my identity in time for him to pretend recognition.

Both disclaimed any part in such an innocent deception, and Georges went on to prove the point.

"I will tell you, Mr. Beebe," he said, "with whom you used to drink in this very room in 1923 and 1924. You often drank with a young Yale man with the peculiar name of Tipton Blish. Sometimes you came in with your uncle, Monsieur Edouard Center, and on one occasion you were in the company of Berry Wall, King of the Dudes, and His Majesty King Alphonso of Spain. Correct?"

He was, in every detail. I had been very fond of Berry, a courtly old gentleman and courteous to brash young college boys who thought they would also like to be fancy dressers, and I had, indeed, imbibed champagne cocktails with him and His Majesty, who was then a regnant monarch, on more than one occasion. Alphonso was the first man I ever saw drinking the arrangement that used to be known in those days as a royal highball or what he sardonically called "King's Death." This consisted of a full bottle of vintage champagne served in an outsized stem glass with three or four shots of a good hard cognac thrown in it, along with a handful of fresh strawberries. His Majesty would drink the glass in three or four installments and then eat the strawberries with his fingers, daintily touching up his mustaches with a huge Charvet handkerchief.

I was immeasurably impressed with such grandeurs, and, on my return to New York, attempted to popularize the King's Death at Jim Moriarty's collegiate speakeasy at 216 East Fifty-eighth Street. It was not a smashing success. Few college boys had the price of bootleg champagne, and the wine list at Moriarty's seemed to be all Hackensack Meadows brut and didn't adapt itself to such spacious gestures.

Georges, as I have remarked, more nearly established continuity with a great era in the Paris Ritz than represented the era itself, for the golden noontide of American expatriate ringing and swinging in the City of Light was the decade that intervened between the passage of prohibition in 1919 and the stock market's Black Friday of 1929.

It was an age of transatlantic razzle-dazzle and high-seas hilarity, with every sailing of the *Aquitania, Berengaria, Olympic,* and the old *France* booked to capacity in every class with thirsty and solvent Yankees—Yale undergraduates, and vice presidents of Kidder Peabody and the Farmers Loan & Trust. Its like will never be seen again. Only the top echelons of celebrities, of course, made the grade to the men's bar at the Paris Ritz and the dreadful smoke-filled cubicle across the corridor assigned to women and known as the Cambon Dog House. The Ritz bar itself was for men only, a rule strictly enforced and never, to my knowledge, violated, despite all tales of Connie Bennett in man's attire.

Frank, whose family name few knew and which escapes me now, was the bar's manager and as arbitrary and authoritative in his province as was the all-powerful, monocled maître d'hôtel, Olivier, in the Ritz restaurant just down the corridor. Nobody took liberties with Frank. Drunks, bad-check artists, bores, and spurious noblemen like Mike Romanoff got short shrift, but Frank was the soul of liberality with stranded undergraduates—a sure source of succor, restoratives, and cheery counsel when bankruptcy or the shakes came with the morning. There was a tiny private barber shop just off the main apartment of the men's bar where hapless patrons caught short in evening clothes in daylight could have street dress sent over from their hotel, and where restorative shaves and hot towels were administered by an expert to twitching patrons who had to meet wives and family for lunch in half an hour. Popular legend maintained that Mme. Ritz, who was then very much alive, used to seat herself in the barber chair while the tonsor was at lunch and listen to the more or less Rabelaisian, and clearly audible, colloquies between masculine customers at the mahogany.

Appearing in Frank's domain before twelve noon was supposed to indicate acute alcoholic necessity, an aspersion shunned by even the most palsied celebrants from the night before, while arriving after twelve was most unfashionable, with the result that the countdown to noon found the corridor outside jammed with the perspiring thirsty who looked furtively at their wristwatches and fussed with gloves, hats, and walking sticks. At precisely noon there was a rush for the door in which a small man could be trampled.

Survivors of the era are few today, bottle-scarred veterans of an age of drinking that will not come again. Possibly Tipton Blish still draws breath in his native Indianapolis. Paul Palmer is one of the moguls of *Reader's Digest*. Basil D. Woon, whose book *The Paris That's Not in the Guidebooks* was the *vade mecum* of a hundred thousand tourists, is a bearded recluse in Carson City, Nevada. With the majority is Jack Thomas whose *Dry Martini* was written about the Ritz. So are Berry Wall and His Catholic Majesty. But it was a wonderful time while it lasted.

THE PARIS RITZ:
Men's Bar Addendum

As an addendum to this department's recent recollections of the old Paris
Ritz men's bar, and the sacerdotal functions of its custodian, Frank, the
confidant and bail bondsman for an entire generation of American ex-
patriates, a correspondent has written to remind me that one of Frank's
prime sources of personal income was the sale of Irish Sweepstake tickets. On one occasion in the early twenties, as closing time for the drawing
of lucky holders was approaching, Frank found himself with a solitary
two-dollar ticket still unsold. Customers at his bar that day were uncooperative, didn't believe in gambling, were anti-Irish, or had already purchased their limit of chances on this improbable source of potential riches,
and Frank was verging on tears at the prospect of being stuck with two
dollars in unsold merchandise. Finally, a gentleman at the end of the bar
who was liberally in wine and tired of hearing Frank's pathetic pitch
purchased the ticket out of charity or boredom.

It won him the sum of $139,000. He was a chap by the name of
Procter, who already owned ninety-nine and forty-four one-hundredths
per cent of Ivory Soap.

THE PARIS RITZ:
Olivier

In a recent issue of *Gourmet,* mention was made in this space of the two Theodores of the New York Ritz, Theodore Titze and Theodore Szarvars. Several readers have written in to ask politely why, while I was on the subject of great maîtres d'hôtel of the legendary past, I didn't mention Olivier of the Paris Ritz, perhaps the haughtiest of them all.

Olivier of the Ritz was indeed the most celebrated restaurant manager in all the long legend of stylish dining, and he was probably the sole world celebrity of his time who was known only by his first name, even by patrons who daily enjoyed his approval and came in more or less frequent social and professional contact with him. His last name, just for the record, was Dabescat, but it was of so little consequence or meaning in his lifetime that even in the memoirs of Mme. Ritz herself one can find no note of it. Everyone knows the name of his creator and employer, César Ritz, just as all educated people know that Escoffier's name was Auguste, but Olivier of the Ritz was sufficient identification for the most arbitrary and respected maître d'hôtel of all time.

Olivier lived well into my time in the Paris of the early twenties, but I, alas, as a college boy who could afford the men's bar of the Ritz on the Cambon side, knew no such affluence as was indicated by dining there. We nursed our traveling money for purposes of more hooray than was represented by gastronomy, and ate well but frugally at Prunier's, where seafood of all sorts was heavenly, and authentic Russian caviar was within our reach—which it certainly wasn't at the Ritz.

Olivier's favor was perhaps more widely sought than that of any of the influential maîtres d'hôtel of his time, and he must have died substantially wealthy. His only peer was the corpulent and courtly Monsieur Albert, who reigned as supreme arbiter at Maxim's in winter and took over at Ciro's at Deauville during the season at that exalted resort.

Those were the times when Sunday evening was the great moment of the week at the Ritz, with full evening attire required and tables at an astronomical premium. The aging and still socially ambitious Mrs. John Mackay, widow of the Bonanza King of the Comstock who had died early in the century, was one of Olivier's most ardent admirers, and the spectacle of the overpainted old lady far gone in years being piloted to a choice table by Olivier with the same reverential obeisances he accorded Berry Wall or the Duc de Gramont invariably evoked smiles among the knowing. What Mrs. Mackay may have tipped is, at this remove, problematical, but those who pretended to know reported it was truly fabulous.

Olivier was most at home with royalty who then clustered in the Ritz thick as autumn leaves in Valombrossa. The handsome young Duke of Windsor, then Prince of Wales, Alfonso of Spain, Manuel of Portugal (usually with Gaby de Lys, who eventually cost him his throne), the Shah of Persia, and the Russian grand dukes, especially Boris and Cyril, were all patrons of Olivier. He, of course, walked backward to show them to their tables, a miracle of navigation, for waiters, wandering patrons, and tables filled with diners escaped collision by the merest hairbreadth. A later generation would have said he had built-in radar.

The Dolly sisters were the toast of the town in those days and could be seen dining at the Ritz under Olivier's benevolent regard at a table strategically located midway between that of Mrs. Stuyvesant Fish and Berry Wall. Berry sometimes dined with Mrs. Wall but always with his chow dog, who was as much a *boulevardier* as his master and, like him, invariably wore an ornate dinner jacket after six in the evening. The chow's stock collars and old-fashioned black satin stock ties were made by Charvet from the same pattern as Berry's, and there used to be a cartoon at Charvet's by the famed satirist Zem showing the dog being fitted for his haberdashery with all the attention lavished on "The King of the Dudes" himself.

Olivier's identifying panache was, of course, his glittering single eyeglass, expertly worn without a cord and with a component of hauteur that, with a single stare, reduced demanding patrons and troublesome old duchesses to the estate of peasants. Cornelia Otis Skinner, in her lively and marvelously well-informed recollections of Paris in its great years, expresses the opinion that Olivier's monocle was his insignia of office, and that he wore it when on duty as other men might wear a tailcoat or Court sword to show that they were invested with their fullest authority. When Olivier, encountering his clients outside the Ritz, bowed to them ceremoniously, he invariably removed his eyeglass to show them that this was an occasion of informality and a purely personal matter.

Olivier is gone now and merely one of the many great memories associated with the Paris Ritz, but it is certain that his spirit hovers over the conduct of its restaurant, still one of the world's finest. As noted above, confirmed old-timers there sometimes find themselves saluting the maître d'hôtel of 1965 as Olivier. It's a tribute to a personality that far transcended his office.

Eatalls and Tosspots

When I had suspended my hat and wraprascal on a peg, I prepared to order terrapin Maryland, anticipated by a dozen or so Lynnhavens.

BOSTON: EATALLS AND TOSSPOTS:
Consommé Julien
The Parker House
Locke-Ober's Winter Place Wine Rooms

The history of gastronomy, the legend of gourmandism in Boston, was inaugurated the day that Julien evolved his soup. The precise date of this event can only be left to conjecture, but it was three of four years before the end of the century.

Scrodded codfish, brown bread, baked kidney beans, and Cotuit oysters are, naturally enough, universally and reverently associated with the tradition of Boston table fare. They are characteristic, indigenous dishes to the region, deriving from its setting, the tastes of its inhabitants, and the genius produced by their early necessities and resources. It comes as a surprise, however, to learn that such an essentially Gallic contriving should have its source, *fons et origo,* within the precincts of Yankee Congress Street as that arrangement through whose agency Julien became known to fame. Consommé, somehow, is not as patently a Down East derivative as, say, quahogs or salt-rising bread.

Jean Baptiste Gilbert Payplat *dis* Julien came to town in 1794, a refugee from the Paris terror. He had at his disposal, it appears from the records, the sum of $6000, and with this he undertook to introduce to an as yet strictly home-faring Boston an authentic French restaurant. Up till then people had eaten in public at cook-shops and taverns, but Julien's "Restorator," as he called his enterprise, set diners-out by the ears with its Parisian elegance of fare, its new and foreign dishes, and their cachet of fashionable smartness. His modest frame establishment at the corner of Congress Street and Milk became the resort of the town. The Restorator thrived. Gustatory symphonies were prepared to the accompaniment of a leitmotiv of clattering dishes and tinkling crystal. Hogsheads of fine claret washed down firkins of Strasbourg *foie gras.* *Crêpes à l'orange* came into ambrosial being over flaming spirit lamps. Truffles from Périgord appeared to ornament galantines of grouse and cold sides of Restigouche salmon. The proprietors of the Hat and Helmet and the Green Dragon waxed vainly apoplectic.

And then one day Julien created a new consommé, and fame and fortune hovered over the tureen of its birth. Overnight Jean Baptiste Gilbert Payplat became the toast of gastronomes, a veritable prince of soups. The recipe for Julien flew out of town with a hundred galloping stage coaches, and from far and wide eatalls and epicures converged on Congress Street in hungry hundreds.

Rumors of this gastronomic Klondike reached Hartford and the most distinguished gourmet of all time simultaneously. Claude Anthelme Brillat-Savarin, whose *Physiology of Taste* was a few years later to become a classic of good living, was on a wild-turkey shoot. He hung up his fowling piece and engaged passage on the first stage to Boston. The Field of the Cloth of Gold palls beside the meeting of these two mighty monarchs of the saucepan.

In return for the boon of a new consommé, Brillat-Savarin taught Julien the secret of cheese fondue, and the proprietor of the Restorator found that in inventing one new dish he had acquired two. Cheese fondue, a sort of lineal antecedent of our own rarebit of Wales, became the favorite late-supper dish of Boston, and when Brillat-Savarin went back to New York on his way home, Julien sent him a fine roe deer which, the father of transcendental gastronomy records, was vastly appreciated at a party he gave on the eve of his sailing. No reigning sovereigns could have exchanged more princely tokens of their mutual esteem.

When Julien died, his wife inherited the property and the recipe for the consommé, and held forth at the old stand a decade before she sold it to Frederick Rouillard. This estimable boniface, unlettered perhaps in the subtleties of Continental cuisine, ran the Restorator as a chophouse.

Julien's was torn down in 1824 after three decades of service, but the name was evidently too valuable a one to be allowed to perish, as is attested by an insertion in the *Boston Advertiser* in 1831 which informs the public that at the Julien House in Congress Street "Gentlemen and ladies from the country who are in pursuit of board and pleasant situation will be most thankfully received."

Until the third decade of the century the various taverns, ordinaries, and stagecoach inns of Boston were sufficient, both in numbers and appointments, to accommodate the transient travel of the city, but in 1828 it appeared that there was a real need for more spacious and impressive facilities for the entertainment of visitors, especially of distinguished foreigners, who were flocking to town in ever-increasing numbers. To meet this need a group of public-minded citizens pooled their resources to build, in the Tremont House, the earliest first-class hotel in America.

The inaugural dinner of this establishment, the distinguished guests at

which included Daniel Webster and Edward Everett, was indicative of
the manner in which meals were served in public restaurants at this
period:

> The waiters [wrote a contemporary] filed into the upper end of the
> room where the landlord, Dwight Boyden, stood with a long white
> apron around him, and carving knife and fork in hand; and at the sound
> of a bell, one seized upon a quantity of plates, another knives, a third
> forks, a fourth a lot of large soup spoons, and a fifth the smaller spoons.
> At the second sound of the bell, they moved into line, and at the third
> marched with sedate steps behind the chairs of the guests, and simul-
> taneously the bearers of plates, knives, forks and spoons, with a flour-
> ish of the hand, placed the various articles upon the table before the
> guests, and then gracefully stepped back into line, ready to carry out
> their orders. In the meantime, the landlord was carving.

Such was the ritual of the host's dinner, a ritual which obtained until
the first à la carte bills of fare made this pleasant regimentation of service
a thing of the past. The Tremont House was for many years the wonder
and glory of American hotelkeepers who came from far and wide to study
its crystal chandeliers, Turkey carpets, French ormolu clocks, its free
New Years' Day dinner to all guests, and its innovation of free slippers
provided for guests while their jackboots were being cleaned and returned to the long row of gleaming footgear in the front office. It was the
Boston residence of celebrities including Charles Dickens, President Van
Buren, the Prince de Joinville, Edwin Forrest, Daniel Webster, William
C. Macready, and President Tyler.

Boston's next great hotel, constructed during the fabulous forties some
score of years later, was the Revere House, then considered a palatial
caravanserai, which in its time sheltered Jenny Lind, the Prince of Wales,
the Grand Duke Alexis, the Emperor Dom Pedro, and General Grant. A
tattered railroad guide of the fifties, in the possession of the writer, rec-
ommends that voyagers who have safely survived the perils of the train
brigade from New York by the Long Island and New London ferry route
may, with confidence, put up at the then new Adams House, the American House, the Revere House, the Tremont House, or the United States
Hotel.

It was Harvey D. Parker, however, who made modern history in the
Boston world of hotels. Parker House rolls were to bear his name and renown throughout the world. Parker's Hotel was to become a Boston institution almost as representative of the town as the proverbial codfish,
whose image hangs in the State House, and second only in fame to the
Athenaeum, the *Transcript*, and the uncontrolled passion of authentic
Bostonians for attending funerals.

Mr. Parker, whose seaman's beard, innocent of mustaches, and sturdily handsome profile you can still see hung in the up-to-the-minute Parker House of today, came to Boston from Paris, Maine, and served his apprenticeship as coachman for a lady of circumstance living in Watertown. His cockaded topper bravely set over one ear, his top-booted feet planted firmly against the dash of a lurching coach which swayed in a seagoing manner over the roads on cantilever springs, young Parker drove her on shopping trips into the city at frequent intervals, and it was his custom to lunch in a modest Court Square restaurant kept by one John E. Hunt.

Whether it was because he found the orders short and indulged that almost universal hanker to be proprietor, someday, of an establishment in which one has received a fancied slight, or because he saw a more secure and affluent future as boniface than as groom, must be a matter for conjecture; but, in any event, in 1832, he bought Hunt out for the sum of $432, and some notion of the shrewdness of the trading involved can derive from the circumstance that items as small as a ten-cent lemon squeezer were listed in the bill of sale.

Parker's restaurant, in the conduct of which he interested as steward John F. Mills, prospered because of the perfection of its service. The Jacks and Pats and Timothys who were its waiters practiced all the little attentive touches long since bequeathed to a Gallic race of Henris and Marios in the restaurants of the land. The Tremont Restaurant fairly coined money.

In 1854, Parker bought the old John Mico house, hung a simple shingle with the word "Parker's" over the busy sidewalk, and set out to test an idea he had harbored in the back of his head for some time: namely, that perhaps hotel patrons might like their meals at other than specified hours. Heretofore, even amid the almost Babylonish elegances of the Tremont House, meals had been served at fixed hours, and he who was late went without. The American plan, as it is to this day known, and continuous dining-room service came into immediately popular being at Parker's.

Subsequent additions to the original Mico house carried the School Street façade of Parker's to the corner of Tremont Street, opposite King's Chapel, and almost as far down the hill as to be opposite the stone and iron gates of City Hall. Parts of its exterior suggested a Georgian mansion, others the Château of Chambord. Its corridors, as most Bostonians recall, resembled gaslit catacombs carpeted in Turkey red and full of improbable angles, turns, and levels. The chances were heavily against a late diner's ever getting to his own apartment, even if the lift deposited him in its approximate vicinage, and one gay old dog used to recall that he slept more frequently in linen closets than in his own bed. Its lobby, with its black-and-white marble floor and mahogany-fitted desks and offices, was one of the sights of the town, and the writer's father was fond of recalling how, as a boy in the sixties, he used to be brought to Parker's for the heavenly experience of seeing the famous wallpaper, gay as it was with steeplechases, departing coaches, and huntsmen galloping across the rolling and perpetual countryside of its pattern.

What the Brown Palace was to Denver, the Planters to Saint Louis, the St. Charles to New Orleans, Brown's to London, and the Windsor to Montreal, the Parker House, as it became formally known after the death in 1884 of Mr. Parker, was to all New England. It was the meeting place of countrymen, with chin whiskers and carpetbags, of the sort known as Silas on every comedy stage in the land, of mutton-chopped bankers over from New York in George Pullman's new plush and maple-walnut palace cars, of white top-hatted sports who matched their trotters of a Sunday afternoon on the "Mile Ground" as the stretch of Commonwealth Avenue was known that lay beyond Cottage Farm Bridge. The whiskered and tattersall-waistcoated blades of Harvard arrived and departed, refreshed, on the hourly horse cars to Cambridge that stopped at the little waiting room on the corner of Bosworth Street. State Street merchants had their first Scotch grouse of the season, washed down with Perrier-Jouet *extra sec* in its sober dining rooms. Drummers, litterateurs, the unspeakable Mr. Dickens who returned America's gracious hospitality with a vulgarian's churlishness, *bon viveurs,* all the world of travelers for a third of a century made their rendezvous there.

For many years Parker's barroom made more than $100,000 annual clear profit, and now that common sense has again been incorporated into the Constitution, it is possible that the new Parker House may approximate this handsome source of legitimate revenue. Heaven knows the place was dismal enough during the great dry spell, and the writer recalls the horror registered on the face of a waiter captain when, in a private dining room, a bucket of ice was commanded for the cooling of a couple of bottles of wine at a dinner for a prospective bridegroom.

The Parker House roll was, of course, the most famous of the contributions to the tradition of gastronomy in School Street, but other things, especially game, were notable as specialties of the house. The following menu, that of a private dinner given in an era of less Spartan table fare than is currently fashionable, gives a fair index of what a Bostonian of the seventies might expect at Parker's when he had, with anticipatory forethought, unbuttoned his Albert watch chain and smoothed his napkin into the folds of his white linen vest:

Château Yquem Grand Vin

Little Neck Clams

Yriarte Pâle

Clear Green Turtle *aux Quenelles*   *Pôtage à la Reine*

Schloss Johannesberger

Soft Shell Crabs, *Sauce Tartare*

Spanish Mackerel *à la Maître d'Hôtel*

Pommery and Gréno "Sec"

Fillets of Beef *à la Triano*

Green Goose Purée of Chestnuts

Sweetbreads *à la Toulouse*   Broiled Fresh Mushrooms

Suprême of Chicken aux Truffles

Pâte de foie gras à la Bellevue

Roman Punch

Château Mouton Rothschild

Upland Plover   Doe Birds

Parisienne Soufflé   Opera Biscuit

Chantilly Cream   *Petits Charlotte*

Roquefort and Camembert   Olives, ripe and green

Hamburg Grapes   Apricots, Cherries

Strawberries   French Fruit

Ice Cream Sherbet

Pousse Café

Café Noir

Cognac 1811

Liqueurs

These casual snacks would not, of course, have been considered anything suitable for a formal occasion. The terrapin, saddle of mutton, canvasback, mongrel goose, grouse, and other essentials of true dining were omitted altogether, but the bill will indicate what was esteemed proper for a small supper tendered to an eminent barrister on the occasion of a notable legal triumph. The rapid whirring sound audible in the direction of The Granary Burying Ground is doubtless the Puritan father who watered his family's soup, lest they should enjoy it overmuch, turning over in his grave.

No account of the annals of dining in Boston would be complete without mention of the old Bell in Hand, of Jake Wirth's immortal resort of

beer and song, and of Billy Park's, beloved of Harvard students, but space
compels us to Winter Place.

The brass sign on either side of the door reads "Locke-Ober's Winter
Place Wine Rooms," and it is here that an entire school of Boston eatalls
and tosspots of enduring fame for more than half a century have resorted.
For here, in a narrow alley, scarcely a long stone's throw from Brimstone
Corner, is a true shrine of the culinary art in its robuster moods, and, like
pious incense, the savors of its service drift through the open windows into
the tranquil evening of the city around it, complemented by an amiable
leitmotif of laughter and clinking crystal.

Early in the eighties Louis Ober hung out his bush in Winter Place.
Eben Jordan, the great merchant, ate there and drank deep and was
pleased, and his patronage brought a prosperity to the taverner. Twenty
years later Frank Locke, a rival boniface, established a similar place of
business next door, and the substantial citizens of the community found it
agreeable to drink a whiskey sling at Locke's before having a Medford
rum at Ober's, where the food was admittedly superior. Sometimes these
potations were retroactive in effect, and the doors between the establishments were kept in a state of abrupt oscillation by customers hurrying
from sling to rum and, conversely, from rum to sling. On such occasions
the food consumption was practically negligible, but everyone agreed that
Locke's and Ober's were essential one to the other, and in 1894 the party
wall between them was torn down with what amounted to a public demonstration. The two taverns were merged as Locke-Ober's Winter Place
Wine Rooms, and the brass sign in the alley still announces this cheerful
circumstance.

Prosperity has always been associated with Winter Place tavern, as it
is commonly known. Even during the years of the great drought, when
its bar was dedicated to oysters alone, the bright youth and chivalry of
Harvard thronged its tables and were careful of the disposition of their
feet, so as not to disturb the bottles under their chairs. The long carved
mahogany bar with its French mirrors, imported from San Domingo at
great expense and installed with public rejoicing, the steam dishes of the
free lunch with their intricate system of chains and counterweights for
lifting the covers, the magnificent barroom nude at the end of the room
with a crystal goblet in her hand and vine leaves in her hair, all are sym-
bolic of physical well-being dating from the days when burgesses in frock
coats and top hats lined the bar and invented the Ward Eight.

The invention of this arrangement was unquestionably the high point
in the history of Winter Place. The precise details of the epochal event,
together with the name of the pioneer in bar craft of its first designer, are
shrouded in the mists of antiquity, but word of the phenomenon spread
rapidly, and it was shortly after this that Locke and Ober jointly partici-

pated in a ceremony which consisted of throwing the key to the front door
into Boston Harbor. The Ward Eight is a sort of whiskey sling based on
ancient bourbon and served in a highball glass. Compared with it, a bolt
of lightning is a very mild form of stimulant. The tinkle of ice in the
glasses appropriate to this toddy became louder than the traffic in Temple
Place hard by, and if the secret of its composition had not become generally known, it is probable that excursion trains from all over New England
would have converged upon the common goal of Boston filled with thirsty
enthusiasts. Locke and Ober, as a result, got rich.

The increased patronage of the house called for a revision of the menu,
and Emil Camus (who succeeded to the property when Locke and Ober
took the Ward Eight with them to the Elysian Fields) and Nick Stuhl,
the manager, designed a bill of fare which became famous for its fish and
game, sweetbreads Eugénie, lobster Savannah, monumental fillets of beef,
and distinguished cellarage full of hocks. Theodore Roosevelt invariably
patronized it when in Boston. Thomas Lawson, between moments of
frenzied finance, projected his urbane personality and inevitable gardenia
upon its festive scene. Thomas Bailey Aldrich and Henry Cabot Lodge
were members of a regular patronage, and Enrico Caruso could hardly be
dragged away when it was curtain time at the opera house up in Huntington Avenue. As a matter of fact, Louis H. Mudgett, old-time manager
of the opera house, used to detail a special agent who was to cut off the
great man's supply of edibles when it was becoming apparent that if he
consumed one more entree he might have convulsions on the stage in the
midst of Aïda.

Nor has the passing of time dissolved in any appreciable degree the
flavor of authenticity which pervades this substantial ordinary. The man
who has fared there on Cotuits and grilled Scotch grouse, complemented
by a bottle of Rudesheimer Oberfeld of that greatest of years, 1921, the
whole served by Charlie, dean of waiters, has dined indeed. By custom,
the older patrons of the establishment who are dining alone are seated
together at a long common table. There H. T. P. of the *Transcript* was for
many years the arbiter of its conversation. Professor John Livingston
Lowes of Harvard has been no stranger to its board, and at one time a
mysterious undergraduate organization, known as the Michael Mullins
Chowder and Marching Society, put in a not-too-reticent appearance,
arriving in horse-drawn herdics and, for the earlier part of the evening
at least, immaculately attired in silk hats and tailcoats. Neither chowder
nor marching gave its members very much concern.

Only masculine persons are permitted in the restaurant proper or at
the oyster bar presided over by the ingratiating Jacimo, but there are
cabinets particuliers upstairs, upholstered in the crimson satin of tradition,
dating from the period when drinking champagne from the slipper of a

dancing lady was considered the very smartest, if slightly daring form. Under its florid and ornate electroliers, Winter Place has seen much of Boston history. For more than half a century it has dispensed sound food and mellow liquors, and it is possessed of the worn quality, the patina of useful age, which only time and good cheer and the passage of stout eaters and happy drinkers can impart.

It will be apparent, perhaps, from the foregoing memoranda on the most important of the arts devised for human comfort and delight that neither as a Puritan community nor as a latter-day Tyre of the Western World was Boston an undernourished citadel of lean fare or languishing trenchermen.

Nor has the passage of time diminished the capacity of the town's gourmets, who celebrated the first year of repeal and the arrival of André Simon, president of the Wine and Food Society of England, with libations whose echoes must have reached even to the vault on the Common where Master Julien dreams of vanished triumphs. At the dinner accorded him in a private home on Beacon Hill, M. Simon was able subsequently to recall that with the hors d'oeuvres was served a very old Madeira, a Cossart Gordon's 1826 Rainwater; a Bâtard Montrachet with the soup; a century-old pale sherry with the fish; a hock with the entree; Burgundies of three distinguished years, ranging from a Clos de Vougeot 1887 to a Grand Chambertin 1915, with the roast (a Mallard duck per guest); a sweet hock with the soufflé; and then, said M. Simon, the real drinking started.

Coffee was supplemented with six brandies: two kinds of Armagnac, two Charentes and two cognacs of 1820 and 1848, respectively. After these came a couple of bottles of wonderful old Medford rum, described by the celebrated diner-out as "a steel fist in a velvet glove," and, finally, a very rare old bourbon and a hundred-year-old rye out of the cellar of the host's grandfather. M. Simon later told newspaper reporters he did not expect to meet such hospitality elsewhere on his grand tour of the United States.

An amusing sidelight on the Puritan caste of thought which has animated the Boston licensing authorities down to the present day is the requirement that the entire interior of taverns must be visible from the street. By this device it was hoped citizens would be ashamed from standing up to bars and drinking in the full view of the populace. But the result has, happily, been the reverse, and strollers, until then quite unconscious of their need, have viewed the happy topers through the window and dashed inside to get themselves in similar case.

Warmed by the genial fires of third-proof rum, Boston has always been a town of eatalls, but it required Julien and Brillat-Savarin to make it a city of gourmets. And the coot stew at Haussman's in Avery Street, like the inimitable cream cheese and *Bar-le-Duc* dear to old gentlemen at teatime in the lounge of Clark's Hotel next to the Adams House, are as much a part of the Boston legend as the elusive accent of its inhabitants, the First Corps Cadets, or the tradition of John L. Sullivan, the strong boy of Roxbury and the wonder and glory of an entire generation of sporting Americans.

ON THE ROCKS

Although the phenomenon has not yet achieved validation in the public prints and the faith it represents is still narrowly guarded in its membership, there is, throughout the length and breadth of the land and twice each day performed, a ritual whose significance is not lost upon perceptive beholders. Participants in this mystic rite face toward the east, raise a votive chalice to their lips, and mutter an incantation more dread than that of any ancient priesthood, the words of which, here to repeat, would carry with them the instant damnation of the impious blasphemer. It is no secret, however, that the initiated are turning their faces in the general direction of No. 8 Berkeley Street, Cambridge, Massachusetts, the true shrine of the True Prophet, Bernard De Voto, the most powerful mediator and advocate of purism in the drinking habits of the enlightened American male.

At the ancient cry of the muezzin, "What will it be, gents?" the believers shout an antiphonal "On the rocks!" and thereafter face the shrine and utter the secret and ritualistic word.

In the Happy Valley at the Sheraton-Palace in San Francisco, in the Pump Room in Chicago, in Brennan's in New Orleans, Willard's hotel in the Federal City, and in Locke-Ober's Winter Place Wine Rooms in Boston (where the worshipers vary the ritual by facing to the north and west in the direction of Harvard Square), at noontime and at nightfall, strong men praise the name of Benny De Voto and acknowledge the righteousness of all his words.

For, in addition to being the ranking historian of the American scene whose *The Year of Decision* and *Across the Wide Missouri* are classic volumes in the matter of the Old West, De Voto is the most articulate champion of the ultimate refinement in the absorption of spirits and purist in the field of gin and whiskey; and it should be said at the outset of this brief devotional essay that it but carries the message of the master and paraphrases holy writ as contained in De Voto's scriptural volume *The Hour. The Hour* is the *vade mecum* of the just, the Mosaic law of the upright in heart when they approach the mahogany. All else, at least since the publication of Professor Jerry Thomas' *The Bon Vivant's Companion,* is, at best, profane, at worst, heresy. The true creed is: bourbon whiskey should be consumed straight.

The De Voto faith probably marks a turning point of some sort in the polite drinking habits of the American people, a divergence, if not a revolution, from the multiplicity of fruit-juice follies and Borgia mixtures of the past quarter century, in search of reasonable standards of alcoholic propriety and the dignity of the inner man.

Any attempt to trace the course of the popularity of various types of drinks down the American decades must end in utter frustration. The champion of booze on the rocks and the elemental essences of the grain may plausibly remark that in the nineteenth century strong men with beards and Albert watch chains stood manfully up to the bar in the Hoffman House, the Southern Hotel, and a primeval Waldorf and drank nothing more complicated than straight whiskey with a modest chaser of Croton water, beer, or ginger ale. But parallel to this robust simplicity of habit, he is confronted with the emergence of the cocktail and whole libraries full of barkeep's guides awash with slings, crustas, flips, phlegm-cutters, pick-me-ups, sangarees, fizzes, smashes, cobblers, juleps, toddies, sours, daisies, skins, punches, cups, nogs, shrubs, and fanciful arrangements of fruit juice, wines, cordials, bitters, and fortified matters whose mere recitation is the occasion for implicit emesis.

Most of them have vanished down the years to become obsolescences like the horsecar. The orange blossom and the entire field of mixed drinks was narrowing down to more or less streamlined proportions when the advent of prohibition revived the business of elaborately mixed and fancifully camouflaged drinks as the natural result of the lamentable liquor available during those thirteen years.

Now, however, good taste is once more abroad in the land. The thoughtful hostess, renouncing all temptation to Alexanders, sidecars, Myrtle Bank punch, and the possibilities inherent in *crème* of violets, imitates the best practice that has always obtained in strictly masculine circles of entertainment, and furnishes forth for her appreciative guests the basic fundamentals of hospitality—namely, the best spirits in the best crystal, complemented by an abundance of ice cubes and a few simple, choice, and also basic hors d'oeuvres.

The more universally acceptable alternative to the basic Continental consumption of caviar and strong waters is found in the American and English spirits, bourbon and scotch, and, perhaps, in one of the almost infinite varieties of light and dark rums, chastely chilled over ice cubes and consumed in the satisfying leisure that can make the cocktail hour a prolonged and urbane tranquility, instead of a morally depraved scuffle with grenadine abominations boiling in the clammy mitt of the consumer.

Dedication to the ideal of simplicity in liquid entertainment imposes upon the host one stringent qualification that does not necessarily prevail when miscellaneous mixed drinks are served: everything must be the best obtainable. For, while it is possible to conceal spirits of less than superlative quality when compounded with overbearing mixes, any attempt at economy of purse, or uninstructed choice of brands, will be alarmingly obvious when whiskey is drunk straight over the rocks. Polonius may be paraphrased: "Costly thy spirits as thy purse can buy, but not expressed in fancy." The very best names in the worlds of scotch, bourbon, rye, gin, and rums are household names, advertised at staggering expense and, through competition, maintained over the years at unvarying standards of quality. To name brand-names of bottled goods here would be invidious, but on every grocer's and liquor dealer's list is a variety of excellent brands, and there is no excuse for accepting anything but the superlative.

To know and acknowledge excellence in drinks is the first requirement of successful hospitality. No bargains come in bottles.

Invariably, in any discussion of alcoholic entertainment, there must come to hand the great schismatic matter of the martini cocktail. Unless you prefer gin on the rocks pure and unadulterated, the whiskey toddy (not an old-fashioned, mark you) and the martini cocktail are the two thinkable arrangements available to civilized practice today. The toddy is whiskey with a little sugar, lemon, and water, and nothing, but nothing, more. The martini is the source of more heresy, strife, argument, debate, and malpractice than any other drink save possibly the mint julep, and where the frosted mint toddy is regional, the martini is universal in its implications.

There is a legend current in circles of masculine fashion of an exclusive club for young gentlemen at one of the acknowledged English universities where, after all other qualifications of station, finance, and acceptability had been met, the candidate for membership was subjected to one ultimate and searching test of manners. He was asked to take snuff. On his expertise with this exacting and ceremonial commodity rested his social future.

Some such standard of accepted conduct might well be arranged in the matter of the martini.

One of the silliest affectations of the current world of drinking fashion in the United States is the vogue, among self-styled sophisticated drinkers, of the extra-dry martini. This, of course, represents a swing of the pendulum from the extremity of sweet arrangements masquerading as cocktails which were in universal style before prohibition—Alexanders, pink ladies, orange blossoms (now a dirty word in the language), and other confections relying variously on grenadine, sirup, and Italian vermouth.

Actually, the martini was originally one of these, or close cousin, since it was made with Italian vermouth in nearly equal proportions, and often with a sweet-type gin. This primeval martini was intended for consumers who used a single *apéritif* before a meal, and it was often enough served without any ice at all, *à l'anglais* as it were. Its name is sufficient clue to the vermouth of the 1910 martini.

Eventually, of course, the cocktail fell into the hands of more robust drinkers who had previously been addicted to nothing more complex than bourbon and branch water, and there started its progress toward a goal that approached zero as a limit: gin on the rocks. The sweet martini of yesteryear didn't lend itself to absorption in quantity. Its function of cleansing the palate became reversed when taken by twos or twenties, and the drink found itself in a process of evolution toward something better suited to long-time stands at the bar. During prohibition, when vermouth was as costly and often unavailable as real gin, the trend toward dryness was hastened and in recent years found its ultimate and logical expression in the martini of the Madison Avenue advertising man, where the vermouth is a mere humorous reference.

Continentals and cultivated persons generally are horrified by the American dry martini, which is nothing more in simple fact than gin on the rocks, but the dry martini has been made fashionable by patrons of the Racquet and Jack & Charlie's "21" and corresponding members of the club in the Sheraton-Palace in San Francisco, and now the merest mention of vermouth in connection with a martini is a source of inextinguishable merriment in the Saddle & Cycle Club in Chicago or the Ship's Bar in the Brown in Denver.

One calls to mind in this connection the brain child of the late and much-loved Ernie Byfield of the Pump Room on Chicago's Goethe Street. It was his notion that as a come-on to the gustatory wonderments of his restaurant, he would serve at the bar a full six-ounce martini at the conventional six bits, elsewhere charged for a two-and-a-half-ounce cocktail. This would pull the customers in in droves where they would shortly fall under the spell of the Pump's legendary magnificence and start commanding pressed duck and magnums of Bollinger. The carriage trade arrived in gratifying numbers, but, alas, failed to explore the resources of the Byfield cellars and menu. After two—or at the most three—of the bargain martinis, the house footmen were helping them into cabs for home, where they spent the remainder of the evening lying on their sides in a cool, dark place.

The author of these vagrant paragraphs has made himself conspicuous for some years by actually asking for a three-to-one martini, and now his appearance is greeted from one end of the continent to the other with glad cries of patrons and barkeeps alike as the man who really wants vermouth, a sort of benevolent eccentric and nice to have around. Unsound, maybe actually idiot, but harmless and rather Old World.

Of course, the manufacturers of vermouth (and "manufacturers" is the word since it is not a natural wine) soon caught on to the dry martini and wanted in on the act. They have produced a completely colorless or, as they like to advertise it, white vermouth whose presence in a martini is indistinguishable to the eye and, after the third or fourth drink, to the palate, and, vermouth being far less expensive than gin, a lot of drinkers aren't getting their martinis as dry as they think they are.

Obviously in the face of the overwhelming and universal esteem in which the bone-dry martini is held, it is folly perhaps compounded with subversion to attempt to set up a formula for the proper mixture of gin and vermouth, that Cole Porter discovered to be the Fountain of Youth. Nevertheless, the above-mentioned Bernard De Voto, a man so fearless of consequences that he preaches soil conservation among the cattlemen of Montana, has gone on record to the effect that with a ninety-four-proof gin, the ideal proportion, neither more nor less, is three and seven tenths part of gin to one of dry vermouth. Who shall raise his voice against De Voto is a blasphemer and will be shunned by the elect as unclean and perhaps a Princeton man, but, bartender, make mine exactly three to one.

Nor is the matter of glasses and ice any mere footnote to the classic martini. De Voto cites a purist who ends every formula for any mixed drink whatsoever with "and five hundred pounds of ice." This can only be improved on by making it a long ton. Ice is the essential, ice in gelid masses, plentiful, limitless, and inexhaustible to chill the compounding chalice and individual container. But beyond the natural temperature of frozen water—say, the use of the deep freeze—lies damnation. During prohibition, Jack Bleeck, at whose mention New York newspapermen of the era will stand and uncover, every night before closing his Artists and Writers' speakeasy in Fortieth Street, hard by Helen Reid's *Herald Tribune*, made up his next day's martinis in gallon jars and set them to chill without contact with what he considered the contaminate ice. The resultant depth charge was acceptable to the race of giants—Harry Staton, Geoffrey Parsons, Bill McGeehan, Percy Hammond, and Bill Houghton of that vanished generation—but not to be advised for mere contemporary heroes.

Let therefore the foundations of your hospitality be elegantly plain: a limited number of distinctive hors d'oeuvres with character and flavor, a gleaming array of bottles and decanters bearing the names of nothing but the best, a carafe of branch or witch water, and perhaps bottled soda for Corinthians, a glacial avalanche of ice cubes, and substantial glasses of the finest crystal. And remember that the best things in life are never cheap.

So, when the challenging sentry in a white apron or butler's tailcoat, as the case may be, demands, "What will it be, gents?" the countersign will be, "On the rocks." This takes care of almost everything.

PITTSBURGH:
Hors d'Oeuvres Traffic Club

For many years I have been, almost without reservation, a member of the dissident group of drinkers who take a very dim view of what pass, at many cocktail parties, for hors d'oeuvres: the miserable fish paste and liver paste squirted from tubes onto damp crackers; the dollops of allegedly exotic delicacies from China, Turkey, and South America; the tinned quail eggs that could be used for shrapnel if it weren't forbidden by the Hague Conventions; the miscellaneous fragments of unidentified delicatessen, fried, frizzled, and furnished forth with dabs of whipped cream; and, especially, the pretzel sticks and assorted Oriental nuts and vegetables encased in shellac that are fobbed off as the noblest products of Islands cookery.

On the other hand, I naturally welcome the sight of fresh caviar, *foie gras*, large black olives, and various smoked fish, if they are served in quantities acceptable for human consumption. Pickled walnuts have always exercised a profound charm upon me, too, and I consider an honest slice of hot buttered toast, layered with half a tin of anchovies or sardines, a fine absorbent for hard liquor. (But my feeling has always been that any canapé smaller than two and a half inches square should be given to Towser before the party begins.)

For the epicure who believes hors d'oeuvres were first discovered by a chef in the service of the Borgias, I would like to report the gustatory doings at a party that highlights the annual meetings in Pittsburgh of the Traffic Club. In case you're not acquainted with the latter, it is a confraternity of railroad moguls and steel manufacturers that still retains vestigial traces of the grand manner once so characteristic of broadgauge industry and its accessories of transport and service.

The ultimate reception, which climaxes a three-day Traffic Club convocation, is to be attended by invitation only, and transpires within the august precincts of the Duquesne Club. I attended this exclusive function at the lordly behest of John W. Barriger, president of the Pittsburgh & Lake Erie, a patron of the arts and letters in the grand manner of years gone by, and an authority on the corporate history of American railroad transport. It is seldom, nowadays, that one encounters a railroad president emerging from the library of the Pacific Union, the Chicago Club, or the Union League; but in Mr. Barriger's briefcase, a fine binding by Riviere is as much at home as a weekly audit of the carloadings of his enviably profitable carrier.

The Duquesne Club reception attracts every major railroad executive and every major shipper east of the Missouri River. It is, believe me, no tearoom collation, but a buffet feast of cold roast pheasants, Guaymas shrimps, Kentucky hams, and chafing dishes simmering with terrapin Newburg. It is something that could be evoked only in one of the period novels of Joseph Hergesheimer, who was, of all American writers, the most appreciative of the grand style and the elegant amenities of wealth. Henry VIII and Cardinal Wolsey, so often depicted in poses of fraternal gastronomy, throwing bits of whole roast cows to the dogs under the table, would have been at home at that Traffic Club reception.

As far as the eye could see, starched chefs stood at attention behind ice carvings of majestic dimensions, ready and eager to urge opulent platters of cold smoked salmon upon vice presidents and trust officers. There was sturgeon in slices the size of an old-fashioned treasury note and as thick as a bookmaker's wallet; there was hot and cold Maine lobster variously served with mayonnaise or *sauce verte*, Thermidor or New-burg, and truffled *foie gras* jeweled with Périgord diamonds as big as hens' eggs; there were oysters Rockefeller, oysters *poulette*, and oysters on the half shell, still dripping with Atlantic brine. There were shrimp from the Gulf of Mexico, and from Lower California, in five varieties of sauce. There was any sandwich the human imagination could devise, manufactured from vast mounds of black bread, rich and sour as the odor of a New Orleans delicatessen.

Three-pound tins of fresh caviar were placed at convenient intervals along the groaning board, with soup spoons for self-service. Cold roast capon and pheasant cascaded in slices, reminding me of the buffet aboard the *Queen Mary*. Behind a hundred-foot table, ten active servitors in high white caps carved "thumbits" of smoking roast beef, corned beef, and hot Virginia ham, and presented these on warm rye bread to the element of corporate hearties who regarded oysters and *foie gras* as frivolous. Strategically located bars dispensed nourishing Niagaras of martinis, spring freshets of manhattans, tidal waves of scotch, and mon-soons of bourbon on the rocks.

The reception is underwritten each year by a different group of the more solvent ironmasters of the Pittsburgh region. This year, we flirted with apoplexy as guests of the National Steel Corporation, Wierton Steel. and the Edgewater Steel Company. May fortune light their footsteps they are hosts of rare magnificence. And for any cynic who thinks the world of good living is shot to hell, a glimpse of that Duquesne Club party could effect a conversion as fervent as the one experienced by Saul on the road to Damascus.

CHICAGO:
The Fabulous Pump Room: I

It is fifteen years since this department reported on the most eye-popping of all American restaurants, the Pump Room, in Chicago's Ambassador East Hotel. It is pleasant to be able still to report that although Ernie Byfield, the creator of the Pump Room's stately satisfactions, has been gone from the scene for almost as long, his handiwork has been so enduring that old-time Chicagoans still speak of going over to "Byfield's" for lunch—quite as though the master himself were still at his corner banquette with Helen Hayes or Ethel Barrymore.

Although Chicago never formally recognized it, Byfield's invention of the Pump Room in the middle of the Depression years gave the city a new existence for a class of travelers it had never had since the heyday of Potter Palmer's celebrated hotel, before the turn of the century. In Palmer's spacious days, of course, the mere possibility of seeing Mrs. Palmer provided an excuse for stopping over. She was herself a national institution, and her clothes, jewelry, and carriages gave the hotel a cachet of elegance that was the most enviable sort of advertising. Then, too, gentlemen could be shaved and singed in the Palmer House barbershop, whose floor, inlaid with silver dollars, so outraged Rudyard Kipling that he stayed at fever pitch all the way across the continent until he got to San Francisco. (There, alas, he heard a well-bred young lady remark that her escort of the night before had been "drunk," whereupon he hit the ceiling all over again.)

But by the twenties these heady delights had disappeared from the Chicago scene, and the stopover between trains became a dreariness that could only be ameliorated by spending unconscionable sums of money at Marshall Field's. At night, to be sure, there was the College Inn, a Byfield property and an oasis of relaxed attitudes. But that night spot was not precisely geared to the conservative carriage trade.

Byfield and his associates came by the two Ambassador Hotels up on the Gold Coast in the depths of hard times, and it required a great deal of faith and some shrewd financing to get the deal underway. Few other ho-

teliers or restaurateurs would have selected the moment as propitious for
the inaugural of a costly luxury restaurant with eight-dollar-a-portion
fresh caviar, double magnums of Krug's private *cuvée*, and pheasant *en
plumage* featured on the menu. Then there were the servants in knee
breeches and tailcoats that caused one anguished patron, during the
Pump's early days, to comment in its guest book that there was nothing
wrong with the restaurant that a good revolution wouldn't set to rights.

But Byfield, like Dave Chasen at the other end of the Santa Fe Railroad in Hollywood, had the loyalty of the theatrical profession. Depression
or no Depression, the film industry had to continue; names of the first
magnitude on Broadway and Sunset Boulevard had to travel between
New York and Los Angeles. They all paused, for lunch or longer, in the
Pump Room. It became a social and professional must for any trouper of
consequence to "have lunch with Ernie" on the way through. So universal
did the claims to having lunched with Ernie become that when
Humphrey Bogart knew Byfield was in Europe, he would trap his pretentious contemporaries. "Who'd you see coming east?" he would ask in-
nocently at the "21" bar. The mendacious answer was invariably: "I
lunched with Ernie."

At one time or another, however, everybody of consequence did indeed have lunch with Ernie—or dinner or supper. His booth overflowed
with celebrities. Many lesser folk, of course, had to come to shine in the
reflected glory of Monty Wooley, Ben Hecht, Charlie MacArthur, and
Gregory La Cava.

The Pump Room was photogenic beyond the wildest imaginings of
magazine editors and publicists. The cobalt-blue walls with their chaste
white trim and pillars, waiters in red tailcoats and smallclothes of the
ancien régime, Miss Barrymore's hats, and Mae West's hairdos, with every
dish on fire all the time, made it a photographer's paradise. Byfield, an
old pro in the matter of promotion, saw to it that all reporters were
sluiced and gentled on the cuff. The resulting press was rapturous.

It was not enough for Byfield that his clientele glittered with such
publicized effulgence. He was a perfectionist; the food had to match the
front. Students of gastronomy agree it was Byfield who first devised the
lyric or adjectival menu where the most prosaic entree was described in
a way that made it sound like the ultimate combination of tender comestibles that a grand master of culinary expertise could devise. An astonish-
ing number of these entrees actually lived up to their billing.

Byfield was also the most effective advocate of having everything on
wheels and everything in flames. From time immemorial, of course, joints
of meat had been rolled to the tables of restaurant patrons on cushioned
dollies and covered with silver shelters big enough to serve as doghouses
for St. Bernards. But Byfield put all his food on rolling tables and substi-

tuted mobile open-hearth furnaces for everything from soups to pastry in a way that had hitherto been reserved only for flaming desserts and other exotica.

After the death of Byfield, disbelievers foresaw an end to the reign of glory at the Pump Room on the theory that it was a one-man inspiration and that nobody could be found to maintain it in the grand manner with which Byfield had invested it. They couldn't have been more mistaken. Ernie had trained a successor every bit as durable and congenial as himself in the person of Jimmy Hart, a hotelier with almost as wide an acquaintance in the world of the theater and communications. Although Hart has now followed his one-time partner to whatever rewards are prepared for distinguished hoteliers, the Pump Room continues to be the first restaurant of Chicago and the logical stopping place between the arrival of *The Super Chief* and departure of *The Twentieth Century Limited*.

The Pump Room's king-size martini is still just about the only really plausible cocktail between the St. Regis and the Sheraton-Palace. In its infancy—before it was limited to one to a customer—the cocktail had been the cause of some consternation. Byfield had devised the six-ounce noggin with the idea that, inspired by its noble dimensions and bargain price, the customers would stay on wildly ordering fresh caviar and duckling *à l'orange*. Quite the reverse. The customers would have two or three of these Henry VIII libations, and would then have to be conveyed to a taxi by members of the staff.

All the old Pump Room specials and stand-bys are on the menu and just as magnificent as they were during the benevolent reign of Ernie. The Caesar salad, I believe, cannot be duplicated anywhere. There is an essence of black mushrooms *au Chablis* that would in itself be the making of a lesser establishment. For Westerners heading toward the Atlantic and crazed for seafood, here is the first place they can safely order Maine lobster. As for the giant shrimp flown in daily from Guaymas, Mexico, served with Mexican tartar sauce, it has to be eaten to be believed.

The likeness of Beau Nash, patron of the original eighteenth-century Pump Room in Bath, England, stares at the Chicago customers from behind one of the most ample bars in North America. In my mind's eye, I see Byfield looking over Nash's shoulder in order to count the house. It is usually full to capacity.

THE FABULOUS PUMP ROOM: II

The motif of the Pump Room is mobility. Everything is on wheels. A great deal of it, too, is in flames.

On the least provocation or none at all, Byfield admires to produce fire and smoke. A buff of the wine bins, neither Vulcan nor Prometheus nor even Mayor Fiorello La Guardia was ever consumed with such a passion for blazing dishes. At stated intervals, although nobody has commanded their service, platoons of knee-breeched servitors race around the perimeter of the Pump Room waving sabers on which are skewered flaming cutlets of veal and other inflammable viands in the hope of exciting the frenzied spectators to further gustatory excesses. Approached on the subject of this pyromaniacal display, Byfield once told the author: "The customers seem to like it, and it doesn't hurt the food very much."

In the course of a recent transcontinental Hejira to the Palace in San Francisco, Dwight Fiske, the author, and Charles Clegg contrived to scurry up among them three orders of crabmeat *crêpes louise*, blazing mightily, a roast pheasant afire from stem to stern with cognac, an order of cherries Jubilee, one of peaches *flambées*, a ditto of *crêpes suzettes*, and three beakers of *café diable*, making a grand total of ten table conflagrations, any one of them calculated to strike terror to the heart of a fire commissioner. All that was lacking was Mrs. O'Leary's cow to lend a pyrotechnic panache to the carnival of combustibles.

THE FABULOUS PUMP ROOM: III

In the matter of promotion and the cultivation of a good press, Byfield combined the special talents of such well-known experts as Billy Rose, Dave Chasen, and Dick Maney, Broadway's most emphatic public-relations practitioner. He inspired his staff to such heights of dreamy elegance that the service of a Waldorf salad assumed the nuances of a stage performance by Maurice Barrymore or Salvini the Younger. José Ferrer, a distinguished character actor, admits he makes notes on performances of waiter captains and *sommeliers* in the Pump Room whenever he passes through Chicago.

The function of the Pump Room flunky is not alone the proper service of a meal which may in itself suggest the Great Fire of London destroying St. Paul's. He subtly insinuates, as well, that the only people he is accustomed to serving are from the class that throws away its Lincoln roadsters when the ashtrays are full. Yet the humblest patron, by the mere act of commanding Beef Tenderloin Steak *Sauté au Beurre d'Échalot* with Mushrooms, is ennobled, or at least raised to the status of a Morgan partner. Bank notes of less than $100 denominations are picked up by bar boys between fastidious thumb and finger and carried to the till at arm's length as if contaminated.

THE FABULOUS PUMP ROOM: IV

Byfield was one of the great champions in the cause of caviar, both on general principles and because it seemed eminently suited to the over-all tone and conduct of his restaurants. On one occasion the Amtorg Trading Corporation, outlet for Soviet products in the United States, came by a shipment of beluga eggs which, through some freak of processing, had turned an alarming shade of bronze. There was nothing wrong with the caviar, but buyers weren't interested in bronze caviar.

Byfield heard about this distress merchandise and put in a bid for it at fire-sale prices. Amtorg sold him a long ton of it. (For some obscure Russian reason, caviar comes by the long ton, 2240 pounds.) Byfield labeled it "Rare Imperial Golden Caviar of the Czars," and put it on the menus at the Pump and Buttery at a price equivalent to five dollars a teaspoon. It was sold out in a year.

ALOFT:
TWA's *Royal Ambassador Flight*

About a year ago, a friend of mine flying Air France to Europe was seated next to an uncommonly knowledgeable as well as nosy gentleman, who expressed profound curiosity and deep interest in Air France's cuisine, and the resources of food and wine with which the line sluiced and gentled its passengers. He observed every detail of the culinary operations, the service, and the presentation of food—even the menu design—and he took copious notes on all he saw. He then grilled the attendants for every available bit of intelligence relating to the problems of feeding and wining the customers, and appeared satisfied with his findings.

So professional was his interest that my friend, in the course of a casual conversation, had no difficulty in identifying the man. He was, he admitted easily, a spy for Trans World Airlines, and wanted to see how Air France managed to establish its radiant reputation for high-altitude cuisine of an order as exalted as the level at which it is served. TWA envied Air France its fair repute, he explained, and was going to cut in on a good thing to the best of its abilities. Hence the presence of an expert observer, who was making several round trips from New York to Paris in order to observe the rival operation.

I was interested in TWA's shrewdness in trying to glean the know-how of the competitor, so, a few weeks ago, when my friend prepared to cross the Atlantic via TWA, I asked him for a report on the chow situation. I was also curious to know if the airline had managed to impart any of the Air France expertise to its own intercontinental operations.

He returned stuffed with food like a Christmas goose, leaking vintage wine at the seams. Bearing as proof of the mission's faithful discharge a bedsheet-sized TWA menu from the Royal Ambassador flight, he asserted that Henri Soulé had better look to his laurels. The menu (truly of a dimension to serve as parachute in the event of catastrophe en route) is before me as I write, and it implicitly suggests that a determined gastronome, taking passage to Paris and back, could easily consume sufficient food and drink to equal the money value of his ticket.

Accompanying the report was my informer's sworn assurance that every item on the bill of fare was as represented. There had been no cheating, under the façade of voluptuous phraseology, to hide mediocrity.

There was fresh Malossol caviar in unstinted portions, and a bewilderment of the best French hors d'oeuvre to accompany a choice of cocktails —martinis, manhattans, vodka martinis, old-fashioneds, or gimlets—as many as the customer thought suitable. There was clear turtle soup with sherry, and seven entrees, including Maine lobster Thermidor, fillets of English sole ambassadeur, prime U.S. sirloin steak or chateaubriand, double-thick lamb chops, *canard à l'orange au Grand Marnier,* and a salmi of guinea fowl. There were conventional vegetables and salads; there was a wide assortment of the best French, English, and Italian cheeses, a *bombe glacée,* fruit, and French pastry, all washed down with limitless quantities of Mumm's Cordon Rouge. Also, thoughtfully tucked away where they might not offend the sensibilities of more sophisticated travelers—and obviously for the benefit of returning Americans who couldn't wait to set foot on native soil—were such items as a hamburger special, corned beef on rye, hot dogs, and malted milks.

This account is printed herewith as a public service, and in no way in mitigation of my fixed and unalterable belief that the Wright Brothers' folly will never get off the ground. If, however, one is determined to take chances with gravity, there seems no valid reason that a meal on high shouldn't be an eminently satisfactory one, Air France *or* TWA.

PHILADELPHIA:
Bookbinder's

During the course of a necessary trip to Philadelphia a few weeks past, I stepped, one evening, into a taxi and said, "Bookbinder's."

"Which one?" the driver asked. I had not been in Philadelphia overnight in something like thirty years, and I was taken by surprise. As it was a stormy evening, and I faced the possibility of having to walk home in the absence of available cabs, I said, "The nearer Bookbinder's." Shortly we drew up to a modest premises, in keeping with the traditional Philadelphia façade, on South Fifteenth Street.

This, I discovered, is not the original Bookbinder's. It does, however, possess a valid claim to the name, as no fewer than four members of the Bookbinder family are involved in the operation. At my arrival, all four were on the floor, as testimony of authenticity.

I was reassured by the multiplicity of representatives of the ancestral name, all of whom looked sleek and contented, and as good advertisements for their own seafood as Elsie the Cow is for Borden's whipping cream. When I had suspended my hat and wraprascal on a peg, I prepared to order terrapin Maryland, anticipated by a dozen or so Lynnhavens.

The Bookbinder's in which I found myself is a no-nonsense, plain-as-an-old-shoe dining room, with a long oyster bar behind which three gentlemen were busy shucking bivalves. I took note of checkered tablecloths, honestly patched coarse napkins, and some of the biggest and most effective martinis you'll find on the Eastern Seaboard.

Unhappily, some customers at an adjacent table who were eating heavenly-looking Maine lobster were attired for this sacrament in coy little bibs provided by the management. But this touch did seem to please the patrons, and it did not harm the food.

Unhappily, too, there was no terrapin Maryland. No terrapin at all, in fact.

"We used to have terrapin on the menu once in a while," I was told by the nearest Bookbinder when I complained of this outrage, "but they really weren't in great demand. They were a chore for the kitchen to cut up, and the customers ate the Maryland part but not the turtle, so we finally gave it up."

I could get terrapin, he thought, in a number of private homes, and at insurance-company annual dinners, but that was no help to a stranger on the town. I therefore turned my attention to the things available on an entirely ample and satisfactory menu, one that fairly crawled with crustaceans, fit to addle the wits of a seafood-starved Nevadan.

The Lynnhavens, I found, were Chincoteagues, and so good that a mere dozen were insufficient; another twelve arrived practically with the speed of light. The snapper soup was, by itself, worth the price of admission. I went on, in my devotional research, to broiled shad, which was then in season and was one of the more urgent excuses for my being in the East at all.

Bookbinder's doesn't scorn to serve a wide variety of steaks and chops, which looked superlative as they passed my table, brought in by motherly-type waitresses who stood by and watched until the patrons got to their victuals, to see that all was satisfactory. I gathered, though, that the big seller was Maine lobster which came chicken, small, medium, jumbo, in stew, Newburg, and Thermidor, and as lobster Coleman, stuffed with lump crab meat, a dollar extra. If the lobster population of the seven seas is declining at an alarming rate, as oceanographers and students of such matters darkly assure us, Bookbinder's is one of the reasons for their disappearance.

WASHINGTON:
Harvey's

Followers of these columns may recall that approximately a twelvemonth back (May 1964) I reported my disappointment at the disappearance of the terrapin dishes from the otherwise ample menu at Bookbinder's, on South Fifteenth Street in Philadelphia. These dishes were long a distinguishing feature and principal glory of Tidewater cuisine, not only in Philadelphia but also in Baltimore and Washington. The management at Bookbinder's explained to me that when in recent times terrapin Maryland had appeared on the menu, "the customers ate the Maryland part but not the turtle" and that, anyway, it was almost impossible to get the skilled labor necessary for skinning and boning the turtles. A short time back, however, my professional occasions took me to Washington, where my search for the errant terrapin was more amply rewarded.

In the years immediately before and during World War II, the affairs of my employer, the *New York Herald Tribune*, not infrequently brought me to the Federal City. I cherish warm recollections of long, leisurely Sunday afternoons spent in the upstairs rooms of Harvey's putting away terrapin stew and Bollinger in double bottles in a manner that would be imprudent if undertaken today. From a window table in the third-floor restaurant at Harvey's we were able to secure an uninterrupted view all the way to the kitchen door. Time was of no consequence on Sunday afternoon, and the service was the reverse of expeditious. It became a ritual with my companion at table of those days and me that between the moment the ancient servitor appeared with our entree, at the far end of the room, and the time it was served at our table we consumed, without effort or haste, a fifth of Mme. Bollinger's best. The halfway mark was invariably achieved as the venerable waiter passed the open grill midway down the course, and the last drop was poured as he started to ladle the world's most savory of all stews onto our plates. It was a pleasant and rewarding ritual, and, of course, there was more Bollinger available.*

* The present laws of Washington do not permit the serving of champagne on Sunday. The customer will have to be content with a chilled white wine of his choosing on the Sabbath.

The founding father of Harvey's—whose likeness, limned by the great cartoonist Thomas Nast, adorns the menu to this day—opened his Oyster Saloon in what had previously been a blacksmith shop, back in 1858. By the time the Civil War was under way, the saloon had become so institutional and its status so revered by both North and South that Harvey's fleet of oyster boats was permitted to penetrate both the Union and Confederate blockades when they happened to be established in the waters where the management planted its shellfish.

In 1866, when hostilities had subsided in a measure and the partisans of the North and South returned to the serious business of eating and drinking, George Harvey removed to larger premises at Eleventh Street and Pennsylvania Avenue. There he could accommodate a fantastic patronage of politicians, statesmen, and international celebrities drawn by the fame of his diamondback terrapin stew and Harvey's famous Musty Ale. Washington was then a world capital where no political business could be undertaken or objective achieved without the ritual of gastronomy and its accompanying consumption of a wide variety of drinks. The precedent had been set by none other than the by now almost godlike Daniel Webster. He had so wined and dined the British emissary Lord Ashburton, in negotiating the terms of the Webster-Ashburton Treaty in 1842, that an entire school of culinary diplomacy had come into being. Terrapin had figured largely in Webster's menus, along with Maine lobster, South Carolina ricebirds, canvasback, and Chesapeake Bay crab meat, and it remained the stuff and substance of political entertainment all through the nineteenth century. Samuel Ward, the greatest lobbyist of them all, relied in large measure on terrapin Maryland to gentle legislators and to smooth a pathway for the projects of his clients. Through such elevated agencies as these, terrapin passed into the folklore of American politics as no other single item of entertainment has ever been able to do.

A few weeks back, in company with John H. White, Jr., the distinguished Curator of Land Transportation at the Smithsonian Institution, I revisited Harvey's after a lapse of fully twenty years. By good fortune we were able to obtain the third-floor corner table I had occupied in the days when Evalyn McLean was the leading hostess of the Washington scene and Roosevelt II was in power.

It is pleasant to be able to report that, with one exception, no detail of the Harvey routine was missing, and that continuity with the well-upholstered past was established without a flaw. The exception is the wine list, where not only is no Bollinger available but almost nothing else in the way of a champagne suitable for the gastronomic sacrament of terrapin Maryland.

The menu,.however, is a noble one, and terrapin Maryland is on it as big as life. Nor is it exorbitantly priced at $4.50 a liberal portion, magnificently rich and exotic in a generously sherried Maryland sauce that would have enchanted Daniel Webster himself if it had been possible to evoke his urbane spirit.

The excellences of Harvey's are by no means exhausted with the terrapin department. We returned the next day for a luncheon that included two dozen Gardiners Island oysters and a dish of baked Alaska crab meat, both of which confirmed the altogether elevated implications of the evening before. The menu is a noble one in the great American seafood tradition, studded with crab gumbo New Orleans style, Harvey's special clam chowder, Maryland crab cakes, Florida pompano, and Chesapeake Bay rockfish. Unable to sample all these wonderments and already straining at the gussets of our Henry Poole trousers, we conscientiously conned the dishes as they passed by en route to adjacent tables, and the report must be that they all looked heavenly.

Harvey's has a special dessert menu, but we had no capacity for frivolities when confronted with such an ample array of seafoods. The service has been accelerated a bit since 1940, but not to an intolerable degree. It does not suggest anything but affluent leisure to enjoy what is one of the really notable bills of fare of the continent.

The menu not inappropriately—indeed, rather gracefully—suggests that in dining at Harvey's you are becoming a part of history. It is a sentiment I subscribe to with much enthusiasm.

LASALLE STREET STATION:
Stylish Chaos

In the lifetime of the late Ernie Byfield, impresario of the Pump Room in the Ambassador Hotel and a dedicated collector of theatrical celebrities, *The Twentieth Century Limited* was regarded by many starring names of Broadway and Hollywood as a sort of extension of the Pump Room's ineffable gastronomy, just as *The Super Chief* was regarded as an extension of Dave Chasen's legendary resort. Iced caviar with Byfield's compliments would be consigned to Helen Hayes or Ronald Coleman, care of the dining-car steward, or James Cagney would find a magnum of Dom Pérignon in his room when he stepped aboard at LaSalle Street. Since these fringe benefits of Byfield's hospitality invariably arrived in the charge of Pump Room footmen whose silk stockings, silver-buckled pumps, satin knee breeches, and gold-frogged liveries didn't make them precisely anonymous, everybody benefited from the ensuing *réclame*.

On at least one occasion, the Pump Room's effulgence, when translated to the train shed of LaSalle Street, engendered a contretemps of musical-comedy dimensions. It was after Byfield's death, and the affairs of the restaurant and the extension of its personality to departing trains and planes was being maintained in the bravura tradition by James Hart. The author of this monograph and his partner, Charles Clegg, were spotted on an adjacent track at the LaSalle depot on their own private car, the *Virginia City*, scheduled to depart at the end of a less exalted consist than *The Century* which, neither then nor at any other time, accepted special equipment. Hart had thoughtfully dispatched a jeroboam of Perrier-Jouet to us in the care of a more than usually ornate delegation which included a waiter captain in a morning coat, two Pump Room footmen in the usual knee breeches and fourragères, and, to lend additional tone to the pageantry, a colored chauffeur in bright lavender greatcoat and top hat with a cockade.

None of the emissaries knew about private cars. They had been told to deliver the wine "to Mr. Clegg's and Mr. Beebe's car," which suggested to them its delivery to their space on *The Century*, a train with which they were familiar and where they had often completed similar missions. Told at the train gate that no such passengers were listed or expected, the Ambassador's bravos had said loudly that they knew better, they had their orders and were going on board. Our first intimation of trouble was what appeared to be an uncommonly dressy mob scene on the platform intervening between the *Virginia City* and *The Century*. Fisticuffs were being exchanged between railroad police, porters, brakemen, a large Negro in ornate attire, and the decorative flunkies. In the middle of the turmoil, like a float in a Mardi Gras riot, there rose and fell perilously a vast bottle of vintage wine in a silver ice bucket. It was a scene of indescribably stylish chaos. It also fulfilled the fondest illusions of the onlookers about the conduct of life among poeple who owned private railway cars. When order was finally restored and the misunderstanding explained to everybody's satisfaction, *The Century* pulled out, on time, but with its staff visibly shaken.

COLORADO:
Central City

I have just returned from an unusually refreshing experience in the Colorado Rockies.

While this brief chronicle of the enchantments of Central City's opera season won't appear until after the last curtain has been rung down on this year's production of *The Girl of the Golden West*, it might be well if readers tied a piece of string around their fingers to remind them of its possibilities next year.

Other ghost towns may make their claims: Virginia City, Nevada, which is where I live, maintains it is "The Liveliest Ghost Town of Them All." The statement is based on the presence of one saloon for every twenty inhabitants, and other recreational facilities in proportion. Panamint City, in the remote Panamint Mountains of California, overlooking Death Valley, is probably the most inaccessible ghost town. Aspen, Colorado, with its music festivals, learned seminars, and kindred doings, may well be the most cultural of ghost towns. But Central City is far and away the most stylish.

It is the only one of the scores of former mining communities, lost in the nearly impenetrable mountains and deserts from Bodie to the Coeur d'Alene and from Alder Gulch to Tombstone, which is entirely accustomed to formal evening attire, chauffeur-driven Rolls-Royces, liveried house servants, champagne in double magnums, cocktail parties in terraced gardens, and grand opera sung by name artists from the Metropolitan. All this activity is seasonal, to be sure, but the summer months find society reporters from the Denver papers in permanent residence in Central City's Eureka Street, and culture finds its apotheosis on first nights that would do credit to Paris or New York.

Central City's revived opera season has been going full blast since the thirties when a small group of historic-minded and well-heeled Denverites rediscovered the once-magnificent and still structurally substantial opera house which, in the seventies, had been one of the most celebrated music halls west of the Missouri. Being descendants of Colorado pioneers, and thus possessed of a strong streak of sentimentality and the means to indulge it, these good folk thought it would be fun to rebuild Central's opera house, restore the adjacent Teller House, an uncommonly well-preserved hostel, import a Broadway cast that included Lillian Gish and stage designer Robert Edmond Jones, and stage for one night's performance the most lavish production of *Camille* ever imagined. Some idea of the expense that went to the gratification of this whim can be gleaned from the fact that a descendant of one of Central's silver nabobs ponied up $250,000 for just one of the stage sets. His name, for the greater glory of Colorado, was Delos Chappelle.

Well, inevitably, the thing got out of hand. The metropolitan press all over the world gave the project space, and, in addition to the five hundred hand-picked guests who had been invited for the one scheduled performance, the opera backers found themselves besieged with entreaties, all accompanied by liberal sums of money, to prolong the one-night run to a week, two weeks, and, finally, for the entire six weeks' summer season.

It was a fantastic success from every aspect—commercial, social, professional, and cultural. Central City became as well known a newspaper dateline as it had been in the seventies when the Boston Mine and the Coeur d'Alene were making millionaires overnight. The whole thing passed in a twinkling from a richly upholstered whim into the realm of public asset and benevolence, and the opera is now jointly administered by members of the Central City Opera Association, the University of Denver, and the State of Colorado. Every summer, for seasons varying from six to eight weeks, it presents one or two classic operas, with stars from the Metropolitan, and visitors from all over the world. *The Ballad of Baby Doe*, a Colorado regional saga translated into operatic form, made its debut there a few seasons back, and promptly moved to New York and world renown. Central City has, in short, become big business, and now functions under the public-spirited administration of Frank Ricketson, who, in other life, is an important figure in film distribution and theater ownership in the West.

The Rolls-Royces, footmen, evening dress, orchid corsages, and names that make news are in no way foreign or exotic in the setting of Central's abrupt and precipitous Eureka Street, for in its golden noontide of mining, it was one of the richest bonanzas of all. The pioneers showered stage favorites with gold double eagles and commanded Niagaras of champagne in the Teller House bar: they were of a piece with Denver and Colorado Springs socialites who now maintain elaborately rebuilt cottages on the surrounding mountainsides, just to entertain for a few weeks every year.

Each year, after opening night, there is a ball in the Teller House's elegant ballroom suite. This year it was suspended for an unbelievably opulent private supper party for the two hundred mink-and-monocled guests of Miss Elinor Weckbaugh, a Denverite who enjoys doing things in a big, handsome manner. The guest of honor was an equally well-placed first citizen who had been born just two blocks up Eureka Street over eighty years ago. The iron foundry where Fred McFarlan made his first million is still there, as a tourist attraction of the first chop. Fred took in his first gold piece sharpening tools and making heavy machinery for the deep mines of Central; today, when any of the bigger bankers in Denver want to borrow the price of a new forty-story skyscraper, they go to Fred, who, in summer, still lives across from the foundry, in the Victorian cottage in which he was born.

It was the sort of social, economic, and sentimental setup which I think could happen today only in Denver: a cheerful homecoming for many old-timers, orchestrated by Puccini, upholstered in orchids and black-pearl evening studs, and perfumed with Dom Pérignon and the most costly of Coty's products. And, of course, there was the wonderful smell of money, in simply staggering abundance.

NEW ORLEANS:
Antoine's

An old-time painting, the reproduction of which appears on all the menus of the restaurant which has come to be the symbol of New Orleans' good way of life, depicts a dinner party at Antoine's in the period *circa* 1880. In it two gentlemen in evening tailcoats are toasting each other's health and good fortune in somewhat contrived poses, while in the background their wives smile at each other with serene benevolence. Everyone is happy, confirmed in the assurance that God is in His gastronomically abundant heaven and that there will be just the right amount of amontillado in the green-turtle soup.

The founding father of what is today the world's best-known restaurant dynasty was Antoine Alciatore. He came from Marseilles in 1839 and in the following year was established in a city which even then attracted well-heeled tourists with Continental tastes in food and wine. In his footsteps there followed his son Jules, who died in 1934. The third generation, represented by Roy, took over the family tradition with a success which today accounts for scores of imitators, hundreds of recipe counterfeiters, and thousands of customers over the world who regard St. Louis Street with the veneration artists reserve for the Louvre. Each of the Alciatores added to the prestige of the establishment. Each added dishes to its menu and resources to its bank account, and, as a family enterprise, it rates with the Mellons, Morgans, Whitneys, and Astors.

As a result of its pre-eminence, Antoine's is the standard by which all competition is judged. Casual bar conversationalists will tell you that the Oysters Bienville at Commander's Palace knock the spots off the Oysters Rockefeller at Antoine's, or that the shrimp Louisiane at the Count Arnaud's is a cut above anything the chef at Alciatore's can run up. "The volume of business at Antoine's!" you will be told. "They just can't give every order its proper individual attention with all those customers. You ought to try French Gaston's [or Henri's, François' or Marcel's]. He has only ten customers at a time."

A discerning diner once remarked to the author, over one of Antoine's incomparable squabs *paradis*, that it might be better if Antoine's were situated in some city where there weren't so many rivals by which to measure the standards at Alciatore's. Alciatore, who himself was present, replied simply that without the competition Antoine's wouldn't be so good.

The real miracle of Antoine's is that it is as good as it is, which is entirely excellent.

The contemporary fame of Antoine's derives mainly from five preparations which are specialties of the house: *huîtres en coquille à la* Rockefeller, orange *brûlot, pommes soufflées, pompano en papillote*, and *café brûlot*. There are many and various other wonderments and delights on the menu, more substantial and sophisticated in the gourmet's lexicon: *bisque d'écrevisses cardinal, filet de boeuf marchand de vin, bouillabaisse à la Marseillaise, gombo Créole, pigeonneaux royaux au sauce paradis*, buster crabs maître d'hôtel. Antoine's serves eggs in more than two hundred styles. Its *filet de boeuf Robespierre en casserole* is a legend among table *aficionados* throughout the known world. The *langouste* Thermidor and *pompano amandine* are celestial. But Antoine's stands or falls on its baked Oysters Rockefeller, its fresh Gulf pompano prepared in a paper poke, its balloon potatoes, burned orange liqueur, and flaming coffee, the last of which moved the late Bob Davis, incomparable globetrotting reporter of the old *New York Sun*, to hail it as the "quintessence of hell's best, brewed in the pit where sinners take their vows and declare that death hath no sting and the grave no victory."

Although the *pommes soufflées* at Antoine's are vastly admired by the customers and form a conversational topic for months after a visit to St. Louis Street, at times the management has wished they had never served them. Back in 1837, Antoine Alciatore was chef at the Hôtel de Noailles in Marseilles, and a close friend was the great Collinet who was practicing at St. Germain-en-Laye. One day, as Collinet later confided to Antoine, he was preparing a command dinner for King Louis Philippe. Collinet had already put the French-fried potatoes in the deep fat when he was horrified to learn that the King was to be late. Collinet mused on the conduct of the great Vatel, who had stabbed himself mortally in parallel circumstances at Blois some centuries before. Dismissing this pleasantly morbid reverie, he did what any housewife would do: took the potatoes out of the fat and set them by to wait. After they had cooled awhile, the King arrived and the chef hastily dumped the potatoes back into the deep fat which was appreciably hotter by this time. To his amazement and delight they puffed up to incredible dimensions and emerged to be served as what are known today as soufflé potatoes.

With Collinet's secret in his breast, Antoine came to New Orleans and started serving the airy *pommes soufflées*, and immediately had cause to regret it: there wasn't a housewife who encountered them without demanding how to make them. (It actually takes two kettles of deep fat at different temperatures and considerable know-how to evolve the dish.) First Antoine and then his son Jules were driven crazy by their importunate patrons. When it became more than human nature could endure, Jules sometimes appeared at a table with a miniature bellows and told the customers that every souffléed pomme was individually blown up with its aid.

The ladies said, "My, can you imagine!" and went home to attempt impossible things in the kitchen.

Oysters Rockefeller were first devised by Jules Alciatore in the latter years of the nineteenth century and, because of their rich sauce, named for the multimillionaire who was at that time first attracting national attention. The house of Alciatore maintains that the recipe is a profound secret. Taking a leaf from the cookbook of Frederick of the Tour d'Argent in Paris, who assigned a number to every serving of pressed duck, Antoine's numbers each order of oysters Rockefeller.

It has been widely imitated and shamelessly so, since it is unquestionably the moral property of the house of Alciatore, but the writer believes that it doesn't merit all the fanfare it has received, and that Oysters Bienville, another New Orleans favorite, or Oysters Kirkpatrick, invented in the kitchens of the Palace Hotel in San Francisco, are superior. The Rockefeller version, however, has a fantastic following.

The fish delicacy *pompano en papillote* is something else again and very special. Jules Alciatore dreamed it up at the turn of the century on the occasion of a dinner in honor of Alberto Santo-Dumont, the balloonist.

Requested by the dinner committee to produce some dish in the shape of a balloon, he recalled that many years before, his father, also an amateur balloonist, had created a fish dish cooked in a paper bag, and had christened it for the Montgolfier brothers who had invented the balloon back in 1783.

Since very few of the customers nowadays are conversant with the great names of ballooning, the pompano appears on the menu realistically listed as cooked in a paper poke. This toothsome fancy is something nobody should miss.

A fillet of the delicate Southern-water fish or entire small pompano is inserted into a greased paper poke, together with a rich sauce of white wine, chopped crab meat, diced shrimp, egg yolks, onions, thyme, butter, and fish stock. The whole business is cooked until the oiled paper turns a deep brown, and is served, at Antoine's, with a superior Chablis or a Meursault. When prepared for President Franklin Roosevelt, champagne was substituted for the white wine in cooking, and the guest of honor found it altogether admirable.

Café brûlot diabolique is one of those flaming arrangements dear to the hearts of amateurs and fancy diners alike, since it requires special apparatus and involved ritual. Cloves, lemon peel, and sugar are placed in a special silver chafing bowl, and a quantity of the best cognac ignited in a substantial silver ladle. The flaming spirit is poured over the contents of the bowl, slowly, until the sugar is dissolved, and strong after-dinner coffee is added until the flames subside. At Antoine's this pleasing little ceremony is accompanied by a dimming of all overhead lights.

A classic on the Antoine menu since the founding of the house is *filet de boeuf Robespierre*, and an interesting story concerns its origin. The first Alciatore, the founding Antoine's father, had been a well-to-do wool merchant in France during the days of the Terror. Among other dark and bloody interludes, he had witnessed the death on the guillotine of the bloodiest tyrant of them all, Robespierre. Young Antoine was familiar with the story from his father's lips. When, as a boy of fifteen, he was apprenticed to the proprietor of the Hôtel de Noailles at Marseilles, he found himself—in the momentary absence of the chef—required to prepare a meal for the great Marquis de Talleyrand. All France knew that Talleyrand ate his beef heavily spiced and blood-rare.

The apprentice outdid himself: the *filet* and the fire had only the merest bowing acquaintance before it was served, superbly seasoned, and red as a Turner sunset. The great man put it away with evident satisfaction, and then asked to have the chef presented. It was a big moment for the boy apprentice when Talleyrand inquired grandly what he called his wonderful beef dish.

Antoine recalled Robespierre on the scaffold, and had the perfect answer: "*Filet Robespierre,* sire!" and Robespierre it has been ever since.

One of the first of the very great to be dined into a coma at Antoine's was Henry Clay. The evening previous he had dined off solid-gold plate amidst the aristocracy of the time at the St. Louis Hotel, and Clay had remarked that there, once and for all, he had seen the rarest and tasted the best. At Antoine's, however, when the dessert was served, the statesman threw up his hands, and, in the voice that had rolled with that of Webster through the halls of Congress, cried, "Truly marvelous! Where did the man acquire his art?"

"I have at last found in America a truly great restaurant," Prince Louis Ferdinand of Hohenzollern said of Antoine's.

"What Jules can do to oysters and fish is what angels must do to them in heaven," deposed Irvin Cobb.

The last time the reporter broke Antoine's beautiful, hot, feathery French bread with Mr. Roy, the snack began with bisque of *écrevisses cardinal,* a wonderment in itself worth a transcontinental pilgrimage; *filet* of trout *amandine* with soufflé potatoes; *tournedos béarnaise* with green beans in butter; a mixed green salad; baked Alaska with the reporter's name touchingly inscribed in the meringue on a ribbon supported by two floating doves; and *café brûlot*. There was a dry sack with the bisque, one of Frank Schoonmaker's Pouilly Fuissés '45 with the trout; a Clos de Vougeot 1943 from the bottling of the *Chevaliers du Tastevin*, of which both the host and his guest are members, with the *tournedos;* and, toward the end, Bollinger brut champagne and Bellows Trésor de Famille Armagnac.

At the conclusion of this simple collation, the reporter was groping for his hat among the hundreds that had arrived since cocktails near the St. Louis Street door.

"Try and get your own," pleaded Mr. Roy. "We have had to declare a liability limit of fifteen dollars on men's hats, and I often find myself astounded by the uniform price paid for their hats by our customers. Nobody ever puts in a claim for a hat costing less than fifteen dollars. It's most remarkable."

NEW ORLEANS:
Brennan's

When the late Owen Brennan—founder of the fortunes of the House of Brennan, in the Rue Royale, in New Orleans—first undertook to promote and popularize breakfast in a public restaurant, his friends, of whom there were many, shook their heads and confidently looked forward either to Brennan's bankruptcy or to a profound and immediate change of gastronomic heart. This was considered a mild view when his friends found that the menu would include a prescribed gin fizz, a claret, a champagne, fruit in brandy, and a dessert flamed in kirsch and strawberry liqueur, in addition to such robust matters as broiled pompano, hot French bread, lamb chops with *béarnaise* sauce, exotically shirred eggs, and *café diable*.

Even in New Orleans, a town where time means nothing and a great tradition of leisurely gastronomy obtains, this sort of thing was flying in the face of Battle Creek—where processed butcher's paper is widely packaged as breakfast food—not to mention the defying of an entire generation of Americans who have been conditioned, by means of one of the greatest national swindles of all time, to a breakfast of orange juice and Melba toast.

Brennan was goaded into prandial rashness when a lady novelist of some local fame had celebrated a rival restaurant in a novel called *Dinner at Antoine's*. Friends, grousing with Owen at this invidious partiality, came up with the alliterative alternative of "Breakfast at Brennan's." The founding Brennan promptly ran up a collation that would have assured him of the patronage of Henry VIII, and began advertising it as "an old New Orleans tradition dating from the great days of the Creoles," although the ink wasn't dry on the menus.

Brennan said that if nobody would eat his breakfasts, he damned well would himself—and promptly had his portrait painted opening a bottle of the best champagne. The portrait was prophetic, and it hangs today in a place of honor in a new and enlarged Brennan's, much of whose fame, fortune, and felicitous repute derive from Owen's stewpot vision of what the morning of a civilized man should be devoted to. Under its benevo-

lent regard, champagne corks mutter decorously of a Sunday morning—
and on weekdays, too—in an overture to a recurrent symphony of shrimp
remoulade and *café brûlot* that is making Owen's heirs and assigns rich.

New Orleans itself is partial to old traditions and was quick to recognize
that venerable antiquity can be established when the right man meets
the right moment in history. Today, to hear the customers talk, you'd
think this sort of thing had been going on since the days when Bienville was royal governor.

The celebrity of breakfast at Brennan's—not to mention luncheon, dinner, and supper—soon began to bulge the walls of the original premises
on Bourbon Street, and Ella Brennan, Owen's sister, who took over after
his untimely death, moved to the present address, 417 Rue Royale. Here
Ella Brennan, whose married name is Mrs. Paul Martin, with her sister
Adelaide, brother Richard, nephew Owen, Jr., and an assortment of other
relatives and in-laws to bewilder a genealogist, has set up a New Orleans
institution of such radiant dimensions that celebrities in its uncommonly
handsome patio are a dime a dozen, and the customers overflow onto
the sidewalk during the tourist season, which is all year.

What Ella Brennan and her associated family have brought to the
façade of New Orleans gastronomy is an absolute, all-out, and overwhelming dedication to perfectionism. The words are not idly used. The
writer has scant respect for the language of transcendent idealism to
describe a poor-boy sandwich or the frying of pork chops. The menu
jargon of radiant superlatives, evolved by the late Ernie Byfield—wherein
every grain of caviar was fertilized by supernal sturgeon, and every leaf
of lettuce grown and nurtured to educated maturity by the rays of a
benevolent Kentucky sun—has no place in the honest, down-to-earth
effort the Brennans make, and make continually, in the hope of approximating perfection.

"The food in the world's worst cat's-meat shop can be glorified with
poetry on the menu and still be cat's meat," says Ella. "It's the dish itself,
when it arrives at the table—its appearance, composition, the perfection
of its ingredients and preparation—that tells the story. I want our waiters
to be cheerful. I want the whole façade and being of Brennan's to be a
place where people have a happy time and go away with golden memories. The food, of course, is the basic ingredient. We're in the restaurant
business, but there are satisfactions that transcend the sauce remoulade.
We want eating at Brennan's to be an experience, something to remember."

Apparently a good many other people do, too. The list of regulars at
Brennan's is studded with local celebrities and national names as well,
representing a port of call with equivalents elsewhere in the land at
Chasen's, the Pump Room, and Soulé's.

More than most cities famous for their regional gastronomy, New Orleans represents a sort of mother lode for recipe prospectors. The long-established celebrity of Creole cuisine, and the mystery which lends fragrance to the mere word "gumbo" have a lot to do with it. Pilgrims to Brennan's shrine of pompano and *crêpes* Fitzgerald demand recipes in wholesale lots, and the management is happy to oblige. If it wonders mentally what treasures may be confected in their dimensions on the banks of the Wabash and in deepest Iowa, the management never begrudges an enthusiastic customer the directions from which to build his own crayfish bisque or chicken Pontalba.

NEW ORLEANS:
Commander's Palace

The transition from French Quarter restaurants such as Antoine's and
Arnaud's to Commander's Palace, an establishment which in the estima-
tion of the writer is, in some aspects, possessed of an even superior cuisine,
is at once geographic and social, but it is not spiritual. The restaurants
of the Vieux Carré are frankly a superlative tourist attraction. Many distinguished New Orleans people go there occasionally, and some, like
Dorothy Dix, have been accustomed to eating at Antoine's, Arnaud's, or
Galatoire's with regularity, but in the main their clientele derives from
out of town.

Commander's Palace, a favorite of the late Lyle Saxon, is located
across Canal Street in what is expansively now known as the Garden
District but what a century or so ago was called "the American Quarter,"
first populated by the newly arrived Yankee inheritors after Napoleon
sold the Creoles out. A large, rambling, white-painted mansion, with a
tower at the corner, which dominates Washington Avenue, Commander's
is a comfortable restaurant of ample dimensions, at once expensive, beautifully managed, and tradition-conscious. It has to be, because the vast
majority of its patrons at either lunch or dinner are New Orleans residents and Louisiana taxpayers, who know at a sniff if the gumbo z'herbes
contains the correct seasoning of sage and borage, and if the redfish is
properly impregnated with bay.

The proprietor of Commander's Palace, which was named not for any
naval functionary but for Emil Commander who built it in 1880, is Frank
Moran, as serious-minded a gustatory disciplinarian as ever burned a
pinch of chervil at the altar of Brillat-Savarin or Escoffier. An American-
born citizen of Mexican parentage with an Irish name running a Creole
restaurant in the American quarter of a French-Spanish town doesn't as-
tonish New Orleans. Rather, folk seem to consider it a tribute to the cos-
mopolitanism of the community.

Commander's menu boasts all the conventional Creole specialties: gum-
bos, bisques, pompano, and the wonderful fresh French bread which is

an almost universal glory of New Orleans eating places, and, in addition —and the addition is a matter of vast gastronomic import—Commander's Palace is the acknowledged home of the soft-shell turtle stew. It is the wonder and glory of Creole gastronomy.

This wonderment of the senses may be encountered elsewhere, for all we know, but nowhere does it partake of the almost transcendental qualities of Commander's. It is a dish that has to be experienced to be believed. The meat of the soft-shell turtle, not to be confused with the terrapin, comes from a large deep-sea turtle encountered in the Gulf of Mexico and its adjacent waters. Stew made from its meat has fewer small bones and pieces of shell than terrapin, and is ambrosia when encountered at Commander's.

Unfortunately, the turtle from which this ambrosial ragout is confected is not always available and, like buster crabs, another Louisiana specialty, is seasonal in appearance. Buster crabs are not a separate type of crab, merely the conventional soft-shell variety, but endowed with buster estate at a certain stage in their development, just after they have shed their old shell, when the newly grown shell is altogether edible and delicious. Commander's has busters, too.

No greater tribute to the truly humane and civilized attitude toward its business on the part of the management can be cited than the occasion of a fire, a few years ago, which threatened the premises. When the kitchen burst into flames, did the management concern itself for the safety of the patrons, for the rare works of art which adorned the walls, for the cash register, or even the priceless *filets* of beef in the storage rooms? In a word, no. With one concerted cry of "Save the bar!" the entire staff rallied to cover this spendid specimen of mahogany craftsmanship with wet towels, carpets, and protective devices of every sort until the *pompiers* should arrive with more effective measures. The ancient bar was saved and to this day stands as a memorial to the selfless devotion of the cooks and waiters, as well as being one of the noblest agencies of human restoration in the entire Deep South.

High Iron

But most of all, the American traveler aboard the cars was delighted by the locomotive engines that drew the whole glittering train brigade, where the engineer sat on the right-hand side, godlike and remote as an earl, his hand and will dominating the most beautiful and compelling machine ever devised by man.

"WAVING AT TRAINS . . ."

Waving at trains is almost as purely American as carrying umbrellas is English.

WHEN BEAUTY RODE THE RAILS

It is no accident of circumstance that the most beautiful devisings and artifacts in the American record have all been associated with motion and movement, the transport of things and people all going somewhere else. In their final aspects and fullest development, they might be incredibly debased by the putrescences of progress and the indignities of improvement, but in their original concept all agencies of travel and transport, even aircraft as represented by the free balloon, came trailing clouds of beauty and wonderment to the human spirit.

The native genius of Americans was seen in its most radiant aspect when it was creating the clipper ship, the floating palaces of the Mississippi and other inland waters, the Concord coach of fragrant immortality, and the first automobiles, those miracles of style, structure, and audacity that were the glory of Duesenberg, Mercer, Stutz, Packard, Pierce-Arrow, and Olds before the world of automation grew gray from the breath of the assembly line.

The first concern of the emergent railroad business when it was born in the thirties was with the basic factualities of transport and the mere fundamental task of transporting goods and people from here to there. To build cars and engines that worked and a permanent way to accommodate their passage with what expedition and safety might be devised occupied the imagination and energies of the first railroad engineers, financiers, and operating personnel. The locomotive engines were utilitarian; the cars they drew through an awe-struck countryside were equally practical.

But in a very few years the whole business of railroads began to be invested with style and character. Primarily the steam cars were in direct competition with the steamboats that plied the coastal and inland waters, and the floating palaces of the Mississippi, the Ohio, and the Atlantic sea lanes had nothing if not style. They were ornate and luxurious to a degree beyond the experience of any but the well-to-do classes until their coming, and the railroads had to meet the competition of gorgeous *décors*, comfortable privacy, an abundance of food and drink, a knowledgeable personnel, and convenient connections.

Yankee ingenuity was quick to solve the operational problems of railroading, and when it turned its hand to creating luxury and, as it were, painting the lily of transportation, it did it with a magnificence that soon became legendary.

From the beginning, railroad travel was an adventure in fantasy. Travelers boarded the cars and, at the end of their journey, were set down in storybook settings—Grecian temples, Moorish arches, French châteaux, the tombs of Egyptian dynasts, in Turkish mosques, Palladian porticoes, Gothic castles, and Italian *palazzi*, all of them representing nineteenth-century vogues in architecture, décor, and letters translated into railroad depots.

One has only to contemplate the old Dearborn Street depot in Chicago, which closely resembled the vaulted chambers of a first-class *hammam*, or the Boston & Maine station at Salem, Massachusetts, which might appropriately have been the castle of a Yankee Dracula, to know that railroad travel, until the age of glass bricks and chromium tubing, was an adventure that had its inception among minarets, crenelated turrets, and Doric columns of purest romance.

Passengers rode in cars that were patently devised for holiday occasions, brightly painted in the liveries of the carriage-building tradition from which they derived, scrolled and fretted with lettering in gilded script and, in the early stages of the game, with their sidewalls bearing amusing and instructive works of art, paintings depicting landscapes and points of interest along the route, wild animals, and scenes of domestic husbandry.

Aboard the cars and in the toyland depots at which they paused, characters out of fairyland ministered to the travelers' wants, or, in premonitions of Madison Avenue, stimulated needs he had not previously recognized. There were vendors of popular periodicals and paperback novels, the ice-water boy whose name on one railroad was Thomas Alva Edison, the chocolate and hard-candy seller who reached his apotheosis on the railroads of New England where he sold miniature red-and-green railroad lanterns filled with checkerberry drops. In the Deep South, Negro-mammy types pressed hot breads on passengers through the car windows, and, in an uninhibited age, members of the train crew, including conductors, did a brisk business in fireman's suspenders, pictorial views of the passing landscape, and, sometimes, Medford rum served in the baggage car to adult males. And at every station there were hotel runners, whose competitive techniques in securing patrons aboard the omnibuses of their employers stopped only at physical violence.

In later and more sophisticated times, as journeys became longer and even lasted overnight, the cars became magnificent beyond all reason, land-roving counterparts of the white-and-gold and crystal palaces that floated on the Ohio and Mississippi, awash with mahogany, plush, French mirrors, fringes, ormolu, and marquetry, and boasting buffets and dining rooms, sleeping compartments, barbershops, and bathtubs attended by servants in uncounted numbers and stylish liveries.

But most of all, the American traveler aboard the cars was delighted by the locomotive engines that drew the whole glittering train brigade, where the engineer sat on the right-hand side, godlike and remote as an earl, his hand and will dominating the most beautiful and compelling machine ever devised by man. In the beginning, the teapot locomotives of American railroads were more notable for their ornate design than for tractive force and acceleration. There was vermilion trim and brasswork all over, the spokes of drive wheels were fine-lined in gold, storm lanterns as big as dog kennels for St. Bernards were splendid with oil paintings on their side panels, bells were cradled in hangers that would have amused Cellini, and, in some cases, the windows of engine cabs were of Gothic design, narrow with pointed tops that might have illustrated a contemporary set of Tennyson.

Fancy dictated much about the steam locomotives of the Golden Age of Railroading. Engines assigned to the personal trains of magnificoes like Commodore Cornelius Vanderbilt or Jay Gould might have a portrait likeness of the patron somewhere on their sidewalls. Deer horns and fraternal emblems rode the smokebox, signal flags floated from beautifully turned brass flagstaffs, and the name of the owning carrier was emblazoned in four or five colors on a ribbon held by a painted eagle on the tender side. The backheads of the boilers on certain choicely regarded engines might be plated in silver. Some of the engines of the New Haven Railroad assigned to limited runs had two headlights, one mounted on each side of the smokestack, and on the pilot beam of a celebrated Michigan Central locomotive there was a diminutive colored boy in cast iron holding out a vase of flowers which the engineer's wife filled fresh every morning for the day's run.

The countryside and right of way through which the trains ran were of intense interest to travelers not yet too sophisticated to take pleasure in a changing landscape of meadowlands, forests, rushing streams, and high passes in the seemingly impervious hills. The tracks were protected by whitewashed fences, and sometimes the cars ran noisily through covered wooden bridges over rivers or the canals which were slowly but certainly being rendered obsolete by steam and steel. On densely trafficked railroads there were signal towers at fixed intervals, little gazebos with turrets and catwalks and jigsaw ornaments like a Swiss chalet, from which telegraph operators controlled brightly painted semaphores or signal lights that were not always, alas, infallible tokens of safety for the rushing cars.

Until comparatively recent times, the wayside stations in country places were frequented at train time by the local inhabitants who strolled the platform for a brief, vicarious experience of life in the great world from which the railroads ran and to know the thrill of contact with events beyond their own placid and changeless horizons. The loungers knew the engines by name and the train crews, too: they were the good, familiar things of American daily life rendered slightly exotic by the implications of adventure which were their freight along with the milk and the traveling salesmen.

The personnel of railroading in the time of which we speak was colorfully attired in a vein of magnificence unknown in a more bleakly utilitarian age. While no car attendants on the American record ever approached the magnificence of conductors on the luxury sleepers maintained in Europe by the *Compagnie des Wagons Lits & Grands Express Europeens* who wore blue knee breeches with white silk stockings, silverbuckled pumps, crimson tailcoats with gold fourragères, and frilled shirts with lace cuffs, American trainmen were not altogether inconspicuous. Conductors of the Wagner Palace Car Company wore a military-type overcoat with a crimson-lined finger-length cape attached, surely one of the handsomest railroad uniforms ever designed. Wagner barbers were cautioned in the company rule book at all times to wear high, stiff white collars and alpaca jackets with five front buttons embossed with the company name on each. The engineer of the New York & New England's celebrated *White Train,* all of whose equipment was painted in cream color and the coal in the tender whitewashed before each run, wore an all-white jumper, gloves, and a white silk cap similar to that affected by jockeys.

From earliest times, when he was known as the train captain, conductors wore frock coats which gradually gave way to the more modern cutaway morning coat in fine blue cloth with gold buttons, although the silk top hats of the first primeval captains were shortly found to be impractical. The universal hallmark of office of the passenger conductor was a heavy, looped Albert watch chain of red or yellow gold, and conductors on crack flyers often wore flowers in the buttonholes to match the boutonnieres of well-dressed gentlemen who rode with them.

In a day when competing boat trains out of Boston connected for New York steamers variously at Fall River, Bristol, and Providence, and rival companies set great store by the style of their service, the Merchants Line out of Providence was generally conceded to take the palm with a magnificently dressed pier manager who shook hands with each passenger as he changed from cars to steamer while wearing a pair of white kid gloves. His gesture of stripping off the gloves, rolling them into a ball, and tossing them into the harbor was the signal for the ship's departure.

Even thrifty Yankees couldn't resist patronizing so stylish a railroad as this!

But what, more than anything else about the railroads, charmed the American fancy and laid hold on the imagination was the aggressive individuality of their properties, operations, personnel, and conduct of their affairs. No two carriers were quite the same. Each possessed a distinguishing character that might verge on the eccentric, as in the case of the New York & Erie which ran on tracks six feet wide, or the Chicago & North Western which, having been financed by Englishmen, drove on the left-hand side of the road. For many years the various connecting railroads of the land were so uncooperative that the cars of one, either for reasons of physical dimensions or the whim of the management, could not ride in the trains of another line, and passengers had to change at junction points of fearful remoteness or inconvenience.

Railroads became celebrated for their excellences, or infamous in reverse degree. The conductors of such New England railroads as the Old Colony and New York & New England were famous for their elevated and gentlemanly character and were the social peers of banker and college professor and, like the famous Asa R. Porter of the Fall River Boat Train, were "Mister" to railroad presidents and justices of the Supreme Court who rode his Pullmans. Conductors on lines west were less formal and inclined to the bonhomie of the frontier so that the Pullman captain on the original *Overland Limited* was in great request because he could play the organ that was part of the equipment of the sleeping car *Palmyra*.

Food aboard the diners became a conversation piece of limitless implications, and experienced travelers boasted of the terrapin Maryland they had encountered on the Baltimore & Ohio, or the scrodded codfish on the Maine Central. On one of the Santa Fe's luxury trains, appropriately named *The De Luxe,* uniformed messengers boarded the cars when they passed into California and presented elaborate corsages to the ladies and pigskin wallets to the gentlemen, the latter with a likeness of the train in gold leaf. In the Royal Gorge of the Arkansas River, trains of the Denver & Rio Grande Railroad paused at Hanging Bridge to let passengers view the immense chasm through which they were passing. On another Colorado run, the narrow-gauge Denver, South Park & Pacific, all trains made the informal practice of stopping to set down and pick up hunters and fishermen at their favorite spots along the route, while an engineer on the Boston & Maine, in a day when engineers were of the status of today's film actors or ballplayers, made a good thing of selling autographed photographs of himself posed beside his locomotive to awestruck passengers.

For many years there was nothing even suggesting uniformity in the accommodations available on main-line trains of different railroads. In time, most carriers came to recognize the superior merits of the sleepers and other luxury equipment built by Pullman, but the New York Central held out for the cars of Pullman's hated rival, Webster Wagner, and there were many other sleeping car patents rolling through the night owned by Mann, Woodruff, Jackson & Sharp, and a score of now-forgotten car-builders. On some of them passengers slept sideways, on others fore and aft, as it were, while aboard cars of the Monarch Company occupants of uppers were wise if they saw to it that their berths were securely locked in position against being jerked into the ceiling by a contrivance of cords and springs designed to hold the bunk aloft when not in use. Some sleepers carried safe deposit boxes with keys for each passenger so that he might secure his valuables on retiring, while on cars of the Fitchburg Railroad in Massachusetts, specially designed to transport visitors to the World's Fair in Chicago in 1893, there was a footbath countersunk below the floor level and concealed by a trap door in each sleeping compartment.

In their period of finest flowering of internal luxury, the cars themselves presented exteriors of great style and individualistic beauty. Passenger cars became known in railroad parlance as "varnish" because the fine woodwork that went into their construction was protected against the wear of travel and the elements with coats of shellac. Many carriers adopted identifying liveries, traces of which survive to this day in the Tuscan red of the Pennsylvania, the orange of the Milwaukee, and the royal blue of the Louisville & Nashville. At one time the cars of the Pennsylvania were painted in the red, green, and white Mexican national colors, a scheme an official had admired on the private train of Don Porfirio Díaz. Mention of the all-cream *White Train* of the New York & New England is made elsewhere in this brief essay. Golden palm trees were painted into the insigne on the name boards of the Florida East Coast; parlor cars built and leased by the Woodruff Car Company had canary yellow exteriors with gold and carmine striping; Harlan and Hollingsworth chose plum or wine color for their exteriors, with lavish gold ornamentation; Monarch cars were finished in natural-color mahogany with heavy coats of protective varnish; and the sleepers of the Wagner Palace Car Company were a rich dark brown with black trucks and roofs.

The aspect of a crack passenger flyer in these opulent times, from the burnished brass flagstaffs on the locomotive boilers to the final and equally burnished platform rails on the observation car, was one to fill the eye of the beholder and lift up his heart with longing to himself ride in such splendor.

The nomenclature that came to identify railroads, their name trains, and even the cars and engines were implicit with romance, riches, continental dominion, and classical mythology. Today, Union Pacific is still perhaps the most radiant name in the lexicon of railroading, but once there were others to charm the ear: the North Star & Mifflin; the Kansas City, Mexico & Orient; the Marcellus & Otisco; the Tallulah Falls; the Colorado Midland; and the Rio Grande, Micolithic & Northern. Their trains were of a richness and variety to beckon the most sedentary with the allurements of travel: *The Flamingo, The Fast Flying Virginian, The Royal Blue, The Ambassador, The Olympian, The Empire Builder, The Golden Triangle,* and *The De Luxe.* In early times the engines themselves were named for local magnates, investors in the company's bonds, and for the beasts of nature—*Lion, Tiger, Eagle, Panther,* and *Black Hawk.*

The names of Pullmans became in time part of the national folklore, but for many years were largely derived from classic mythology and the place names of antiquity: *Hector, Pharos, Attica, Hera, Ulysses, Hesperus, Delphi, Dorcas, Prometheus, Aida, Nestor,* and *Argo.* It was a liberal education in the humanities just to take passage on *The Midnight* from Chicago to Kansas City.

Once and for all the steam cars put to rest the notion that Americans were members of a classless society, and, from the very beginning, social and economic barriers were erected to separate all travelers into the categories to which a just God had assigned them. Aboard the first train brigades, which were made up of a series of stagecoaches mounted on trucks and insecurely joined together in transit, the preferred place was inside the body of the cars, while hoi polloi rode the roof where they were exposed to the elements, live coals from the engine boiler, and the possibility of being thrown off the train by the inequities in the roadbed.

As soon as things became better organized and the impropriety of all classes riding together in a common compartment was recognized, parlor cars with special conveniences and limited seating capacity were placed in service for people of a certain social and economic standing who preferred to travel in comparative privacy at a slightly elevated tariff. On all trains carrying Pullman equipment, coach passengers were forbidden to penetrate to the diners, club cars, and lounges reserved for first-class patrons. In time there came into being all-Pullman and often extra-fare trains running on specially expedited schedules with upper-case amenities of comfort, such as valets, barbers, baths, lady's maids, and stock tickers, and in which no coaches or coach passengers were carried at all. And, finally, among the all-Pullman name trains there came into being certain prestige runs such as the Santa Fe's *De Luxe,* the Union Pacific's *Overland Limited,* the New Haven's *Merchant's Limited,* the New York Central's *Twentieth Century Limited,* and the Southern Pacific's *Sunset,* whose occupancy and use by great names and the privileged of the world in itself assured travelers of a cachet of aloofness and the grand manner. A measure of distinction could be achieved through no more complicated agency than regular patronage of the Milwaukee's *Pioneer Limited* or being on terms of familiarity with the dining-car steward on the Illinois Central's *Panama Limited* between Chicago and New Orleans.

In the bright noontide of their splendor, riding the cars exercised so great a hold upon the public imagination that crack reporters for the national periodical and newspaper press were assigned at frequent intervals to write feature stories on the wonderments of new equipment, specially speedy runs, or the daring and achievements of the men who rode the cars and engines for a living. Enterprising metropolitan dailies had railroad editors, even as they had staff members specially charged with society, the theater, and the stock market. Distinguished foreigners, many of them titled, came to the United States specially for the experience of riding the great transcontinental limiteds that were coming into operation and recording their impressions for the English and European press. The illustrated periodical press that was developing coevally with the railroads was admirably adapted to portraying the comforts and excitements of overland travel, and the pages of *Harper's, Leslie's, The London Illustrated News*, and their Continental contemporaries devoted frequent and lavish spreads to ranking American achievements in railroading such as the new Pacific Railroad, Pullman's improved sleeping cars, and the overnight service of rival flyers between New York and Chicago.

But, whether its purview was along the lines of the homely bread-and-cheese railroads that followed the waterways of the American countryside and cemented the economy of grange and meadow with the great world beyond, or if it embraced the gorgeous gold-railed flyers whose mahogany palace cars were peopled with captains of industry and names that made news everywhere, railroading was the great preoccupation of the American people. It permeated the thinking and dreaming of countryman and city banker. The glory that rode the cars night and day toward distant horizons of achievement was part of the national time-spirit of America for three entire generations.

Railroading, until the ultimate modernities of centralized traffic control and tight lock couplings, was a curious synthesis of the old, the established and institutional, and the newest devisings of pioneer thinkers. The first train brigades drawn by locomotive engines were something absolutely new in the consciousness of mankind, a product of emergent evolution without premonition or foreseeable coming, yet they retained vestigial traces of what had gone before. The cars were known as carriages; the engine tender to this day is a hostler; travelers booked passage as they had on the stagecoaches; and the gauge of tracks was determined by transportation conventions reaching back to the gauge of Roman military chariots. In the roundhouses, like horses, the engines slept in stalls.

In some places trains paid toll as had travelers on the turnpikes of an older time; they were dispatched from terminals by the ringing of a bell such as was the practice on departing ships; in strongly Sabbatarian communities no trains ran on Sunday and, eventually, it was found prudent to buy off the disapproval of clergymen generally with free passes. Until only recently the conductor was known as captain, and the kitchen of dining cars was the galley, as in nautical parlance. Until the coming of air-conditioning, experienced travelers often covered their garments with dusters, a practice borrowed directly from the drivers of Western stages on plains where the alkali was thick. Before electric signals, train movements were governed by highball, a painted metal globe hoisted to a yardarm that for generations had been used by harbormasters to control the movements of vessels at sea.

No survey, however fleeting and cursory, of the delights of railroad travel in the nineteenth century but must make mention of the element of Gothic thinking and feeling that entered into the design of railroad properties in the opening decades of their emergence.

Stewart Holbrook, one of the most profound and perceptive students of the American folk scene, has remarked that in his early awareness of railroading, which was in New England shortly after the turn of the twentieth century, two words characterized travel aboard the cars. They were "genteel" and "elegant." Had he been one of an earlier generation of American wayfarers who, with Gladstone valises containing a copy of Young's *Night Thoughts* and a flask of Lawrence's Medford rum, boarded the primordial Pullmans, Wagners, Mann, and La Mothe sleepers, he might also have included the word "Gothic."

For railroading both here and in England had its genesis at a time when Gothic was enormously in vogue and when Horace Walpole's *The Castle of Otranto* and other novels of Gothic gloom and terror had a profound influence on English literature everywhere, as witness many of the writings of Edgar Allan Poe. Romance at the time flourished in the dim crepuscular vaults and chambers of ruined castles in which ancestral portraits came fearfully to life at a fateful juncture of events in which Manfred, the long-missing rightful heir, confronted his scoundrelly uncle with the words: "Traitor, what dost thou here? I had thought thee immured in the lowest dungeons of the North Tower!" The novels of Walpole and imitators such as William Harrison Ainsworth were directly and immediately reflected in the literature of the forties in the United States and in a remarkable array of mansions along the lordly Hudson River at Rhinecliff, Poughkeepsie, Camelot, and other strategic points, so moated, turreted, battlemented, and generally menacing as to form a school of architecture known as Hudson River Gothic. In them the disinherited Dutch patroons who had once been manorial lords of the Hudson Valley were supposed to dwell in rich, monastic seclusion, while the steamboats that plied Hudson water paused briefly at their private piers. Numerous ancestral retainers in somber livery served these exiled grandees, and grounds and gardens were garnished and attended by appropriate domestics in the dark of night so that privacy and seclusion might not be violated when their owners, in theatrical cloaks, might choose to stroll in meditation.

Inevitably this delicious gloom left an impression on the emergent outline of railroading. One had only to turn to the Boston & Maine passenger depot at Salem, Massachusetts, or its Fitchburg Railroad counterpart in Boston to come upon the Castle of Otranto itself, enlivened by the presence of train callers and steam whistles announcing the arrival and departure of the cars. Locomotives were built by the first firms of engine erectors at Taunton and Amoskeag with tall, pointed windows in their cabs from which engineer and fireman peered through mahogany frames and sashes that would have been appropriate to the vestry chambers of Westminster Cathedral. Other cabs came in circular, curved, and even hexagonal and octagonal shapes like gazebos or country summerhouses and were topped with gilded finials on domed roofs. The finials caused contretemps in tunnels and bridges with low clearance, and these decorative embellishments were soon eliminated, but other traces of authentic Gothic were not so easily supplanted.

Shortly after the Civil War, the then-building Chicago & North Western Railway out of Chicago was in funds to commission the purchase of a special car on which its directors might travel and admire their property. It came with narrow, pointed windows fitted with colored glass in leaded panes like a chapel. The main salon, countersunk between the trucks to the level of the journals, was available via staircases at either end of the car whose risers were of solid silver, and its occupants sat in tall-backed episcopal thrones around an altarlike table draped in purple velvet. On the table was a massive silver service, much like those used in communion in well-to-do churches, designed for the service of ice water in silver chalices. The North Western directors used it for scotch whiskey.

Largely the vogue of Gothic in the décor of railroad properties stopped at the Mississippi River and was lost to inhabitants of the Old West who never heard of *The Castle of Otranto*, but here and there traces of its essentially gloomy gaiety showed. Early mail and baggage cars on the California Central, built, to be sure, in Massachusetts and New Jersey, had pointed windows with colored glass set in leaded panes, and several of the early locomotives of the Central Pacific had hexagonal mahogany cabs. In the over-all railroad scene, the last traces of Gothic were the windows of washrooms and toilets in Pullman cars, many of which as late as 1920 were still made of colored glass panes set in lead. Intimations of Horace Walpole rode the cars right into the administration of Warren G. Harding.

With the passing of time, there began to emerge on the general awareness the cast of characters that rode the cars or were associated with railroad travel to take their place in the dramatis personae of America, along with such already-established personalities as the Yankee peddler, the Kentucky frontiersman, the absent-minded professor, Mr. Bones of the minstrel show, and the Mississippi River pilot.

Starred performer was the brave engineer, who was destined in a few years to take his place in the national pantheon of god-images along with the cowboy and the baseball professional. Associated with him was the tallow pot or fireman, a player of minor importance save upon such occasions as he might crawl along the footboard of a speeding locomotive and from the pilot beam scoop up a child from sudden death on the track.

Then there was the water boy, who passed an ice-water jug before the coming of patent coolers; the news butcher who sold periodicals, candy, popcorn, and sometimes novelties in the form of postcards of questionable propriety; the brakeman who called the names of the stations and opened the platform gates; the ticket agent in the depot; and, sole occupant in the demonology of railroading, the baggageman, whose special talents were directed to smashing luggage and dispatching it on the wrong train.

To this playbill of well-defined personalities, George M. Pullman added the most popular performer of all and that in a usually semicomic role, the Pullman porter. Together with the Pullman upper berth, the Pullman porter, usually named George but sometimes Steve or William, was destined for a bright and enduring immortality in the American lexicon of fact and humor.

The traveling salesmen, or drummers, and the stories they recited in the Pullman smoking compartment became a special and well-defined element of American folk legend. So did the virginal women who, when risking all by occupying an open section berth whose only protection against predatory manhood was a thin baize curtain, advised each other to travel armed with hatpins whose lethal design made them admirable weapons of defense in an emergency. The element of mischance implicit in the open sleeping accommodations of Pullman Standard design are a recognized component of American national humor, as are the misadventures of traveling minstrel shows and burlesque choruses en route through the agency of sleeper hops between the cities of the land.

These and some of the other practices, amenities, and eccentricities of

American railroading in a time when a glory shone about the cars and their goings are the theme of this pictorial record.

The modern eye can see, and not without justification, beauty in the profiles, silhouettes, and images of giant industrial installations where railroading is integrated to mines and mills and manufactories of massive presence and far-flung implications of economy. The eyes of the collaborators of this book, however, reach backward into a time of pastoral simplicities when the railroads and their properties were beloved as faithful domestic animals were beloved and their names were household words in a time of gold coinage, church suppers, open trolley cars, and free lunches in saloons whose patronage was exclusively male.

A reporter for *The New York Times* covering a recent rail-fan excursion through New Jersey overheard one of its participants, as the train emerged from a high pass in the wooded hills to a land of meadows with only an occasional farmhouse in sight, exclaim, "Now we're in railroad country!" He wanted his railroading free of industrial smokestacks and oil refineries, and to run in a land of stone walls, whitewashed silos, and covered wooden bridges, with occasional branches controlled by an attended signal tower running to even more remote and ineffable Ultima Thules of imagination.

Blow, hogger, high on the right-hand cushions, aloof as an earl without strawberry leaves, an earl in denim cap and goggles; blow for the grade crossings of remembrance; wind a trump for the yard limits of Bangor and Schenectady, La Junta, Cheyenne, Burlington, Walla Walla, Billings, and El Paso. Blow for green from the signal towers of destiny. Blow down the long vistas of American consciousness and for the order boards of eternity. The horn you wound was one with Roland's at Roncesvalles, one with the bugles of far hunting in ancestral memory. No nobler or more melancholy trump will be winded till Gabriel. And perhaps not then.

THE TWENTIETH CENTURY LIMITED

It is the dawn of a fine spring day late in May of, let us say, the year 1934—take away or add a page of the calendar—for the scene we conjure up in the mind's eye of remembrance lasted for a decade backward and another forward into the then-unforeseeable forties. The viewer is invited to envision over the years, from a vantage point on the Hudson at Manitou or Peekskill, the broad waters of the lordly river flecked with early-morning shipping, and the Jersey Palisades in the misty distance. In the foreground, gleaming and sinuous, are the four main-line tracks of the New York Central Railroad curving out of sight around a headland on their way to Albany or, if you prefer, Ultima Thule.

It is just five o'clock, and around the bend, running fast under a curving banner of coal smoke that hangs stationary on the morning air, comes the first train of The Parade. It is No. 36, an undistinguished bread-and-cheese sleeper called *The Genesee*. Ten minutes later comes *The Iroquois*, Train No. 30, Pullmans only; that is followed, in another ten minutes, by Train No. X4, *The Fast Mail;* and right on its heels comes a train with some suggestions of style in its going. It is *The Montreal Limited*, Pullmans only from Montreal to New York and a club car over the connecting Delaware & Hudson. And behind it, with only moments to spare, comes its companion on the Montreal run, *The Mount Royal*, with coaches and sleepers over the Rutland through deepest Vermont.

Next on the time card and clicking through like clockwork is a truly massive consist, No. 4, *The New York Special*. A flash of synchronized side motion, a hail of cinders, a long-drawn muted thunder of trucks over rail joints, and *The New York Special* has gone, leaving the stage set for the big event of the day.

This is the passage in glory of Train No. 26, *The Twentieth Century Limited*, all-Pullman extra-fare flyer from Chicago to New York on the tightest schedule known, with deluxe standard Pullmans, drawing rooms, staterooms, and compartments; single and double bedrooms; and valet, barber, and maid service. It has porterhouse steak on the menu, fresh flowers on every table, a steward on bowing terms with the great of the great world, a conductor with a pink in his buttonhole, and Pullman porters who are the *haute noblesse* of the social milieu in which they move. The names on its sailing list are the names of headlines; and besides a passenger list of exalted dimensions, *The Century* carries an intangible but equally glittering freight, the pride of a great operation with a tradition of excellence unmatched by any railroad in the world.

Showpiece, legend, article of railroad faith, *The Twentieth Century Limited* is a national institution, moving with the exactitude of sidereal time, as implacable as Fate.

In its turn, too, *The Century* is gone in a torrent of green and gold under a canopy of coal smoke, in the direction of Harmon and Manhattan. But its going has given an imperial dimension to the day. Other fine trains will follow inexorably in the order of The Parade—*The Fifth Avenue Special, The Southwestern Limited, The Wolverine*—but they are anticlimax. *The Century,* for fifty years, was the star performer.

The New York Central's *Twentieth Century Limited* was for over half a century, and beyond all reasonable argument, regarded as the finest train operation in the world. There were, and are, other trains of great distinction and enviable celebrity. Elsewhere in the world were comparable trains of lustrous memory and exalted prestige, but none of them quite approached *The Century* and the connotations of its name.

It was a train apart, aloof, serene, incomparable—the sum of all excellences wrapped up in all-Pullman extra-fare schedules that none might let or hinder. It was at once a force of nature and a national showpiece. When it sailed each afternoon from its terminals in New York and Chicago and the red carpet of its going was rolled up for the night, each of its several sections became a self-contained microcosm of security, composure, and the best of everything.

The author's experience of *The Century* was not only as a fairly regular patron in the thirties and forties, but vicariously through the agency of one of the first of the now numerous and familiar sound effect recordings of steam railroading on phonograph discs. A friend had presented me with a primordial version of this now commonplace rail-buff artifact purporting to recreate on a phonograph the sounds of *The Century,* complete with a train caller at Grand Central, whistles, crossing bells, engine changes at Harmon and Albany, conversations with the dispatcher, and other noisy fakements of robust steam motive power.

The writer lived at the time at the Madison Hotel at the corner of Madison Avenue and Fifty-eighth Street directly under an apartment maintained—and occasionally occupied when away from Albany—by New York's Governor Herbert Lehman. It was sometimes our whim, late at night and usually in wine, to play this disc at its fullest volume.

The Governor shortly showed signs of apprehension, and finally approached Bertram Weal, managing director of the Madison, in the matter.

"Mr. Weal," he said warily, "do you ever hear anything unusual around your hotel at night, train noises for instance, as if *The Twentieth Century Limited* were going by under your window in Madison Avenue at full speed? I'm not a drinking man or subject to hallucinations or anything, but every so often late at night I get the impression this hotel has just crossed the long bridge into Albany and is slowing down for the station there."

Mr. Weal took the matter under advisal and had no great difficulty in tracing the source of the bells and whistles. It was pointed out that the Madison leases contained clauses strictly enjoining tenants from running railroad trains at speed through their apartments, and thereafter the Governor slept better at night.

For many years an identifying hallmark of *Century* cuisine was a particularly delectable pickle made of watermelon rind and served along with the olives and celery. So closely did the condiment become associated with *The Century* that once or twice when it failed of delivery or was suspended during momentary waves of economy, regulars protested in no uncertain terms and the management hastened to restore it to circulation. Research discloses that the relish is known as Old Honesty Brand and is manufactured by the Johnson-Appleby Company of Cambridge, Massachusetts, who cannot establish the date when their product was first an item of *Century* commissariat. Nor can they state authoritatively how much is used by the New York Central, but allow that they use twenty carloads of Georgia watermelon annually in its manufacture and that the largest purchasers are S. S. Pierce & Company, the ancestral Boston grocers, and the Central. It comes in eight-pound tins, and the number of these opened between Mott Haven and LaSalle Street over the years may well be astronomical.

The invaluable Merle Armitage, whose souvenirs of *The Century* are a repository of concert-hall lore *en route,* recalls good times on The Greatest Train in the World in the days of operatic giants:

"One season we were preparing to go west to commence the thirty-six-city tour contracted for by John McCormack, when he learned that Dame Nellie Melba, whom he knew well, would be crossing the continent on the way home to Australia. He asked Melba to take passage on *The Century* on the day we were leaving, for the sake of company on the overnight run to Chicago, and Dame Nellie accepted with great enthusiasm, considering her formidable *hauteur.*

"The party, therefore, consisted of Dame Nellie Melba and her maid,

John McCormack, his accompanist Edwin Schneider, and myself, and we occupied drawing rooms and compartments in the same car. Walking down the red carpet to *The Century* that evening, we encountered Fritz Kreisler, who was also westward bound. We invited him to join us for dinner.

"Shortly after leaving New York, the dining-car steward punched the bell on my apartment door, and announced that the chef was preparing a special dinner for the party, which would be served in the drawing room in just one hour. I informed all concerned, and we ordered cocktails.

"The dinner came promptly, served by smiling Negroes in gleaming white uniforms, and supervised by the steward. We could scarcely have fared better at the Pavillon or the Colony. There were hot hors d'oeuvres in the true style of Sweden, crayfish court-bouillon, English Channel sole in wine and herbs, followed by chateaubriand and crisp salad. All with proper wines. And the dessert, served with a perfectly straight face, was, of course, peach Melba with a fine Tokay wine, and then the coffee. In a silver tray which came along with the dessert was a note which read, 'Compliments of The Twentieth Century Limited.'

"An unprecedented evening which I recall with utter nostalgia, as a tribute to a train with character and personality, and a mode of traveling which was superb!"

By the year 1916 *The Century* was so well established as a status symbol as to provide an interlude—grievous at the time, hilarious in retrospect—for Henry Sell, later to become the irreproachable and august editor of *Town & Country*, itself a coated-paper *feuilleton* of impeccable social acceptability. But in that earlier time, a youthful Sell, avid for fame and fortune, was appointed book editor of the *Chicago Daily News*—or rather was told that he could call any space he could steal from other departments "The Wednesday Book Page." The stealing took place among the makeup tables one morning at five o'clock, when Sell induced the makeup editor to give him the much desired billing, and that afternoon Sell purchased bedroom space on *The Century* with an eye to rustling some business among the New York publishers.

"Kind friends warned me that less expensive train passage would be more acceptable to management," Sell recalled forty-five years or so later, "but I persisted in folly, using my own money to avoid any recriminations. I was full of confidence and wanted no part of second-class travel, then or now, a state of mind that has changed little with the passing years at either management or Sell level.

"Aboard the most elegant of trains, I moved to the club car where I posed as a bored sophisticate waiting the dinner hour. It came and I was conducted to an empty chair at a table for two, opposite (may I use the cliché 'of all people'?) the owner of the *Chicago Daily News*, Mister, in every possible sense of the title, Victor F. Lawson. He made austere acknowledgment of my presence. I offered an embarrassed smile. Some moments later he cleared his throat and asked, 'We have met? I have seen your face!'

" 'No, sir, we have not met, but I am Henry Sell, the new Book Page editor of your *Chicago Daily News.*'

"Lawson touched his Prince Albert beard, made a neat crescent of his mustach ends, looked out the window, and spoke as to someone just over the horizon. 'There must be some mistake. Employees of the *Chicago Daily News* do not travel on *The Twentieth Century Limited.*'

"Dinner was not easy, but somehow I managed the bouillon and creamed chicken as planned. Not hours later, although it seemed like it, but later, again the clearing of the throat . . . 'Mr. Sell, may I suggest that you try these stewed figs for your dessert? They are a little sweet, but quite tasty.' A faint smile. Picking up his dinner check and mine, he paid for both and departed. As an employee of the *Chicago Daily News*, I journeyed to New York many times in years to come, always on *The Twentieth Century Limited.*"

Once, when the author of this monograph had tarried overlong in Chicago laying waste its ordered social curriculum in the course of a transcontinental whoobab with Lady Suzanne Wilkins whose husband, Sir Hubert, was providentially under the Arctic ice cap in a submarine, Mrs. Peggy Harvey, a well-placed Chicago hostess whose resources of patience and wine had been taxed, sent a singing chorus of six Western Union messengers to see him off on *The Century*, bleating, "Happy Good-by, Mr. Beebe, Happy Good-by to You," from the platform.

Early in the 1930s, *The Twentieth Century Limited* became the name and central theme and setting of one of the most hilarious of all Broadway farces of the period. Charlie MacArthur, en route to join his wife Helen Hayes in Hollywood, was spending the evening doing things with bottles in the company of Ernie Byfield and Ben Hecht in the College Inn, a grotto adjacent to the furnace room in the Sherman Hotel, and had occasion to remark on the elevated moral tone of *The Century* in which he had arrived from New York that morning.

"The club-car porter wouldn't serve me White Rock for my whiskey because I had kicked my shoes off and there was a hole in my sock," he complained. It was prohibition and passengers brought their own.

"I know," said Byfield. "Ethel Barrymore complained of the same thing last week. Said she threw a hard roll at John Drew in the dining car and hit an Anglican bishop. The conductor spoke to her about it."

"They wouldn't let Jesus Christ in the diner if he wasn't wearing a tie and waistcoat," said Hecht, MacArthur's collaborator in a number of disorders including a play called *The Front Page*. "That gives me an idea."

Hecht and MacArthur went into a trance together a few weeks later in a suite in the Ambassador East, another Byfield hotel where the servants were used to them, and came up with a play whose entire action was to take place aboard *The Century* eastbound and whose characters included a demented Broadway producer with delusions of grandeur, a disillusioned press agent, and a Christus from a stranded troupe of Oberammergau Passion Players. The producer, a transparent synthesis of Morris Gest and David Belasco, was eventually played by Moffat Johnson, with a Scottish accent, opposite Eugenie Leontovich in the role of his Russian ex-mistress. The press agent was drawn to correspond with startling fidelity to Broadway's own Richard Maney, a celebrated coiner of Shubert Alley superlatives who, in fact, acted as press agent when *Twentieth Century* was produced by George Abbott.

The action and dialogue made infamous jape of the propriety which hung around the Central's flagship like an aura. The bearded Christus in search of employment, attired in a Gethsemane suit, invaded the drawing room of Moffat Johnson to exhibit his virtuosity with passages from *The Passion Play*. Saul of Tarsus, also bearded like Moses, was trapped in his stateroom by Leontovich who mistakenly fancied him as a Chicago multimillionaire in search of dalliance. A religious fanatic identified with the stranded Christus pasted labels with the admonition "Prepare to Meet Thy God" on the backs of unsuspecting members of the train crew.

As the train was passing through Elyria, Ohio, in the midnight hours, the harassed train conductor forsook all dignity and roared at Christus: "God's blood and blizzards, Jesus, this is *The Twentieth Century Limited!* Take off those false whiskers and that nightshirt in my club car, or I'll have you jailed at Buffalo!"

Twentieth Century was an instant and hilarious success on Broadway and only succumbed when the bank holiday darkened its marquee.

In recent years the affairs of *The Twentieth Century Limited* have been of a nature regarded by its admirers as melancholy, if not downright disastrous.

The new regime that assumed control of the New York Central after the great proxy battle of the early fifties showed little awareness that for more than five decades *The Century* had been the most radiant imaginable advertisement for the over-all operations of the railroad and its greatest recommendation to public favor. Railroaders everywhere were horrified when in the fall of 1957, after a particularly disheartening audit of its passenger revenues, the management ordered coaches carried in the once lordly all-Pullman consist and abolished the extra fare. Other curtailments followed. There were complaints about food and downgraded service and the shabby condition of equipment. Employee morale achieved an all-time low, and the future was a grim one for the flyer that had for so long been touted as "The Greatest Train in the World."

Happily, however, the long and stirring saga of *The Century* does not end on such a note of gloom unmitigated.

Few trains in the record have been able to evoke the loyalty and devoted regard that *The Century* has aroused in people not otherwise prone to abundant sentimentality. Arthur Dubin refers to it unabashedly as "my beloved of all trains." Christopher Morley described the electric engine which powered the cars as far as Harmon as "the father who takes the bride up the aisle on his arm." "There are trains and trains," said *The Christian Science Monitor* editorially, "but no train has ever received such adulation as does *The Twentieth Century Limited*." The author himself many years ago encountered at the now long vanished bar at Romano's in London an English Army officer of general rank who had only once been in America as a member of a purchasing commission during the 1914 war. The only things that remained impressed on his memory were Delmonico's Restaurant and *The Century*. "Riding it was the great experience of my life," he said, quite literally with tears in his eyes.

Such fierce loyalty helps in part to explain the rage and anguish in the most unexpected quarters encountered by the Central management after the humiliation of *The Century* in 1957. People whose blood pressure would not have mounted at an affront to the Flag regarded its downgrading as a desecration transcending the destruction of Louvain by the Germans in the first war. The torrent of abuse and vilification that arrived in the mail at 466 Lexington Avenue horrified officials who had no idea they were tampering with what amounted in many quarters to an article of faith. The world of railroading was unutterably shocked.

It became evident in 1961 that *The Twentieth Century Limited* was once more a matter of concern to the ranking brass who order the affairs of the New York Central. Word went out that trains Nos. 25 and 26 were again in favor and managerial regard. Old patrons who ventured an exploratory trip on *The Century* reported that once more the best of everything obtained, and an old romance between the train and the traveling public was revived. The quality of the train's clientele immediately reflected the new order of things, and, as a final panache to the over-all restoration, the red carpet, banished for the period of austerity, reappeared at Grand Central to make the departure of No. 25 the ceremonious institution in the life of a great city it had always been.

Whatever could be done to repair the damage and establish a continuity with the happy past was being done, and a personal voyage of exploration by the author of these paragraphs confirmed the happy tidings that had come to his ears.

As he boarded the cars on a bleak winter's evening at Chicago while car tonks were thawing out the brake rigging with flares, the old *Century* panache of elegance was visible the moment he stepped through the train gate. Immaculate porters stood rigidly at attention as of old at each car platform, a superintendent of service welcomed him by name, a dinner-jacketed dining-car steward was at hand to be commanded. Through the gloom of the train shed, the cut flowers showed in the windows of warmly lit club cars, and on the end of the train was, as of yore, the name in neons of The Train of Trains. I was home again.

As a coda to these brief vignettes of The Greatest Train in the World—which has entered the folklore of the American people as surely as Buffalo Bill Cody, the Winchester rifle, mint juleps, or the Model T Ford—it may be appropriate to quote from an editorial on the naming of deluxe trains from the now vanished *New York Evening World* for January 9, 1930:

And then, of course, there is the name of names for anything pulled by the Iron Horse, the name so superb that one would almost be tempted to say that after it there are no others. It was given that train of which the New York Central is so proud, and is so magnificent that it should never be printed save in capital letters, thus:

THE TWENTIETH CENTURY LIMITED!

THE CENTURY:
A Gastronomic Footnote

Mention of *The Century* in this space a few months back (*Gourmet*, October 1963) evoked fragrant souvenirs of its cuisine and luxury appointments from a number of readers, none more entertaining and instructive than those of William B. Plummer of Warrington, Florida, who added a gastronomic footnote to the ambrosial legend of *Century* cuisine.

"My complaint," wrote Mr. Plummer, "is that you did not mention my favorite steward by the name of Burns. You also failed to mention one of the long-time specialties of *The Century* diners, which was lobster Newburg on toasted cornbread. The reason I bring this up is to exemplify the service that *The Century* used to perform. One night I got on the train and wanted this special lobster, but it wasn't on the menu. So I spoke to Burns about my problem and pointed out that there was cold lobster on the menu so that the chef at least had a starting point. Burns said it would be arranged but that it might take a little time. So I had a drink and waited for some minutes, when Burns finally came back and reassured me that it was in the works but would take a few minutes longer. So I had another drink and waited a bit, and ultimately Burns came back with the lobster Newburg on toasted cornbread and apologized for the delay. It seems that while they had the lobster, there was no cornbread in the galley so they had been forced to make a pan of fresh cornbread, cook it, and then toast an appropriate amount in order to fill my order. That is what I call service."

STEP INTO MY PARLOR

In the sometimes confusing and always colorful lexicon of railroad usage the word "parlor" does not mean parlor car. A parlor car is cushions, varnish, or any one of several more or less oblique synonyms for mobile luxury, but the word parlor itself is one of the more common jargon terms for caboose. There are many others: way car, palace, shack, crummy, van, doghouse, shanty, cabin car, mansion, pavilion, bouncer, buggy, bedhouse, cage, glory wagon, drone cage. The writer once heard a brakeman, evidently one of a modern generation of college-educated boomers, refer to it as the château. A certain panache of Old World charm was carried with the appellation, and one half expected the conductor to appear in the person of a threadbare aristocrat in a skirted coat which had seen better days.

It is also buggy, chariot, shelter house, gocart, hack, hut, monkey wagon, brainbox, zoo, diner, and perambulator. There are probably others in a variety bounded only by the limitations of human imagining and the vocabulary of profane and uninhibited men.

It is the freight crew's home away from home, a rolling microcosm of domesticity, a shelter against the blast, a premises as masculine in its implications as a corner saloon, a light to guide a man in the dark, the period and apostrophe at the end of the completed sentence of a train. To the perfectionist there can exist no symphony without a coda, no finished repast without the benediction of cognac. So to the railroad perfectionist there can be no train, in the technical sense and as an esthetic entity, distinguished from a cut of cars, without a caboose complete with markers. There are, shamefully enough in a degenerate age, transcontinental Pullman trains without observation cars. There are also pork chops without apple sauce. Either is more thinkable than a freight, whether redball manifest or modest local, effacing itself on passing track for every other train on the employees' card, without a crummy.

Quite aside from the realms of fancy, however, it is not only the spider who addresses the fly with a courtly invitation to come into his parlor. On at least two railroads, all unsuspected by a vast general public to whom a railroad caboose is as delightful a mystery as the lamasery of Tibet, passengers may and do ride in the caboose as a regular thing (verified correct August 1967.—Ed.), if for no other reason than that there is no coach or combine available to the run. Such passage may lack the white-coated stewards and modernistic décor of the last word in stream-lined club cars aboard the *City of San Francisco* or the *Congressional Limited*, but it is a traveler of mean perceptions and lean imagination who would not rather go a country journey in a crummy than amid the most upholstered devising of modern luxury.

Most folk know that drovers, sheepherders, cattlemen, shippers, and custodians of livestock of all sort are customarily carried in cabooses and sometimes envy them the privilege, but any passenger who has cash fare will step aboard an atmospheric bouncer if he buys a ticket on the Tucson, Cornelia & Gila Bend Railroad.

The Tucson, Cornelia & Gila Bend Railroad is located roughly a hundred miles southwest of Phoenix and a hundred miles northwest of Tucson and it operates a round-trip train of mixed freight and passengers over its forty-three-mile long line daily except for Saturday and Sunday. Passengers ride in the caboose in style in seats probably cabbaged from the line's last passenger coach when it was scrapped, and a trip through the Arizona desert with the train crew for company from Gila to Ajo, the southern terminus just bordering the Organ Pipe National Monument, is a trip to remember.

About a hundred miles to the east of Flagstaff, Arizona, lies the town of Holbrook on the mainline of the Santa Fe Railroad, and it is here that the little Apache Railroad's seventy-two-mile line takes off and heads due south to McNary. Passengers ride in the neat little silver and red caboose on reversible-back seats probably taken from some long-forgotten trolley car. It is a night operation, however, and passengers are rare.

Probably there is more warmth of homeliness and sentiment about a hack at the end of a string of high cars, a little self-contained world of animation and reality as it diminishes down the tracks behind a hustling symbol freight, than exists for any other of a railroad's tangible properties. Neither the drowsing water tank in the desert nor the semaphore giving green in a cut in the high hills nor even the glitter and crisp linen and fresh-cut flowers of the deluxe dining car are possessed of quite the qualities to captivate the imagining that belong to the red-painted caboose with a wisp of smoke from its disreputable chimney pot, canted at a rakish angle and secured against complete disintegration by a length of rusty baling wire.

Because of its unique status in the roster of railroad equipment, too, the caboose achieves an individuality unshared by rolling stock in any other category, freight or passenger. Because, unlike all sorts of freight and some passenger cars, a crummy seldom rides any rails but those of its home company, it is not subject to the qualifying regulations which govern the design and maintenance of stock cars, reefers, or tanks which must operate over a vast multiplicity of different systems. It is an individualist, a maverick, proud of its own eccentricities of character and disdainful, in its usually shabby raffishness, of the well-bred uniformity of Pullmans and high cars alike. The caboose is the bohemian of railroad rolling stock society.

Because of its comparatively humble function and utilitarian design, the history of the evolution of the caboose is largely a matter of conjecture. Unlike the proud designers and builders who left specifications and architect's elevations of their every locomotive for the wonderment and imitation of posterity, there was no William Mason of the crummies to leave his imprimatur on the hacks that came into emergent being in the sixties and seventies to roll across the Western lands or through the woodlands of the Deep South. The caboose came into being conditioned by the imaginings and necessities of finger-shy link and pin brakemen and chin-whiskered freight conductors who required a shelter from the storm in which to light their ponderous globular lanterns and tally their waybills, and who begged or stole a disused high car or rigged a precarious pavilion on a flat to serve their purpose.

The word caboose in a variety of more or less germaine meanings has been a part of several languages since it first appeared as *cambose* or *camboose* in the records of the French navy in the middle of the eighteenth century. Its initial appearance in English literature, according to the *New English Dictionary,* was when in 1805 in the record of a New England shipwreck the New York *Chronicle* reported that a member of the crew, "William Duncan, drifted aboard the canboose." Its latest example, dated 1884, the *New English Dictionary* merely attributes to a "Dakota newspaper" and describes "four cars and a caboose running down the track," so that after that it may be taken as sufficiently current usage not to attract the attention of historians of the vernacular. The caboose was running down the track with sufficient momentum to carry it right down to the immediate, twentieth-century present.

It was in the summer of 1863 that Conductor T. B. Watson of the very English Chicago & North Western was assigned to regular freight runs between Cedar Rapids and Clinton, Iowa, according to Mr. Knapke. His regular shack was being shopped and he was temporarily the unhappy captain of a somewhat disreputable boxcar which had, in some manner, come by a large circular hole in the roof. Shamed by his makeshift buggy and being something of a card or character, Watson determined to make the best of things and decided that comedy was indicated. As his consist clattered over the sixty-pound switch points into the Clinton yards, other trainmen and loiterers were fascinated to observe Watson's portly person, obviously supported by a requisitioned chair or packing case, protruding from the unseemly aperture while the fellow raised his hat and made courtly bows to all and sundry. In the course of his little act, however, Watson discovered that a clearance of a couple of feet above the roof of his car was an ideal vantage point from which to con the progress of his train, and he forthwith persuaded the road's master mechanic to enclose the position with glass against the weather and install a permanent deck underneath this clerestory. Thus the cupola was born.

The parallel between the caboose of railroad operations and the original and antecedent cook shack on the deck of a sailing ship is in no way merely one of etymology. Their exterior resemblance was obvious from the beginning and consideration of their function further heightens the resemblance. Both are designed as strictly functional parts in the integrated economy of travel. Both are made to withstand the assaults of nature upon man's inherent frailties, to stay and comfort him when the rains descend and great winds blow upon the earth. Both are destined to voyage into far places and see strange and wonderful things, and each of them nourishes and strengthens a breed of men at once individualistic and disciplined beyond the ordinary run. And, of course, the ship's galley and the little red caboose are both dedicated, primarily, to that great equalizer and most common of all human common denominators: food!

The baked beans and bread puddings, the pork chops and pan-fried potatoes, and the illimitable varieties of hot breads evolved by generations of chariot chefs sustained many and many a famished brakeman and conductor on desert divisions before the days of Harvey Houses and in times when it was not uncommon to tie up for rest on the road miles from the nearest eating place.

Least homely of the uses of the caboose, but of necessity a primary one, is that of office for the conductor and supply department for the entire freight crew. The train's operating headquarters is represented by the conductor's desk, among the pigeonholes and filing devices of which that functionary may spend as much as half of the running time of his trip receipting waybills, drawing up his wheel reports, which furnish the basis for the home office's statistical records of all freight and merchandise movement, and doing the other paper work necessary to the orderly conduct of a vast business enterprise.

Lockers, variously located in accordance with the details of the design of the individual hack, but all convenient to the hand of the crew, are provided for the storage of heavy supplies: chains, journal brasses, knuckle pins, rerailing frogs, and wrecking tools for emergencies. Signal fuses, torpedoes, signal flags, lanterns, and fuel oil, too, are stored away as neatly and ready to instant use and availability as the signal flags and code books on the bridge of an oceangoing liner. There is also the conductor's emergency air control and in some cases an air horn for calling the attention of the engineer up ahead.

West of the Mississippi—as might be expected, where divisions are longer and cities fewer—cabooses are more than ever self-contained homes for train crews, and Bill Knapke recalls living and eating in a Southern Pacific crummy for a year on end without inconvenience of any sort. In such setups a good cook is beyond rubies and many a conductor has been known to ask to have assigned to his run brakemen who were noted more for their ability to run up a creditable tin pan of hot biscuits than for their railroading competence. In the West, too, cabooses are frequently made longer and more on the order of Pullmans to accommodate in folding berths the drovers who, on stock trains, ride to market with their cattle and sheep to assure their arrival in good order. Such elaborate cabooses are usually assigned permanently to a single train crew who spend their own money for their commissary and fittings with the result that shacks sometimes boast such details as radios and elaborate sets of cooking utensils.

If the caboose has figured in legend it has also been written large in the ballad lore of the land. It has probably been dramatized on the stage and it has certainly furnished a favorite theme for several generations of railroad artists and photographers. Be it, however, a swallowtail hack or a less fanciful model, it is probable that the crummy lies nearer to the heart of railroad men everywhere than anything except the wonderful steam locomotives that for many decades have rolled them over the main lines and short hauls, the standard iron and the slim gages of the nation's roads. The all-steel streamlined, airflow shacks of the Peoria Road, the Rock Island, and the Erie, and the old-time four-wheel bouncers of the valiant little roads such as the Raritan River and the Morristown and Erie, the doghouses of the stormy mountain divisions of the Rio Grande, conditioned against the winters on the Great Divide, and the buggies of the Santa Fe rolling across the August wheatlands of Kansas, the bright-painted way cars of the St. Louis Southwestern rolling south toward the heart of Texas, and the Tuscan-red cages of the Pennsy hotshotting through the green fields of Indiana, all have been and still are, most of them, colorful players in the pageant of overland travel by the iron highroad. The saga of the high iron would be the poorer had they never been.

ELEGANT PRIVATE VARNISH

It is difficult in a generation in which any sort of rail travel is regarded as faintly exotic and many of whose members are not even familiar with the once commonplace amenities of travel aboard the steam cars to imagine the position occupied in the scale of material assets and luxury appointments by the private railroad car.

In an age when the phrase "status symbol" had yet to be invented, the private Pullman was probably the most exalted and enviable of all available indexes of economic preferment and social inaccessability. Beside its implications of wealth and exclusiveness such recognized properties as a Fifth Avenue address, titled sons-in-law, social recognition at Newport or Palm Beach, galleries of old masters, English servants, and entire garages filled with Rolls-Royces and Bentleys paled to insignificance. Only the oceangoing steam yacht of acceptable dimensions and the maintenance of a top-flight racing stable possessed comparable connotations of grandeur.

The reason for this supremacy in common acceptance and the general imagination of a comparatively inexpensive artifact lies in the hold that the entire business of railroading held on the minds of the American people for three quarters of a century. A château on Bellevue Avenue or Nob Hill might cost from $3,000,000 to double that amount at a time when the most princely of private cars could be built to the owner's specifications for no more than $50,000. The dowry that went with a Vanderbilt heiress when she married an English duke could come to $2,500,000. A seat in the United States Senate at a time when it was the most exclusive club of rich men in the world might carry a $1,000,000 tab and often did. The price tag on a single art masterpiece such as Gainsborough's "Blue Boy" when acquired for an American collector by Sir Joseph Duveen could come to $620,000, but Henry E. Huntington, who bought "Blue Boy," maintained no fewer than four private railroad cars whose total value was the merest fraction of this sum.

At the period of its greatest costliness a private Pullman stood its purchaser $500,000 and in the period of its greatest multiplicity in the twenties $150,000 would get something extremely nice from American Car & Foundry. The private car was very far from being the most expensive evidence of upward mobility in American society and finance, but as a symbol of success it had few peers and was topped by nothing.

Its possession combined luxurious convenience with the romantic hold railroading had for the popular imagination and the combination exalted it above ownership of the Hope Diamond or a claim on the favors of the ranking Hollywood Cyprian of the moment. Swimming pools were for successful greengrocers and electrical contractors. Palm Beach and charge accounts at Cartier were for well-placed stockbrokers. The private Pullman, its dark green varnish and brass-railed observation platform headed for Florida or Del Monte or the Adirondacks, was for grand seigneurs and the feudal overlords of the American economy. Each lent a dimension of magnificence to the other.

In few other tangible properties—excepting homes and steam yachts —could the whims, prejudices, and taste for the exotic of the well-to-do find expression in such a dimension as the design and construction of a private railroad car. He was inhibited only by the standards of the American Association of Railroads, the clearances of individual carriers, and the limits of his bank account, and within these limitations his imagination could and did run riot.

In general, the ground plan of one private car closely resembled that of any other. It included a dining room, usually seating eight or ten, an observation salon whose dimensions might vary at the whim of the owner, a master stateroom usually with its own bath, three or four slightly smaller staterooms for guests, a galley and kitchen offices and quarters for the crew which traditionally numbered two and were known as cook and waiter. To call them chef and butler would be a departure from accepted railroad usage of a parvenu.

The galley with its storerooms, iceboxes, and repositories of linen and other necessities was traditionally located at the head end of a private car, while the rear end was devoted to a brass-railed observation platform from which occupants might take the air or enjoy the view. The number of staterooms and size of the drawing room depended on each other. It was possible to have more private sleeping space and less room for general assembly, or the reverse. A corridor along one side of the entire length of the car gave access to its various apartments and to the rear platform for the members of the crew working the train.

It was in its special appointments that the tastes of private-car owners found their fullest gratification. Marble bathtubs, gold-filled plumbing, jewel safes, cedar wardrobes, king-size beds, and other built-in equipment were fairly standard. One car of recent record had a steam bath activated by the main train line. The private car *Adolphus* of August Busch, Jr., reportedly had beer piped to all its rooms.

In the earlier days of railroading there was little or no distinction drawn, as there later came rigidly to be, between the Pullmans and varnish cars owned by private individuals and those maintained by railroads for their officers and executives. In the middle nineteenth century well-to-do individuals were very often also railroad directors and the distinction meant nothing. A later generation of railroaders prefers to refer to their executive varnish as "business" or "official" cars and they are carried in the books as railroad property rather than personal assets of their proprietors.

The first record of anything resembling a private car in the United States appears in the tariff rates of the Boston & Providence Railroad for 1834 among whose items appears a round trip rate between Boston and Dedham Township, "private cars holding twenty passengers: $15." Their next mention would seem to be when, in 1841, William H. Harrison went to Washington as President-elect of the United States, and the general manager of the Baltimore & Ohio asked his superiors if he should supply this dignitary with "a distinct car." Twenty odd years later the military car shops at Alexandria built for President Lincoln the first armored car designed in this country for a chief of state.

From these first beginnings, the private car rose rapidly in general use and in the public imagination until, in the eighties and nineties, the millionaire, society figure, or railroad or industrial nabob who did not own at least one private car, and in many instances two or three, simply had not arrived socially or financially speaking. William H. Vanderbilt's favorite private varnish car was named, somewhat redundantly, *Vanderbilt* and another, *Duchess,* was available if his guests were numerous. General William Jackson Palmer was outraged at the infringement upon his privacy when the Colorado press reported that his *Nomad* on the Denver & Rio Grande, a narrow-gage drawing-room car, rejoiced in a bath with both hot and cold running water. Life in a later generation of railroad tycoons was even less austere. In his diaries, published many years later, Count Boni de Castellane told how, when he was courting Anna Gould, guests aboard the private train of her brother George Gould were expected to wear full evening dress at dinner.

With the turn of the century when railroad executives became increasingly inhibited about the use of private equipment the custom became general among railroad officials to remove fanciful or colorful names from their business cars and substitute plain and functional numbers, so that to this day a railroad president may travel in comparative anonymity aboard *Car 100* or *Car 1,* numbers widely favored by railroaders of presidential rank. Although comfortable, well staffed with servants, and unavailable to any but qualified persons, the modern business car is, by comparison to its ornate and orchidaceous predecessors, a paradigm of Spartan simplicity.

Private varnish of the nineties and early 1900s reached an all-time high in luxurious appointments, ornamentation, and physical conveniences. Pipe organs, solid gold and silver dinner services, period furniture, costly upholsteries, rare paintings, and air-conditioning long before it was commonly available to standard railroad equipment were the merest commonplace. *Loretto,* the celebrated Pullman-built car of Charles M. Schwab, boasted marble plumbing fixtures, plate-glass mirrors of heroic dimensions, brass beds, and ceiling murals in its master bedroom executed by an Italian artist specially imported to Chicago for the commission. *Ranger,* belonging to Cissy Patterson, publisher of the *Washington Times Herald,* was kept fully staffed twenty-four hours a day in the Southern's Washington yards and possessed seven complete sets of slip covers for its furniture so that its passengers might not become fatigued with the same décor on successive days.

Jomar, the car inherited from his uncle John Ringling by John Ringling North, owner of the circus, has in its dining salon a series of circus murals by Charles Baskerville, a fashionable painter of animal life. The personal car of Brigham Young, president of the Latter-day Saints, had a frieze of heavily gold-plated angels around the transoms in its clerestory, and the car of Arthur E. Stilwell, a railroader of religious leanings, had a pipe organ installed as an adjunct to divine services which were held every Sunday wherever the car might be spotted. When Estelle Manville, the roofing heiress, married the Count Folke-Bernadotte of Sweden a few years ago, Mrs. Edward F. Hutton, a friend, took two of her own private cars from Grand Central to Pleasantville, New York, a distance of thirty-one miles for the wedding. Charles Clark, son of famed Senator William F. Clark of Montana, reportedly commissioned the Pullman Company to build *Errant* for his wife so that she might travel with her pet dog, forbidden in public conveyances. The first air-conditioned railroad car in the world was *Edgewood,* the property of Major Max Fleischmann, the yeast tycoon, and Mrs. J. P. Donahue's *Japauldin,* perhaps the most costly private car ever outshopped by Pullman, had solid gold lighting fixtures, quartered oak beams running the length of the drawing room ceiling, and a wood-burning fireplace equipped with an electric blower for draft.

When J. P. Morgan hired a special train of Pullman Palace cars, his major-domo was Louis Sherry.

Valets, ladies' maids, secretaries, and paid companions went with their employers by the score, and a total of six bedside push buttons in mother-of-pearl in her personal bedroom on her husband's *Loretto II* testified to the number of domestics at the call of Mrs. Charles M. Schwab.

Jay Gould was troubled with dyspepsia, and his entourage when he boarded *Atalanta*, or another of the several private cars owned by or available to him in his lifetime, included not only a personal physician but a French chef specially skilled in the preparation of lady fingers and other featherweight pastry allowed by his regimen. Sometimes he was accompanied on long trips by his daughter Helen who brought her own *Stranrear* along for the ride.

The son of James Jerome Hill of the Great Northern and famed as an empire builder, known to intimates in St. Paul as "Pooch," maintained a Great Northern car with a garage that occupied its forward portion, access to which was achieved by a ramp that could be let down like a drawbridge. In the early days of automobiling, Hill was a Rolls-Royce addict and, in a time of few and uncertain highways, traveled with a Park Ward tourer on board. There was sleeping space, too, for a chauffeur.

The private car of one Georgia nabob with a taste for mushrooms had a mushroom cellar slung from the underside of his car between a storage locker and the batteries.

It was aboard Mrs. Donahue's *Japauldin*, while it was spotted at Palm Beach in the early twenties, that an invited guest strayed from the observation salon to investigate the resources of the rest of the car and returned awe-struck to tell a friend in a stage whisper: "You ought to get a load of the dining room; all the silver's solid gold!" Another gold table service of railroad legend was that manufactured by Shreve, the great San Francisco silversmiths, for *Salvador*, Pullman-built palace car of James Ben Ali Haggin which traveled between California and the owner's vast stock farms in Kentucky with a chef from Foyot's in Paris in the galley. The crew on August Belmont's private electric car in which he used to ride from the Belmont Hotel in New York to the races at Belmont Park were attired in dress uniforms from Wetzel, the costliest of all gentlemen's tailors.

In the years between the company's formation and 1930 when it outshopped its last private railroad car for Harry Payne Whitney, the Pullman Company, according to its records, built a total of 350 such items of equipment. Many others were built by American Car & Foundry and the carshops of individual railroads.

As a result of the Second World War when rail equipment of all sorts was in great demand for the military, the private cars of yesterday were largely turned back to the railroads for official or government use. *Curley Hut*, the handsome varnish car of Franklyn L. Hutton, is now business car No. 25 of the Chesapeake & Ohio. Barbara Hutton's car with its elaborate Tiffany silver service and spacious bedrooms is the business car of the president of the Western Pacific.

Henry Ford's *Fair Lane* is reserved for the president of the Cotton Belt.

Atalanta, the sumptuous car built for Jay Gould in the eighties at a cost of $50,000, a fabulous sum for the times, ended its days as a yardmaster's shack on the Missouri Pacific in Overton, Texas. Joshua Cosden's Pullman, on which the then Prince of Wales toured the United States in 1924, is now grounded as the residence of a coal-stripping gang at Hazelton, Pennsylvania. For private cars, the paths of glory lead but to the rip track.

As part of its function of public service, the Pullman Company still maintains a number of drawing-room cars with kitchens and observation salons which can be rented for a fixed daily sum with a staff of two attendants. Rental is in addition to the eighteen full first-class railroad fares required by law, taxes, parking, and sanitation charges.

FOLKLORE OF MANIFEST DESTINY

The engines and the cars clattered smokily into the consciousness of the American people when the first train brigades commenced rolling through the meadows of New England and past the cotton fields of the South and they have remained there ever since, less poetic, perhaps, but fully as valid a symbol of national destinies as the American eagle and starry empyrean that figure in the Great Seal of the United States.

It is difficult at this remove to suggest the altogether compelling fascination which almost every aspect of railroading possessed for the national mind from its earliest inception. It became at once apparent, both to thoughtful and informed intelligence and to the common apprehension, that America was both literally and figuratively riding the cars to splendid destinies beyond dimly seen horizons. Almost overnight the steam locomotive became an instrument of continental implications. Only fifteen years after the coming of the trains the country was swept to a crescendo of emotional tensity by the phrase "manifest destiny." The United States was going places and, by tunket it was going there in style aboard the railroad.

For three full generations the railroad was to be the essential tangible fact of American life. With the exception of a very few mileposts of the years such as the Dred Scott decision, woman suffrage and the boll weevil, almost every fact of life in the American record has been in some way affected by the railroad.

With this background combined with the incomparably romantic appeal of railroading, its sights, smells, and sounds, it is no wonder that there grew up around the cars and engines, the men who served and rode them, their depots, operations, achievements, and catastrophes, a national folklore which expressed itself in song, story, and ballad, in music, pictorial art, and on the stage, in the national vocabulary and in artifacts and legend.

These manifestations are so various and so innumerable that their complete tally is obviously impossible in this space. Their existence is suggested by hundreds of geographic locales, "Railroad Gaps," "High

Bridges," and the literally thousands of communities ranging from great cities to flag stops that were named after railroad builders, engineers, superintendents, and mere track layers. The national vocabulary is the richer for such phrases as "across the tracks," "tank town," "high-ball," and "asleep at the switch."

In the realm of popular art one has but to consult the roster of Currier & Ives prints to discover its universal and overwhelming dominance in the mid-nineteenth century. In the annals of music the railroad theme runs from "I've Been Working on the Railroad," which is an American folk song of Stephen Foster dimensions, to Arthur Honneger's classic "Pacific 231." "The Wreck of Old 97," "The Chatsworth Wreck," and "In the Baggage Car Ahead" are securely rooted in the body of native American music, while "Union Pacific" is the title of a ballet not infrequently included in repertories of the dance. In letters, the bibliography of American railroading has engaged the attention of learned confreries and occupies a bulletin of some hundreds of pages of fine-type references published by the Railway & Locomotive Historical Society, which has its headquarters at Harvard University.

A simple generation unaccustomed to the radio, streamlining, or atomic fission was thrilled and delighted by the brave girl who threw the switch in time or flagged down the limited at the washed-out trestle. The roaring, smoky locomotive at the head end of a swaying string of varnish cars became a symbol of American resolution, one with the charge of the United States Calvary and the bold fireman mounting his precarious extension ladder amid the flames.

Music-hall tenors assumed the vigilant pose of the locomotive engineer with his hand upon the throttle. The public consciousness was orientated to railroading. The first commercial motion-picture film ever released depicted *The Great Train Robbery*. Novels like *The U. P. Trail* had railroading as their setting. The first successful legitimate drama of railroading, *Under the Gaslamp* was followed by scores of plays such as *The Ninety and Nine, The Fast Mail*, and *The Denver Express*. Only a few years ago Ben Hecht and Charles MacArthur confected a hilarious comedy-melodrama called *Twentieth Century* in which the entire action was realistically staged aboard the cars of the New York Central's most celebrated varnish flyer. A ponderable number of early film thrillers were railroad melodramas and such mature, semidocumentary films as *Union Pacific* have made fortunes for Hollywood. As a matter of fact this film, directed by the great Cecil B. De Mille, netted $5,000,000 for Paramount and proved to be fabulous publicity for the U. P. Railroad.

It is probable that the first aspects of railroading to become established in the national imagination and hence in its folklore were the visible attributes of the engines and cars themselves.

At a very early age of railroading, probably well before the year 1853 when William Mason of Taunton first undertook to design locomotives that should "look somewhat better than cook-stoves on wheels," the decoration and embellishment of railroad engines began to recommend itself both to professional and amateur artists. From the day when the first engineer left his terminal one fine morning with a pair of deer's antlers rakishly attached to his smokebox down to comparatively recent times, engines were possessed of personality and character, sometimes an individuality that verged on eccentricity. In a generation when locomotives carried names rather than numbers and were often assigned to service with a particular engineer and fireman and never operated by anyone else, it was not unnatural that the imagination and native artistry of the men who came to feel themselves the actual owners of engines should be represented in their appearance.

Most locomotives of the mid-nineteenth century were characterized by varied and beautiful paint jobs. Driver spokes were painted fire red, drive rods were silvered, Russian iron on boilers was finished in steel blue, and the trim and scrollwork on engine cabs, running boards, and tenders as well as all lettering were characteristically engrossed in gold leaf and red varnish. Gleaming brasswork for handrails, bells, candlesticks, and nameplates was universal.

One of the early Baldwin locomotives delivered to the Pennsylvania Railroad in 1856, a 4-4-0, was named *Tiger* and an artist's graphic representation of a crouching Bengal man-eater in full color appeared on each side of the cab, but mostly such complicated scenes of landscape and natural life were reserved for enhancing the beauty of early coaches rather than engines.

Regionally there seems to have been little difference in the tastes of the amateurs who sat about dressing up the iron horse. By far the greatest universal favorite was a set of deer's horns or stag antlers mounted either on the smokebox or atop the great storm lanterns of the period. It was visible on main lines and branches, great trunk railroads and short hauls alike from Maine to Florida and from Georgia to California.

Another favorite everywhere was an Indian profile cut from sheet metal by some mechanic in the railroad shops. Sometimes this was varied by a mounted brave or a warrior with drawn bow and arrow.

Still a third was a brass spread eagle similar to those which long ago added a panache to the top of the high-pressure cylinder of every steamer to boast expansion engines. On locomotives the eagle usually rode the sand dome. Sometimes it gladdened the eye from a position on the smokebox.

The storm lanterns of the old wood burners are a subdivision of engine art by themselves. As long as engines were assigned by common usage and custom to a single engineer for their maintenance and operation the custom also obtained by whose terms the engineer supplied and owned his own headlight. Usually he removed it at the end of each run and often he took it home with him as a symbol of ownership and independence. The metal panels and glass sidelights of these lanterns offered illimitable possibilities for native artists, and the subject matter was bounded only by the imagination of their owners.

The death knell of decorative locomotives and their brass trim and scrollwork was probably sounded by old Commodore Cornelius Vanderbilt despite his own gaudy business car also named, appropriately enough, *The Vanderbilt*. When the story got around that parts of the Central's locomotive *Cephas Manning* were finished in plated gold, antirailroad agitators pointed to this as gratuitous voluptuousness and Vanderbilt gave the order to begin a regime of decorative austerity. Henceforth the Central's motive power was characterized by a general absence of the gingerbread and frosting which before that had been thought essential on any progressive railroad, and the other roads of the land followed its lead.

Perhaps no other occupation ever fetched the American fancy as did that of the locomotive engineer. Not even the cowboy, the Indian scout, the vision of Washington at Valley Forge, or the swift facility of "Tinker to Evers to Chance" quite so effectively captivated the national imagination as the steam locomotive, its drive rods flashing obedient to the crossheads in their guides and the dynamic whole obedient to the visor-capped man at the throttle. His eagle eye pierced the impenetrable storm and saw to the farthest horizons; his controlling hand on the airbrake lever was the hand of Fate itself. The aviator of a later generation, a mere military mechanic cleaving his wide blue yonder, was never in the same league with the brave engineer.

And second only to the engine driver in mobile majesty was the conductor. His authority was and, indeed, still is absolute, comparable to that of a ship captain with the possible exception of solemnizing marriage and decreeing death. His insignia of office were his blue frock coat with brass buttons and heavy gold Albert watch chain festooning a liberal bay window. The conductor in the old days was the peer of senators, millionaires, and, possibly, Buffalo Bill.

Less exalted than the train captain or the brave engineer, but nonetheless facinating to a generation of American youth to which pluck-and-luck and work-and-win were a fact rather than a humorous myth was the news butcher, a sophisticated gamin who was wise in the ways of the world and peddled tobacco, candy, cigars, joke books, tourist guides, sandwiches, soft drinks, and periodicals in the aisles of the cars. From news butcher to railroad president was the theme of many of Horatio

Alger's fictional exhortation to ambition, and Thomas A. Edison, who for a time worked the cars on the Grand Trunk, and William A. Brady, a gaudy theatrical impresario of the early twentieth century and father of Alice Brady, was another. Brady's route was over the lines of the Union Pacific and Central Pacific in the Far West in the early seventies when railroading was robust and the pickings for a smart lad not' overburdened with professional ethics were often substantial. The cars in those days and places crawled with drunks and to these and gullible Easterners Brady sold collections of fancy colored rocks labeled "Mineral Specimens," while aboard the immigrant cars he peddled bedding, soap, tinned foods, and other such substantial matters. "Brady," says Stewart Holbrook, "was a general store on two legs."

Many of the American types who rode the cars in the years of the great riding were so well defined and established as to achieve for themselves an association with railroading almost as close as that of the train personnel itself. Drummers, professional gamblers, smoking-room raconteurs, newly-weds, bunco steerers, and the genus *rusticus Americanus* became so identified with the coaches and Pullmans that, in varying degrees, they were translated to the estate of stock characters on the stage and in the repertory of national anecdote. Each had his identifying characteristic; the gamblers wore ratcatcher suits, smelled strongly of Macassar hair oil, and possessed winning ways which covered devious designs; newlyweds were invariably on their wedding trip bound for Niagara Falls; the bunco steerers slyly exhibited gold bricks beneath the skirts of their traveling coats in the manner of Paris postcard vendors; the smoking-room raconteurs involved the drummers in their anecdotes which invariably began: "It seems there were three traveling salesmen . . ."; and the hick pulled the conductor's cord at the wrong time, had trouble with the toilet facilities, and wore a duster coat and straw in his hat.

The homely types who rode the cars in the simple times of the dollar dinner in the diner and red-plush upholstery in the coaches may not have realized it, but they were riding on a one-way through ticket to national immortality.

The ballad lore of American railroading, while by no means as voluminous as its bibliography, is still both representative and extensive. True to established tradition, most songs and verses of the rails and railroaders are of a plaintive or downright melancholy order. A susceptible and highly sentimental generation was admonished that life was like a mountain railroad and that if it wanted to achieve its earthly terminal it should keep its hand upon the throttle and its eye upon the rail. The singer inquired if you heard the foreman calling: "Dina, blow your horn?" The terrified imagination knew that old 97 was going downhill at ninety miles an hour when its whistle broke into a scream. Americans rode vicariously on the little red caboose behind the train. A hundred lives were lost when the bridge was burned at Chatsworth and mother rode in a casket in the baggage car ahead.

But the words and music that have rocked Americans right down to their boots and probably will for generations to come were sold for a pint of gin by a roundhouse hostler and concerned an Illinois Central engineer named John Luther Jones.

Casey's name derived from the town of Cayse, Kentucky, where he had once lived and at the time of his death he was a well-known engine driver along the I.C.'s divisions in the Deep South. He was killed in 1900 in a rear-end collision when the fast passenger train, the *Cannonball*, on the Chicago-New Orleans run, of which he was engineer crashed into a freight which had failed to draw completely into a passing track near Vaughan, Mississippi.

Jones' Negro fireman, Sim Webb, who lived for half a century after the accident, jumped before the crash and spent the rest of his days in the reflected glory of the event. His sentimental regard for the late Casey was shared by Wallace Saunders, a hostler at the Illinois Central roundhouse at Canton, Mississippi, where Jones's engine was regularly stabled. Saunders had a native talent for improvisation of plaintive melodies and his musical lament for his hero achieved a certain local vogue among the railroad men in the region. In the proper ballad tradition it was designed by its original author only to be sung or harmonized so that the imperfections of its metrical structure were inconsequential.

There is more legend than fact in the precise manner in which Saunders' roundhouse dirge became sublimated to a national institution, but one version has it that an itinerant music-hall performer, passing through town, gave the author a bottle of Saturday night gin in return for permission to write down the words. From there its progress toward sheet-music publication was a saga of popular success which ended in nearly fifty years of litigation, claims of proprietorship, and suits over copyright infringements. Casey Jones was valuable property.

Casey's widow, who was known to both the authors of this book as a lively old lady living in Jackson, Mississippi, enjoyed much the same celebrity as Sim Webb. She visited conventions of railroaders, was regularly interviewed at suitable anniversaries and became a landmark of consequence in the countryside. Her greatest personal triumph was a trip to New York to appear on a national radio hour, an instrument of immortality of which Casey, in the Jackson cemetery these many years, never dreamed.

BEEF AND BOURBON

"My mother and father came west in the eighties, on the 'steam cars,' as they called them then," said the well-preserved woman in covered-wagon tones as she sipped a double Gibson and looked out of her drawing-room window. The *City of San Francisco* was barreling along at eighty on its westward run through the Wyoming uplands. "I suppose they'd be really amazed at the way we travel across the continent nowadays. Things must have been really rough on the Old Frontier."

She ordered lunch from the upstairs boy from the diner: a small *filet*, very rare, fresh asparagus with drawn butter, Camembert, and a split of Bollinger.

"I suppose they carried their food with them," she continued. "Pemmican or whatever—or perhaps buffalo steaks."

She brightened visibly at the thought of fresh buffalo hump, of which she had read at some length in Bernard De Voto.

"They certainly were made of sterner stuff than we are, in those times," she concluded, and had another Gibson to fortify herself against the thought of the deprivations they must have suffered on *The Overland Limited* in the year 1880.

It would have done no good—and she probably wouldn't have believed it—if anyone had told her that things weren't so tough at the time she mentioned, and that the sufferings of the Mormons crossing the Great Plains in winter had by that time been history for nearly four decades. The continuity of luxury travel reaches further into the American past than many people know. On the very *Overland* run in which our well-brandied lady envisioned her ancestor roughing it, there were three kinds of imported champagne on the breakfast menu, and lounge cars carried "the new improved Burdett organ," which must have been an improvement over the radio programs picked up from Denver today.

Our lady-traveler-to-the-Coast was following the classic route of the forty-niners who go west today, only a century after the first white tops set out from Kansas, except that she was bound for San Francisco and the Sheraton-Palace instead of the bar at Dave Chasen's in Hollywood. After

lunch at Soulé's, she had departed from New York aboard the crimson-
carpeted splendor of *The Twentieth Century Limited*, had spent the
late hours of the next morning shopping at Marshall Field's, and arrived
at the Pump Room in Goethe Street for lunch. She headed west late in
the afternoon aboard the *City of San Francisco*, while her counterparts
in social and professional fashion were heading, in equally stylish circumstance, toward Kansas City aboard *The Super Chief*. In the years of
the covered wagons, the wagon trains for Northern California via the
Great Overland & Pike's Peak Route diverged a few miles west of Leaven-
worth from those heading for the Old Pueblo of Los Angeles via the Santa
Fe Trail. Today, the trails diverge at Chicago or Ogden, Utah, as the
case may be, but the fork in the trail is still there.

In the year 1957, the beef-and-bourbon route of professional and fashionable necessity between the Atlantic and the Pacific is perhaps even
more rigidly decreed by convention than was the route of the seventies
and eighties by practical necessity. To the names that make news and
persons of consequence today, it consists of a single terminal at either
end of the continent's three thousand miles, and two or, at most, four
possible trains of "steam cars." There are, to be sure, some people so
uncertain of their own importance as to feel compelled to attract attention to themselves by flying, but in this brief essay we will confine ourselves to the transport of persons so securely established in the world
that they have no need to pretend their time is more valuable than it is.

Comfort, dignity, and security still ride the steam cars, and the air lanes
may be surrendered for present purposes to the cinema starlets and lower
echelon of Madison Avenue hucksters who cherish the *arriviste* delusion
that air travel is classy, which is, indeed, just the word to describe it.

From New York, the point of departure is Jack & Charlie's No. 21
West Fifty-second Street. From Grand Central to LaSalle Street, the
only thinkable conveyance is—as it has been for better than fifty years—
The Twentieth Century Limited. The halfway house is the Pump Room.
From Lake Michigan to Southern California there is a possible choice
between the Santa Fe's *The Chief* or *The Super Chief* and the Union
Pacific's *City of Los Angeles*. For dinner at the far end of the continental
dimension, one reassembles at Chasen's. By following this rigidly defined
routing, it is possible to be assured of the best the world has to offer of
everything, and, consequently, the risk of seeing more than an irreducible
minimum of strange or foreign faces is practically nil. Everyone anyone
knows travels the same way, and it's as safe—from the social and professional point of view—as heading directly from the Ritz-Carlton to the
Royal Poinciana and back aboard the *Florida Special* in the early Otto
Kahn age.

Ben Fairless, Josh Logan, Bill Hearst, J. Edgar Hoover, the Harvey

Firestones, Judy Garland, Mrs. Perle Mesta, and Mrs. Grover Loening dined last night at Chasen's. Today, Ben Fairless, Josh Logan, Bill Hearst, J. Edgar Hoover, the Harvey Firestones, Judy Garland, Perle Mesta, and Mrs. Grover Loening are lunching, either in the restaurant car of *The Super Chief* or in their private apartments, aboard the same train. Tomorrow they will be on view, under the benevolent aegis of Jimmy Hart, at the Pump Room. *The Century's* train secretary will check them aboard at LaSalle depot that afternoon, and next night they will all be at "21." It's like a Greek frieze—restful, uncomplicated, and always the same wherever you encounter it.

Transcontinental rail and hotel travel in the eighties—despite its seemingly primeval simplicities when compared with the Pump Room's knee breeches and rolling tables of caviar, and the streamlined Diesel-powered consist of *The Super Chief*—differed mainly in the matter of time taken in transit. Nobody suffered much, even though air-conditioning was undreamed of and dining cars didn't run everywhere.

Voyagers heading for the Far West from a gaslit Manhattan had their last lunch at Delmonico's or the Hoffman House, checked out of the Windsor Hotel on Fifth Avenue, took a growler, or closed horse cab, around the corner to the splendid new Grand Central Station (which for some years now had replaced the old Harlem Depot on Forty-second Street), and entrained aboard the New York Central and Hudson River Railroad's crack passenger flyer *The Pacific Express*, which made the run to Chicago in thirty-six hours.

And just in case you imagine this to have been a teapot-drawn string of day coaches out of a Culver City Civil War costume job, *The Pacific Express* sometimes left for the west with twenty-two cars—five more than regularly comprise today's *Century*—and more than half of them were Wagner's Palace Hotel cars, which delighted their generation with mahogany-finished exteriors and interiors of rare paneled woodwork, Turkey-carpeted private drawing rooms, crystal lighting fixtures, plate-glass picture windows, and looped and ball-fringed draperies. They reminded passengers of the residences of the various Vanderbilts even then rising on upper Fifth Avenue in florid architectural profusion.

Arrived in Chicago, the voyager took a cab of the Parmelee transfer—still in operation in the Windy City to this day—to Potter Palmer's superb hotel, in whose restaurant it was the chef's boast that any dish available anywhere in the accepted restaurants of the civilized world could be produced on short notice.

In the age of which we speak, the railroad dining car was by no means universal. It was more rare in the Far West than among the railroads of the East. Beyond the Mississippi, the various on-line depots, where the cars pulled up three times a day for meals, contributed to the fair fame—or the reverse—of the region and the railroad that traversed it.

Which brings us inevitably to Fred Harvey. The pioneers of the Old West—and say their names with bugles—Kit Carson, Jim Bridger, Lieutenant (later Brigadier General) Zebulon Pike, Peter Skene Ogden, and Benjamin Louis Eulalie de Bonneville, all have been remembered by a grateful posterity. And their names are still fragrant in legend and ballad lore, in historic record, and in the geography of the Western continent.

But aside and apart from the Mountain Men and the Long Hunters—the Fremonts, the Woottons, and the Custers—there were pioneers of another sort to whom the West owes a debt of gratitude not too often mentioned even though their explorations contribute daily, by indirection and direction, too, to the well-being of millions.

Somebody should raise monuments to the pioneers of good living: François Pioche, who imported an entire shipload of French chefs to give San Francisco gastronomy its first beginnings in the gold-rich fifties; the godlike Ernest Arbogast, first chef of the first Palace Hotel in New Montgomery Street, whose memory is reverenced by informed diners and oenophilists to this day; and, perhaps most of all, the English Fred Harvey who preached salvation through the agency of sauce remoulade and brought civilization in its fullest and most fragrant flower to the entire Southwest. From the Great Plains of Kansas, then through the high passes of the Raton, across the High Plains to Santa Fe itself, and to the Old Pueblo of the Angels among the adobes of Southern California, the name of Fred Harvey rolled triumphantly on a tidal wave of souffles and salads, *potages* and purées that from the seventies even to this day has never diminished.

Honored with potations and revered among the entrees be the name of Fred Harvey!

For one thing, Harvey established a family dynasty which even now does things the way he would have wanted them done, eschewing cheapness and shortcuts in a world where the shabby devisings of economy are almost universal. Although the Harvey restaurants and hotels and other enterprises—dining cars on the Santa Fe Railroad, service units, and other installations—cover a sixteen-page mimeographed list that is still expanding, no least compromise has ever been made with the ultimate superlative in merchandise and its presentation. Matching such standards of perfection is difficult enough for an exclusive, individual restaurant in New York or Los Angeles; the problem it presents in an establishment which has a payroll of thirty-five hundred is something to imagine.

For the first time in a decade and a half, this reporter journeyed westward a month or so ago aboard the Santa Fe's incomparable and incomparably maintained *Super Chief*. There are defects about this train, but not conventional ones. For one thing, it makes the trip between Chicago and Los Angeles with time for only five meals aboard its diners. This is a mistake, for there must be many travelers who would gladly endorse a schedule twice as long that would include twice as many meals. But *The Super Chief* is the jewel box and display case of the management, and the reporter rode it for this reason.

The antelope steaks and sage hen which Fred Harvey first included on his abundant menus are, of course, one with the buffalo and the passenger pigeon; but time has not diminished the massive proportions of Fred Harvey steaks, the freshness of Colorado mountain trout, the incredible dimensions of the strawberries, or the lush salads which illustrate the menu in epic profusion.

The founding Fred was a perfectionist. In a wilderness of ptomaine nests masquerading as stagehouses and of other resorts dreadful to contemplate, where passengers on the first primeval transcontinental trains were systematically poisoned in graceless surroundings (by Borgias who knew that the chances of a return to their premises were slight), he insisted not only on the best things to eat and drink, but on the style of service and presentation that compared favorably with Delmonico's and the Albermarle Hotel in far-off New York. His table linen was the finest that Irish looms could weave, his silver service was solid, his crystal immaculate. Cow pokes, boomer conductors, cattle shippers, drummers from Kansas City, and the gamblers who frequented the steam cars ate in a style and in surroundings fit for nabobs.

No train in the land today—neither *The Twentieth Century Limited, The City of San Francisco, The Burlington Zephyrs,* nor the haughty *Empire Builder*—presents meals any more graciously than does *The Super Chief.* Its staff of stewards, waiters, maîtres d'hôtel, and chefs are, of course, Harvey veterans of the first chop and, as they should aboard an extra-fare limited, the patrons of its restaurant car set great store by the conventions of polite travel. Fred Harvey, in his own remote and uncouth time and place, insisted that patrons wear ties and jackets to his table, and this tradition continues today. Dinner aboard *The Super Chief,* if lacking the almost unearthly formality of similar occasions aboard crack Cunarders, is at least an occasion of spirit and grace, something to look forward to as a fitting conclusion to a day of relaxed progress upon a superlative train.

A good many years ago, William Allen White, "the Sage of Emporia," writing in his *Emporia Gazette* of the Harvey diners on the Santa Fe, remarked: "Harvey meals are so much better than meals on other railroads east, west, north, or south that comparison seems trite." The sentiment is true today, as it was in 1920. Now the Harvey system spans three thousand miles of highway and railroad between Cleveland and the Pacific Coast and can boast of matchless hospitality the entire distance.

Much has been written during the past quarter century about the two terminal or anchor restaurants, "21" and Chasen's, and the swing station, the Pump Room, and their various careers. So much, indeed, as to make it the most remarkable aspect of their continued existence that each is the standard of eating and social excellence in the community in which it operates, and none shows any least sign of abatement with the passing years.

It is well established that ordinary human beings, not smitten with delusions of self-importance, do not see history in the things around them and in which they themselves participate. Yet it is an absolute certainty that "21," the Pump Room, and Chasen's, as well as the streamlined restaurant cars and rolling oases that connect them, are irretrievably a part of the pattern of American folklore, one with the Waldorf of an older generation, the Brevoort, and Antoine's on St. Louis Street. The years are already investing them with an aura of romance imperceptible to the regulars who have been complaining about the martinis for a quarter of a century and lamenting that the age of giants passed when Harold Ross made his last exit into Fifty-second Street and the night of all things. The mantle of greatness and splendid ways has fallen so gently over the participants in these souffléed sarabands that not until tomorrow dawns will they stand revealed as History.

But already their names, the foibles and characters of their customers, the epic witticisms that have transpired at their bars are slipping into anthologies of folklore and the regional record of the American scene. Time is having its way with them, and they are in the position—not unique, but not common either—as were Buffalo Bill Cody and the old Hippodrome, of having become legends in their own lifetime.

The beef-and-bourbon scheme of things, it will be seen, supplies food not only for the inner being of men, but for thought among the perceptive as well. Life in America in the second half of the twentieth century wouldn't be half so pleasant without it.

"THE MOST HEROIC OF AMERICAN LEGENDS . . ."

The most heroic of American legends is the chronicle of railroading. It is heroic not only in the integral sagas whose synthesis constitutes the body of any legend, but in the spaciousness and breadth of its entire pattern, its concern for the affairs of men on a scale essentially epic, and its inescapable association with a national destiny.

What her armadas and merchant fleets, her ships and admirals of the ocean-seas have been to England, what the legions and proconsuls ruling the *orbis terrarum*, the known world, were to Rome, steam locomotion and the great railroad builders have been to America. For a full century, railroads and railroading have dominated the story of the nation, and they have left a stirring, a breathlessly vivid impress upon the American consciousness. The chapters have been written by the Collis Huntingtons and the Jack Casements, the W. W. Fairbankses and William Masons, the generations of engine-drivers who have wheeled their Taunton-built diamond-stackers, their latter-day Mikados and Mallets over the illimitable steel of the illimitable and compelling Western land, and the whole of it is possessed of an urgency and a magnificence that is, in the essential meaning of the word, unique. For no other machine has ever exercised a fascination for the human imagining comparable to that of the steam locomotive.

In the introduction to one of the collected volumes of his poems, John Masefield tells of the sailing ships that peopled his youth standing into the distant roadsteads of the world—"beautiful unspeakably."

The writer has stood in the late afternoon at the end of a bay in the long train shed of the St. Louis terminal watching the coming and going of many trains. There were locomotives from nearly a score of roads on the tracks surrounding that Pharos of all switching towers that divides the hemispheres of the East and West: the ponderous but fleet passenger greyhounds of the Missouri Pacific, after whose first 4-6-2 type the Pacific locomotive was named; one of the celebrated tribe of the Pennsylvania's K-4s, panting from a scorching run across the whole of Indiana and Illinois under a July sun; the immaculate heavy Pacifics of the Alton, their boiler shells the fine blue-gray of daily polishing, rods and cross-heads and tires gleaming like mirrors; the lovingly tended power of the Frisco with burnished brass bells and handrails in the old manner, blue and gold and rakish, backing in for the through varnish for Oklahoma and the great Southwest. And there were the locomotives and the rolling stock of the Burlington and the Wabash, the Illinois Central, the Nickel Plate, the Southern, and the Mobile, and Ohio.

He has paused by night in the yards at Cleveland where the feline Hudsons of the New York Central panted in the hot darkness, mousing for green lights among the switch points, and the yard engines throbbed with a subdued tensity waiting for *The Century,* in three sections, to thunder through like the implications of destiny itself. He has rolled as smoothly as on a bath of oil and almost with the speed of thought into the Colorado uplands aboard a Burlington streamliner, and he has sensed the conquest of a continent as the Overland has borne him, in the tranquil security of his drawing room, within a few miles of Promontory where once Engine 119 and the Jupiter, "pilots touching, head to head," enacted the closing scene of an epic of empire. The symphony of the twelve driving wheels, obedient to the main rods, of a Union Pacific Challenger-type gliding implacably westward in the yards at Omaha with a mile of red-ball freight behind them has moved him as some men are moved by the "Eroica" or the opening verses of *The Song of Roland.* And the sight of *The Chief,* double-headed and with a pusher, breasting the high iron of the Glorieta Pass, has been what Masefield's ships were to him, "beautiful unspeakably."

William Rose Benét once wrote a delightful poem beginning:

> Green aisles of Pullmans sooth me like trees
> Woven in old tapestries . . .

and to many and many an American the long green cars, the compact staterooms, those secret mansions and microcosms of all luxury, the flowers and crisp linen of the diner, the burnished brass of the observation platform, the ghostly whistle of the locomotive far up ahead in the enveloping night, and the flickering markers of the passing limited receding down the iron are implicit with all that spells wonder and romance and delight.

The function and office of the railroad historian are difficult of definition, since his subject matter requires exposition rather than interpretation and, unlike so many aspects of history, demands little orientation to other parallel aspects of the record. The saga of steam and overland steel is largely self-contained, self-evident, and self-sufficient. Its operations are almost wholly devoid of figures and personalities. The most vivid and colorful characters to emerge from the American railroading saga of the nineteenth century were not so much Jack Casement, William Mason, or

Theodore Judah as the scoundrelly capitalists of Wall Street and Nob Hill in black broadcloth tailcoats and General Grant whiskers. It was the Commodore Vanderbilts, Leland Stanfords, and Daniel Drews who have proved such fearsome fellows in the biographies written by men who, in their proper lifetimes, never quite paid off the mortgage on the house.

The closest approximation to honesty in any writer of consequence remarking on the great princes of the rails was achieved by Ambrose Bierce, who, one San Francisco morning in the nineties, was observed by a friend to be speculatively, even longingly, eying the fine swinging doors of Flood and O'Brien's Saloon in Sutter Street.

"There," sighed the noisiest crusader against vested corruption of his generation, "there, lapped in luxury and upholstered in Babylonish devisings, sipping rare vintages of great cost and plotting further brigandage against a toiling people, are those arch-thieves and conscienceless pillagers, Leland Stanford, Charles Crocker, Mark Hopkins, and Collis Huntington. Even now, no doubt, they scheme to loot more outrageously than ever the people and commonwealth of California. I wish I might be one of them!"

There has never since been and never again will be a time of such inherent, characteristic romance in railroading as in the 1850s and '60s. It was the period of the eight-wheeler, the American-type locomotive, with its diamond stack, its four high drivers, its brilliant lacquerwork, and such balance of design that the makers signed their product as an artist writes his *fecit* forever on a canvas. It is legendary that in winter, when the sound carried clearly, the engine bells ringing across the hillsides of New England were so beautiful of tone as to be loved like the church bells and so familiar that the country folk in villages many miles from the line would say, "There is the General Putnam," or, "The Minerva is behind her time today." In cold weather the brakeman carried the key to the cannonball stove in every car against fares who might be prodigally inclined with the chopped wood. The roads had about them the romantic promise of great things to come and the friendliness which until recently existed on country trolley routes, where cars waited at corners for regular passengers and the crews did errands in town for the neighbors along the way. Railroading, too, was once a country affair, innocent of the grim necessities of urban commerce as was the national spirit of the times, and to many this charm and flavor has never entirely been lost amid the urgency of a latter industrial age.

It is conceivable that the end is in sight for much that is picturesque and stirring to the imagination in the railroad scene. Diesel power and the frequently fatuous devices of streamlining do not quicken the heart. Romance and glory are implicit in outside motion, in side rods, crossheads, eccentrics, and the implacable rhythm of counterbalanced driving wheels reeling off the miles as the chapters of history were once written by the measured *passus* of the Roman legions. Railroading has become too involved and costly an enterprise to concern itself with legend and sentiment. The expenditures of the Santa Fe for a single year recently equaled the total appropriations for the same period of three states through which its iron passed. The brass-railed observation platform, so dear to the hearts of passengers, has been supplanted by, God save us, inclosed lounges of nightmare shapes and paneled with health glass.

Joaquin Miller spoke for uncounted millions when he wrote that "there is more poetry in the rush of a single railroad train across the continent than in all the gory story of burning Troy." Edna St. Vincent Millay expressed an almost universal urge when she proclaimed that there wasn't a train she wouldn't take no matter where it was going.

During the greater part of their life span the locomotives and cars were individualistic, possessed of character, and railroad travel exercised a charm upon the human spirit. The rails running to the horizon were indeed a royal road to romance. The cars were palaces in microcosm and a whole people rode them to far places and happy destinations in fact and in fancy, both literally and metaphorically. Manifest destiny lay around the curves and down the tangents.

The past beats against them as the night wind against a storm lantern. Their import and symbolism is that of Stephen Benét's "riders shaking the heart with the hooves that will not cease," and they stand as reminders still of heroic times in the land. And they are one with the placer diggings and the Jingle Bob, the hallmarks of California and the Chism steer, the C.C. on the minted gold of Carson City, the Wells Fargo scales, the Conestoga wagon, and the Starr's Navy pistol, all the identifications and styles, the devices and coat armor of a way of living as vanishes as the longhorn and as distinctive as Medford rum.

As the star of railroading dims, the steam cars that had been good familiar things for seven generations of American life and movement begins to recede from the general awareness, never to return. They rolled, obedient to the rails, through woodlands and meadows, over lofty trestles and in the high passes of the hills toward the final coach yard of forgetfulness, their locomotives, proud in the ancient ritual of reciprocating side rods, housed for all time in the last roundhouse. The cars went freighted with happy memories of a nation's bearded youth and of the brave years, of destinies beyond the horizon and a good time on the way. They had quickened the pulse as only the ships of the ocean-sea had done before them, and they were unseated from the wonder and admiration of men by the melancholy uses of progress and discomforts of modernity. The age was happy that had ridden the red-plush seats and watched the coal smoke roll over the winnowed farm lands. The generation which followed and was going conspicuously nowhere was to ride with more expedition surrounded by the décor of an operating room. Fortunate was the world that had heard the train blow.

The West: Nevada and California

"Fine," asserted a ten-year-old visitor. "We'll steal from the rich and give to the poor."

"That's not the way we play Robin Hood in Hillsborough," corrected his hostess. "Here we steal from the poor and give to the rich."

THE BEST OF POSSIBLE WORLDS

Nevada is my adopted state and I will defend it to the death. Nowhere in the Union is so low and comfortable a way of life available as in the One Sound State, the Hard Money State, the Sagebrush State. It is, among other things, the only state in the Union with no public debt, no income, inheritance, sales, or other nuisance or confiscatory state imposts. It is the only state where gambling, high, wide, and handsome, flourishes around the clock, and one of two—Louisiana, I think, is the other—where the saloons never close. Storey County, where I reside in the seedy grandeur of a Victorian mansion, is so poor that no offense requiring a jury trial ever reaches the bar of justice. Malefactors, including a recent murderer, are booted across the county line and told not to return.

Best of all, there are hardly any people in Nevada, only about one inhabitant for every square mile, which is as dense a population as I, after twenty-odd years on Madison Avenue, care to put up with. When, from my dressing room in the morning, I look across the 175 miles separating Virginia City from the Reese River mountains, I can comfortably reflect that there are hardly twenty-odd people in the intervening countryside.

As I say, Nevada is the best of possible worlds.

GOING FOR THE MAIL

A tie with the American past establishing continuity with a simpler age, the morning walk to the post office is still the identifying hallmark of the fast-vanishing country village. Going in person for the mail is one of the few American folk habits that connect the urban here and now with the country ways that were evident almost everywhere in the United States a century or so ago.

In such small towns as Virginia City (where I make my legal residence and spend the clement months of the year), going for the mail is almost the only common bond between the somewhat haphazard citizenry of this abode of the ancient glories of the Comstock Lode. Meetings of Their Honors, the Storey County Commissioners, are apt to be slimly attended unless matters of great moment, such as the annual debate over licensing the girls in Six Mile Canyon, are to be discussed. The subject of the girls is brought up every summer when one group of insurgent taxpayers insists they be licensed for county revenue, while another group demands their suppression on moral grounds. The result is always the same. The district attorney rules that licensing them is illegal but that the maintenance of love stores is in itself no violation of Nevada law. So the girls remain *in situ,* doing a roaring summer-month trade in a disreputable trailer camp down Sutro way.

Even the great community drunks on the occasion of the full moon, once common in many towns where the old frontier has died slowly, have now fallen into the discard. A full Comstock moon, than which there is none fuller or more mysterious anywhere on earth, used to set the patrons of C Street's saloons and other resorts at each other's throats to such a degree that the maimed and contused lay all night in the gutters and had to be swept up in the morning amidst general cries of "What seems to have happened?" Now the old-timers who liked to wrap a bar stool around each other's heads are all in the town's several cemeteries.

Only the nine o'clock walk to the post office for the morning mail remains. One must take part in this ritual in person, since sending an emissary or surrogate is invariably taken as a sign that a Comstocker is *in extremis* and won't last the day. Preferably one goes on foot to participate in the exchange of news (fallacious) and views (malicious) that takes place among the enlightened electorate on the sidewalk while waiting for Tex and Marion Gladding to finish putting up the second class.

In the West, where we all like to imagine vestigial traces of the Old West still linger in the most palpable tourist traps, the mail has an even greater significance than it does in, say, Vermont or Nantucket. The time when Horace Greeley's *Tribune* took eight weeks out of Missouri to get here is only yesterday in the general awareness. The well-known sketches, in all the Western histories, of the first San Francisco settlers waiting in long lines at the post office for the arrival of a steamer from Panama are evidence of a heritage of dependence on the safe arrival of mail. The morning ritual in Virginia City in 1966 has the best imaginable bloodlines.

Nine o'clock, when Virginia City sets its face toward the post office, finds an almost full tally of its first citizens hastening, ambling, or slouching (as their several natures suggest) toward the lockboxes. First on the scene, in her official capacity of picking up the county business, is Shirley Andreasen, the all-powerful functionary who, as Clerk, administers the county's affairs in their remotest detail. Nominally, the commissioners are the regulatory body, but in practical fact authority rests in the Clerk's office in the vast and venerable Storey County Court House near Piper's Opera. The courthouse was built in the seventies, when the Comstock still boasted 25,000 permanent residents, and now absorbs the microscopic taxes and records the deeds and legal business of a scant 350.

Hard on Mrs. Andreasen's heels comes Judge Edward Colletti, former partner and senior barman at the Delta Saloon now elevated to the magistracy, and as formal of attire and habit as any Montgomery Street broker over the hill in San Francisco. The town takes pride in Judge Colletti's decisions, but regrets his loss as a bartender.

In the early van of Virginia City's notables will be Florence Edwards, proprietor of the Silver Dollar Hotel and perhaps the community's most celebrated character. Mrs. Edwards, whose middle name is Ballou and who, on its basis, claims elevated connections in the East, came to Virginia City twenty years ago on a sight-seeing bus and awakened next morning in the Silver Dollar with a deed to the property, all properly sworn and attested, in her hand. Florence has never been away since. One day a week, she takes off for Reno and the hairdresser in her museum-piece motorcar, "The Spirit of Nausea," and the town makes book on whether she'll get it back up the hill by dinnertime.

Early on the scene, too, will be the town's only certified artist, Cal Bromond, whose Western canvases, mostly on a heroic scale, command really startling figures and can be discovered behind the bars of some of Reno's best sluicing places.

By nine-thirty the daily rite of picking up the mail is over, and the news of the day has been circulated with far greater celerity than in larger communities served by the rotary press. Everybody knows who is in jail for what from the night before, and Florence Edwards has recited the entire register of her guests at the Silver Dollar, together with their pedigrees, incomes, and social connections.

With this observance of the rite of going for the mail, Virginia City does more than pay its respects to a ceremony deep-rooted in the Western consciousness. It also prepares itself to honor an even more compulsive tradition. In the days of the deep mines of the Comstock, the town's multiple saloons were crowded with workers of the night shift who went off duty at eight in the morning, pausing on their way for an "after-shifter." The custom, which would raise scandalized eyebrows in New England, still obtains. Everyone of consequence still has an after-shifter when the mail has been cleared.

Occasionally, when the mail is late, the after-shifter takes on overtones of mild abandon, because the most natural place to wait for the mail is the place where one is eventually going anyway. "An old Western custom," everyone assures everyone else, as they teeter out into the cold light of day.

JULIA BULETTE:
The Comstock's First Cyprian

In many ways Julia Bulette, the Comstock's first and most enduring Cyprian, was of classic stature, the very model and prototype of what the frontier came to require of its fair but frail women. She was type cast according to the strictest imaginable conventions, one with the Pullman porter, the stage coach driver, the down-at-the-heels Shakespearian actor, and the end man in the minstrel show, her character as irrevocably defined as the unities in French classic drama.

The pioneer prostitute had to be beautiful or at least passably attractive. It was preferable if she had a mysterious but romantic background and antecedents. It was completely necessary that she be a ministering angel in frontier times of calamity and disaster. She must be a refining influence among the crude and uncouth characters of the placer mines and shack towns. The respectable element of woman must envy and despise her, and she must come to a tragic end.

All these attributes and characteristics Julia Bulette had in abundance. She subscribed to every convention of her role, playing it with the fidelity a member of the D'Oyly Carte Opera Company accords to the Lord High Executioner or Modern Major General. She missed no cue, fluffed no lines, and, from her emergence on the Virginia City scene to her ritualistic elevation to immortality in the legends of the Old West, she was a Sarah Siddons of the Sagebrush, a Mrs. Fiske of the gas lamps and wooden sidewalks.

The consequences of the character created by Julia Bulette in time became tangible far beyond the confines of Virginia City and Nevada, for just as mining towns everywhere were cast in the pattern of the Comstock, so she became the glass of fallen fashion in Last Chance Gulch and Candelaria and Tombstone, and had her lesser counterparts in a hundred Virgin Streets and Maiden Lanes from Bannack to Dodge City. In her lifetime, the Bulette was the archetype of frontier light-o'-love and in death achieved, as a characteristic institution of the frontier, a status far more elevated than a mere aspect of regional folklore.

Julia, according to contemporary evidence, came to Virginia City in its first wild flowering on the slopes of Sun Mountain from New Orleans. The putative pictures—there is no accredited likeness—show a trace of Creole cast and coloring, and it is notable that the fortunes of the Comstock attracted many adventurers from the Deep South of antebellum times, most notable of whom in a different sphere of activities was the fire-eating Judge David S. Terry, whose biography was largely written in .45 caliber and achieved a final period in the same dimensions.

Virginia City in 1860 was still largely a ragtown, one of tents and packing cases or a combination of both for private dwelling and public assembly alike. Intimations of urban permanence were, however, visible at the corner of A Street and Sutton Avenue where *The Territorial Enterprise* was being published from an edifice fashioned entirely and sumptuously of boards, kitty-corner from a structure actually built of brick and jointly occupied by Charlie Sturm's Saloon and the agency of Wells Fargo & Co., the latter's presence proclaiming the camp a proven diggings and destined for greatness.

Julia's arrival was not of sufficient consequence to rate mention in the public prints, although if it had been gifted with prescience, *The Enterprise* would have certainly hailed her coming with a suitable nosegay of agate or long primer. She took up her abode and presumably circulated professional tidings from a small, pretty cottage in the lower town, perhaps D Street where residences, miners' shacks, saloons, and structures of commerce were going up side by side amidst the mine hoists and headframes of the deep workings which were almost daily uncovering new bonanzas in the dark treasure houses of geologic time.

A contemporary oil painting in the primitive style, perhaps executed by an itinerant artist in payment for services, in the possession of the author of these vagrant paragraphs, shows her abode of joy flanked within its own fence by a flower garden on one side and the blank wall of some sort of manufactory or warehouse on the other. At the hitchpost, a gentle appearing mount decorously side-saddled awaits its owner, and in the background the slope of Sun Mountain ascends endlessly into the Nevada sky.

The tradition of the red-lit doorway was still in the womb of time, not to be established until train crews of the Kansas Pacific, when enjoying relaxed moments in Abilene, made a practice of hanging their switch lanterns outside to aid the dispatcher's call boy in finding them. But the miners of Con Virginia, Best & Belcher, and Burning Moscow beat a path to Julia's door without professional illumination, and it was soon known in every saloon in C Street that not only had Virginia City achieved its first bagnio, but something pretty special into the bargain.

For not only was the Bulette a prostitute with the proverbial heart of gold beating under lacy underthings, she was a woman of taste who permitted no coarse language or conduct in her premises and who was destined in a short period of time to show the Comstock the essential difference between a saloon and a salon.

Legend has it that her dinner table groaned under its load of Lucullan wonderments, fresh oysters, hot-house grapes, and vintage champagnes bearing the great marques of Reims and Épernay. Perhaps it did indeed, since the fast stages of the California Staging Company were already in operation to San Francisco, a metropolis of notable culinary achievements, but whatever Julia's menu, it must have seemed like a glimpse of Delmonico's to grizzled prospectors accustomed to sourdough biscuits and the cheap whiskey of the frontier.

Conversation at Julia's table was elevated for its time and place. She tolerated no obscenity or profane language, an innovation of startling dimensions in itself. Julia's fees were high, legend sets them at $1000, but even if this figure is perhaps apocryphal, she still achieved overnight success both socially and economically. The circumstance of her social status is attested by her elevation to honorary member of Virginia Engine Company No. 1, the highest accolade within the gift of the Comstock's most exalted circles. Her financial solvency was indicated when, a year after her advent in Nevada, she enlarged her operations to embrace a dozen adjacent cottages, each occupied by a vestal of her own shrewd selection while she herself entertained only the most exclusive carriage trade as became a madame of acknowledged position in the community.

It was during the first terrible Comstock winter, too, that Julia undertook the role of ministering angel when influenza swept the ill-sheltered shacktown and carried away scores of miners for lack of medical care and nursing. Heroic figures of this fearful period were Father, later Bishop, Patrick Manogue, the beloved priest, and Julia, the beloved prostitute braving the winter storms and terrible winds of Washoe on errands of mercy in lowly hovels and wretched lodging houses. Assisted by the only other woman in camp, the seeress Eilley Orrum, who was soon to become the first of a long succession of Comstock millionaires, Julia gave unstintedly of her store of drugs and medicinal brandies, and many a miraculous recovery was credited to her by sentimental sourdoughs.

With the coming of better times as new bonanzas were uncovered and scientific mining replaced the unsophisticated surface diggings of the first discoverers, Julia emerged as Virginia City's most controversial figure if not its undisputed social leader. The ever-growing circle of "respectable" women, miners' wives and superintendents' ladies, who arrived as Virginia achieved civic status, frowned at Julia's unrepentant ways with great frowning. The diamonds she wore at first nights at Maguire's Opera did nothing to abate their envy, nor did the Paris evening gowns, rare silks and sables, and the fine landau with two matched horses in which she took the air of an afternoon, the gift of a particularly enthusiastic admirer. The honor of being a member of the Virginia Engine Company, one shared by no other woman, rankled as did Julia's position at the head of the procession at all firemen's musters, outings, picnics, parades, and other municipal jollifications.

Ladies were not asked to share in these delightful excursions, but Julia, no lady assuredly, was in the greatest requisition in a predominantly masculine society. Her soirees at the cottage in D Street were attended by judges, mine superintendents, and foremost political figures including, so it was reported over a hundred backyard fences on Sun Mountain, portly James W. Nye, first Territorial Governor of Nevada and owner of the first silk hat ever to be worn in Virginia City's riotously informal precincts. Nye's splendid presence, his senatorial voice and charm of person dominated dinner parties in the cottage in D Street where a "fallen woman" poured wine from silver ice buckets. Whatever was the world coming to?

But Fate was digging a mighty and, indeed, final pitfall for the wicked. Julia's wealthy ways were attracting unfavorable attention and not alone from the upper stratum of Virginia City's churchgoing society. Sharp eyes followed her triumphal arrival at opera and charity bazaar for the benefit of the Sanitary Fund, Civil War predecessor of the Red Cross. Acquisitive minds made note of her comings and goings, of the hours kept by her clientele, and the nightly disposition of the vestals in her service. Stealthy glances as she passed in C Street appraised the rubies that gleamed at her throat and the rich sable stole that trailed from shapely shoulders.

And then, one morning the Comstock rocked to the intelligence that Julia, the beautiful, witty, and animated Julia of a thousand firemen's balls and picnics at the Bowers Mansion, Julia of the first nights and cotillions and intimate buffet suppers at the cottage in D Street, was dead, murdered for the loot of her jewel caskets and fur vaults.

Virginia City was accustomed to murder. It stalked unabashed through the town's early years, so little regarded that *The Territorial Enterprise* seldom bothered with its particulars but ran a standing head reading "Last Night's Violence." On one occasion the victim of a stabbing in a C Street saloon lay for two days under a billiard table before the coroner bothered to sign a certificate permitting its removal.

But the murder of a woman, and she the town's darling of the hose reels and supper parties at the International Hotel, that was something different. Virginia City seethed with speculation and the details of the great crime.

The good women of Virginia were outrageous with satisfaction and wore I-told-you-so expressions of unbearable smugness as they shopped for bonnets at Barnert's Clothing Emporium or smoked oysters at Fulton Market. Virtue was, in their book, victorious, but Julia dead had one more triumph at the expense of respectability: she had the finest funeral ever seen in Nevada either before or since.

Every place of business in Virginia City was closed the day they buried Julia. Funereal pomp in the form of countless yards of crepe and black-bordered portraits of the deceased was displayed in front of many commercial premises. Father Manogue ordered the tolling of a passing bell at St. Mary's-in-the-Mountains. Led by Julia's own Virginia Engine Company, every red-shirted fire group, every hose wagon, pumper engine, and ladder company, with representations from neighboring Gold Hill and Silver City, formed in solemn procession behind the hearse. Every military company of the Comstock, parading to the Dead March from *Saul*, marched with turned musket butts behind the band of the Sarsfield Guards. Every politician, saloonkeeper, businessman, and gambler of the Lode, in black frock coat and equally somber gloves, was in Julia's last and largest cortege. They buried her, in unhallowed ground perforce, on a ridge overlooking the town she had, perhaps, loved too well and marched back to C Street to the tune of "The Girl I Left Behind Me."

The respectable women of Virginia City were speechless with rage at the honors paid to the woman they regarded as The Enemy. In death, Julia had had the last laugh at virtue.

Even in her grave Julia was the occasion of one more, almost equally splendid Comstock holiday when they hanged one of her murderers the following year. A Frenchman who spoke little English, John Millain, was apprehended by sheriff's officers when he attempted to dispose of some of the loot from the Bulette robbery. Convicted of complicity in the crime, he was sentenced to be hanged, and immediately became the caged darling of the women of the Comstock who had hated Julia and now regarded him as their own personal instrument of vengeance and retribution.

Millain lived high for his last few weeks in jail. Sentimentalists, admirers, and publicity seekers, all of them female, deluged his keepers with mash notes and chicken potpies in equal quantities. But Millain was taken out at last and hanged at the north end of town from a gallows whose expert design and pleasing appointments aroused universal admiration.

The occasion was the second greatest holiday in Comstock history. All business was suspended save that of the souvenir hawkers and pitchmen who circulated among the crowd estimated at five thousand that flocked to the place of execution. Flasks of whiskey, small meat pies of a sort known locally as Cousin Jack pasties, seegars, viewing glasses, cheap cushions, and ballads and broadsides detailing the life of the condemned sold like the proverbial hotcakes. Reporters representing *The Territorial Enterprise* and *The Gold Hill News* were at hand on the scaffold as witnesses. A woodcut artist from *The California Police Gazette* dodged about making sketches from which to cut a sensational woodblock for next week's paper.

Millain made a long address in French which nobody understood but was generally felt to lend *éclat* to the occasion. The noose was adjusted. The man from *The Gold Hill News* took a quick pull from a bottle and handed it hastily to *The Enterprise*. The trap was sprung and "a tremendous roar clearly audible at the Gold Hill Divide" rose from a thousand throats.

It was generally felt to be a production that did credit to Julia Bulette's memory and one in which everyone concerned, especially the condemned, had given a fine performance.

That night another treat was in store for the Comstock. Mark Twain was billed to give a lecture at Piper's Opera House on "My Adventures in the Holy Land."

SAN FRANCISCO'S PALACE: 1955

When the Sheraton Hotel management, a corporation with headquarters just about as far from California as it is continentally possible to maintain them in Atlantic Avenue, Boston, purchased the stately and long-established Palace in San Francisco from the heirs of Senator William Sharon, San Francisco, from the Ferry to Van Ness, was completely outraged.

Its columnists and editorial writers to a man, spearheaded by Mr. San Francisco himself, Herb Caen in the *San Francisco Examiner*, took an extremely dim view of the whole matter. The Palace was part of the very foundation, social and economic, of San Francisco's peculiarly well-integrated existence. It had been in operating business for eighty years, in the possession of the same family, with time out for an earthquake and fire. Sentimentally, it was the undisputed heart of the community, a repository of a legend of grandeur, hospitality, and warmth of being which few hotels anywhere and none elsewhere in the American West possess.

When the Sheraton management, having acquired the Palace from Mrs. William Johnston, Senator Sharon's granddaughter, and other heirs of the Comstock millionaire, added insult to sacrilege by renaming it the Sheraton-Palace, San Francisco was fit to be tied.

"General Grant visited the Palace when he was near the height of his popularity and could easily have had the name changed to the Grant-Palace," wrote Abe Mellinkoff in the *San Francisco Chronicle*. "He declined the honor, and the Sheraton people might at least show the same degree of modesty. After all, this is the only hotel in the city where you can have two-way motorcycle traffic in the corridors with complete safety to pedestrians and drivers. This is the Palace and nothing else."

Sentiments such as these were heartily applauded all over San Francisco. To be sure, nobody from the Wells Fargo Bank & Union Trust Company across the street or even the archconservatives of the San Francisco Wine & Food Society seriously considered boycotting the Sheraton-Palace, but there was an undercurrent of dissatisfaction about the whole deal. Every detail of the management was subject to microscopic and hostile examination. An overdone lamb's kidney at lunch or a neglected potted palm in the Great Court, and the conventional comment was: "Just what you'd expect! Chain management! Foreigners!"

And then one morning shortly after the change, San Francisco awoke to a startling and in some ways disconcerting discovery. Not only hadn't the old Palace gone to rack and ruin under the new dispensation, dammit, they'd made improvements!

An entire reversal of community feeling, a revolution in thinking had been accomplished through the seemingly innocuous agency of a single operation: the price of martinis. The old Palace martini had held an ounce and three quarters and sold for seventy cents. The Sheraton-Palace martini sold for the same basic price, but the new glasses held three ounces. By the same token, bar whiskey remained at a stable sixty-five cents, but the container rose from an ounce and a half to two ounces.

The news traveled like gee-whiz.

Brokers in Montgomery Street stopped in mid-career to pass the tidings. Mayor Elmer Robinson was induced to issue a statement. "Most gratifying," said the Mayor. Elmer Brown, head bartender for all of the Sheraton-Palace bars, was interviewed as a ranking diplomat might be on a move of international import. Mr. Caen came in personally from the *Examiner* Building next door to see if it were true. Noontime patrons, three deep in the Happy Valley and Palace Corner (the management hadn't changed it to Sheraton-Palace Corner) consumed unprecedented numbers of cocktails to appraise their relative potency with those of the day previous. The town hadn't been in such a pleasant dither since the mythical, never-never era of Before the Fire.

It is still possible among the die-hards at the Pacific Union Club on Nob Hill to discover ancients, conditioned to being against everything, who mutter that Sheraton-Palace is a dirty word; but with San Francisco as a whole, the revised martini, plus a few other and incidental marks of managerial know-how, put the hotel right back on everybody's good books where it had always been.

One of the other saving gestures was the retention as general manager of Edmond Rieder, dapper Paris-born *viveur*, wit, and public character who, as viceroy of the Sheraton heirs, is generally credited with having put the Palace in grade-A running shape so as to command the fancy price paid by the Sheraton purchasers. Still at the old stand behind the legendary mahogany of the Pied Piper is Elmer Brown; in the Palm Court, the same courtly staff of captains and graying waiters still serve the same tables occupied by the same patrons (or their forebears) from time out of mind. In the kitchen, Lucien Heyraud, ranking *chef de cuisine*, is still feudal overlord of the pots.

To understand the suggestions of civic upheaval implicit in the change of the original name of William C. Ralston's Palace, it is necessary to understand how, for a full eight decades, the Palace has come to represent—more probably than any other American hotel in the record except possibly the original Waldorf-Astoria—the community and its way of life and thought.

The hotel was conceived by Ralston and his associate, William Sharon, the Bank of California's Virginia City representative, at a time when California was riding the very crest and apex of the Comstock bonanzas in Nevada. The Mother Lode and its comparatively small recoveries in precious metals were, to all practical purposes, a thing of the past. Now Nevada was what Oscar Lewis has called "the wishing well of the nation." Its fabled bonanzas in the silver mines under Mount Davidson were largely being diverted from Virginia City to San Francisco, where the nabobs Flood, Fair, Mackay and O'Brien, Sutro, Senator John Percival Jones, Sharon, Ralston, and Darius Ogden Mills were acquiring property of every glittering sort from palaces on Nob Hill to Turkish baths in Market Street, and from fantastic villas on the Peninsula such as Ralston's at Belmont to the mahogany-stalled stables of Lloyd Tevis.

Ralston, whose infatuation with grandeur was to know no limit short of the grave, conceived for his dream city a dream hotel that should surpass in opulence and splendor anything yet reared in the Western World, and, when it was completed by Sharon after Ralston's untimely death, the Palace was just that.

From its very inception, the Palace was the paramount showplace of what was easily the most ostentatious city in the world. Here were celebrated the community's most gaudy municipal sarabands; here, upper-case society reveled discreetly, but richly, in an age of champagne in magnums and a hot grouse on everybody's plate for supper; here, reigning kings and emperors were housed when viewing the wonders of the Western continent; here, two heads of state, King David Kalakaua of Hawaii and President Warren G. Harding saw fit to shuffle off their mortal coil.

In time, the Palace came to share with Shepheard's in Cairo the distinction of being one of the few hotels in the world to which guests came with no other business or social purpose than simply to spend a weekend at the Palace. After a few decades, it was able to count on reappearance, at stated intervals, of folk who had spent their wedding trips there and returned, years later, to recapture in wistful recall that sentimental time of long ago.

The Palace seldom lost a patron. Newer and more fashionable hostelries might rear themselves in marble wonderment atop Nob Hill and in more socially select portions of the city, but when a Tevis or Flood or Sharon or Hearst or any other great name out of San Francisco's heroic past wants to celebrate a debut, a charity ball, a state dinner, or business luncheon of importance, the Palace gets the business. Film stars or Texas tycoons may register elsewhere; Californians know there is no place but the Palace.

It was for a synthesis of all these sentiments, obligations, loyalties, and emotional and economic attachments that San Franciscans were concerned when the Palace became the Sheraton-Palace. And, like many other affairs of the heart that are proverbially reputed to have their seat and origin in the stomach, much of the fair name of the Sheraton-Palace has been derived from its cuisine which, for eight decades, has sluiced, gentled, and delighted so many and so exacting palates as to elevate it to the estate of one of the world's truly great and distinguished restaurants. Born in an age when gold plate, side-whiskered waiters, and the masterpieces of the chef known as *pièces montées* were considered essential to exalted gastronomy, its tradition of good living has survived, with only a minimum of scathe at the hands of time, into an age of drive-ins and hamburgers.

First *chef de cuisine* at the Palace at its opening was the now almost godlike Jules Harder who had run the *cursus honorum* of his exacting profession at Delmonico's, the New York Union Club, and the celebrated Grand Union Hotel at Saratoga Springs—twenty-six years of apprenticeship in the service of the most meticulous gourmets of a well-fed generation.

The Palace *chef de cuisine,* whoever he might at the moment be, has by virtue of inherited position always been the dean of San Francisco's restaurant hierarchy. Harder gave way to Fred Mergenthaler, descendant of a long line of European cookstove nobility and at one time personal chef to the Queen of Holland and the Grand Duchess Marie of Russia. And after Mergenthaler, the hotel's kitchens entered into the spacious regime of sunny-tempered Ernest Arbogast.

Arbogast announced his entry to the San Francisco culinary scene in the grand manner with the invention of an oyster omelet. This was followed by Oysters Kirkpatrick, named for the manager, John Kirkpatrick, and has appeared on Palace menus from that day to this. Arbogast went on to even loftier triumphs: he created the California oyster omelet, pronounced by the Grand Duke Alexis to be the world's finest restorative in the morning if consumed with a double bottle of the best chilled champagne. The Grand Duke ate one every morning of his stay. The Palace oyster omelet swept first the West Coast and then the continent until it became a standard on menus from Bangor to Seattle.

The earthquake of 1906 and subsequent fire which reduced San Francisco and the Palace to "the damndest finest ruins, nothing more and nothing less," while it provided an effective demarcation between an old and new city, only temporarily interrupted the tradition of the Palace as a going concern.

The new hotel occupied the same site and identical dimensions of the first Palace, and its construction was ordered on the same princely scale as had guided its architects in the seventies. San Francisco's entrepreneurs were providing competition farther uptown in the form of the lavish Fairmont which also rose from the ashes in threatening splendor. To meet the competition, the new Palace was constructed and furnished on a scale of magnificence not again to be seen west of the Mississippi until Spencer Penrose built the Broadmoor at Colorado Springs.

When the second Palace opened its doors, local satisfaction was adequately expressed by a first citizen named Ned Hamilton who was the first customer to elevate a tall one in the new Pied Piper bar under the Maxfield Parrish painting.

"Thank God," apostrophized Hamilton, "the town has a two-bit bar once more."

The Sharon family had been agreeable to the rebuilding of its most expensive, and what may prove most enduring, monument at a cost of $12,000,000. When, on December 16, 1909, the new hotel was opened to the public, the younger Ralston opened the massive front doors with a golden key, which was then taken ceremoniously to the roof and attached to five gaily painted balloons that soon bore it out of sight over the Golden Gate.

That night, society turned out for the formal opening—some fifteen-hundred members of society. The *Chronicle* declared it to be a world's record in number for service at small tables. There was no speech making, and the orchestra, located in one of the balconies of the Garden Court, "came in subdued tones to the halls beneath."

It is improbable that any single era in its long annals will be remembered in the Palace legend as comparable to the days of World War II when the eyes of the nation and the world were turned toward the theater of the Pacific and life in San Francisco became a pageant of history on a radiant scale. The forces of land and sea moved through the Palace's apartments and public rooms in a resistless surge.

It was during the sometimes dark and always strenuous days of the war that a curious synthesis of up-to-the-minute efficiency and a revitalized grandeur came to the Palace in the person of Edmond A. Rieder, late of the superlative Ritz-Carlton in New York in the spacious times of the great Albert Keller, late of the upholstered Park Plaza in St. Louis.

Like the best hoteliers in the world, Mr. Rieder had a hotelier for a father. Reared in the military tradition of an officer of cavalry, Mr. Rieder combined the perfectionist ideals of Continental hotelkeeping with a dollars-and-cents attitude toward business which would do credit to a Yankee horse trader.

But it was in a realm that lay notably close to the Rieder heart that the new managing director performed most brilliantly and with a Gallic flair for the theatrical: he set about restoring the fame of the Palace kitchens to the estate of glory they had known in other years.

The Palace cuisine had always, and without serious interruption even by two world wars, been one of the glories of San Francisco life. During the darkest hours of the 1941 war, its food, service, and wines maintained an approximation of the grand manner, partially perhaps because the average age of its waiters removed them, in some cases by decades, from the likelihood of military service.

At the conclusion of hostilities, however, Mr. Rieder felt the need, as part of his over-all program of rehabilitation of a panache of superlative radiance, to re-establish the Palace in the imagination of the dining world. This he shortly unearthed in the person of Lucien Heyraud, one of the last truly magnificent *chefs de cuisine* in the old tradition of ortolans, champagne, and gold service plates.

Mr. Rieder found Heyraud at Romanoff's in Beverly Hills muttering maledictions on cinema stars who made an entire luncheon off salad, and producers who didn't know claret from Chianti. He painted for the thwarted genius of the soufflés illimitable vistas of fat and happy diners in the Palm Court, the Rose Room, and private apartments, none of whom considered dinner with fewer than seven courses and who commanded caviar as though it were birdseed.

From the day of Heyraud's arrival in the kitchens, San Francisco was aware that bonanza times were again on the town. The menu took on overtones of supernal grandeur. Truffled pheasant and *foie gras* in aspic issued from the kitchen portals, wafted dinerward in clouds of savory aroma, and Gaye, the red-jacketed wine steward with his gold chain of office, began demanding an apprentice. People were drinking more Bollinger, Romanée-Conti, and Châteauneuf-du-Pape than ever before in his memory.

The Sheraton-Palace is, in all truth, one of the last hotels in the land and perhaps the only one west of the Rocky Mountains equipped for the preparation and service of vast quantities of food in the grand manner. Heyraud ran up public banquets beginning with *homard cardinal* and running through *faisan en cocotte périgourdine,* and private dinner parties ending with *cerises Jubilées* and *café des princes.* He skirmished mightily with smoked sturgeon and *coeur de filet de boeuf Coquelin* and strawberries Romanoff. Oysters Kirkpatrick, of course, remained on the menu along with Palace raisin toast, and all the other good things that had delighted San Franciscans since the days of the railroad rajahs, and there were added *vol-au-vent de crêtes de coq* and *bombe* "Cable Car."

Inevitably, San Franciscans take chauvinistic pleasure in speaking of the Sheraton-Palace as the Palace, just as though nothing had happened in its well-ordered scheme of dynastic succession, but guests in the hotel continue to report surprising little niceties that were not there in the old days: a new and wonderful type of hanger in the closets, wide enough to accommodate something beside pegleg pants of the 1900s without throwing them on the floor, agreeable paintings on the walls of apartments where a bare décor was thought sufficient, and radios everywhere.

Continuity into the new regime has been maintained by a remarkable staff of personalities such as Elmer Brown and Frank Douet, his able assistant, born appropriately enough in Nevada's Gold Hill, a suburb of ancestral Virginia City, and who is a fathomless repository of folklore and legend. Jimmy Maars, the timeless cigar boy with his tray and harness, is one of San Francisco's institutions on a par with Caen and Jake Ehrlich, the greatest mouthpiece of them all. Dino Perini is a maître d'hôtel in the grand manner, and Henry Gaye, the *sommelier* in his gold chain of office, is the only authentic wine steward dedicated to his cellars and nothing else west of Chicago's Pump Room.

The hotel stationery, the design thoughtfully retained by the new management, shows a forty-niner guiding his covered wagon across the Great Plains, following the lofty mirage of a splendid hotel. The legend reads: "At the end of the trail there is the Sheraton-Palace." San Francisco hopes it may be so forever.

THE TOP OF THE MARK

Although many thousands of earnest sight-seers and, perhaps, some dedicated drinkers (although it is not noted for the liberality of its martinis), make yearly visits to the Top of the Mark in San Francisco, many of them with sentimental wartime memories of it as the established San Francisco rendezvous of servicemen, few realize that the handsome premises were not always the town's most spectacular saloon. Even informed San Franciscans are often surprised to learn that the Top of the Mark, in a previous incarnation, was one of the most opulently upholstered private apartments in the world.

Its fantastic vistas and twenty-foot ceilings, enormous space, and handsome dimensions were, in the hotel's beginnings, the private residence of Daniel C. Jackling, one of the great nabobs of the old mining West and a grand seigneur of such staggering resources that, after his death, it required five years to tally his holdings.

Jackling was a hardrock miner from the Colorado diggings at Cripple Creek where he made his first few millions in the company of other nabobs-to-be such as Spencer Penrose, Charlie Tutt, and Bert Carlton, all of them men of fantastic wealth who left their impress on Colorado Springs and gave Colorado a cachet of urbanity and sophistication it has never lost. Just being millionaires, however, wasn't enough for Jackling and Penrose, both of them far-sighted enough to predict that eventually even the richest true fissure must pinch out and that the mining of precious metals might someday come to an end. They wanted to be rich millionaires and had the highly rewarding premonition that copper might be just the thing to achieve this.

An accomplished metallurgist and a superb geologist, Jackling secretly perfected in the early years of the century a process for milling low-grade copper ore which he and Penrose and a small group of Cripple Creek insiders first financed into operation at Bingham Canyon, Utah. The birth of the Utah Copper Company uncovered a bonanza that, over the years, made all the gold and silver recoveries in the Mountain States look like the merest interest on its investment. In no time the Jackling milling process was making spectacular profits on one per cent copper ore and had produced pure copper to the extent of $1,500,000,000 with dividends of $500,000,000 to the lucky Jackling and his grubstakers—if such a homely mining phrase could apply to the patrician and lordly Spec Penrose and Charlie Tutt. At the lowest ebb of his fortunes, Penrose's income from Utah Copper was $200,000 a month, and he was peanuts compared to Jackling. Penrose, Carlton, and Tutt chose to remain in Colorado, where they enriched the community with vast benevolences and foundations and an even richer heritage of frontier folklore, but Jackling, who had no roots in the Centennial State, elected to live in California.

The stately apartment that is now the Top of the Mark was his San Francisco town house. A truly baronial country seat occupied his attention at Woodside, and when the mood to travel was on him, the Colonel had in succession three private railroad cars, two of them named *Cyprus* for that island's association with copper in classical times, and a yacht also named *Cyprus*. When he purchased additional choice building lots near San Mateo on the Peninsula, the town limits of Hillsborough were promptly enlarged to include his holdings, and that was the beginning of San Francisco's most socially exclusive suburb of today.

But from 1927, the year after the Mark opened for business, until 1937 when Jackling removed to Woodside, his apartment on the top floors of the hotel was the showplace in town for those fortunate enough to be on terms of intimacy with the rather retiring Croesus of copper. In the two-year interval between Jackling's removal to his country place and the opening of the Top of the Mark, the space was rented for occupancy by important guests and for parties of a spacious order.

Even in a community that was accustomed to the elegance of the railroad barons and Comstock kings of the nineteenth century and didn't rate a residence as being a mansion unless it had a minimum of forty rooms, the Jackling apartment on the roof of the Mark Hopkins bugged the eyes of San Franciscans. Each of its ten bedrooms had a bath approximately the size of a family dining room. The twenty-foot ceilings which are still a stately feature of the Top of the Mark were constructed to accommodate rare tapestries and heroic oil paintings that required an outsize dimension. Jackling's personal retreat, perhaps the greatest mining library in the West, was so large that, as one awed beholder remarked, a cavalry charge would be only a minor inconvenience.

Jackling has been dead now for a full decade, half of which was spent sorting out the properties in his estate, but the Top of the Mark carries on his spacious ways in its own commercial manner. In a mutable world where many millionaires' residences have been turned into religious premises and funeral homes, and put to other debased and dreary purposes, Colonel Jackling's home maintains at least a facsimile of continuity with its glittering past. The number of drinks that have passed over its mahogany in the twenty-five years of its lifetime might well gratify even a graduate of Cripple Creek.

PISCO PUNCH

One of the best of the ambrosial legends wafted down the San Francisco decades since that dreamy period of unearthly wonderment known as Before the Fire, part myth, part recorded fact, part recollected grandeur consecrated by long acceptance, concerns the Pisco punch.

Around this sacramental brew the regional mythology of San Francisco's Golden Age of Nabobs and Splendid Living gathers, perfumed by names that will live as long as the Old West recalls its heroes and its magnificoes: Duncan Nicol, Leland Stanford, Joaquin Miller, and John Mackay. Others are shadowy or substantial as the light of time glances over their remembered profiles: the Emperor Norton, François Pioche, David Scannell, Isaac Requa, John Percival Jones, Mark Twain, and the godlike William Morris Stewart.

As with the Palace Hotel, there was scarcely a personality of consequence or character in nineteenth-century San Francisco who cannot be associated, as one of the faithful at Duncan Nicol's Bank Exchange Bar, with the miracle and benison that all men of good will and sound judgment universally admitted the Pisco punch to be. No regional drink, not even the benevolent julep of Kentucky, the Medford rum of Yankee New England, or the Taos Lightning which brought civilization to the region the *Denver Post* likes to call the Rocky Mountain Empire, was more truly indigenous to the place of its most appreciative consumption. To be sure, the basic spirit from which Pisco was compounded was imported in great earthenware pipkins by sailing ship from far-off Peru, where the volcanic soil gave to the grapes an essential genius encountered no where else on earth. Until it reached San Francisco, however, Pisco remained merely one more of the ardent spirits that inspired men have evolved over the centuries from the grapes and grains of the earth.

Once in the hands of Duncan Nicol it was translated, as by consecration in the name of a divinity more benevolent than all others, into Pisco punch, the wonder and glory of San Francisco's heady youth, the balm and solace of fevered generations, a drink so endearing and inspired that although its prototype has vanished, its legend lingers on, one with the Grail, the unicorn, and the music of the spheres.

Like much of the vocabulary of California and many of the customs, artifacts, and social institutions of early San Francisco, Pisco was an inheritance from the Spanish days of the great ranches. Along with the Golden Gate and the Presidio at Monterey, the inheritors of California took over a number of pleasant aspects of Old Spain: the *talma*, or short cloak of the mounted grandee, the siesta and the love of ease it represented, a habit of calling the highways *caminos*, and a pronounced taste for Pisco.

Pisco punch, so far as anyone can discover, originated in the premises called Parker's Bank Exchange, which opened in 1853 in the Montgomery Block, an edifice built by General Halleck and representing to its generation in San Francisco all that the Empire State Building was to represent to New York three quarters of a century later. The Montgomery Block, at the junction of Washington, Montgomery, and Columbus Avenues, speedily became the most admired professional address in San Francisco and was filled with the offices of lawyers, top-ranking merchants, and the private bankers of the time. On its second floor was a splendid red-and-gold billiard parlor; directly beneath, and under the same management, was Parker's Bank Exchange Saloon.

Somewhere in the shifting mists that obscure San Francisco each evening as the sun goes down beyond the Golden Gate, the original Parker disappeared from behind the bar of this favored oasis. In his place there emerged—and name his name with bugles—Duncan Nicol, an authoritative, almost clerical figure, clad in immaculate white, his eyeglasses hanging over his right ear.

In the fifties in San Francisco a saloon for gentlemen that was run by men of breeding and manners was an extreme rarity. Barry and Patten, themselves New Englanders from fine families, set the style when they opened their saloon in Montgomery Street next to the first office of Wells Fargo and Company. Their walls were hung with choice paintings, nudes not among them. Gambling was forbidden and the wines and liquor were irreproachable. There were no libraries or reading rooms, and many patrons came to the town's better saloons to read their mail and the local newspapers. The New York and Boston papers, usually about three months old, which had come around the Horn in sailing ships, were on racks for all to peruse. Barry and Patten are still known to a later generation of San Franciscans for their gentle and illuminating book of recollections of the town in pioneer times.

It was the success of Barry and Patten in attracting a clientele of respected merchants, professional men, and first citizens generally that inspired Parker and his successor, Nicol, to undertake a similar project in the Bank Exchange.

Nicol was like no bartender or saloonkeeper before or since. In a generation when most San Francisco bartenders were recruited from the slugging carnivals of the Barbary Coast and acted as their own bouncers, he fairly radiated respectability. Merely to be admitted to the Bank Exchange was a patent of social and financial probity. Nicol tolerated no *arrivistes*. "Two of my punches are enough for any gentleman," he would say serenely, "and I'll have none others in the Bank Exchange."

He meant it, too, about the two drinks to a customer. If a favored patron like Fire Chief Scannel or James Flood, the Nevada bonanza king who was himself once a saloonkeeper of note (both of them were known tosspots), wanted more, he could walk around the block, thus qualifying as a new customer. When millionaire John Mackay, perhaps the richest man in America at the time, wanted a third, he, like everyone else, raked his silk hat off the stag-horn rack, walked demurely around the block, and returned to get it. Nobody took liberties with Nicol.

It wasn't long before the ritualistic imbibing of Pisco achieved wide fame. Passengers of distinction who arrived from Panama aboard the Pacific Mail steamers strode down the gangway and told cab drivers in resolute tones to take them to the Bank Exchange; they could register at the Palace after they had presented their credentials to Duncan Nicol. After 1869, when the steam cars came through from Omaha in a miraculous five days and patrons of the Central Pacific Railroad in Inverness cloaks and Sherlock Holmes caps were brought over from Oakland, as they are to this day, on the ferry, the first stop for knowing travelers was still the Bank Exchange. What "21" is to New York, or the Pump Room to Chicago, the Bank Exchange was to San Francisco celebrities in the sixties, seventies, and eighties.

Pisco came into the fullest flower of its celebrity, became a generic term, and entered the local language. A writer in the *California Alta* elegantly referred to a drunken character as "more than piscoed." Neill C. Wilson, the Western historian, coined the simile "as comfortable as a Pisco jag." Scores of lesser places advertised "The Original Pisco Punch," but Nicol, serene and secure in unimpeachable supremacy, smiled on the competition and steadfastly kept the secret of the greatest mixed drink of the age.

The speculative contents of a Pisco punch were as much a conversation piece of San Francisco as its undeniable authority, its guileless approach, and its invariable triumph over the partaker who partook too well. Topers who managed to countervene the two-drink regulation, or who were susceptible to this maximum allowance, lapsed into unconsciousness with the docility of sleepy kittens, wreathed in smiles and dreaming heavenly dreams. Nobody ever got fighting drunk on one of Nicol's punches. On the contrary, communicants acquired a perhaps unwonted courtliness of manner; benevolence radiated from features usually stern, noted curmudgeons were gentled into fraternal attitudes of good will. Under its spell, misers donated liberally to good causes. The Pisco drinker was at peace with himself and the world around him.

Nicol gradually achieved international fame. Of the Bank Exchange special, Rudyard Kipling wrote: "I have a theory it is compounded of the shavings of cherubs' wings, the glory of a tropical dawn, the red clouds of sunset, and fragments of the lost epics of dead masters." Before Kipling, Thomas W. Knox had written: "The second glass was sufficient, and I felt that I could face smallpox, all the fevers known to the faculty, and the Asiatic cholera, if need be." Lesser singers have hymned Pisco in less Arcadian cadences but with no less veneration.

The Bank Exchange in Nicol's consulship was, according to all contemporary testimony, quite unlike most of the well-upholstered San Francisco bars of its age. No barroom nudes profaned its hallowed walls. The décor was of a classic austerity commensurate with the exalted status of management and guests. Tessellated black-and-white marble was on the floor, the bar was of simple polished walnut, steel engravings of irreproachable theme adorned the walls. The champagne buckets were of sterling silver, and the handles of the beer pulls were made of authentic Wedgwood china.

A free lunch of fabled variety and viands in keeping with the character of the Bank Exchange was served daily from an enormous mahogany table in the middle of the main room. Awed customers remarked that the steel engravings in the back room—scenes of the French Revolution—were identical with the ones in the robing room of the House of Lords in London, and were valued at $1500 each by connoisseurs of such matters. The bar had been worn smooth at its outer edge by generations of drinkers, and old-timers were fond of recalling how, in the sixties and seventies, its well-to-do patrons often varied their noontime dice games for drinks by side bets for gold double eagles piled in neat stacks among the Piscos.

Duncan Nicol and the Bank Exchange remained honored institutions in San Francisco, as nearly immutable fixtures as mortality allows, until well after the fire of 1906. Pauline Jacobson, quoting from an old-timer in the *San Francisco Bulletin* in 1912, describes the remarkable uniformity of performance on Duncan's part even though his hands were by now trembling with the years. "E-v-e-r-y one of them is mixed the same," deposed the old-timer. "I had nine of them punches once and e-v-e-r-y one of them was mixed the same." (Duncan by that time must have relaxed his mandate of two to a customer.) "If you came there for thirty-five years, every one of them would be mixed the same."

And so we take leave of Duncan Nicol, gentleman, perfectionist, austere acolyte of a noble priesthood, who could have flourished only in San Francisco's golden noontide, and who will remain forever among her most durable legends.

On the true contents of the mysterious Pisco, who shall speculate with authority? Until only a few years ago, a saloon calling itself "The House of Pisco" did business among the honky-tonks in Pacific Street and served a not-unrefreshing arrangement which the management maintained was the True Sacrament as first devised by Nicol a full century ago. The drink wasn't a bad one, and contained pineapple juice, and what passed in those days for Pisco, but it embodied none of the magical qualities associated with the legend of the Bank Exchange, and a few of them served to induce torpor without exaltation, something like the effect of a slug at the base of the neck.

Only recently, a lineal successor to Nicol, Jack Koeppler of the Buena Vista Café in San Francisco, who has proved himself worthy of his noble heritage as an innovator by first launching Irish coffee on the American market, prevailed upon a fellow San Franciscan, Kenneth Prosser, to reveal to this writer what purports to be the recipe of the True Elixir. Mr. Prosser swears on a formidable stack of assorted books that the following recipe was recorded in his late father's own handwriting and may be taken as Revelation. It comprises 2 jiggers of Pisco, 2 jiggers of white grape juice, 1 teaspoonful of pineapple juice, and 1 teaspoonful of absinthe, Pernod, or Herbsaint.

The problem which presents itself, even with this formula in one's possession, is, of course, the procurement of the Pisco on which research must be based. A recent inquiry failed to disclose a single bottle of the essence.

And even assuming the prescription to be accurate, what was the secret of compounding the ingredients, the secret that required a good ten minutes of the master's time and the special skill of his matchlessly knowing hand?

Perhaps it is best not to delve too far into forbidden lore. Let us rather leave the secret of the Pisco punch a holy mystery for all time to come, like the language of Etruria and the divinations of the Chaldeans, the circles of Merlin, and the expertise of those chemists who produced the vanished dyestuffs of Tyre. Let its legend hover wistful and unobtainable over San Francisco as the mists roll in around Telegraph Hill at sundown. Let it not be profaned by a generation of haste and ineptitude, but let it remain a memory to be carried through the ages and to eternity only by Duncan Nicol, his eyeglasses lodged over one ear and on his face a smile of transcendent wisdom as inscrutable and timeless as that of the Sphinx.

THE BARBARY COAST:
A Body Could Feel at Home There

Once, in the long ago past, I worked for a newspaper that is now with the ages called the *Boston Telegram*, whose moral tone, because it was in direct afternoon competition with Mr. Hearst's *Boston American*, was so low and its editorial stances so depraved as to freeze, by the very mention of its name, the marrow and congeal the spine of Bostonians who walked the sunny side of Commonwealth Avenue and read the irreproachable *Boston Evening Transcript*.

This is not the occasion to recall the impious scheme of things we evoked through five editions a day on the *Telegram* other than to mention that the word "orgy" was required by a standing editorial regulation to appear somewhere on the front page of every paper every day of publication in something larger than 72-point Cheltenham bold. We specialized in orgies, especially among Harvard students and the Codfish aristocracy of fashionable Back Bay. The banner headline "Society Matrons Seized in Fashionable Orgy" was a recurrent commonplace. The fact, revealed when one read below the banks, that the society matrons were named Suzie Slottnick and Jessie Krassmeyer and that the scene of their apprehension was a bagnio on farthest Huntington Avenue made no difference. It was our orgy of the day, the chef's suggestion in the department of elevated depravity.

The *Boston Telegram* would have been the ideal paper for reporting San Francisco's Barbary Coast in its golden noontide of tumult, but, lacking it, a fair stand-in was a weekly *feuilleton* called *The California Police Gazette*, a file of which in the rare-books section at the Bancroft Library will give the reader food for comparative thought as he scans today's tidings of switch-knife juveniles, Hong Kong bonbons among the beatniks, and slaughter below the Slot.

The heyday of *The California Police Gazette* was the middle fifties, and it had no connection with Richard K. Fox's *National Police Gazette* in New York, which had yet to achieve fame and circulation during the Civil War through the publication of long lists of Union Army deserters.

Our *Police Gazette* could have shown Colonel Fox aces and spades, as the phrase goes, when it came to orgies; and it unhesitatingly identified the Barbary Coast of San Francisco as the uncontested orgy center of the known universe. Rome in the time of Caligula or the Court of the Restoration in London might compare favorably, but the *Gazette* defended the title and crown of depravity for the Barbary Coast against all comers. Alongside it, Sodom itself, aye, the unmentionable Cities of the Plain, were as the Bohemian Club's Low Jinx among the big trees. The Barbary Coast was bottoms.

The *Gazette* was possessed of a picture file, ample in its time and place, of ten or a dozen woodcuts used in weekly rotation on the front page with captions identifying them with one of last week's outrages. The scenes themselves were durable and included two gentlemen in silk hats wrecking the joint in a brothel where they had been rolled; a gentleman in a silk hat holding a Chinaman by his pigtail with one hand while cutting his throat with the other; a State Senator in his underwear fleeing a love store that had been unsettled by an earthquake while the girls, in pretty disarray, flee in the opposite direction; and a gentleman in a silk hat making a flying leap from a second-story window with the inevitable caption: "It Is My Husband, You Must Flee and Quickly!" These and half a dozen others in similar graphic vein represented life on the Barbary Coast as seen by *The California Police Gazette*. It may be imagined that, confronted by such rich disorders, miners on the Yuba and upper Stanislaus panted urgently to cash in their pokes and take the first Wells Fargo stage to Babylon on the Bay.

Everybody had a good time on the Barbary Coast: the inmates who sniffed nose candy and knocked each other over the head with bung starters as a matter of nightly course; the visiting firemen from the East who couldn't wait to leave their families in suites at the Russ House on the pretext of an important business conference with Sam Brannan; or the reformers who raised mitted hands to heaven to testify to the horror of it all and to invoke celestial aid in its suppression.

Murders on the Coast, be they accomplished by hatchet or derringer, had class and a bravura, something that was missing in homicides elsewhere. The shanghai trade in sailors made use of Rube Goldberg devices like trap doors in the floor and chloral in the already lethal whiskey. Prostitution had a flair about it, a panache of the rowdydow when it christened its practitioners Minnie the Pig, the Galloping Cow, and Iodoform Kate. Even such comparatively innocuous occasions as picnics to Contra Costa or Marin Counties had style, as the merrymakers often took along a cannon and supply of ball ammunition with which to flatten interlopers or, lacking intrusion, their own members.

What picnic in this degenerate age takes along a cannon?

And everywhere, but everywhere, there were orgies past counting and description, lovely rousing orgies of sex, depravity, mayhem, the dancing of clogs, and the breaking of glass. "Behind the painted scenes of the melodeon," wrote an enchanted contemporary, "are orgies that may be imagined but not described." The inventory of wickedness was as limitless as a Sears catalogue.

Church folk cheered through the smoke when, on that Day of Doom in 1906, flames finally claimed the Barbary Coast. Me, I would have wept, because the Barbary Coast and I would have gotten along very well. It was a place I could understand. A body could feel at home there.

POLYNESIAN TRAPS

I would like to take a long, hard, and not altogether approving look at a gastronomic manifestation that, in recent years on the West Coast, has been making millionaires of third-rate entrepreneurs and ruining the digestions of millions of customers who probably don't deserve any better but should still receive a certain measure of personal protection, as they do under the provisions of the Pure Food & Drug Act.

I refer to the dismal rash of quasi-Polynesian traps which now have been spawned from coast to coast but flourish in their most lethal abundance in California, probably on the reasonable grounds of geographic proximity to their alleged source of origin in the islands of the Pacific. It seems probable that, since the contaminated-meat scandals of the Civil War, or at least the horsemeat hamburger revelations in Chicago a few years back, no undertaking of mass pollution of taste and wholesale poisoning of innocent men and women has been attempted on a magnitude to compare with the neon-lit squalor now being presented on every hand in the name of Polynesian dining.

Let us fix the blame for this epidemic of submediocrity right where it belongs: on the doorstep of Trader Vic Bergeron of San Francisco, a restaurateur of blameless professional reputation and, especially in the field of drinks, positively humanitarian instincts. Unfortunately for millions of people, he made a superb go of the first of all of these Chinese vegetable places and has incited imitators by the thousands, none of whom has been characterized by a jot of Trader Vic's integrity or the faintest suspicion of his flair for endowing the commonplace with romantic overtones.

Overnight quasi-Polynesian restaurants became as common in the American countryside as drive-ins and milk bars. They have a common décor depicting the beach at Waikiki teeming with surfboards and happy natives assembled for *luaus* or potential sex orgies. Fishnets snag the unwary on the way to the men's room. The menus are the size of Wamsutta bedsheets printed on coconut fiber manufactured by the American Celotex Company. The food is fabricated from fish heads and boiled newspapers, and listed on the bill of fare under names that make Oriental visitors snicker.

Many of these grottoes carry their steal from Vic Bergeron to the point of advertising themselves as "Trader Nick" or "Trader Dick." "All of them," states *The Wall Street Journal* in the understatement of the year, "command good prices for food and drinks made with relatively inexpensive ingredients." What the oracle of finance really means is that a good many of them charge outrageous prices for food, at least, that is worthless. But curiously enough, in the experience of your reporter, most of these el dumpos run by straw-skirted Borgias give the customers a relatively fair shake at the bar.

The sophisticated diner who isn't beguiled by the insane music of steel guitars and hypnotized by the tropical fish in the tanks on the back bar into ordering from the Gum Mop Toop department, with an exotic dessert of Clum Blum Yoy made from genuine Ceylonese guano, can do pretty well for himself at table if he knows the ropes at even the most notorious ptomaine *poi* places. Few of the proprietors would for the period of a split second think of ordering from their own assortment of authentic Polynesian entrees, and some of the best Kansas steer meat available is stashed away for the informed clientele and friends of the management who admire the Mai Tis at the bar but want Christian food when they sit down at table.

I am given to understand, although do not report the circumstance on my own authority, that in San Francisco the steaks at Skipper Kent, for some years the best accredited imitation of Trader Vic's, are of remarkable excellence, and I myself can certify that one of the best *filets* in the entire Burlingame-Hillsborough complex along the Camino Real, where I spend some of the inclement months, can be had at a surfboard stoop named the Lanai, which is one of the components of a deluxe hotel-motel-restaurant setup four miles south of San Mateo.

If you must eat in the dark amidst papier-mâché waterfalls while Polynesian natives from the University of California graduate schools perform tribal rites with drinks in coconut shells, the fact stands that hidden in the tidewater trash on the menu in many a South Seas deadfall there lurk other dishes of surprising excellence.

HILLSBOROUGH

When, a short time back, Bing Crosby moved his lares and penates to Northern California and bought himself and his family a home in Hillsborough, residents of San Francisco's most conspicuously conservative residential suburb were gratified. They weren't as gratified as the San Francisco newspapers, which made a real-estate deal into something approaching an apostolic visitation, and for weeks had devoted space to speculation as to which of the available properties the crooner might select.

Hillsborough has gathered around itself a more substantial body of regional folklore than has any other place near San Francisco. Located eighteen miles south of the city, it is a residential subdivision of aloof and aristocratic Burlingame and nestles—manicured, policed, and Rolls-Royced, a secluded enclave of uppertendom—in the green hills of San Mateo County.

Brookline, Massachusetts, shortly after the turn of the century, was statistically designated as the wealthiest incorporated township in the United States. East Hampton or Southampton, or possibly Scottsdale, Arizona, might lay claim to similar laurels today. Such concentrations of vast financial resources can obviously be attributed to Palm Beach, and once might have applied to Lenox or Stockbridge or Newport, but these are, or were, seasonal resorts. On a year-round basis of permanent residents and voters they are low on the economic totem pole.

Hillsborough's grandeur has none of this transitory quality. It is permanent (for all the exoduses of its notoriously restless residents to Palm Springs, Lake Tahoe, the Monterey Peninsula, or Paris), a lineal inheritor of San Francisco's great suburban wave of the seventies and eighties when magnificoes such as William Ralston, Darius Ogden Mills, Senator William Sharon, and Milton S. Latham began building wedding-cake country estates at Millbrae, Atherton, and Menlo Park.

Today Hillsborough is the bright particular gem of the Peninsula, the Kohinoor of suburbia, inclined to patronize even its parent town, Burlingame, whose post office it shares, and barely acknowledging San Mateo, where it does its shopping. For no trade or profession may be pursued in Hillsborough; no doctor may hang out his shingle nor may boarders be taken in. Hillsborough is residential and nothing else. Ernie Gann, one of California's foremost contemporary novelists (*The High and the Mighty*, etc.), is reputed to have rejected Hillsborough residence for fear his professional livelihood might be curbed within its stainless confines. He lives instead at Pebble Beach, where Sam Morse, the Duke of Del Monte, permits writers to practice their calling and is himself an artist of note.

There isn't even a restaurant or public bar in Hillsborough, the only approximation of such conveniences being the Burlingame Country Club, which has never been rated an abode of transcendental gastronomy even by its stoutest partisans, but rather as an emergency facility for moments of crisis.

Perhaps as adequate an anecdote as any to indicate the lofty *ton* of life in Hillsborough relates to the occasion of the disastrous fire at the Jackson Moffetts' last year. Fires are rare in the community, as is attested by the almost microscopic insurance rate attributable to a superb fire department at Burlingame and another at San Mateo, which cover all regional alarms and back up Hillsborough's own facilities. Anyway, the Moffetts' mansion, surrounded by lordly grounds and pools, caught fire downstairs during the dark hours. The servants slept in a nearby converted stable, and the first thing Nancy and Jack knew, there they were, cut off at the pass by several stairwells of vaguely Tudor and highly inflammable design. Dialing the operator, Mrs. Moffett told her of their plight and hung up, forgetting to identify herself or give the location of the blaze.

The operator quickly checked to see where the call had originated, notified the appropriate fire stations, and, for good measure, alerted not one but two regional hospitals to send ambulances. She then rang back the Moffetts, reported her actions to Mrs. Moffett, who still had the presence of mind to answer the phone, and suggested that should there be any delay in the advent of the *pompiers*, knotting sheets together might provide an emergency exit from a second-floor bedroom.

It may also be noted that Ah Sam, the Peninsula status symbol in florists, conducts a service in keeping with the character of his shop's clientele. It's a baby-sitting service for orchids. In a benign climate and with plenty of room for greenhouses, a number of Hillsborough residents raise their own orchids, and a commuter boarding the Southern Pacific train for the city in the morning with an orchid in his lapel instead of a mere camellia is rated pretty high in the butler-and-bucketseat sweepstakes. Not all orchid growers, however, have their own full-time gardeners, and if they leave home for extended periods, Ah Sam takes in their plants for them, cherishes them as Nero Wolfe himself might, and returns them in prime condition (and, for all I know, multiplied) when their loving owners return from Paris or the grouse moors of Scotland.

This thumbnail sketch of ineffable Hillsborough would not be complete, I think, without the contribution of Charles Clegg, proprietor of one of the community's moderately ducal demesnes, who, while walking his St. Bernard near the property line of his nearest neighbor, chanced upon a revelatory pearl.

The neighbor's children had out-of-town guests, presumably not schooled in the Hillsborough scheme of things, and were setting up to play a game of Robin Hood.

"Fine," asserted a ten-year-old visitor. "We'll steal from the rich and give to the poor."

"That's not the way we play Robin Hood in Hillsborough," corrected his hostess. "Here we steal from the poor and give to the rich."

THE ROYAL FAMILY

In 1965 the *San Francisco Chronicle* at long last was able to celebrate the downfall of its only considerable rival newspaper *The Examiner* in a realignment of the city's publishing field which relegated *The Examiner*, proudest of all Hearst properties, to the category of an afternoon and secondary paper while leaving the *Chronicle* in undisputed control as the town's only morning publication.

The event marked the conclusion of seventy years of feudal warfare and baronial infighting that would not have been out of place among the city-states of medieval Italy.

It marked the final and overwhelming victory of the descendents of the almost incredible Mike de Young in the last field of endeavor and activity in which they were not already pre-eminent. For a full generation the de Youngs and their collateral families had dominated the San Francisco social scene with princely hospitality, exercising absolute authority with unabashed ferocity toward upstarts.

Financially the de Youngs in their present various redactions as Camerons, Tobins, Tuckers, Coopers, Thieriots, and Martins had been beyond all necessity for even thinking about money, although it didn't deter some of the younger members of the family from doing so. It remained alone for the dynasty to establish itself as top dog in the professional field of newspaper publication from which its original fortunes had been evolved.

The *Chronicle*'s victory over the *Examiner* achieved this last objective in overwhelming degree. In a sense it left the de Young dynasty with nowhere left to go. To paraphrase Dr. Holmes's young lady from Beacon Street, Boston, it might collectively ask: "Why should we travel when we are already there?"

It had been a long, hard road with social, economic, and professional ambush at every bend, and gunfighting and factual assassination in its accustomed incidentals. The road began in a San Francisco which every filmgoer or connoisseur of the Old West would recognize in its every detail: a rich, sprawling, uninhibited, hard-drinking, gold-rush frontier whose frock-coated inhabitants carried derringers in their coattails as habitually as they drank vast quantities of Pisco punch at Duncan Nicol's Bank Exchange Saloon before venturing into Montgomery Street to take potshots at rival editors, bankers, or politicians. Its terminal was in the precincts of Floribunda Avenue in ineffable Hillsborough, an enclave of property and privilege south of San Francisco so perfumed with folding money and decorum that its chauffeurs made a practice of lightly dusting the bonnets of immaculate Rolls-Royce town cars with mink dust cloths, and its butlers still wear white gloves at dinnertime, a practice long since outmoded in less scrupulously administered parts of the countryside.

What made the de Young family's triumph of dynastic succession and financial and professional statesmanship notable in the annals of American brass knuckles was the style in which its warfare had been conducted. The brass knuckles of the de Youngs, at least in the second, third, and fourth generations, were fashioned of fourteen-karat gold. San Francisco has always evoked style, even in the bashwhacking of the opposition, and the de Youngs handed style on from generation to generation along with their lodges in the Sierras, private duck clubs north of San Francisco, and membership in the Pacific Union Club on top of Nob Hill.

When royalty visited San Francisco it was and is habitually entertained by Mrs. Helen Cameron, a second-generation de Young and matriarch of the clan, or by the Charles de Young Thieriots, a third generation that provided the *Chronicle* with its publisher in the big moment of final triumph. Charlie Thieriot possesses the finest cellars in San Francisco, whose bins afford a 1904 Mouton as readily as an 1868 cognac, and Princess Margaret and the Earl of Snowden naturally gravitated to their carriage drive off Floribunda Avenue.

Less regal names that made news for decades have been conspicuous in the family guest lists. When Barbara Hutton, whatever her name of the moment, visits San Francisco she is inevitably entertained by the Sheldon Coopers. Sheldon Cooper is head of the law firm that handles the family's and the *Chronicle*'s affairs, and Patricia Cooper is a daughter of Mrs. Joseph O. Tobin, one of the four durable "de Young girls."

"I was nobody and didn't have a pot," said Hedda Hopper, "when I was playing at the Curran Theatre in *Dinner at Eight* and Phyllis and Nion Tucker came backstage after the performance to ask me to their home. I was less than nobody, but it made no difference to any member of the de Young family," and she was a sort of daughter-in-law until her recent death. "Your Bradstreet rating never matters in San Francisco," said Hedda, but this generality may be excused in an excess of loyalty to old friends and liberal benefactors.

In San Francisco the de Young descendents are known collectively as "The Royal Family"—a reference, it is generally felt, not so much to the

Barrymores in the play of that name as to some unidentified but equally cohesive and resplendent clan whose influence and prestige extend everywhere and, like the ruling houses of Europe before 1914, have connection, influence, and affiliations in London, Paris, Long Island, and Washington, D.C.

MR. STUYVESANT FISH'S WILD BOAR

When the world's socially and financially well-placed turn to winegrowing, stock raising, or gentleman farming, the product of their efforts is likely to be something pretty superlative. And even if their motives are completely selfish, it is usually the consuming public that benefits in the end.

Take the Rothschild family as a glittering example. Its imperial economy hardly needed a vineyard to make ends meet. But Nathaniel Rothschild bought the Mouton vineyards near Bordeaux merely to improve their product and to see his own cachet upon his claret bottles; Mouton-Rothschild has been a dazzling name on wine cards ever since. Baron James Rothschild paid four million francs for the Lafite vineyards because the name resembled that of his Paris address, and another extraordinary label—Lafite-Rothschild—emerged.

A comprehensive list of well-placed persons who have made a good thing of their greenhouses, stables, dairy farms, and orchards would consume more space than is available to this essay, but it would have to include the socially exalted and presumably well-heeled Stuyvesant Fish, of Palo Corona Farms in Carmel, California. Mr. Fish, whose grandmother made history in several ways on Newport's Bellevue Avenue and among New York's Four Hundred a generation or two ago, raises, improves, and merchandises wild boar. He is thus making history in California in somewhat the same way the late Mrs. Fish did when she decided to serve nothing but champagne at her dinners, and set the world of polite dining on its ear by so doing.

Stuyvie's impeccable background and Harvard accent lend a new dimension to the hog-raising business. He is in trade under the stylish name of the Imperial Wild Boar Company, with its business address at Carmel, as aloof a premises for a stockyard as any on record; and his wild boar are the lineal descendants of a breed brought, during the twenties, by millionaire George Gordon Moore from his North Carolina estate to his ranch in the Santa Lucia mountains.

Moore had intended the boar for hunting, restricted, of course, to his friends and guests. But the boar flourished in their new environment, and before long, wild piglets roamed all the way from Monterey to Big Sur, enjoying the finest view of the Pacific available anywhere. Since they were unprotected by game laws—no California legislators had foreseen this particular contingency—they were slaughtered indiscriminately by poachers who were rarely apprehended. Then Mr. Fish conceived the idea of breeding the animals for the market, and today he is in trade up to his eyes. The breeding is necessary to eliminate a strain of tame or garden pig which, understandably, got tangled up with the wild article: the Santa Lucia mountains are a very romantic setting.

I have eaten Mr. Fish's wild boar, roasted as a rack, and I am willing to go on record as saying, unreservedly and whole hog, if such a phrase may be pardoned, that it is some of the most wonderful table fare I have ever encountered. The meat is slightly on the pink side, like veal, and the flavor is something that must be tasted to be appreciated: gamy, rich, and as opulent as it is unusual. The wild boar is a fighting animal, dangerous in the extreme to handle, and its wildness is the priceless ingredient of its meat. It is safe to say that it will neither be imitated by synthetic-flavor merchants nor be available to bogus aging. Nor is wild boar recommended to dietary cultists, as it is veined in perfectly heavenly fat and probably has a caloric content that would give Gayelord Hauser the vapors. It is strictly for folk who know the McCoy when they encounter it, gastronomically speaking.

Cooking wild boar is a nice trick, and not to be approached in a spirit of frivolity. It takes considerable time to cook the pig. Constant and devoted basting with a sauce compounded, according to Mr. Fish, of Burgundy, honey, soy sauce, butter, lemon juice, and freshly ground black pepper is also called for.

It is a game dish fit for kings—which may well be the reason that four wild boar were incorporated in the coat of arms of Richard III of England.

Observations and Prejudices

Every now and then, when not contemplating other significant problems in a far from perfect world, I am prompted to wonder whatever became of the derby hat.

ON THE SUPRÊME

Certain amateurs of good cooking believe that they can judge a restaurant by the way it chills and serves its wines. Some rely on the chef's attitude towards beef. Others use the strength of the establishment's vichyssoise as a yardstick. As for me, I judge a restaurant by its use of the suprême. It is, I believe, the symbol of a restaurant's fraudulence or veracity; an appraisal on the basis of its use or misuse is explicit, instantaneous, and usually comes early in a meal.

So far as I know, the suprême—a double container for chilled fluids or solids which allows them to be served surrounded by a bed of ice—is indigenous to the United States. At least I don't recall ever seeing such in Rule's or in Maxim's, or on the Cunard steamships, which, in my book, are established hallmarks of excellence in food and its service.

The suprême dish is widely used in American dining, usually as a suggestion of quality, with overtones of elegance generally. Oysters, from time immemorial, have come on a bed of crushed ice. But the service of seafood cocktails and a whole range of summer soups in an elaborate and often fanciful chalice (the bowl is immersed in the source of refrigeration, which is concealed by an apron of silver or the like) is comparatively new. The dish is often so elaborately designed that its utilitarian aspect is eclipsed by its fraudulence.

I dined one evening recently at a San Francisco restaurant that shall here be nameless because of its long and honorable tradition. The premises had recently been redecorated at hideous expense. The customers needed snowshoes to enter over a carpet as thick as the snow pack on the high Sierra. Fiddle music was wafted from a small orchestra attired like Slovenian squat dancers or Magyar cavalrymen. The menu appeared on bedsheet-sized bills of fare embossed in gold leaf and glittering with the names of exotic dishes ravished from Brillat-Savarin and Fisherman's Wharf. The wine list, its prices in Federal Reserve figures, was presented by a captain—in a tailcoat by Henry Poole of London—who bowed as low as an imperial chamberlain soliciting the favorable regard of his monarch.

On every hand, diners of financial and social consequence were being sluiced and gentled with rare viands and vintages of museum-piece status. Across a double magnum of Mme. Bollinger's best, I was able to perceive the direct descendant of the old Spanish dons who owns the local ball park. A genuine cliff dweller from Nob Hill, who had recently achieved celebrity by being stabbed by his fifth wife, was wielding a dainty gold toothpick in a sequestered alcove reserved by the management for the authentic old noblesse of Gold Rush times. Millie Robbins of the *Chronicle*'s society staff, followed by Bill Young, her favored photographer, tripped between the tables in a state of positive radiance induced by the profusion of eligible faces. It was a scene of such dazzling dimensions, so richly endowed with implications of elevated social rank, that the *plat du jour* was unthinkable, and the only possible recourse was to the à la carte menu and ultimate bankruptcy.

In this pass my guest and I, hopeful that the management would not eject us for bypassing the fresh beluga caviar at ten dollars the spoonful, ordered a chaste but select list of nutritious items, the total cost of which would have staggered the late Henry Clay Frick. We began with something I hadn't had in years, a hearts-of-palm salad. (Remember, this is the American West, where salad is something consequential, not a dab of foliage intruding itself inconspicuously just before the arrival of the *bombe soufflée* or the *fraises Grand Marnier.*)

The six waiter captains who took our order retired backward as from the presence of a reigning monarch, bowing to the waist with each retreating step, and narrowly missing incineration at a table where one of their peers was engulfing the customers in a sheet of flame while preparing *crêpes suzettes*. The orchestra played gems from *The Chocolate Soldier* and *The Student Prince,* and the ball-park owner departed in a snowstorm of currency suggesting the exit from Bustanoby's of the late Diamond Jim Brady. Millie Robbins noted that press time was approaching and left, trailing names of glory as from the Duchess of Richmond's ball before Waterloo.

Time passed—enough time to have frozen solid all the hearts of palm in a Cecil B. De Mille production of *Samson and Delilah*—and at length there issued from the kitchen a flying squadron of servitors. Wagons were wheeled into position with the military precision of the horse artillery. Bus boys stood at attention. A respectful waiter handed to a captain —and the captain placed before us—the hearts-of-palm salad. To state that it was a production number would be a triumph of understatement. Scallop shells perhaps a foot across (made of gleaming silver that might have come from the workbench of Cellini) were mounded high with crushed ice. Atop tastefully arranged grape leaves and lightly strewn with ornamental paprika lay the biggest, handsomest hearts of palm ever seen by mortal eye. The orchestra leader stilled his musicians, waiting for us to raise our forks as a signal to render "Land of Hope and Glory"—it was an epic moment in the annals of gastronomy.

There was but a single flaw in the objects of all this solicitude.

The hearts of palm were, if not positively hot, still at the fairly elevated temperature they had achieved reposing in tins on the top shelf of a superheated kitchen. At no time had they come in contact with anything to make them cold.

The emphasis on the ceremony of dining, at the expense of the food itself, is, I maintain, the foremost curse of the contemporary restaurant scene. Elaborate fakements of elegance have been designed: pepper mills of rare tropic woods, three feet high and as big as howitzers; rolling hot dishes with silver covers like bank vaults; coffeemakers of a complexity to bemuse Rube Goldberg; duck presses that would do credit to Youngstown Sheet & Tube's most monstrous open hearth—the list is endless. There are patent brandies guaranteed to produce a huge fireball when ignited on cherries Jubilee, Italian coffee brewed in boilers of a dimension fit to power the *Queen Mary*. Waiters stagger in with champagne in ice buckets of iceberg proportion.

All to no avail as far as the food is concerned.

No heat penetrates to the breast of pheasant because the sumptuous chafing dish has been designed for show, not for service, and no flame from the fire pot comes within several inches of the surface it supposedly warms. The champagne, after regal frivolities with napkins and chilled glasses, is just below boiling point because the wine steward has put it on top of a bed of crushed ice instead of immersing it in a bath of ice water. The coffee, when it is finally distilled from the junior chemical set in which it makes its appearance, is a Borgia potation fit for truck drivers and newspapermen who know no better.

I have discussed this unhappy state of affairs with various restaurateurs and hotel men who, if in a candid mood, almost without exception admit its melancholy aspects, but pass the burden of blame on to the customers themselves.

"Since the war we have had an entirely new class of well-heeled patrons, who are willing and even eager to spend lavishly on food and drink as a status symbol," one well-known New York restaurant owner recently told me. "They don't know the least thing about either food or wine. Their experience hasn't taught them much about quality, but they are uniformly delighted and impressed with ostentatious service. . . . I have obviously well-to-do customers who come into my place. They ignore the menu, but they look around the room and if a table is having something in flames or another attention-attractor, they say, 'Give me what that guy is having' . . . We're in business. We'll feed the dolts what they want, but it isn't food. Half the time it's nothing but a demand for ostentation and the chance to show off. It's a by-product of the times. . . ."

ON MILK

President Kennedy's determined pitch for the milk industry a few weeks back (and the Washington rumor is that immediately after heroically downing a glass of the stuff, he washed his mouth out with a stiff brandy and soda) opens almost illimitable potentialities for Presidential endorsement of any product that may allegedly be having rough sledding.

There is a school of adult thought that regards milk as an essential to the restorative brandy milk punch, and it is surely essential to the production of cream and butter, without which life would not be worth living. But many highly placed medical practitioners are of the mind that milk itself is totally unsuited to human consumption.

The French people, on whom such a reaction reflects the greatest imaginable credit, not so long ago threw out of office a premier who was so imprudent as to advocate the consumption of milk instead of the other potable matters that have given France its long-standing reputation as the seat of the cultural humanities and amenities of life in general. No such tempest of disapproval followed Mr. Kennedy's skirmish with the Borgias; but should he endorse, either explicitly or inferentially, patent cake mixes, "light" beers, nicotineless cigarettes, or any of the other infamies of mediocrity dreamed up by Madison Avenue, there could be political consequences of the gravest nature.

Milk, a seemingly innocuous product, arouses ardent passions of distaste in some people and mystic devotion in others. Personally, I would as soon lift a cheery cup of the hemlock that poisoned Socrates as drink a glass of milk whose toxic potential had not been abated by a liberal infusion of proof spirits. My father before me, *per contra*, held cows in such veneration that we suspected a Hindu strain was somewhere concealed in the family genealogy. He collected rare cows, Guernseys, Alderneys, Holsteins, Brown Swiss, as other men pant for philatelic treasures or rare examples of colonial furniture. Although he was a near man with a dollar in most aspects of finance, no cow could be too high priced, and he and another notable cow *aficionado*, the late Clarence Barron, publisher of *The Wall Street Journal*, used at intervals to descend on those Channel Islands celebrated for breeding the beasts and buy herds like drunken sailors. The legend ran that the King of the United States and the Crown Prince (Mr. Barron had whiskers and looked like a monarch) now and then came to Guernsey and enriched the natives beyond the dreams of avarice by buying up rare and desirable cows.

My father could stand in silent and contemplative admiration of a row of cows in his barns, as J. P. Morgan is reported to have stood entranced by the frescoes of the Sistine Chapel. His admiration is inherited only in moderation by his son. I admire a cow vastly more than I do the run-of-the-mill of the human race, but I see it divided in those quartering lines of the butchers' charts, subdivided as it were into sirloin, *filet*, brisket, tongue, prime ribs, oxtail, and oddments, the whole nourishing vista surrounded by a border of fine cheeses. Utilitarian, that's me about cows.

A HOLLOW MOCKERY, A SHABBY SWINDLE

A week or so ago, the perpetrator of this column threw caution to the winds, became lost to all prudence, and blew the works on a case of Dom Pérignon champagne. In the event you don't know about Dom Pérignon, it is a specially reserved bottling of the best wine manufactured by the old, established firm of Moët & Chandon. First produced in the now legendary 1921 vintage, allegedly as a salute to Dom Pérignon, traditionally the inventor of champagne but, in fact, a mere pleasant myth, the Pérignon Cuvée was an enormous success in restaurant circles from the beginning. For one thing, it was put up in a squat, heavy, and uncharacteristic hand-blown bottle, hand-corked with the product of contented cork trees in Portugal, and the conventional wire to secure it reinforced by knotted cords, the whole handsomely and impressively sealed with great gobs of dark green wax.

It was an impressive presentation, and the wine was as good as its billing, which is to say excellent. It was also very costly and remains the most expensive item on the champagne card today in such restaurants as can afford it on their inventories.

For the service of this treasured nonesuch, I selected an auspicious evening when there was company of an exalted social status and when the cook had outdone herself. The champagne arrived, chilled as the Antarctic in a silver bucket that had belonged to the last of the Czars.

Mindful of the solemnity of the occasion, I undertook to open the bottle myself, and reached for it with a knowing ceremonial flick of the rare Irish linen napkin that would have done credit to Oscar of the Waldorf, when suddenly I recoiled as from the presence of a swamp adder in the centerpiece. Beyond all question it was the familiar green bottle; undeniably I had paid a king's ransom for the stuff. But all was now a hollow mockery, a shabby swindle, a treacherous and deceitful fakement, for where once had been the noble and useful green sealing wax was twined around the cork in its stead a nasty blob of miserable plastic.

As God is my judge, there was a plastic foil on the cork of a bottle of Moët & Chandon's Dom Pérignon Cuvée Champagne, the noblest and most exalted handiwork of nature contaminated by the nastiest devising of man's infinite genius for trash.

At that precise moment a cock crowed, and I heard the echo of the horn of Roland, betrayed by Ganelon; Brutus and Benedict Arnold walked across the lawn and peered in the window. No treachery more damnable, no chicane more debased had been contrived since the betrayal of the Great Inca.

It was as though the radiator ornament on a Rolls-Royce had turned out to be pinchbeck, or the trade name of F. W. Woolworth were to be discovered on the hem of the Veronica. No greater imposture would be involved if the Declaration of Independence were found to be a forgery, or John Kennedy exposed as having worn a wig.

ON ADVERTISING MENDACITY

If I were asked where I would lay my money in the advertising mendacity sweepstakes—surely the widest potential field for possible selection in the whole world—I wouldn't go to the bookmaker for odds on the various commodities that claim nine secret ingredients, or the gasoline that alone contains diophrasnitone (which nobody ever heard of or cares about), or even the hooligan advertising that defames the competition by name and whose product chained horses couldn't drag us to buy. I would lay my money on the nose of the restaurant wine card that flatly asserts that a half bottle of Napa claret "serves two" or a quart "serves six."

Two what? Dyspeptic inmates of an orphanage for dwarfs?

Six what? Members of Alcoholics Anonymous?

Of all the mendacities commonly practiced at the behest of avarice and dishonesty, this, for my money, is the most offensive. It not only explicitly concedes that the vendor is a cheat, but also suggests that the consumer is a cripple, senile, unable to take nourishment, or an inmate of a charity hospital. To suggest to any wine drinker, either amateur or dedicated, that a single sleazy glass of any beverage, unless perhaps it's green Chartreuse, is sufficient for his needs is an affront of the first order and suggests that the management's contempt for the customers is as limitless as its bad judgment. Half bottles of wine are intended for invalids or infants. Memory recalls the Traveler's Club in Paris where the champagne glasses come in only one size: sufficient to hold a full bottle of Bollinger or Mumm's. In the civilized service of wine, less than a bottle per person is unthinkable.

One couldn't ask for a pleasanter invitation to raise glasses than the amiable legend "serves six," but it is one that should only recommend a half case of conventional bottles or three magnums.

LOBSTERS AND THE WRIGHT BROTHERS' FOLLY

As a world traveler and globetrotter of international repute (an accolade of my own based on an annual trip to London to eat mutton at Simpson's-in-the-Strand) who has yet to take passage in the hell carts powered by jet, I couldn't care less about flying, or about what happens to the dolts who climb into cartridges of death under the delusion that their time is valuable. Living, as I do, near an "international airport," I am restrained from taking shots at the flights that roar overhead only by the existence of a Federal statute that forbids this sort of target practice. I couldn't care less, also, how fast my mail gets to me from distant places, and so far as I am concerned the entire aviation industry, civil and military, could disappear overnight with nothing but universal benefit and rejoicing.

There is, however, an interesting gastronomic aspect of fast transport which may yet justify the Wright brothers' folly, and that is the vista of potentiality opened to the procurement of edible Maine lobsters in California. This feat hasn't been accomplished, but laudable efforts are being made in this direction, and success may yet crown the risks and probable financial losses of the pioneers in this field.

Let us grant at the outset that Eastern lobster is at its best no farther than a hundred yards from Atlantic tidewater. It is at its ineffable superlative broiled or boiled—and the hell with all fancifying of the noblest of crustaceans—on the beach at Sconset, at the pier restaurants of a score of Connecticut shore resorts, at Watch Hill, at Locke-Ober's in Boston, or hard by the cold waters of Casco Bay at South Harpswell, or farther north, within hailing distance of the Mount Desert ferry. From there inland, lobster becomes progressively less noble, but nothing to be despised in the Pump Room or Well of the Sea in Chicago. Its present traveling radius seems to be about a thousand miles inland, but after that it becomes suspect and should be approached cautiously.

Several well-accredited restaurants in the San Francisco Bay Area currently undertake to import live Eastern lobsters in brine and seaweed, notably Grison's in Van Ness Avenue and the Villa Chartier in El Camino Real, San Mateo, but somehow, although indisputably animate when taken from the tank by the chef, they lack something both in flavor and in texture when plain boiled or broiled. They are, however, entirely adaptable to more elaborate preparation, and, served in Newburg sauce or *à l'américaine*, can be as sumptuous as they must once have been in the days of Diamond Jim Brady and the lobster palaces—Rector's, Shanley's, and the Knickerbocker grill.

The only live Maine lobsters I have encountered in this part of the world that were really successful from the viewpoint of broiling or boiling were shipped to me from Boston via special handling in surface express. I picked them up in Reno in a small barrel filled with ice and seaweed. The ice was unmelted, the lobsters indignant and vicious. We parboiled them practically with the speed of light and put them in the frigidaire whence they emerged as they might have at Damariscotta or Prouts Neck. The explanation seemed to be that they had been shipped with just the right rail connections all the way at a cool season of the year in unheated baggage cars. All the auspices were right. If the super jets with three-hour schedules out of New York with which we are currently threatened can meet this standard, they may, at least in part, justify their pestilential existence.

"FRENCHMEN HAVE SOME ODD IDEAS . . ."

Frenchmen have some odd ideas about Americans, and they all pertain to our eating habits. There are, of course, a certain number of American tourists who persist in demanding hot dogs and Cokes instead of examining and understanding French cuisine in its more exalted aspects. But the most consistently irritating delusion suffered by French restaurateurs is that all Americans exist solely on a diet of frozen foods, and that everything edible, even in the best-managed American homes, stays in the freezer for a year. I encountered this bizarre notion a few seasons back on a French liner, when I complained that the steaks, fish, and fowl had all been frozen, and were, therefore, not for me.

"But, sir," the chief steward said firmly, "Americans demand that all their food be frozen, and we try to make them happy. It's all they eat at home."

This dismal hallucination cropped up again this year, in a sort of reverse form. When it was suggested to an executive board of a French hotel association that restaurants in France now rely more on frozen foods in order to cut costs, the accusation was rejected with gratifying firmness. But the board then added that what might be good enough for Americans was *not* up to French gastronomic standards.

If the French want to preserve the superior tourist trade, it would be prudent for them not to continue assuming that all Americans eat nothing but frozen steaks, and can't tell a frozen fowl from a freshly killed bird. There are hundreds of thousands of American homes in which a freezer is regarded primarily as a convenience to preserve out-of-season delicacies and as a source of emergency ration when strictly fresh food isn't available.

In fact, if France, or, for that matter, any other country, doesn't realize the truth about better American eating habits, it will be doing both itself and the general cause of gastronomy a notable disservice.

WHATEVER BECAME OF THE DERBY HAT?

Every now and then, when not contemplating other significant problems in a far from perfect world, I am prompted to wonder whatever became of the derby hat.

A few years back the hard-topped bowler enjoyed a momentary resurrection, presumably at the caprice of hat manufacturers, but aside from this brief interlude, the record of the derby has been one of decline and, in the United States, almost total disappearance. It is easy to see why the short renaissance of 1950 wasn't crowned with overwhelming success: the hat shops did no business. Anybody who already had a derby in the front closet didn't buy a new one: he just put on the one he had purchased twenty years back and was instantly à la mode.

For a hard derby is as indestructible as a Rolls-Royce. It is well established both in fact and folklore that in the sixty-odd years the firm has been in business, no Rolls-Royce has ever worn out or disintegrated from mere wear. Nor has a well-made derby. A model purchased from, say, Scott, Locke, Brooks Brothers, Cavanaugh, or Collins & Fairbanks is still most certainly in operable shape and needs only dusting off to become the most comfortable, the most durable, and the most practical hat ever devised.

The most beautiful man's hat, the silk top hat, was awash with inherent vice. It was highly vulnerable to the elements; it dented on the least provocation; and it was constantly in need of the ministrations of a professional hat smoother with hot wax and a lure. The opera hat or collapsible topper, while a manifest boon in crowded places and impervious to getting brushed the wrong way, was highly perishable. Its inner economy of spines and springs was easily upset, and its life span was brief. No soft hat yet devised will hold its shape, and even the perennial homburg, if worn close to the head, leaves a crease across the middle of the scalp like a misplaced hair part.

The derby was the universal hat, congenial to almost every scheme of attire except evening and sports dress. It took no heed of weather and resisted the elements as it resisted misuse; it never got out of shape and seldom required brushing. It was the paragon of hats, not aesthetically beautiful, but morally and spiritually reassuring beyond all compare.

I have seemed to be the last practicing derby wearer west of the wide Missouri and perhaps in the entire United States, and this state of affairs has caused me grief. My appearance on the streets of San Francisco occasions only latent and diligently concealed amusement, for San Franciscans are the politest people in the world, at least this side of the United Kingdom. I do not, however, purpose to abandon the practice of a lifetime merely to gain the suffrage of fashion and the approval of the moment's style. There are at least four, perhaps five, hard black bowler hats in the hall closet and they will, with easy assurance, last out my time. You don't throw away good, only-ten-year-old Cavanaugh bowlers just because nobody else wears them.

In Virginia City, a derby elicits no remark at all, possibly because Nevadans don't know it has gone out of fashion, but more probably because they recognize in the derby the true and authentic Hat of the Old West.

This is a demonstrable verity and deserves the attention of students of Western mores—if only to erase the delusion that the only headgear for men in the classic West was the Stetson sombrero, a hat that in actual fact never existed outside of Texas and Kansas during the cattle drives but which was widely if spuriously exploited by the painter Remington about the turn of the century.

The most casual reference to the iconographic record will reveal that everywhere west of the Mississippi in frontier times, when firearms were universal and before the stages were preempted by the steam cars, the derby hat was universal in almost every walk of Western life save two: banking and driving a stagecoach. The man of money wore a silk tile; the knight of the ribbons was identifiable by a finely textured, usually white, low-crowned felt hat known regionally as a Mormon.

The derby was the approved headgear of both good guys and bad guys. The most widely circulated photograph of Bat Masterson depicts him in a gray bowler of sportive mien. Wyatt Earp, the toughest peace officer of them all, was an inveterate derby man. Black Bart, the versifying highwayman who specialized in the gold-bearing coaches in the California Mother Lode, wore a derby—surmounted, to be sure, by a pillow slip—as his occupational attire. His photograph in the ensuing Wells Fargo "Wanted" poster shows him in a low-crowned, curly-brimmed bowler of jaunty dimensions. When the Hole-in-the-Wall gang relaxed in Kansas City, they got themselves photographed wearing bowlers to a man. Train robbers especially admired them, but no more than did the engineers whose trains they held up, for whom the cast-iron derby served as a sort of primeval crash helmet, the equivalent of today's tin hat for working stiffs. Also confirmed hard-hat wearers were roundhouse crews and back-shop mechanics for whom loosened pieces of machinery were an occupational hazard. But the derby was scorned by the godlike master mechanic. His symbol of office was a well-brushed silk top hat.

Another unlikely stronghold of the pot hat was the timber industry in Oregon, Washington, and Idaho, where riggers, sawyers, stationary engineers, tool dressers, and bull cooks alike rejoiced in the protection of a well-built bowler, both on duty and on Saturday night forays on the skid road. When Stewart Holbrook, who was later to become the recognized minstrel of the lumber camps, arrived from Boston in 1915 wearing a five-dollar Collins & Fairbanks derby, he discovered that he was completely à la mode in the bunkhouses of Snohomish and Tillamook.

The derby was, of course, brought into the remote places of the Old West by the traveling salesmen who swarmed aboard the cars and stage-coaches as soon as the last Indians were safely out of the way, and in some cases before. Local historical societies and other repositories of such matters can furnish scores of yellowing prints by the town photographer of arriving stages in Austin, Eureka, The Dalles, Helena, Goldfield, Redding, and Encampment Valley. The outside seats are peopled with gents in ratcatcher suits and the hard derby—gray, brown, or black—of the fashionable moment. The waddies, the railroaders, the timber stiffs, and the rest of the frontier saw the obvious advantages of a weatherproof and well-nigh-indestructible hat, and the derby was very emphatically "in."

As additional evidence that the derby was indeed the Hat of the Old West, it may be worth noting that the only mechanical derby-hat-tipping device of which there is available record was the invention not of a New Yorker, a Bostonian, or even a Chicagoan, but of a Mr. James C. Boyle of Spokane, Washington, a community not notably given to dudes or Eastern elegance of attire. The Boyle Patent Derby Hat Tipper was an intricate mechanism of wheels, springs, levers, and ratchets, controlled from the palm of the wearer's hand like a camera shutter and devised to eliminate the bother of constantly snatching at one's hat when encountering ladies or other acquaintances. Activated from the rear, somewhat in the manner made famous by Charlie Chaplin, the hat invested with Boyle's patent elevated itself in a stately manner without the apparent agency of human hands, and then returned to its position of repose.

The invention did not, alas, meet with public acceptance, and to this day it reposes in the U.S. Patent Office in Washington, Patent No. 556,248. But it was as Western as silver dollars in payment for bourbon and branch.

That the derby and not Remington's Stetson was the authentic Hat of the Old West would be the worthy subject of a well-researched doctoral thesis, and any student of Western folklore is welcome to the suggestion.

Today, except for your correspondent, the derby this side of the

Missouri has vanished almost as completely as the frontier it once ornamented and comforted.

But not quite.

There is the heartening example of a San Francisco youth named Reginald Stocking II, known to Sunday editors as a foremost amateur of vintage Rolls-Royces, and sometimes proprietor of a one-man car-hire livery with very British overtones. Mr. Stocking often makes a springtime pilgrimage to London for the purpose of picking up a replacement for his hard-hat rack, and, when he was recently commanding a snappy Bond Street model, a shop clerk, misled by his youth, made mention of its being his "first derby hat." He was put in his place instantly.

"My fourth," said Stocking sternly.

ON GOLF: PEBBLE BEACH:
"The Crosby"

Unlike the principalities of Liechtenstein, Andorra, and San Marino—with which it is most frequently compared and where the national preoccupations are beer drinking, dueling, and folk dancing—Pebble Beach is devoted first and foremost and last and hindmost to golf. Golf is practiced throughout the daylight hours by all Pebble Beachcombers as a sort of religion, and its discussion and recapitulation go on far, far into the night in private homes and in the bar at the Lodge. Pebble Beach's morbid preoccupation with the world's silliest form of competitive athletics spirals to an annual climax of macabre dementia complete with propitiatory rites, known formally as the Invitational National Pro-Amateur Golf Championship; more familiarly as "The Crosby" for its patron and sponsoring supernatural, Bing Crosby.

On the occasion of this recurrent orgy of inanity that traditionally takes place in mid-January, as many as fifteen thousand people of unbalanced mind strangle in their own traffic at Pebble Beach, shred the shrubbery of houses adjacent to the jousting lists, lacerate the lawns, and participate in orgiastic tribal rites the length and breadth of the three major golf courses of the Peninsula, ending at Pebble Beach on the final day. Almost invariably, the Crosby can be relied on to invoke divine recognition in the form of torrential rain, and the spectacle of fifteen thousand of the Smitten of Allah in waterproofs and waders sloshing through the inundated lowlands of California has to be seen to be believed.

ON THE ADVERTISING PITCH THAT DESCRIBES . . .

Easily baffled by many aspects of the low comedy provided by American taste and purchasing habits generally, I am simply graveled by the advertising pitch that describes its product, which usually happens to be a beer, whiskey, or cigarette, as "mild," "light," or "pale"—for all the world as though these negative and discouraging adjectives somehow endowed with positively wholesome qualities commodities that by nature should be the precise opposite. To be instructed in advance that a beverage or smoke possesses none of the characteristics for which, presumably, it is being purchased, and that it is warranted to be deficient in any quality at all, seems to the Madison Avenue mind a stroke of sheer, supernal genius.

To me it suggests outright mental derangement.

Of course it is to the advantage of the manufacturer or vendor to merchandise cigarettes without tobacco and beer without hops, since these ingredients are costly to come by. Americans have for generations now been sold on the peculiar concepts of food without nutriment, bread without flour, milk without butterfat, and coffee without caffeine. This unparalleled swindle, on a positively cosmic scale, has made the allegedly richest and most resourceful nation on earth incomparably the worst fed. There isn't an Italian peasant who wouldn't throw a loaf of the plaster-of-Paris-cum-kapok that masquerades in the United States as bread right back through a baker's window, and there isn't a Hollander or Dane who, confronted with a bottle of milk from which all nutritional qualities have been removed, wouldn't have the dairy burned to the ground come nightfall.

It's not for a minute that the merchants of these trash products care a hoot about the health fads and dietary delusions of their customers. Selling food and drink from which the essential properties have been removed at the same price usually charged for the legitimate product is big business. It thrives on the gullibility of idiot customers who have been brainwashed into the belief that something "light" is preferable to something that is dark or heavy merely by the advertised repetition of a patent and demonstrable lie.

It's big business in the food and drink industry to downgrade the entire American standard of living through the agency of widely financed campaigns to promote the notion that somehow inferior and devitalized foods are health foods and will contribute to a slimmer waistline. So will a diet of sawdust.

The will to be cheated is, apparently, a deep-rooted and inherent American instinct, but it seems a pity when it leads to the rejection of the all-too-infrequent natural pleasures that make life bearable at all. As somebody once remarked, the customers at diet-fad groceries always seem to look as though they had got there ten years too late.

JOHN BARRIGER'S NO. 99 AND MAJORDOMO CLIFF

Regular perusers of this department may recall that until comparatively recently it has been able to report favorably and even with admiration on the activities of John Barriger of Pittsburgh, president of the enchantingly solvent Pittsburgh & Lake Erie Railroad and, perhaps, the last of the long tally of magnificoes who made railroading the most aristocratic of American occupations for a full century. Mr. Barriger's disappearance from directoral junkets, anniversary dinners at "21," and other stylish events on and off his famous business car, New York Central's No. 99 (all of them more than adequately underwritten by the P & L E's swaggering profits), has been occasioned by the major catastrophe of enforced retirement. He achieved the boyish age of sixty-five, a time when most men of bounce are just getting their second wind in the world of affairs, and his boss, the all-powerful Al Perlman of the New York Central, upheld the letter of the law, an act of folly rarely encountered in the Perlman record. Other organizations find room for displaced competence in advisory capacities, but neither the Central nor the P & L E did, so Mr. Barriger moved over to the Missouri-Kansas-Texas Railroad. The "Katy" is not a lush property, but its board apparently appreciates talent, for it named Mr. Barriger to be chairman as well as president, and gave him the possibility of an interesting new career in upgrading.

A final report on the Barriger legend in its days of well-upholstered opulence suggests that greatness in an authentic magnifico is communicable and that spacious ways can be absorbed through a process of social osmosis, as it were.

Majordomo of the Barriger household while the Master administered the affairs of the P & L E in Pittsburgh was an amiable and highly effective Negro named Cliff. When his employer occupied the private car to which his position entitled him, Cliff administered its affairs on a scale in keeping with the topmost flights of Barriger hospitality.

A short time back a friend of the railroader observed No. 99 in LaSalle depot in Chicago as he was about to board *The Twentieth Century*

Limited for New York. He paused briefly to step across the intervening platform to pay his respects.

Barriger was not present, but Cliff, rising to the occasion, undertook to entertain the caller in a manner suitable to his estate, which was an exalted one. The guest refused a drink because time was short and his own train was ready to highball. Coffee, too, was rejected on the same grounds. Neither did he smoke cigars, thanks just the same.

Only momentarily nonplused, Cliff rose to unprecedented heights of hospitable persuasion: "Please have something, do!" he exhorted the visitor. "Mr. Barriger will be most vexed with me if he knows you have gone away without accepting something. Just take along a case of whiskey!"

WHAT WAS WRONG WITH 1905?

Now and then some dolt rises up in meeting, in the columns of the inquiring reporter, or letters to the editor with the horrid pronouncement that, if elected, Senator Goldwater "will set the country back fifty years." Were it indeed possible, by some superlatively benevolent tinkering of the time machine, to turn back the clock and replace the scattered pages of the calendar, it would be to restore an infinitely better world than anybody now alive is likely ever to see again.

Envision, if you will, a world where the most hideous manifestations of contemporary barbarism were mercifully unknown, one which was innocent of even intimations of jet travel, radio commentators, television comedians, mendacious opinion polls, the graduated income tax, women in trousers, nuclear fission, sports shirts, television dinners, peace marchers, sit-ins, plastics, condominium apartments, parking meters, Hollywood diets, beatniks, tailfins, the thirty-cent dollar, Bobby Kennedy, the Rev. Billy Graham, zippers on men's pants, Hilton hotels, and once-a-day mail delivery.

I am aware that a hanker for the irrevocably vanished past, the *temps jadis* of the poet, has existed in all ages and that a dim view has been taken of it by the deluded gulls in the community who subscribe to the illusion of progress. Somewhere in *The Iliad,* Homer complains bitterly of contemporary degenerate times and looks backward to a more heroic age when warriors were bashing in the heads of the opposition with rocks no man of today can even lift. To look backward in admiration and affection is supposed by partisans of the dreadful here and now to be an index of insufficiency, an inability to cope with the changing condition of life which has confronted every generation of recorded time.

It seems to me that Senator Goldwater could do a lot worse than promise to turn back the clock to the first decade of the century which now appears to most people to have been a radiant time of ineffable serenity, prosperity, and abundance. At least it lacked the disasters, say, of women's suffrage, the universal motorcar, credit cards, international airports, repudiation of the national currency, tranquilizers, freedom riders, digit dialing, and the one-ounce martini.

ON TELEVISION AND A TELEVISION SPECTACLE

Last Friday evening, and against my better judgment, I saw my first television show. It was the staff's night out and my partner induced me to look at a production on the servants' set since I won't have one in the front of the house. Of course, I have seen snatches of these things in bars, but never a whole, consecutive, and deliberately envisioned production.

It was devised by Leland Hayward, a great gentleman, whom I have known since about 1919, and called *The Good Years*, based on a bestseller by an extremely able chronicler of catastrophes, Walter Lord, who has set off a chain reaction of book jobs that now cover every morbid event from the Johnstown Flood to yesterday's street accident on your corner.

Let me digress: In 1919 or 1920, or thereabout, Mr. Hayward was married to a lady named, if memory serves, Lola Gibbs, reputedly the possessor of the most beautiful back in New York. People looked at women's backs in those days, and one evening Phil Plant, Hayward's half brother and my roommate in a reformatory that specialized in cramming juvenile delinquents for Yale, took me to the old Palais Royal, then a night club at the northwest corner of Broadway and, I think, Forty-seventh Street.

Charlie Journal was the waiter captain, an unknown thin man named Paul Whiteman led the band, and we all sat in boxes. It was all very grand, until, upon some real or fancied provocation from her husband, Mrs. Hayward tried to stab her husband to death with a steak knife.

There followed an epic chase over tables, across boxes, through thickets of potted palms with customers screaming and glass smashing in as handsome a scene of chaos as ever escaped Mack Sennett. Mr. Hayward fled, Miss Gibbs pursued, waiters waved their arms and dropped trays of White Rock on the customers, while Plant and I trailed afterward endeavoring to disarm the outraged beauty.

It was an interval of loveliness that I will remember to the grave. On the end, Mr. Whiteman smashed a four-dollar fiddle on Miss Gibbs's head as she dashed past the orchestra, and what passed for order in a New York night club in 1920 was gradually restored. Charlie Journal, whose hair shortly afterward turned to snow white, making him the handsomest maître d'hôtel in town, attributed it to that evening.

What I am getting at is: We should have let his wife stab Mr. Hayward to death.

ONE VIEW OF BOBBY

A year or two back, before the assassination of President Kennedy had established the Kennedy cult of adulation which has, for the time being anyway, eliminated all touches of humor from the image of a man who in his own person had an uncommonly fetching sense of it, the story was widely being told of the occasion when the three Kennedy brothers were in a plane together and the other passengers were speculating on the possibility of eliminating all Kennedys forever by tossing them from the window.

"We could throw out John Fitzgerald," proposed the first conspirator, "and make the Republicans happy."

"Or we could throw out Ted," proposed another, "and make the other Kennedys very happy indeed."

"Better than that," suggested a third, "let's toss out Bobby Kennedy and make everybody happy."

ON PACKAGED BREAKFAST FOODS

Perhaps it is a tribute to the lyric prose of advertising copy writers in charcoal-gray Brooks suits in Madison Avenue and maybe again it is irreproachable evidence that the birth rate of the American sucker has been vastly accelerated since Henry Ford originally estimated his emergence on the scene at one every minute, but the American buying public last year spent a cool $300,000,000 on breakfast foods that were conspicuously and demonstrably trash. This is the amount spent on ready-to-eat dry cereals whose nutritional value was a good deal less than that of so much warmed up butcher's paper, especially if the butcher's paper had been casually exposed for a brief interval to even an odor of meat.

Hundreds of millions of supposedly adult Americans who would laugh heartily if you tried to sell them gold bricks or unlisted mining stocks ponied up this fantastic sum of money for dried breakfast food products from which every last particle of actual food value had been removed but which were advertised at mammoth expense and in complete violation of fact as "concentrated vitamins" or "power-packed goodness." They might have spent this incredible sum for sausages or eggs or kippered herring or scrapple or Kentucky ham or salt codfish, all of which were designed by Providence to be eaten for the human breakfast and all of which taste good and have character, but no, the sagacious American housewife who is supposed to pinch every penny made a variety of cereal firms incredibly wealthy by purchasing, variously, pellets made from compressed tissue paper, acorn husks, and hay woven into attractive loaf patterns because the advertisements said to.

The truth is that, one and all, the patent breakfast foods and dried cereals known by the brand names to literally millions are so much complete and utter trash without the least vestigial trace of food value or nutriment of any sort other than that contained in the milk and sugar with which they are made vaguely edible.

Whether the wholesale consumption by Americans of mountains of such rubbish is in fact a determining factor in the decline of the national character through the agency of malnutrition or whether the purchase of totally worthless merchandise is merely a symptom of the decline in our mental processes can be debated endlessly, like the hen and the egg.

Perhaps someone will rise up in meeting to examine the moral aspect of commercial ethics which will manufacture, exploit, and distribute on a practically cosmic scale merchandise of no value at all. This isn't the point: the American buying public has been discovered to be gullible beyond the dreams of "Get Rich Quick" Wallingford. Crispy, crunchy particles of inferior-grade cardboard attractively packaged have proven irresistible to the great American jake and rustic, and it leaves more beefsteak, eggs, and grilled kidneys for his betters. Of course, the man who has breakfasted exclusively off the product of the cereal-swindling syndicate usually keels over in mid morning and has to have a hot ham on rye to get him through until lunch, but he started the day in the radiant delusion he was filling up with vitamins and other wonderful if nonextant foodstuffs, so why tell him the truth?

The joke on the American public is of such staggering dimensions that it can only be appreciated by the man of sense who starts the day with a tureen of hot oatmeal covered with a pint of whipping cream and then goes on to more important things such as a six-egg omelet and two-pound breakfast steak before hitting the coffee.

The Dog: Mr. T-Bone Towser

That night in the storm he heard a call from somewhere far off, something that only a dog could hear, and he sensed it on the storm wind that came down from the north where he had been born. A long, atavistic call from beyond the realm of senses and beyond his memory of puppyhood. He knew it then and wanted to tell me, and I never understood. It breaks my heart that I was so stupid and insensible.

THE DOG:
Mr. T-Bone Towser

That Mr. T-Bone Towser who came to us at the age of six weeks some eight years ago from the St. Erin Kennels at Deer Park, Washington, has been a major force in shaping my life, one with Jack Daniels whiskey and the *Herald Tribune* style book, is so obvious as to reject comment. The entry of 165 pounds of absolute love with big ears into one's life is nothing to take lightly.

From the very beginning he has demanded and received special attention and extra handling. When, in the sixth week of his puppyhood, he was about to be shipped to Virginia City from Spokane by air—the only traffic he has ever had with this peasant form of transport—there was a dog embargo on due to a rabies scare, and I had to get the Governor of Washington to clear his passage. It took some pressure from well-placed friends, and the Governor has been known to say "Yes, sir" to passing St. Bernards ever since.

When, at a later date, my partner, who is half owner of T-Bone, and I chanced to pass through Washington on our railroad car, the dog was photographed shaking hands with Mr. Ralph Budd, president of the Great Northern, whose own car happened to be on the adjacent track, and the local papers captioned the photo: "Home Town Dog Makes Good, Returns on Own Private Car!"

That a private car was the only solution to the travel problem is obvious in the face of the Pullman Company's ruling in the matter: "Dogs will be tolerated aboard room cars if they can be brought aboard *secretly or unobtrusively* by their owners."

As a railroad dog, T-Bone became well and, I believe, favorably known to stationmasters in terminals where there were still private-car tracks available. Terminals rated with Tows in direct proportion to the availability of trees and grass. Seattle and Palm Beach: Grade A. Lots of both right at the car door. Washington, D.C., and San Francisco were further down the scale in walking availability. Los Angeles has a private park for the use of private-car patrons, and Denver is absolute heaven. Right smack dab in the middle of the platform, there is a massive hydrant.

Laundries for outsize dogs are not always easily available, and I will not soon forget T-Bone's indignation upon being called for by a representative of Le Petit Pet Shop in Dallas and returned with a large red ribbon around his neck and smelling of some sort of poodle perfume.

Tows takes a dim view of Texas generally even though he is well received and the restaurant fare is generally excellent in terms of beef. The homes of well-to-do Texans are so large as to make it impracticable for him to attract attention by lying across doorways and causing traffic to be rerouted. At the spacious home of Lloyd and Elizabeth Smith in Houston, house servants merely walked around him and gave him what was later diagnosed as a Humble Oil neurosis.

Ownership of a St. Bernard is educational in directions other than those implied by T-Bone's own natural superiority and gives an insight into the seemingly boundless capacity for harmless self-delusion and wish fulfillment of a substantial portion of the American populace.

Along with the inevitable how-much-does-he-eat imbecilities, we are subject to a continuous leitmotif whose refrain is "We used to have a St. Bernard just like him when we were children." Now granted St. Bernards were probably, for a variety of reasons, more frequent in Edwardian times than they are today, their numbers as suggested by these remembrances would have been astronomical. It seems likely that over the years memory is able to translate any mastiff-size woofer into a veritable St. Bernard and that the recollected vistas of childhood are easily populated with dream dogs that never existed. To hear tell, these dearly cherished images of dogs that never were are all St. Bernards.

Although today St. Bernards are infrequent enough to cause comment in public, they are by no means a vanishing race either in esteem or numbers. Mrs. Virginia Graves, editor of *The Breeder's Digest*, a periodical devoted entirely to St. Bernards with the motto "The Biggest and the Best," assures me that her circulation and pedigree figures indicate a St. Bernard population of 225 in the Nevada-Northern California area alone. Fired with this intelligence and himself an admirer of T-Bone, the press agent for Harrah's Club, one of the major Reno casinos, was recently fetched by the idea of a St. Bernard convention to be staged on the handily adjacent shores of Lake Tahoe.

Co-hosts at this congress of canine chivalry were to be T-Bone and Clancy, mascot of Guy Michael's Christmas Tree Restaurant on the Mt. Rose Road. Prudence suggested a sort of dry run or committee meeting between Clancy and T-Bone before issuing invitations to several hundred St. Bernard neighbors all the way from Reno to Pebble Beach, and it was as well this precautionary measure was taken.

The meeting, far from being a doggy Field of the Cloth of Gold, was, as one spectator remarked, more like an animal version of *High Noon*. Only the intervention of state patrolmen with fire hoses, mops, and ball bats prevented Clancy and T-Bone from mutually reducing each other to rag dolls.

The great St. Bernard convention was dropped.

As a puppy, T-Bone couldn't have cared less about mirrors. Encountering a full-length glass with himself in focus, he would let out a puppy woof and dodge the issue by getting away from there, fast. Now in his maturity he is growing more tolerant, even affectionate, toward his likeness coming down the hall head-on. He's taken especially to sleeping with his nose against its own image in a floor-length wall mirror in the front hall and holding what I imagine to be tentative conversations with himself. This isn't narcissism, for we have never told T-Bone that he is the handsomest and most intelligent dog in the world and could be best dog in show anywhere he wanted. We've kept that sort of thing from him for fear he'd ask for a raise in beef hearts and kidneys.

But he obviously finds that during the long watches of the night, when the hall lights are turned low, the dog in the mirror is good company. He doesn't make any trouble and agrees perfectly with everything T-Bone says and does. If the big lug says "Hello, Handsome" to the looking glass, the friendly dog in there returns the compliment. If he winks, he gets a reciprocal leer; if he wants to lie down and take it easy, his companion in the glass is agreeable to that, too.

The aphorism attributed to Samuel Butler, that the great pleasure of a dog is that he will make a fool of himself with you, is admirably corroborated by T-Bone's mirror acquaintance. Anything he wants to do, the dog in the window is agreeable to doing, too. Most satisfactory. Also it disproves the snob philosophy to the effect that "I have best company when I am alone."

November 1, 1960

I want to set this down, while I remember it.

The Thursday night just a week before Towser died, there was a great wind and rain storm on the Comstock, the first heavy storm of the coming winter. It blew hard from the north with sleet in the rain, stripping the leaves from the trees and filling the pool with dead leaves, so that we cut short our stay two days later and closed the house for the season. In the night I had occasion to get up to see that all was secure in the house, and The Dog was standing out on the terrace in back, clearly visible in the night lights from the house. He was facing directly into the storm, rigid, with all his senses straining into the night as though he was seeing something far off and dim and strove to make it out more clearly. Half an hour later he was still there, pointing into the storm and rain, and I called to him to come into the house and out of the wet. From then on, until the following Thursday when he died, he never left me for a moment. He followed me everywhere, even from one room to another, and spent the night at the foot of the staircase looking up toward our bedrooms. I know now that he was trying to tell me something: that he was going to die. That night in the storm he heard a call from somewhere far off, something that only a dog could hear, and he sensed it on the storm wind that came down from the north where he had been born. A long, atavistic call from beyond the realm of senses and beyond his memory of puppyhood. He knew it then and wanted to tell me, and I never understood. It breaks my heart that I was so stupid and insensible. He died just a week later.

I often think the most fetching of all James Thurber's dog-inspired drawings is the one depicting an astral Thurber man and equally astral Thurber dog facing the west on a horizontal plane with the stars for background to show that they are no longer of this earth. When and if I am allowed company elsewhere but here, it will be, by my choice, the dog T-Bone. I shall not want better. Together, except for pauses at celestial hydrants and other checking points, we will explore things of interest in the hereafter, guiding our progress on the certain astronomy which all men of intelligence most eventually concede to be the sure navigational fix of the possibly valid universe, the Dog Star.

LUCIUS BEEBE
A Biographical Sketch

Lucius Morris Beebe was born on December 9, 1902, at Wakefield, Massachusetts, near Boston, the son of Junius and Eleanor (Merrick) Beebe. The first Beebes had come to America in 1650 and had prospered in their various ventures, so that by 1750 the descendants, scattered throughout New England but concentrated chiefly in Somerset County, Massachusetts, were landed and wealthy men of property. Lucius' father was no exception to this tradition, and during his lifetime was head of his own large leather business in Boston, president of the Wakefield Trust Company and of the Brockton Gas Company, director of the Atlantic National Bank of Boston, and director of the Mutual Chemical Company of New York. The Beebe farm at Wakefield was a sizable 140 acres, and it was here and, during the winter months, in Boston that the "Boy Beebe" grew up.

Beebe's early schooling was peripatetic: from the North Ward School in Wakefield he went at the age of fifteen to St. Marks in Southboro to be sent home, almost instanter, for a dynamiting episode comparable to the one he describes in "Wakefield: The Town That Will Never Forget Me;" he then went to the Berkshire School in Sheffield and was in due course returned for having discovered alcohol in Boston and bringing it, Beebe-Prometheus, to Berkshire; his third prep school was the Roxbury School, in Cheshire, Connecticut, which he survived to enter Yale in 1922. At Yale he would have graduated with the class of 1926—with Peter Arno, John Hay Whitney, Rudy Vallee, Henry C. Potter, and other extraordinaries of the time—had he not in a letter to the *Yale Daily News*, with zeal born of his own and the Jazz Age, attacked the Yale Divinity School lock, stock, and barrel for its lunacy in supporting prohibition. Professor Henry Hallam Tweedy of the Divinity School was not amused, nor was President Angell of Yale. Two weeks later, moreover, Beebe locked himself in one of the stage boxes of the Hyperion Music Hall Theater, and, at an appropriate moment in the performance, rose tall (6′ 4″), white-bearded, and clerically dressed, and shouted, "I am Professor Tweedy of

the Yale Divinity School!" and hurled an empty bottle on the stage.
President Angell, with an administrative assist from Dean Jones, sent
Beebe, in the middle of his sophomore year, north to Boston and Cam-
bridge.

Following a year on the *Boston Telegram*, whose purple works and
72-point orgies are set forth in this collection, Beebe entered Harvard to
graduate as a Bachelor of Arts in 1927, but not without having been first
suspended by President Lowell for having clobbered a classmate and
given him a near concussion. The reason for the attack was literary: Beebe
had, through access to some hundred-odd manuscript lines of Edwin
Arlington Robinson's verse, conceived the idea of publishing them privately in a rare edition limited to seventeen copies. Without the poet's
permission. He did so, distributed copies from Amherst Library to the
British Museum, and all would have been reasonably well had not an
undergraduate by the name of Wetherby informed Mr. Robinson of it.
The poet was pained, but forgave Beebe since the project had been purely
bibliophilic with no commercial overtones. Wetherby, however, was hos-
pitalized, and Beebe suspended pro tem.

After graduation from Harvard and following a stint on the *Boston
Transcript* as contributor to its literary section, Beebe's New England
days ended. He was ready for the champagne and damask fields of New
York.

In June 1929, at the age of twenty-seven, Beebe became a member
of the *Herald Tribune* staff and remained with the paper for twenty-one
years. Stanley Walker, mesmerized by Beebe's six-foot-four and sartorial
elegance, hired him at thirty-five dollars a week. Beebe started as a reporter frustrated by garden-club doings, annual conventions, minor fires,
and occasional assignments as ships'-news reporter. Appearing once
in top hat and morning coat among flames and snaking hoses, he was
quickly moved to the drama department of the paper. This was again
temporary, a mere way station on the road to the ultimate depot:
Beebe came into his own on September 9, 1933, with the first tryout in
the *Philadelphia Inquirer* of his column to be called "This New York." The
column was further tested in outlying papers as far west as Wyoming,
proved successful, and given the final cachet with its appearance in June
1934 in the *Herald Tribune* itself.

The weekly syndicated (Cleveland, Kansas City, St. Louis, and points
west) column dealt only with the good things of this life as enjoyed by
a limited five hundred members of Café Society. Beebe was not only a
fascinated observer and reporter of this Café Society but was himself an
active member of it. His wardrobe, spectacular at Yale and Harvard,
where he not infrequently brightened morning classes wearing the top
hat, tails, and gold-headed walking stick of the evening before, now blos-

somed to meet the greater demands of the metropolis and his position. He is reported to have owned forty suits, not an excessive number for an individual of means, but certainly a fantastic wardrobe for a working newspaperman during the Depression era. One of his overcoats was mink-lined with an astrakhan collar, another mink-lined with sable collar. His top hats ranged from sporting dove gray to formal black, and his gloves from fawn-colored doeskin to evening white. It is doubtful that he ever went abroad without a stick.

The New York which he graced included Bleeck's Artists and Writers Saloon, an extension of the editorial offices of the *Herald Tribune;* the Biltmore Turkish Baths where he presumably dripped Bollinger; the restaurants and night spots: Le Pavillon, the Colony, El Morocco, "21"; the hotels: the Plaza, the St. Regis, the Madison; and, of course, theater first nights, cocktail scuffles, gourmet dinners, and assorted sarabands in the tight inner circle of socially acceptable Manhattan. Leaving the pleasant confines of this inner island, nothing existed westward until Beebe reached the Pump Room in Chicago via *The Twentieth Century Limited.* Comparable vast spaces separated him from the civilization of Antoine's and Commander's Palace in New Orleans to the south, and Locke-Ober's in Boston to the north. New Jersey was an unmentionable wilderness, but Pennsylvania securely saved by a railroad, Bookbinder's, and the Stotesburys, Cadwalladers, Mellons, and such.

He was referred to generally as "Mr. New York," an honorific which delighted him and which went down well beyond the Hudson. Walter Winchell irritatingly enough called him "Luscious Lucius," and he was also enviously described as "the orchidaceous oracle of café society." Kyle Crichton termed him "a sort of sandwich man for the rich," and Walter Pritchard Eaton, reviewing Beebe's book *The Boston Legend* (a chapter of which, "Eatalls and Tosspots," is included here) disapprovingly (and bless him for his words!) reported: "He betrays an incomprehension of moral fervor and high humanitarian purpose hardly reassuring in a historian."

In 1937, eight years after his assault on the Big City, Beebe was the subject of an entertaining two-part profile in *The New Yorker* by Wolcott Gibbs, and, in 1939, made the cover of *Life:* "Lucius Beebe Sets a Style." Gibbs did other pieces on Beebe, also for *The New Yorker,* including a wonderful parody of Beebe's *Tribune* style and material. The closing lines of *The New Yorker* profile deserve a place between these hard covers: "Whatever admirers or detractors say, however, one tribute must be paid. . . . The words of it, with one tiny exception, are from a song made popular in his own time by Miss Ethel Merman, and they can be sung when he is gone: 'Beebe had Class, with a capital K.'"

He was an indefatigable worker, and his production from the time of his arrival in New York to his death in 1966 was constant in quantity and high in quality. He was a "pro." There were fifty-two weekly double columns for the *Herald Tribune;* a book a year for a total of at least forty books; the once-a-month "Along the Boulevards" feature for *Gourmet* Magazine; six to ten full articles a year for *Holiday, Town & Country, The American Mercury, Cosmopolitan, American Heritage, The Ford Times, Gourmet, Status, Playboy, Esquire, Collier, Railroad, Trains,* and other periodicals; and added related matter including book reviews, irate "letters to the editor," a script stint for Hollywood on a film dealing with Café Society, consultant to Hollywood on the railroad film *Union Pacific,* and personal appearances before clubs and such until he cut these off as a waste of his time. In addition, of course, were the activities providing the material about which he wrote: ranging from white-tie first nights and champagne suppers in New York, Central City, and San Francisco to the patient waiting, with focused camera, for the engine of a great or little train (he loved them both) to come thundering or puffing around a bend in Colorado, Missouri, New York, or Texas.

Lucius Beebe, in the year 1950, opted for Nevada. The decision can be traced back to the Warner Brothers junket which he joined from New York to Nevada for the premier of the film *Virginia City* in 1939. The town at that time fascinated him on all counts: the citizens were completely normal and uninhibited characters who drank, if they felt like it, firm slugs of scotch or bourbon at the bars with their bacon and eggs, or skipped the eggs and bacon altogether: the residents were descendants of miners and mine operators who had built the town, and, if they ever noticed them, gave not a damn for the opinions of anyone; there were no confiscatory income taxes of any sort whatsoever: this made supreme sense; lastly and above all, there was a newspaper on which Mark Twain had worked, *The Territorial Enterprise,* one of the most famous papers in the history of the land, up for sale: Beebe and his associate, Charles Clegg, bought it together.

With Clegg, he published for eight years an exciting newspaper, one which took no guff from any quarter and which, as the occasion warranted, fired grapeshot or slammed broadsides at any and all.

In 1960 the paper was sold and Beebe and Clegg took to living during inclement Nevada months in ineffable Hillsborough on the Peninsula south of San Francisco. Beebe contributed from 1960 to his death in 1966 a weekly column to the *San Francisco Chronicle* titled "This Wild West," balancing his earlier "This New York." The opinions expressed in it were at poles removed from the *Chronicle's* editorial policy and horrified the owners, who, however, allowed their San Francisco urbanity to triumph over liberal prejudices. A variety of pieces, selected and trimmed down from the full columns, were published in book form in 1966 by the

Chronicle under the title *The Provocative Pen of Lucius Beebe, Esq.*

While maintaining their residence in Nevada, Beebe and Clegg continued their annual visits to New York with occasional trips via Cunard to London. They also traveled the United States in their jointly owned, fabulous private railroad car, *Virginia City,* an eye-popping legend in its own right, complete with Venetian décor, fireplace, wine cellar, and Turkish bath. Beebe continued producing books and articles to the last: his entertaining *The Big Spenders* appeared after his death, and for more than a full year magazines printed articles of his which had been submitted before he passed on.

Beebe lived a full and expansive life to the end. He died suddenly, of a heart attack, on February 4, 1966.

—Duncan Emrich
Washington, D.C.

CHECKLIST OF SOURCES

Metropolis with Manners from *Town & Country*, April 1962

Dime Novel Destiny from *Gourmet*, August 1962

Uncle John from *Gourmet*, May 1963

Wakefield, Massachusetts: The Town That Will Never Forget Me from *Lincoln and Mercury Times*, July–August 1956

Uncle Ned from *Gourmet*, November 1949

Uncle Ned's Wine Preferences from *Gourmet*, March 1963

The *Boston Telegram*—previously unpublished

Beverly Wagon Living from *Ford Times*, December 1958

Aunt Alice at the Opera from THE PROVOCATIVE PEN OF LUCIUS BEEBE, ESQ., The Chronicle Publishing Co., 1966

Boston Revisited: 1963 from *Gourmet*, July 1963

The Depression Years from *Gourmet*, January 1965

The Grand Closing at 42 West Forty-ninth Street from THE BIG SPENDERS, Hutchinson, 1967

Café Society from SNOOT IF YOU MUST, Appleton-Century, 1943

Café Names Made News from SNOOT IF YOU MUST, Appleton-Century, 1943

Bleeck's Formerly Club from SNOOT IF YOU MUST, Appleton-Century, 1943

Father Visits Bleeck's from THE PROVOCATIVE PEN OF LUCIUS BEEBE, ESQ., The Chronicle Publishing Co., 1966

Dorothy Kilgallen's Victorian Drawing Room from *Gourmet*, March 1949

The Plaza: 1947 from Plaza Hotel fortieth anniversary brochure, 1947

Le Pavillon: 1953 5 East Fifty-fifth from *Holiday*, May 1953

The Elegant Colony from *Holiday*, August 1958

Café Society Revisited from the *New York Herald Tribune Magazine Section*, April 19, 1964

I Saw the Elephant from *Holiday*, September 1950

". . . for me England means London."—previously unpublished

The Wisdom of Polonius from THE PROVOCATIVE PEN OF LUCIUS BEEBE, ESQ., The Chronicle Publishing Co., 1966

Showcase Afloat: 1959 from *Town & Country*, September 1959

Sir James Charles from THE BIG SPENDERS, Hutchinson, 1967

Ship's Pool from THE BIG SPENDERS, Hutchinson, 1967

"It is an article of faith . . ." from *Gourmet*, November 1962

The Old Cunard Club Hatband from THE PROVOCATIVE PEN OF LUCIUS BEEBE, ESQ., The Chronicle Publishing Co., 1966

Henry Poole, Gentleman's Tailor from *Holiday*, February 1960

"The end of civilization . . ." from THE BIG SPENDERS, Hutchinson, 1967

Spendthrift Tour of London from *Holiday*, March 1960

The Savoy of London from *Holiday*, March 1963

Southdown Mutton—previously unpublished

Peal & Company, and Alan McAfee from *Gourmet*, July 1965

Tourist Travel Literature: Scotland, 1965 from *Gourmet*, July 1965

Rolls-Royce from THE BIG SPENDERS, Hutchinson, 1967

Rolls-Royce: Horsepower from *Gourmet*, September 1963

The Paris Ritz: Men's Bar: Georges and Frank from *Gourmet*, January 1964

The Paris Ritz: Men's Bar Addendum from *Gourmet*, April 1964

The Paris Ritz: Olivier from *Gourmet*, November 1965

Boston: Eatalls and Tosspots: Consommé Julien
       The Parker House
       Locke-Ober's Winter Place Wine Rooms from
BOSTON AND THE BOSTON LEGEND, Appleton Century, 1935

On the Rocks from *Town & Country*, October 1955

Pittsburgh: Hors d'Oeuvres Traffic Club from *Gourmet*, June 1963

Chicago: The Fabulous Pump Room: I, II, III, IV from *Gourmet*, October 1963; SNOOT IF YOU MUST, Appleton Century, 1943, and (III and IV) *Holiday*, April 1950

Aloft: TWA's *Royal Ambassador Flight* from *Gourmet*, January 1963

Philadelphia: Bookbinder's from *Gourmet*, May 1964

Washington: Harvey's from *Gourmet*, April 1965

LaSalle Street Station: Stylish Chaos from TWENTIETH CENTURY, Howell-North Books, 1962

Colorado: Central City from *Gourmet*, September 1962

New Orleans: Antoine's from *Holiday*, January 1953 and March 1951

New Orleans: Brennan's from *Town & Country*, April 1960

New Orleans: Commander's Palace from *Holiday*, March 1951 and *Town & Country*, November 1953

"Waving at trains . . ." from HIGHLINERS: A RAILROAD ALBUM, Appleton-Century, 1940

When Beauty Rode the Rails from WHEN BEAUTY RODE THE RAILS, Doubleday, 1962

The Twentieth Century Limited from TWENTIETH CENTURY, Howell-North Books, 1962

The Century: A Gastronomic Footnote from *Gourmet*, January 1964

Step Into My Parlor from MIXED TRAIN DAILY, Howell-North Books, 1961, and from HIGHBALL, Appleton-Century, 1945

Elegant Private Varnish from MR. PULLMAN'S ELEGANT PALACE CAR, Doubleday, 1961, and from HEAR THE TRAIN BLOW, Dutton, 1952

Folklore of Manifest Destiny from HEAR THE TRAIN BLOW, Dutton, 1952

Beef and Bourbon from *Town & Country*, April 1957

"The most heroic of American legends . . ." from HIGH IRON: A BOOK OF TRAINS, Appleton-Century, 1938

The Best of Possible Worlds from *Gourmet*, May 1953

Going for the Mail from *Gourmet*, January 1966

Julia Bulette: The Comstock's First Cyprian—previously unpublished

San Francisco's Palace: 1955 from *Town & Country*, June 1955

The Top of the Mark from *Gourmet* March 1965

Pisco Punch from *Gourmet*, September 1957

The Barbary Coast: A Body Could Feel at Home There from the *San Francisco Chronicle*, September 10, 1961

Polynesian Traps from *Gourmet*, April 1962

Hillsborough from *Gourmet*, June 1964

The Royal Family—previously unpublished

Mr. Stuyvesant Fish's Wild Boar from *Gourmet*, August 1963

On the Suprême from *Gourmet*, July 1962

On Milk from *Gourmet*, May 1962

A Hollow Mockery, A Shabby Swindle from THE PROVOCATIVE PEN OF LUCIUS BEEBE, ESQ., The Chronicle Publishing Co., 1966

On Advertising Mendacity from *Gourmet*, May 1966

Lobsters and the Wright Brothers' Folly from *Gourmet*, February 1965

"Frenchmen have some odd ideas . . ." from *Gourmet*, April 1963

Whatever Became of the Derby Hat? from *Gourmet*, May 1966

On Golf: Pebble Beach: "The Crosby" from *Town & Country*, November 1961

On the Advertising Pitch That Describes . . . from *Gourmet*, March 1964

John Barriger's No. 99 and Majordomo Cliff from *Gourmet*, October 1965

What Was Wrong with 1905? from THE PROVOCATIVE PEN OF LUCIUS BEEBE, ESQ., The Chronicle Publishing Co., 1966

On Television and a Television Spectacle from Terence O'Flaherty's TV column, January 23, 1962

One View of Bobby from THE PROVOCATIVE PEN OF LUCIUS BEEBE, ESQ., The Chronicle Publishing Co., 1966

On Packaged Breakfast Foods from *The Territorial Enterprise*, December 6, 1957

The Dog: Mr. T-Bone Towser—previously unpublished